THE ARTIST,
THE PHILOSOPHER,
AND THE WARRIOR

ALSO BY PAUL STRATHERN

Napoleon in Egypt

THE ARTIST,
THE PHILOSOPHER,
AND THE WARRIOR

*The Intersecting Lives of
da Vinci, Machiavelli, and
Borgia and the World They Shaped*

Paul Strathern

BANTAM BOOKS

Published in the United States by Bantam Books, an imprint of The Random House Publishing Group, a division of Random House, Inc., New York.

BANTAM BOOKS and the rooster colophon are registered trademarks of Random House, Inc.

Originally published in hardcover in the United Kingdom by Jonathan Cape, a division of The Random House Group Limited, in 2009.

Library of Congress Cataloging-in-Publication Data

Strathern, Paul, 1940–
The artist, the philosopher, and the warrior : the intersecting lives of da Vinci, Machiavelli, and Borgia and the world they shaped /
Paul Strathern. — Bantam hardcover ed.
p.   cm.
Originally published: London : Jonathan Cape, 2009.
Includes bibliographical references and index.
ISBN 978-0-553-80752-3 (hardcover : alk. paper)
1. da Vinci, Leonardo, 1452–1519.   2. Machiavelli, Niccolò, 1469–1527.
3. Borgia, Cesare, 1476?–1507.   4. Renaissance—Italy—Biography.
5. Italy—History—1492–1559.   I. Title.

DG540.8.A1S77 2009
945'.060922—dc22   2009006950

Printed in the United States of America on acid-free paper

www.bantamdell.com

2   4   6   8   9   7   5   3   1

First Edition

To
Amanda

The Renaissance is not so much a period of history as the repository of the myths we have created about western civilization.
—Roger Osborne, *Civilization*

Am I politic, am I subtle, am I a Machiavel?
—William Shakespeare, *The Merry Wives of Windsor*

In Italy for thirty years under the Borgias they had warfare, terror, murder and bloodshed, but they produced Michelangelo, Leonardo da Vinci and the Renaissance. In Switzerland they had brotherly love; they had five hundred years of democracy and peace—and what did that produce? The cuckoo clock.
—Orson Welles in *The Third Man*

Contents

Contents

List of Illustrations

Leonardo da Vinci, from Notebook 88A, courtesy of Dices/The Victoria & Albert Museum, London

RL 12278– Leonardo da Vinci, Recto: *Bird's-eye view showing Arezzo, Borgho san Sepolcro, Chiusi and Siena*. The Royal Collection © 2008, Her Majesty Queen Elizabeth II

Map of Sinigallia drawn by Reginald Piggott

Pera bridge design by Leonardo da Vinci © Photo RMN—Gerard Blot

Leonardo da Vinci (1452–1519): Drawing from the period of the Battle of Anghiari (facsimile). Florence, Gabinetto dei Disegni e delle Stampe degli Uffizi. © 1990. Photo Scala, Florence—courtesy of the Ministero Beni e Att. Culturali

Page from a notebook showing figures fighting on horseback and on foot (sepia ink on linen paper) by Vinci, Leonardo da (1452–1519), Galleria dell' Accademia, Venice, Italy/Cameraphoto Arte Venezia/The Bridgeman Art Library

Raphael, *Portrait of Pope Julius II* © The National Gallery, London

Mona Lisa, c.1503–6 (oil on panel) by Vinci, Leonardo da (1452–1519), Louvre, Paris, France/Giraudon/The Bridgeman Art Library

Illustration of the diversion of the River Arno drawn by Reginald Piggott

Facsimile of *Codex Atlanticus* f.1v-b Excavating Machine (original copy in the Biblioteca Ambrosiana, Milan, 1503/4–7) by Vinci, Leonardo da (1452–1519) Private Collection/The Bridgeman Art Library

La Bataille d'Anghiari dit aussi *Le Combat pour l'étenard*. Rubens, Pierre Paul (1577–1646). Paris, Musée de Louvre © RMN—Michelle Bellot

RL 12726– Leonardo da Vinci, after *A Portrait of Leonardo*. The Royal Collection © 2008, Her Majesty Queen Elizabeth II

RL 19095– Leonardo da Vinci, *Recto: Drawing of external genitalia & vagina, with notes*. The Royal Collection © 2008, Her Majesty Queen Elizabeth II

Maps drawn by Reginald Piggott.

Images Appearing Only in the Color Plate Section

Leonardo da Vinci (1452–1519): *Self-Portrait* no. 15741. Turin, Biblioteca Reale (Royal Library). © 1990. Photo Scala, Florence

Melone, Altobello (15th–16th cent.): *Portrait of Cesare Borgia.* Bergamo, Accademia Carrara. © 1990. Photo Scala, Florence

Santi di Tito (1536–1603): *Portrait of Niccolò Machiavelli.* Florence, Palazzo Vecchio. © 1990. Photo Scala, Florence

Pinturicchio (1454–1513): *Disputation of St. Catherine.* Vatican, Borgia Apartments. © 1990. Photo Scala, Florence

Barbari, Jacopo de' (c. 1440–1515): *Portrait of the Mathematician Luca Pacioli and Unknown Young Man.* Naples, Museo di Capodimonte. © 2003. Photo Scala, Florence—Courtesy of the Ministero Beni et Att. Culturali

Spanish School: *Portrait of Alexander VI.* Vatican, Pinoteca. © 1990. Photo Scala, Florence

Leonardo da Vinci (copy): *Battle of Anghiari.* Florence, Palazzo Vecchio. © 1990. Photo Scala, Florence—courtesy of the Ministero Beni et Att. Culturali

View with the Palazzo Vecchio. Florence, Piazza della Signoria. © 1998. Photo Scala, Florence

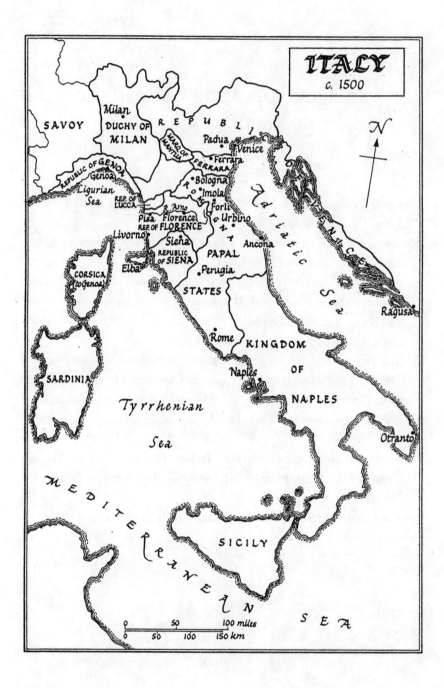

Map of Italy c.1500

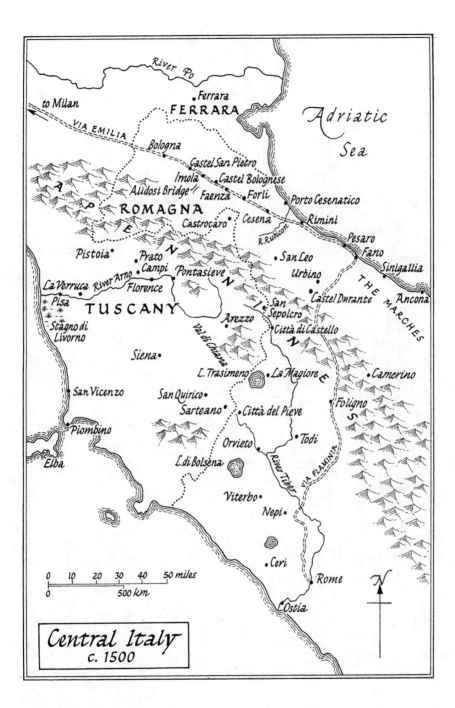

Central Italy c.1500

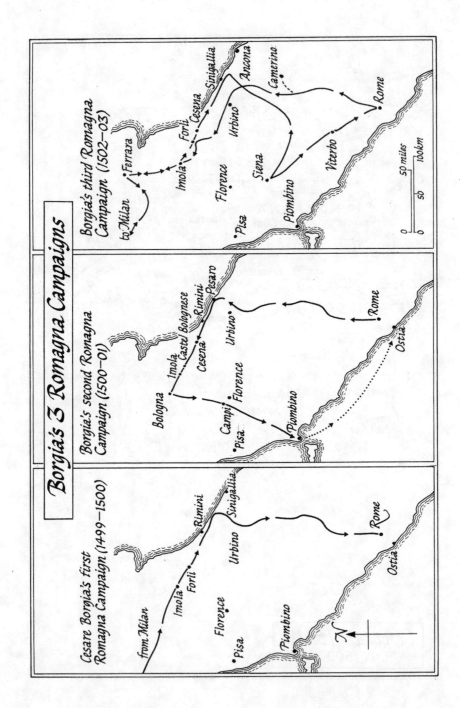

Borgia's 3 Romagna Campaigns

Cesare Borgia's first Romagna Campaign (1499–1500)

from Milan · Imola · Forlì · Rimini · Urbino · Sinigallia · Florence · Pisa · Piombino · Ostia · Rome

N

Borgia's second Romagna Campaign (1500–01)

Bologna · Imola · Castel Bolognese · Cesena · Rimini · Pisaro · Urbino · Campi · Florence · Pisa · Piombino · Ostia · Rome

Borgia's third Romagna Campaign (1502–03)

to Milan · Ferrara · Imola · Forlì · Cesena · Sinigallia · Ancona · Camerino · Florence · Urbino · Siena · Piombino · Viterbo · Rome · Pisa

0 50 50 miles
0 100km

Timeline

Leonardo enters the service of Cesare Borgia

Piero Soderini made *gonfaloniere* for life in Florence

Machiavelli sent as an envoy to Borgia in the Romagna

1503   Machiavelli returns to Florence

Leonardo leaves the service of Borgia and returns to Florence

Death of Alexander VI

Machiavelli travels to Rome to observe the papal elections after the death of Pius III

Election of Julius II, downfall of Borgia

Leonardo starts work on the *Battle of Anghiari* fresco, and works on the *Mona Lisa*

1504   Attempt to divert the course of the Arno ends in disaster

1506   Machiavelli establishes a Florentine militia

Leonardo returns to Milan

1507   Death of Cesare Borgia

1512   The Medici are returned to power in Florence

Fall of Soderini; Machiavelli dismissed

1513   Machiavelli accused of taking part in a plot to overthrow the Medici

Machiavelli imprisoned and tortured before returning to exile on his estate

Winter

1513–14 Machiavelli writes *The Prince*

1515   Francis I invades Italy

1519   Death of Leonardo in France

1527   Sack of Rome by troops of the Holy Roman Emperor, Charles V

The Medici are deposed from Florence, but Machiavelli receives no appointment in the new republican government

Death of Machiavelli

Dramatis Personae

D'Albrecht, Charlotte Younger sister of Jean, who became Cesare Borgia's long-suffering wife

D'Albrecht, Jean King of Navarre and brother of Charlotte

Alexander VI, Pope Formerly Cardinal Rodrigo Borgia, father of Cesare, Juan, Jofre, and Lucrezia.

Alfonso, Duke of Bisceglie Lucrezia Borgia's unfortunate second husband

Alfonso, King of Naples Fled from Naples in 1494 at the approach of the army of Charles VIII

Alfonso d'Este Son of the Duke of Ferrara and Lucrezia Borgia's third husband

D'Amboise, Charles Older brother of Georges. Became French governor of Milan

D'Amboise, Georges Became Cardinal of Rouen. Power behind the throne at the court of Louis XII when Machiavelli arrived as envoy from Florence. Leader of the French cardinals at the papal elections

Baglioni, Gianpaolo Unsavory ruler of Perugia and commander for Borgia

Bentivoglio, Ermes Son of Giovanni

Bentivoglio, Giovanni Ruler of Bologna and sometime ally of Cesare Borgia

Bisceglie, Duke of See Alfonso, Duke of Bisceglie

Borgia, Cesare Oldest son of Alexander VI by his mistress Vannozza de' Cattanei

Borgia, Giovanni The mysterious "Infans Romanus" who was probably born to Lucrezia Borgia. His officially acknowledged father was Cesare Borgia, but her father, Alexander VI, privately acknowledged his paternity

Borgia, Jofre Third son by Vannozza of Alexander VI

Borgia, Juan, Duke of Gandia Second son by Vannozza of Alexander VI, appointed *gonfaloniere* of the papal forces. Murdered in suspicious circumstances in Rome, 1497

Borgia, Lucrezia Daughter of Alexander VI; much beloved by her father and her brother Cesare

Borgia, Cardinal Ludovico One of the Spanish cardinals appointed by Alexander VI, upon whom Cesare so relied

Borgia, Cardinal Rodrigo See Alexander VI

Burchard, Johannes Diarist and master of ceremonies at the Vatican during the reign of Alexander VI

Carvajal, Cardinal Spanish cardinal appointed by Alexander VI, upon whom Cesare Borgia would come to rely

Caterina The peasant girl who was Leonardo's mother

Cattanei, Vannozza de' Strong-willed mistress of Alexander VI, mother of Cesare Borgia, as well as his siblings Juan, Jofre, and Lucrezia

Charles VIII of France The unprepossessing young king whose 1494 invasion of Italy to take possession of Naples instigated a period of instability

Clement VII Second Medici pope, whose disastrous reign saw the sack of Rome

Colonna One of the powerful aristocratic Roman families. Prospero Colonna became a commander of the Spanish forces at Rome

De Predis brothers Florentine artists in Milan with whom Leonardo worked

Don Michele Borgia's notorious Spanish commander; the strangler

Ferdinand, King of Spain, "the Catholic" In fact he was King of Aragon and Sicily, becoming joint ruler of Spain with Queen Isabella of Castile (although Granada was still a Moorish kingdom). Played an increasingly influential role in the kingdom of Naples, and appointed Gonsalvo de Cordova as his governor there in 1503

Ferdinand II, King of Naples Took over from his father, King Ferrante

Ferrante, King of Naples Fled in the face of Charles VIII's army

Francis I of France Succeeded Louis XII; his 1515 invasion of Italy finally deposed the Sforzas from Milan. Met Pope Leo X and Leonardo at Bologna in 1515

Giustinian, Antonio Venetian ambassador to the papal court in Rome

Gonsalvo de Cordova Commander of the Spanish forces in Naples; defeated the French at the Battle of Garigliano and became Spanish governor of Naples

Guicciardini, Francesco Renowned historian and relative of Luigi Guicciardini, Machiavelli's friend in the Florentine administration

Guidobaldo da Montefeltro, Duke of Urbino Son of the great *condottiere* Federigo da Montefeltro, and periodically ruler of Urbino during the time of Borgia's campaigns in the Romagna

"Infans Romanus" See Giovanni Borgia

Innocent VIII Pope prior to the election of Alexander VI

Isabella of Castile Became joint ruler of Spain with King Ferdinand

Julius II, Pope Formerly Cardinal Giuliano della Rovere. Implacable enemy of the Borgias. Succeeded to the papacy in 1503, the year that Alexander VI died

Leo X First Medici pope, who succeeded Julius II

Liverotto da Fermo Small city despot and treacherous commander for Cesare Borgia

Lorqua, Ramiro de Borgia's cruel Spanish commander, who ruled the Romagna in his absence

Louis XII of France His invasion of Italy in 1499 drove Ludovico Sforza from Milan. His army later took the kingdom of Naples, which was unwisely divided with the Spanish

Machiavelli, Bernardo Illegitimate scion of an ancient Florentine family, and father of Niccolò

Machiavelli, Marietta (née Corsini) Niccolò's long-suffering wife

Maximilian I Holy Roman Emperor, whose German court was visited by Machiavelli

Medici, Giovanni de' Son of Lorenzo the Magnificent, cardinal and later Pope Leo X

Medici, Giuliano de' Patron of Leonardo in Rome, briefly ruler of Florence

Medici, Lorenzo de' Known as "the Magnificent," ruler of Florence and patron of Leonardo

Medici, Piero de' Ruler of Florence, deposed after the invasion of Charles VIII

Melzi, Francesco Young Milanese aristocrat who became Leonardo's pupil and secretary, and who took charge of Leonardo's notebooks after his death

Michelangelo The Florentine artist who was Leonardo's bitter rival

Michiel, Cardinal Wealthy cardinal who fell foul of Alexander VI

Moncada, Ugo de One of Cesare Borgia's most loyal Spanish commanders

Orsini One of the powerful aristocratic Roman families

Orsini, Cardinal Giambattista On-and-off crony of Alexander VI; summoned the meeting of anti-Borgia conspirators at La Magione

Orsini, Giangiordano The unpredictable Orsini, whom Borgia refused to attack

Orsini, Giulio One of Cesare Borgia's military commanders

Orsini, Paolo The weak link amongst the anti-Borgia conspirators

Pacioli, Luca Mathematical monk and close intellectual friend of Leonardo's

Perotto Lucrezia Borgia's favorite manservant, who may possibly have been the father of the "Infans Romanus"

Petrucci, Pandolfo The wily and despotic ruler of Siena, the brains behind the anti-Borgia meeting at La Magione

Ramires brothers Borgia's ultra-loyal commanders, who held out at Cesena

Remolino, Cardinal Leading Spanish cardinal

della Rovere, Cardinal Giuliano See Julius II

Salai Leonardo's scallywag assistant, who later became his lover

Sansavino, Antonio di Humanist, appointed by Cesare Borgia as *"Presidente"* of the Romagna; established popular government for Borgia

Savonarola The fanatical priest who came to power in Florence after the Medici were ousted

Sforza, Cardinal Ascanio Brother of Ludovico and the man who cast the deciding vote for Cardinal Rodrigo Borgia

Sforza, Caterina The formidable ruler of Imola and Forli

Sforza, Gian Galeazzo Rightful young Duke of Milan, who was deposed by Ludovico Sforza

Sforza, Giovanni, Lord of Pesaro Disgraced first husband of Lucrezia Borgia

Sforza, Ludovico "Il Moro" Ruler of Milan during Leonardo's first stay in the city. Deposed by Charles VIII of France

Soderini, Francesco, Bishop of Volterra Brother of Piero. Traveled with Machiavelli to Urbino to meet Borgia

Soderini, Piero Appointed *gonfaloniere* for life in Florence; worked closely with Machiavelli

Vannozza, see Cattanei

Vespucci, Agostino Machiavelli's friend and colleague in the Florence administration. Related to Amerigo Vespucci, after whom America is named

da Vinci, Francesco Leonardo's favorite uncle, who played a leading role in his childhood

da Vinci, Ser Piero The Florentine lawyer who was Leonardo's father, a distant figure during his childhood

Vitelli, Paolo Treacherous mercenary in charge of Florentine troops at Pisa

Vitelli, Vitellozzo Often referred to simply as Vitellozzo—brother of Paolo and one of Borgia's commanders

Acknowledgments

My thanks to Ellah Allfrey at Jonathan Cape, whose understanding editing enabled me to overcome many difficulties. Also to Katherine Murphy, who was always helpful, and other editorial staff including Mandy Greenfield and Peter McAdie, who each made significant contributions to this work.

I would also like to thank the helpful and understanding staff I encountered in various libraries in Britain and Italy, but most of all the ever-sympathetic staff in the Humanities 2 Reading Room at the British Library.

No acknowledgment would be complete without mention of my agent, Julian Alexander, who played such a vital role in initiating the project (and even supplied its title).

Paul Strathern

Prologue: A Unique Constellation

IN JUNE 1502 Cesare Borgia led his troops across the Apennine mountains of central Italy, sweeping north towards the Romagna, occupying town after town, his every move spreading terror before him. This was the third time in as many years that Borgia had launched an aggressive campaign of conquest into the Romagna, the remote north-eastern region of Italy between Bologna and Ancona. On the previous two occasions he had shown himself to be increasingly hostile towards Florence, whose unguarded territory bordered the region. The city had no standing army with which to defend itself, and its worst fears were quickly confirmed. Soon Borgia's men were encroaching on Florentine territory, and he sent word to Florence that he wished to discuss a matter of great importance. This message caused consternation amongst the ruling Signoria, and forthwith on June 22 they dispatched Francesco Soderini, Bishop of Volterra, and Niccolò Machiavelli, their most able diplomatic negotiator, on a two-man delegation to meet Borgia and discover his intentions. After riding at full tilt, later that day Soderini and Machiavelli reached Pontasieve, where they were informed by a fleeing priest that Borgia had suddenly and dramatically deviated from his advance and seized the strategically vital city of Urbino, without losing a single man. No one knew for certain what was happening: some said the Duke of Urbino had fled, others that he had been taken prisoner, others still that he had been killed. On only one thing were all agreed, that Borgia had gained possession of the city by means of treachery. As Machiavelli wrote back to Florence: "Your lordships should take note of this stratagem, as well as his combination of remarkable speed and extraordinary good fortune." Borgia's tactics were "to install himself in someone else's house before anyone else noticed it," as in the case of the Duke of Urbino, "whose death was reported before he was even known to be ill."

Riding as fast as their horses could carry them, Machiavelli and Soderini reached Urbino two days later, shortly after dark. Borgia had already heard that they were on their way and ordered that they be brought immediately to see him, giving the emissaries no time to prepare themselves, or even change from their worn, sweat-soiled riding clothes. In the darkness they were hustled through the courtyard up the stairs in the ducal palace, where Borgia had now taken up residence. The doors were bolted behind them, with armed sentries posted outside; Soderini and Machiavelli found themselves alone in the empty palace, where Borgia was waiting for them

> by the light of a single flickering candle which showed only dimly the tall figure clad in black from head to foot without jewel or ornament, the still, white features as regular as a Greek statue and as immobile. Perhaps the cold beauty of those marble features was already beginning to be marred by the pustules which led [Borgia] later on usually to wear a mask.

Borgia launched into an attack on the Florentine delegation, threatening them: "I am not pleased with your government. How can I trust you, how can I be sure you will not attack me? You must change your government and pledge to support me—for I have no intention of letting this state of affairs continue." Borgia's attitude was clear enough: he would no longer accept Florence's neutrality towards him. If Florence did not replace its independent-minded republican government with one that was sympathetic to his cause, he was liable to take matters into his own hands. He ended ominously: "If you do not want me as a friend, you will find me your enemy."

Machiavelli was certainly chastened and impressed by this performance. Borgia's murderous legend had preceded him: this man, who "made Florentines tremble and Rome weep," was liable to do anything. Yet Machiavelli also had sufficient diplomatic experience to recognize that Borgia's declaration was not quite all that it seemed. He sensed that Borgia was bluffing. Yet why?

Machiavelli and Bishop Soderini knew that Borgia had the powerful backing of his father Pope Alexander VI in Rome, and understood that he also had the support of King Louis XII of France, who was with his army in Milanese territory to the north. Florence lay between the two, vulnerable on all sides. Machiavelli knew that Florence could not give in to Borgia, but he also knew that the city was in no position to resist.

In an attempt to mollify Borgia, Machiavelli appears to have made a suggestion. Subsequent evidence points to a secret agreement being struck at this meeting between Borgia and the Florentines. Borgia was most anxious to have in his service the man he considered to be the most talented military engineer in Italy. This was Leonardo da Vinci, who was at present living in Florence.

After a long absence, Leonardo had recently returned to live in his native city, his notebooks filled with designs and coded descriptions of all manner of fiendish military machines. Some of these drawings Borgia had probably already seen, when he had met Leonardo three years previously. On that occasion Borgia had been so impressed that he had offered to employ Leonardo, an offer that Leonardo seemingly turned down. Now, because Florence was under threat, or possibly owing to some previous assurance, Leonardo would be obliged to take up Borgia's offer.

Machiavelli was well aware that Borgia's proposal was fraught with danger, but it meant that Florence would have a spy attached to Borgia. This spy would perhaps be able to relay back to Florence the exact nature of Borgia's intentions, and precisely why he was bluffing.

Leonardo da Vinci, Niccolò Machiavelli, and Cesare Borgia: a unique constellation—each, in his own way, emblematic of a distinct aspect of humanity.

Borgia has become a byword for monstrous deeds—his very name summoning up images of betrayal, murder, and depravity. Here was a man who acted on impulse, who judged people intuitively with a cunning, almost animal acumen. He was a savage, but he was also a man of the Renaissance—a highly educated savage, a brilliant mind utterly attuned to its basest instincts.

Leonardo, on the other hand, has become a supreme exemplar of higher human aspiration. Here is Renaissance man in excelsis: possessed of wide-ranging knowledge and great accomplishment in numerous fields. His paintings and drawings are among the finest of the period, his voluminous notebooks contain the most intricate scientific researches and technological inventions—yet, curiously, the man himself remains something of an enigma. We know so much about his thoughts and his works, but the actual person who produced this cornucopia of treasures remains a shadowy presence whose "colossal outlines ... can never be more than dimly and distantly conceived." In this, he strangely resembles Shakespeare. Two of humanity's greatest creative spirits, each of whose works are so utterly characteristic, have come down to us themselves as peculiarly characterless. Or so it would seem. But there is a way for us to gain a clearer picture of Leonardo. When he is viewed beside his contemporaries Borgia and Machiavelli—two very vivid characters—certain surprising and unexpected aspects of Leonardo's character begin to emerge. What was it precisely that made Leonardo agree to work for Borgia? And what were his real intentions? How did he become involved with Machiavelli? These questions, so often overlooked, hold vital clues to Leonardo's character, helping to dispel the clouds of mystery that have gathered about this great sage.

Machiavelli, by comparison, was very much a normal man: someone who liked joking and drinking with his friends, who enjoyed sexual peccadilloes, who had ambition and strove to ascend the slippery pole of civic life. He fibbed, negotiated, spied, and wrote reports for his political masters—here was the ultimate civil servant. Yet he did so much more than simply obey orders. His exceptional quality lay in his need to try to understand the workings of the political world in which he operated, and in his attempt to discern a science in human behavior. But it was this very search for truth, for a philosophy that underlay human affairs, that would bring him infamy. In his masterwork *The Prince* he would describe how human beings actually behaved (rather than how they ought to behave), and how a powerful leader could manipulate this to his own advantage. As a result, Machiavelli's name would become notorious, condemned by the Church and by all upright citizens. After his death, this notoriety would spread throughout Europe; so that by the end of the century William Shakespeare in far-away England could have a character protest his straightforward honesty—"Am I politic, am I subtle, am I a Machiavel?"—and be confident that his entire audience, from the knights and their ladies to the raucous groundlings in the pit, would understand what he meant.

Leonardo, Machiavelli, and Borgia: as the lives of these disparate individuals unfold, we see how each illustrates an aspect of the Renaissance—its art, its philosophy, and its wars. Borgia was the actor strutting the boards, Machiavelli plotted the devious script, while Leonardo painted the set and designed the ingenious mechanical devices that shifted the scenery.

The tempestuous history of Italy during the Renaissance produced men of genius as well as ogres, many of the greatest works of art known to humanity, and ambitious schemes the like of which had never been seen before. Dark and horrendous events frequently underlay the glories of the Renaissance, and both glory and horror ran through the lives of Leonardo, Machiavelli, and Borgia.

Just as the Renaissance was coming into full flower, these three men would, for some months, travel the same road, drawn towards one another partly by fortune, partly by elements within their own characters. During 1502, from the mists of autumn until chill muddy midwinter, Borgia, Machiavelli, and Leonardo journeyed alongside one another through the mountains, remote valleys, and hill towns of the Italian Romagna. This was a period of extreme significance, and considerable danger, for all of them—when each, in his own different way, was playing with fire.

The time all three spent together may have been brief, but it would have a continuing influence on each of their lives, in ways both great and small. Whilst working with Borgia, Leonardo would discover the landscape that would one day appear as the mysterious background to the *Mona Lisa*; he would also develop some of his most revolutionary schemes. One of these he would discuss with Machiavelli, and later the two of them would launch a vast project that attempted to realize Leonardo's ambitious idea.

Borgia, for his part, had ambitions to carve out his own personal kingdom in the Romagna, the first step in a grandiose dream of uniting Italy and returning it to the glories of the Roman Empire. Not for nothing did he adopt a motto featuring his classical namesake: "Either Caesar, or nothing." As a result, Machiavelli would make Cesare Borgia the "hero" of his notorious work *The Prince*, which shocked the world, revolutionized political thinking, and would ultimately transform humanity's view of itself.

Astonishingly, this encounter between three such disparate characters would prove to be a decisive meeting of minds, particularly where Machiavelli was concerned. Prior to this encounter Leonardo had been developing his scientific view of the world: the truth could only be reached by perception, by careful observation of the world around us, rather than by relying upon the ancient authorities such as Aristotle. Meanwhile Machiavelli's experience on diplomatic missions for the Florentine government had taught him to see through the pretenses of political behavior and attempt to discern the truth of what was actually taking place. His encounter with Leonardo would lead him to seek a scientific basis for what he had learned. Machiavelli too would come to realize that the truth could only be reached by perception, by careful observation, rather than by referring to precedent or authority. But instead of applying this view to the world itself, he would apply it to the behavior of the people around him. In politics, power was the effective principle. To gain this, and hold on to it: here lay the truth underlying human affairs. And to Machiavelli, Borgia would come to embody the ruthless application of this political truth. There was no room for illusion in the pursuit of political power.

The political situation in Italy at the end of the fifteenth century was ripe for such a cynical approach. The entire peninsula was in disarray, dominated by the city-states of Milan, Venice, Naples, and Florence, as well as the ever-vacillating influence of the pope in Rome. Each of these powers was constantly seeking to extend its territory, or defend itself from its perfidious neighbors—by means of intrigue, fragile alliances, or simple treachery. Florence, for instance, was loosely allied to Milan, fearful of its former ally Venice, and suspicious of the papacy in Rome. Meanwhile Pope Alexander VI had plans for extending the territorial power of Rome by reconquering the Romagna, which had previously been part of the papal domains, a move that would inevitably be seen as a distinct threat by both Venice and Florence, whose territory bordered the Romagna.

This fragmented situation left Italy as a whole in a particularly weak and vulnerable condition. A short distance across the Alps to the north lay France, the most powerful country in Europe. Spain, bolstered by the influx of treasures from the New World, would soon seek to extend its traditional influence in Naples. Meanwhile to the east the whole of Christendom lay under threat from the expanding Ottoman Empire, whose armies were sweeping north through the Balkans, advancing up the eastern Adriatic coast.

Such was the background to the early years of Leonardo, Machiavelli, and Borgia. This precarious situation would quickly disintegrate in a succession of disastrous events, which would affect each of the three protagonists in different ways. As we follow their lives before they met, we see the same succession of events from three very different points of view, each time enabling us to see deeper into the complexities and implications of this crucial period in Italian history. It was the events of these years that would eventually bring together Leonardo, Machiavelli, and Borgia for their fateful meeting in the Romagna.

What precisely happened during these months can be gleaned from a number of firsthand sources. Most important, we have Machiavelli's often daily diplomatic dispatches back to his masters in Florence. We also have various descriptions and cryptic remarks that Leonardo jotted down in his coded notebooks. From these two sources it is possible to piece together a vivid, if incomplete, picture of the daily life lived by their authors. Yet it is these very gaps that are often most revealing. Both Leonardo and Machiavelli had good reason for caution in what they described: such close proximity to Borgia placed them in very real danger of their lives. Our sources for Borgia during these brief months are similarly ambiguous. We can, for the most part, glean the contents of his secretive dispatches to Rome by the effect these had on his volatile and demonstrative father, Alexander VI. The pope's reactions were reported in vivid detail by the various confidants he had amongst the ambassadors to the papal court.

After their winter months together in the Romagna, Leonardo, Machiavelli, and Borgia would disperse in pursuit of their different destinies. Each would be influenced by what he had experienced: each would succeed and fail in his own characteristic fashion. Leonardo would seek to distance himself from political upheavals in order to pursue his private speculations, yet these very speculations would draw him back into the fray. Machiavelli would seek to influence events, yet his very failure to do so would confirm for him the truth that underlay the political world. Borgia would seek to play a leading role in Italy, using every means at his disposal, especially treachery; yet it was treachery that would eventually prove his undoing.

The Italian Renaissance was a stage on which art and history, literature and politics, science and warfare were inextricably entangled: Leonardo, Machiavelli, and Borgia were as much involved in this entanglement as any others. In order to understand these three figures—the artist, the philosopher, and the warrior—we must first examine their lives before they encountered one another.

Part 1

The Artist, the Philosopher,
and the Warrior

I

Leonardo Learning

LEONARDO DA VINCI was born in 1452 in the hilly Tuscan country-side near the village of Vinci, some twenty miles west of Florence. He was the illegitimate son of Ser Piero da Vinci, a twenty-six-year-old notary, who during Leonardo's childhood remained for the most part in Florence, pursuing a successful career. All that is known for certain of Leonardo's mother, Caterina, is that she was a twenty-five-year-old peasant girl, who may have been the daughter of a local woodcutter.

Few facts are known about Leonardo's early years and we have to rely upon occasional, often enigmatic, remarks made years later in his notebooks. A prime example is the comment made by Leonardo whilst he was writing on the flight of birds, in this case observing the flight of the fork-tailed kite, a bird that often flew over Vinci from the slopes of nearby Mount Albano:

> Writing in such detail about the kite seems to be my destiny, since in the first memory of my childhood it seemed to me that whilst I was lying in my cradle a kite flew down and brushed open my mouth with its tail, and struck me several times with its tail on the inside of my lips.

Out of this suggestive fragment Freud would construct an entire psychological history for Leonardo, leading from the trauma of separation from his mother, and his consequent ambivalent feelings towards her, to his homosexuality and his reluctance to finish projects upon which he embarked. Unfortunately the German translation used by Freud mistakenly rendered the Italian word for kite (*nebbio*) as "vulture," lending an altogether more lurid tone to this memory. Despite this error, Freud's claim that Leonardo's memory of the tail probing his lips was a masked image of his mother's nipple, when he was suckling her breast, seems plausible enough. And there is little doubt that Leonardo did suffer a trauma on separation from his mother. Years later he would write down a series of riddles, amongst which there is a recurrent theme of violent separation of a mother and her child. A typical example reads: "Many children will be torn from the arms of their mother with pitiless blows and be thrown to the ground to be mutilated." The answer to the riddle is in fact "Nuts, and olives and acorns," but the power of the prior image is suggestive.

In 1456, when Leonardo was four, Tuscany was devastated by a great storm, possibly a tornado. Years later he could still vividly recall:

> I have witnessed movements of air so furious that they have
> borne away, mixed up within them, the largest trees of the forest
> and the whole roofs of great palaces, and I have seen the same
> fury bore a hole with its whirling force, digging out a gravel
> pit, and carrying off gravel, sand and water more than half a
> mile through the air.

Several years after this, the River Arno would overflow its banks, causing severe floods throughout the Val d'Arno. The power of these two natural disasters that Leonardo experienced in his youth would long remain in his memory, the latter initiating a fearful fascination with deluges and floods that would last throughout his life.

Leonardo was brought up in the household of his paternal grandfather, Antonio da Vinci, where he seems to have become particularly attached to Antonio's youngest son, Francesco, who despite being Leonardo's uncle was just fifteen years older than he. Unlike Leonardo's ambitious father, Francesco had remained behind in the country, where he busied himself looking after the da Vinci farmland and vineyards.

We can imagine the impressionable young Leonardo dogging the footsteps of his uncle as he oversaw the laborers on the estate. Francesco was almost certainly the first of the several powerful figures to whom Leonardo would be drawn throughout his life. Significantly, all these figures would be young men: initially older than Leonardo, later younger—but mostly in their twenties, the age of Francesco when the child Leonardo would first have become attached to him. (For example, Cesare Borgia was just twenty-five when the middle-aged Leonardo first encountered him.)

Francesco must have passed on much country lore to his young nephew. The ways of nature—how it appeared, what was happening, what this meant—would remain one of Leonardo's constant preoccupations throughout his life. This curiosity may well have been what initially prompted him to draw.

At least temporarily, Francesco would be the father figure who was missing from Leonardo's life. During this period the young boy was also virtually motherless, for within a year of his birth Caterina married a returned soldier, not long after which Leonardo seems to have been left largely to his own devices. Far from being lonely, he soon began discovering the joys of solitude, of which he later spoke so warmly: "While you are alone you are completely yourself; and if you are accompanied by even one other person you are but half yourself." This solitude was from the beginning associated with drawing nature: "You should say to yourself, 'I will go my own way and withdraw apart from others, the better to study the form of natural objects.'" Years later he would recall an occasion when he was walking alone in the countryside:

> Driven by my eager desire and wishing to see the multitude of
> varied and strange forms created by nature, and having wandered
> some distance amongst overhanging rocks, I came to the entrance
> of a great cavern, in front of which I stood for some time,
> astonished, having never seen such a thing before. Bending
> forward, I rested my tired hand on my knee and held my right
> hand above my furrowed eyebrows as I peered down. I shifted
> from side to side, to see whether I could discern anything inside,

but this was prevented by the deep darkness within. After having remained there for some time, I felt the contrary emotions of fear and desire arising within me—fear of the forbidding dark cavern, and my desire to see whether there was anything marvelous within it.

This description exhibits a riveting particularity—one can vividly picture the young Leonardo amongst the rocks, leaning on his knee, peering forward in the bright sunlight. Yet at the same time he consciously introduces elements that allude to something more: his desires, his fears, the very nature of his individuality. It is as if Leonardo is prompting us to read this passage imaginatively, as one might read an occasional poem. Under such circumstances we become aware of the sexual undertones of the cave and the primeval fear of the unknown that lurks in the darkness, as well as the longing to discover the "marvelous" truth of that very same unknown.

Soon, of course, curiosity overcame Leonardo's fears and he entered the darkness of his metaphorical cave to explore its secrets. Such curiosity suffused his dreams, which included great and strange ambitions. Later, in one of his riddles, he would describe dreaming in the following words, which reek of subjective experience:

Men will seem to see unknown destructions in the sky. It will seem that they are flying up into the sky, and then they are fleeing in terror from the flames that pour down on them. They will hear animals of every kind speaking in human language. Their bodies will glide in an instant to various parts of the world without moving. They will see the greatest splendors in the midst of the darkness. What a marvel is the human race! What frenzy has led you to this? ... You will see yourself falling from great heights without harming yourself. Torrents will sweep you along and whirl you in their rapid course....

It is as if we are seeing Leonardo's future ambitions in embryo, and yet these are the very dreams we all experience. Leonardo's life would be spent trying to realize the dreams of humanity itself. He remained deeply attuned to the promptings of his unconscious mind—its wish to fly, to understand the secrets of nature, to survive a torrent of water. Instead of being taught what to do, what to think, he dreamed of what he wanted to do, and no formal schooling persuaded him otherwise.

Leonardo's father, Ser Piero, would certainly have visited his own father, Antonio da Vinci, and his brother, Francesco, at the da Vinci estate for feast-day family gatherings and during longer summer holidays. And he would of course have brought along his young wife, Albiera, whom he had married in Florence, just as he would bring along his second wife, Francesca, whom he married when Albiera died. Both of these women remained childless. Leonardo may have been a lone motherless child, but it appears that his growing good looks and precocious skill in drawing charmed both his childless stepmothers. From the beginning, he exhibited the self-certainty of one who is used to being the center of attention, of a boy who has grown up experiencing worshipful and unquestioning female love. The fact that both these adoring stepmothers would die when he was still young doubtless caused him sorrow, and may have contributed to the reserved self-possession that he began to display.

Around the mid-1460s, at the beginning of Leonardo's adolescence, he went to live in Florence, where his exceptional talent for drawing enabled him to become apprenticed to the studio of the leading artist Andrea del Verrocchio. Here Leonardo would learn drawing, painting, anatomy, sculpting, and architectural design. This led him into new fields, extending his intellect even further. Drawing would lead him to the study of perspective, which then interested him in geometry; anatomy would lead him to ponder the workings of mechanical devices; architecture would lead him to a study of arithmetic proportions; and this would in turn lead him to learn about harmony in music. His intellectual curiosity coupled with his lack of formal education prompted him to an endless quest for new knowledge. But this would be knowledge that he insisted upon acquiring in his own way: not from books (most of which were written in Latin, which he could not understand), but from experience; not systematically, but as and when the appropriate opportunity presented itself. He began jotting things down in notebooks, without overall order or consequence, just as he would throughout his life. There was no encompassing plan beyond the pure initial impulse, which led with childlike power and wonder in its own direction. Yet his education was not entirely without book learning. It was at around this period that he started reading, in Italian translation, the first-century BC Roman author Lucretius, whose epic poem *De Rerum Natura* (On the Nature of Things) sought to explain the world in scientific terms. Although Leonardo's investigations may have appeared serendipitous, they were increasingly guided by an overall vision, a consistent empirical view of the world, and this he probably drew from Lucretius.

Many of Florence's finest artists would gather at Verrocchio's studio, including Botticelli, the favorite painter of Lorenzo the Magnificent, head of the powerful Medici family that ruled Florence. Lorenzo's "magnificence" extended into many fields. As a ruler he would make Florence great; his bravery in jousting was legendary; he was one of the most accomplished poets of his time, and the circle he maintained at the Palazzo Medici on the Via Larga included the finest poets, artists, philosophers, and scholars. Amongst these were the poet Angelo Poliziano, the philosopher Giovanni Pico della Mirandola, and the Platonic scholar Marsilio Ficino, all leading luminaries of the Renaissance that was taking place in Florence.

Inevitably, it was not long before the handsome and talented Leonardo da Vinci came to the attention of Lorenzo the Magnificent. Here was another powerful young man to whom Leonardo would find himself drawn, and Leonardo would soon be regarded as part of Lorenzo's circle of artists, philosophers, and poets. In the course of his musical studies Leonardo had learned to play the lyre and had developed an exceptionally harmonious singing voice, with which he would now entertain Lorenzo and his friends. This personal connection with the city's ruler was to have serious consequences for Leonardo. Partly in self-conscious assertion of his own exceptional abilities, and partly in bravura compensation for his illegitimacy, Leonardo had developed into something of a dandy. Tall and handsome, he cut a fine figure striding through the streets of Florence in his thigh-length boots of soft Cordoba leather, his long hair falling in curls about the shoulders of his short pink tunic, his passing presence wreathed in rose-water scent.

In April 1476 Leonardo was denounced, along with three others, in an anonymous note to the authorities claiming that he had practiced sodomy with a young man called Jacopo Saltarelli. As a result Leonardo was charged, and almost certainly spent some time in the cells, before being released pending a trial in two months' time. The charges were finally dropped after a word to the authorities from Lorenzo the Magnificent. The accusation against Leonardo appear to have been engineered by one or other of the powerful families who resented Medici rule, as an attempt to discredit Lorenzo and his circle.

It was a deeply humiliating episode, yet the only evidence we have of Leonardo's feelings is characteristically oblique and ingenious. Amongst his drawings from around this period there is a sketch of one of his earliest inventions—a powerful and meticulously drawn "design for a device for unhinging a prison door from the inside." One can but imagine him sitting in his soiled finery in the dimness of his cell amidst the stinking vermin-ridden straw, bitterly piecing together in his mind a machine that would have enabled him to escape.

Florence may have been the early epicenter of the Renaissance, but the ripples of its effect were now beginning to spread far and wide, beyond the realm of art, literature, and philosophy, and into geometry, astronomy, exploration, and even technology. Yet here too there remained that poetic element which characterizes so much Renaissance endeavor. Some time after 1480 Leonardo met and began to study with the astronomer and geographer Paolo Toscanelli, of whom Poliziano wrote in a Latin poem:

> Paulus crosses the earth with his feet
> And the starry sky with his mind,
> both mortal and immortal simultaneously.

As early as 1474, Toscanelli had drawn a map of the world in the shape of a globe, indicating that a ship that sailed west would eventually reach India. Toscanelli's map would inspire Columbus to attempt this voyage. Leonardo too would acquire one of these maps, and years later would list it among his most treasured possessions, referring to it in his notebook: "my map of the world which Giovanni Benci has."

Leonardo's portrait of Ginevra de' Benci.

By 1477 the twenty-four-year-old Leonardo had left Verrocchio's studio to set up on his own. The influence of Lorenzo the Magnificent certainly enabled the young artist to gain several important commissions—most notably his *Portrait of Ginevra de' Benci*, the first work in which he begins to demonstrate an original vision. This painting features a number of striking novelties: the sitter gazes unabashedly out of the portrait, and the landscape behind her is both precisely realistic and psychologically metaphorical. Her head is encapsulated by the dark prickly foliage of a juniper tree—in the Italian of the period *ginépro* or *genévre*, a pun on her name, as well as a subtle indication of her character. Behind her a still, deep river recedes towards distant misty hills. Most striking of all is the pellucid skin of her face, and its heavy-lidded enigmatic expression, hinting at a brooding, willful personality. This is much more than the portrait of a beautiful young woman: it is a profound reading of her individual nature.

Leonardo's relationship with Lorenzo the Magnificent and his circle had by now cooled somewhat. Quite simply, Leonardo did not fit in amongst the brilliant and privileged group of intellectuals who gathered at the Palazzo Medici. Their humanist erudition, their ability to speak Latin (and even Greek), their sophisticated behavior—all these excluded the ill-educated country boy from Vinci, who spoke with a yokel's accent and was more interested in drawing strange machines and animals, while they composed their witty poems for the extravagant festivals that Lorenzo staged to keep the populace happy and defuse any anti-Medici resentment.

Yet this method of courting popularity was not entirely successful, and in 1478 Florence witnessed a tumultuous event: Lorenzo the Magnificent just managed to survive an assassination attempt backed by the powerful Pazzi family, who had the covert support of Pope Sixtus IV in Rome. When the plot failed, Florence was plunged into turmoil as the mob went on the rampage in search of the conspirators. Machiavelli, who was a boy of nine at the time, later recalled these events in his *Florentine Histories,* describing the fate of the conspirators: "They fled in terror and attempted to hide themselves; but when they were found later they were killed and their bodies dragged through the streets in disgrace." Other conspirators, who were caught upstairs in the Palazzo della Signoria, the official residence of the ruling council, "were either butchered immediately or thrown alive out of the high palace windows." Leonardo too witnessed these events, and when one of the conspirators who had escaped was brought back to Florence a year later to be publicly hanged, Leonardo would draw a sketch of him dangling on the end of the rope. These events would undoubtedly have had an effect on Leonardo, but in characteristic fashion his notebooks contain no mention of them, besides this one oblique reference.

Two years later Lorenzo the Magnificent engineered a difficult rapprochement with the powerful pope, and to cement this he dispatched a number of leading Florentine artists to Rome to decorate the chapel recently built by Sixtus IV, which became known after him as the Sixtine (now Sistine) Chapel. Significantly, Leonardo was not amongst the painters chosen for this diplomatic mission. He had begun to develop an unsettling trait—despite the undoubted brilliance of his painting, he found it increasingly difficult to finish the works for which he had been commissioned. This was at least partly because his interests had now begun to turn elsewhere: to scientific studies of nature, drawings of increasingly ingenious projects, plans for military machines, and so forth. This inability to complete his paintings has also been ascribed to his ever-evolving artistic ideas, which often made it impossible for him to achieve any uniform vision in a single work. At the same time, it also has all the hallmarks of some obscure psychological block.

Probably as a result of Leonardo's unfinished commissions (and increasingly angry patrons), Lorenzo sent him in 1482 on a mission to Milan—to deliver, and demonstrate to its ruler Ludovico Sforza, a magnificent silver lyre that Leonardo had produced in the form of a horse's head.

Leonardo evidently saw this as his opportunity to leave Florence on a more permanent basis, and wrote to Ludovico Sforza listing his abilities as a civil and military engineer. He even went so far as to suggest that he be given the task of casting the huge bronze equestrian statue that Ludovico wished to erect in honor of his father, the great *condottiere* (mercenary general) Francesco Sforza, who had taken over Milan and founded the city's present ruling dynasty.

Leonardo was to spend seventeen years in Milan, and this was to be the happiest and most productive period of his life. Although it would be some time before he was taken on by Ludovico Sforza, he readily stayed on in the city, initially accepting joint commissions with his fellow Florentine artists the de Predis brothers. Leonardo relished the brasher and more vibrant commercial atmosphere of misty northern Milan after the hothouse of Florentine snobbery and high culture. And it was here that he took on a ten-year-old assistant whom he

Profile of a youth, by Leonardo:
thought to be Salai.

nicknamed "Salai" (scallywag), whose irrepressible ways and burgeoning adolescent beauty would eventually captivate his master's heart. Leonardo would buy fine clothes for Salai, who would reward him by stealing money from his purse. Leonardo's notebooks become littered with references to this "little devil," this "imp"; at one point he exasperatedly describes him as a "thief, liar, obstinate, greedy," yet at the same time his loving drawings of Salai depict a captivating young man of exceptional beauty.

In a very different way, Leonardo was drawn to the powerful Ludovico Sforza, who was just a year older than he. Ludovico, known as "Il Moro" (The Moor) on account of his dark complexion, was described by the great Swiss historian of the Renaissance Jacob Burckhardt as "the perfect type of tyrant," alluding to his firm government of Milan and his wish to turn the capital of the dukedom into a Renaissance city. Portraits of Ludovico depict him as a distinctly chubby, almost somnolent figure, but such a reading is belied by his actions, which betray a complex, enigmatic man. When his older brother Duke Galeazzo Maria was assassinated in 1494, the dukedom had fallen to the duke's eight-year-old son Gian Galeazzo, but "Il Moro" soon usurped his young nephew's power and took over as regent, ruling in a secretive fashion from within the vast dark-walled Castello Sforzesco, whose grim sillhouette dominated the northern skyline of the city.

Ludovico took as his mistress the attractive, intelligent fourteen-year-old Cecilia Gallerani, and one of Leonardo's first important commissions from Ludovico was to paint her portrait. In this, she appears almost chastely self-possessed in her beauty, holding in her lap a white ermine, a symbol of purity. Yet the way her long fingers fall caressingly over the animal's fur gives a frisson of erotic suggestion. After being sexually besotted with Cecilia, Ludovico had come to love her, and this painting subtly reflects her new position in his life, precisely as Ludovico had doubtless wished. Leonardo evidently established a rapport with Ludovico, yet he remained under no illusions about his master, commenting in his notebook in an unusually direct observation: "The justice of the Moor is as black as his skin."

When Leonardo began working for Ludovico he moved into an apartment in the Corte Vecchia (Old Court). This was where the young rightful heir Gian Galeazzo had initially been kept under house arrest, but now that he had been removed to a residence outside Milan, the palace was for the most part empty. Leonardo's apartment overlooked one of the large inner courtyards that were lined with porticos, and he also had the vast former ballroom at his disposal as a studio.

To begin with, Leonardo was mainly employed in producing entertainments for Ludovico and his court. He would play to them on his silver lute, give singing recitals, write riddles, and tell stories. For the grand pageants he would provide ingenious artifacts designed to astonish and delight Ludovico and his guests—such as ice statues, a complex masque of moving planets, and spectacular firework displays.

Equally astonishing were some of the military devices that Leonardo continued sketching in his notebooks—such as a large mobile mortar that "fires stones as if it were a hailstorm," and a tank-like armored vehicle in the shape of a flattened cone, accompanied by a drawing of its underside showing how its cogwheel engine worked. These designs were way ahead of their time: not until three centuries later would a remarkably similar armored military vehicle be tried out in the American Civil War. It is unlikely that these designs were actually built, but recent experiments have shown that most of them would have worked. One notable exception was the armored car, whose cogwheel engine was such that it would have driven the front wheels and the back wheels in opposite directions. This is such an elementary mistake that it may well have been made on purpose, so that any inexperienced thief attempting to construct one of these on his own would have been unsuccessful. On the other hand, this mistake may well have been due to Leonardo's early misgivings about this kind of work. Despite his growing expertise in designing weapons of war, throughout his life he remained secretly (that is, in his notebooks) opposed to "the cruelty of men . . . who will always be fighting against one another, inflicting the greatest losses and frequent death on both sides."

In a similar vein, Leonardo designed locks for controlling the canals that watered the fertile plains outside Milan, but also conceived of "a method of letting a flood of water loose on an army, and bridges and walls of cities." Such plans may well have been inspired by the Arno deluge that he witnessed in his youth. At the same time, possibly in order to overcome any future flooding of the Arno, he sketched a map outlining a plan to divert the river from near Florence into a canal that would lead it directly to the coast, giving the city a navigable route to the sea.

Given all these preoccupations, it is hardly surprising that Leonardo had little time for painting. In fact, during his seventeen years in Milan he completed only six works, though amongst these were some of the finest that would come from his brush—most notably, *The Last Supper.* This mural, painted in the refectory of the Dominican monastery of Santa Maria delle Grazie in Milan, reveals Leonardo at his superlative best. His ever-innovative painterly skills had reached their zenith, and in his tireless quest for originality he chose an entirely new approach to fresco painting. A firsthand description of Leonardo at work by the young Matteo Bandello, a novice at the monastery, shows the immense pains that Leonardo would take over his work:

> He would arrive at an early hour, climb up onto the scaffolding, and start working. Sometimes he would stay there from dawn until sunset, not once setting down his brush, forgetting to eat or drink, and painting without cease. On other occasions he would go for two, three or four days without taking up his brush, but spending one or two hours a day standing before the work, arms folded, scrutinizing and assessing the figures in his mind. I also saw him, driven by some sudden urge, set out from the Corte Vecchia at midday when the heat of the sun was at its height, without seeking the shade . . . and come straight to Santa Maria delle Grazie, clamber up onto the scaffolding, take up his brush, add one or two strokes, and then go away again.

Every face, every feature, every position and gesture of the twelve disciples at the table with Christ was the result of profound artistic meditation. Each figure is individual, each taken from someone he had noticed—and covertly sketched in the pocket-book he kept hanging from his belt. Yet each figure is both psychologically and symbolically recognizable—from doubting Thomas with his fated raised finger, to the effete intellectual Luke—all enclosed within the strong geometric shapes of the upper room, whose perspective continually leads the eye back to the central figure of Christ, then allows it to pass away along each line of gesturing disciples, creating a drama filled with prescience.

Unfortunately, Leonardo took so much time completing *The Last Supper* that eventually the prior of the monastery, who had commissioned the painting, became exasperated beyond all patience and complained to Ludovico Sforza, who summoned Leonardo to account for himself. Leonardo explained that the painting was all but finished, except for the face of Judas; this was because, despite searching through the most notorious streets and taverns of the city, he had yet to find a face imbued with sufficient perfidious evil. However, if the prior required the painting finished at once, Leonardo assured Ludovico that he was willing to use the prior's face for Judas. Ludovico is said to have laughed at this, and Leonardo got his way.

The result is what Burckhardt would aptly characterize as "this restless masterpiece." But if this was Leonardo at his best, it was also Leonardo at his worst. Despite the length of time he spent on the painting, he proved he was unwilling, or unable, to finish it. One of the reasons he was able to spend so long on the painting was his innovative approach to fresco technique, which involved using oil and tempera rather than fresh plaster. This enabled him to proceed in an unhurried fashion, and to alter the figures as he went along, rather than limiting his painting to the short period while the surface was still fresh (*fresco*). Leonardo's bold experiment would result in disaster: over the years the surface would begin to deteriorate, a situation made worse by the dampness that began appearing on the wall, so that by the time the Florentine artist and biographer Giorgio Vasari saw *The Last Supper* just over fifty years later, "all that could be seen was a blur of paint-dabs."[*]

Leonardo saw painting as one of the sciences, and he believed that all the sciences were underpinned by mathematics. The mathematical basis of painting and poetry related them to the more obviously mathematical art of music. Echoing Plato, Leonardo would write: "Let no one who is not a mathematician read the elements of my work." Leonardo had developed an interest in mathematics during his childhood, but it was not until now that it came to its full flower. While he was painting *The Last Supper* he met one of the leading mathematicians of the age, Luca Pacioli, who arrived in Milan around 1496.

---

[*] The modern version that appears on the wall of Santa Maria delle Grazie, as well as the reproductions of the painting, are merely a ghost of the original. What we now see is the result of several "restorations," which, according to most experts, obliterate much of the subtlety and nuance that are presumed to have existed in Leonardo's original. Even so, *The Last Supper* remains recognizable as an iconic masterpiece.

Leonardo's celebrated drawing of the Vitruvian man.

Pacioli was born in 1445 in the town of San Sepolcro, in the Apennine mountains fifty miles south-east of Florence, where he learned the geometry of perspective from its pioneer, the painter Piero della Francesca. At the age of twenty-five he became ordained as a Franciscan friar, and consequently spent much of his time traveling about Italy teaching (and learning) mathematics. Two years before his arrival in Milan he had published the work for which he is best remembered, his *Summa de arithmetica, geometria, proportioni et proportionalita*, which gathered together all the mathematical knowledge current in Europe at this period. This would include the first explanationi in print of double-entry bookkeeping, which gave birth to accountancy as we know it. This may appear a somewhat mundane topic, but it had in fact already provided the mathematical underpinning of the great expansion of commerce that took place during this century—the prosperity that financed the Italian Renaissance (it was no accident that the Medici rulers of Florence, the great patrons of the early Renaissance, began as merchant bankers).

Leonardo quickly became close to Pacioli, whom he referred to as "maestro Luca," and began taking mathematical lessons from him. Leonardo exhibited talent and even originality at his mathematical studies: he discovered a method for estimating the center of gravity of a tetrahedron, and also found an equally unrigorous method for inscribing regular polygons inside a circle. The latter studies would lead to his famous drawing of the Vitruvian man, named after the first-century BC Roman architect Vitruvius, who wrote on the proportions of the human body that Leonardo's drawing was intended to illustrate. This drawing inserts a naked figure with extended arms and legs inside a circle and a square: the square demonstrates Vetruvius' idea that the width of a man's outstretched arms is equal to his height, while the circle shows how the man's raised arms and legs reach to the edge of a circle whose center is his navel. The potency and poetry of this image derive from the juxtaposition of its fully realized naked humanity and the abstraction of the geometric lines within which it is encompassed. It can be seen as anything from an emblem of humanity's scientific self-discovery to a resonant image of unprotected man pinned like a butterfuly within the limits of the mathematical world. Significantly, the individualized head of the Vitruvian man, with its flowing center-parted locks and grave unflinching gaze, is almost certainly a self-portrait of the middle-aged Leonardo.

Here Leonardo's mathematics is poetic, while elsewhere it is essentially practical. Nowhere is this more evident than in his collaboration with Luca Pacioli, who in 1498 finished his *De divina proportione* (On Divine Proportions). Leonardo would provide the geometric illustrations for this work, which included many superbly realized and often complex figures—such as a masterful visualization of an icosi-dodecahedron (a three-dimensional shape with twenty faces). Interestingly,

The most complex of all Leonardo's geometric illustrations:
a masterfully realized depiction of an elevated icosidodecahedron.

Leonardo chose to depict these not as abstract figures created out of lines, but as actual physical entities—either palpable solids or see-through structures made of wooden spars. This suggests that he understood geometry as a matter of real shapes rather than abstract mental concepts or Platonic forms—a materialist view of the world that certainly informed his scientific investigations, and even (in the view of some) his paintings of religious subjects. Pacioli's influence on Leonardo, arguably the strongest of anyone to whom he was close, would not only be mathematical, but also personal. Pacioli managed to overcome Leonardo's block about bringing his ideas to completion; a finished manuscript of *De divina proportione* would be presented to Ludovico Sforza in 1498, and eleven years later this work would be published in Venice.

Where *De divina proportione* had seen the coming together of wood-work and mathematics, the most ambitious work that Leonardo under-took in Milan would seek to be an embodiment of metalwork and mathematics—and much, much more. When Leonardo at last gained the commission from Ludovico Sforza to make the great equestrian statue of his father, sometime in 1489, he knew that his reputation was at stake. He may have studied under Verrocchio, one of the leading sculptors of the period, but as yet he himself had no reputation as a sculptor—and now he was embarking upon a project greater than any attempted since classical times. Verrocchio had died in 1488 after success-fully completing a massive equestrian statue of the *condottiere* Bartolomeo Colleone in Venice; and now Ludovico Sforza had decided that the statue to his father should be even larger. The project, which became known as the *"gran cavallo"* (great horse), would occupy Leonardo on and off for several years, during which he made all kinds of sketches and models, before embarking upon plans for the casting of the huge statue, for which more than seventy tons of bronze were gathered. Eventually Leonardo set about constructing a full-sized clay model of the statue that gradually grew into life amidst the vast empty former ballroom of the Corte Vecchia, which is said to have been almost a hundred yards long and twenty yards wide. The finished model would rise to nearly thirty feet—more than four times life-size—and all who saw it were filled with wonder. Il Moro's court poet Baldassare Taccone wrote of the *gran cavallo:*

> Look up at its vast beauty with awe,
> Tis greater than anything man saw,
> Even in ancient Greece or Rome,
> And it is created by Leonardo Vinci alone.

Ludovico Sforza was becoming increasingly extravagant, and the citizens of Milan were being forced to support his excesses with ever-growing taxes. He was also becoming increasingly ambitious politically. In 1492 Lorenzo the Magnificent had died in Florence, and according to Machiavelli "his passing was mourned by all the citizens and all the princes of Italy." Lorenzo had played a major role in upholding a precarious peace between the constantly squabbling Italian states, but now the country once more descended into vicious rivalries, with Ludovico Sforza playing a major role. Machiavelli records that "it became impossible for anyone to find a way of satisfying or withstanding the ambition of Ludovico Sforza, regent for the Duke of Milan . . . bad seeds began to flourish . . . and the ruin of Italy was at hand."

The rightful Duke of Milan, the young Gian Galeazzo Sforza, had by now come of age, but Ludovico Sforza refused to hand over power. Gian Galeazzo was married to Isabella, granddaughter of Ferrante, King of Naples, and she appealed to her grandfather to rid Milan of its usurper. Rulers throughout Italy were sensitive on the topic of usurpers: they all faced more or less serious claimants who would have usurped them, given the right backing. Sensing his vulnerability, Ludovico took a rash and unprecedented step: he appealed for help from outside Italy, promising to support Charles VIII of France, who had a claim to the throne of Naples. As it happened, this was just the opportunity for which Charles VIII had been waiting. In 1494 he led a vast French army of 60,000 across the Alps, marching south to Milan, passing virtually unopposed through Florentine and papal territory to take Naples. The whole of Italy was plunged into turmoil, and in the midst of this the Medici were ousted from Florence, which fell into the hands of the fanatical priest Girolamo Savonarola. But in 1495 the newly elected Borgia pope Alexander VI used all his influence to draw up a Holy League against the French invader. Ludovico Sforza was so shocked by the turn of events he had unleashed that he was even persuaded to join Milan's traditional enemy, Venice, in the Holy League. As Charles VIII marched north to return to France, he was met at Fornovo by the combined forces of the Holy League, under the command of Francesco Gonzaga, the Marquis of Mantua. Although the ensuing battle resulted in a victory for the French, it only served to hasten the retreat of Charles VIII's army back across the Alps.

During the course of the upheavals, Ludovico Sforza's enemy King Ferrante had fled Naples and died, while in the same year his rival for the dukedom, Gian Galeazzo, had also died (poisoned on orders from Ludovico). Ludovico now became Duke of Milan in name as well as reality. Then, to cap it all, Charles VIII graciously decided to make peace with Milan. Ludovico Sforza was overjoyed, and now saw himself as the leading ruler in Italy; he "boasted that the Pope was his chaplain, the Signoria [ruling council] of Venice was his chamberlain, and the King of France his courier."

This delusive euphoria came to an abrupt end in 1498 when Charles VIII of France died and was succeeded by his cousin Louis XII, who was descended on his mother's side from the Viscontis, the former dukes of Milan who had been deposed by the Sforzas. Now Ludovico was hoist by his own petard—it was he who had created the precedent of inviting the French into the Italian political arena, and this time he was faced by the prospect of their return, with Louis XII enforcing his claim to Milan.

Ludovico Sforza became a changed man. The would-be Renaissance prince was transformed into an angst-ridden recluse, locked in his fortress overlooking the city. Instead of listening to poets and musicians, he began consulting astrologers and soothsayers, desperately donating large sums to the Church in an attempt to buy his salvation. Despite further increases in taxes, the exchequer began to run dry, and soon the members of his court were all owed back-wages. Leonardo found himself resident in a palace, yet barely able to support himself and the assistants who were helping him put the finishing touches to the model of the *gran cavallo*. Then he heard that the seventy tons of bronze set aside for casting the statue had been requisitioned, to be cast instead as cannons in preparation for the French invasion. Leonardo began making his own preparations, writing in his notebook, "Sell what you cannot take . . ." But for some reason he did not leave the city. Instead he collected all his cash assets, which amounted to some 1,280 lire.* This he bundled up into several paper packets, tucking them away in various secret hiding places amongst all the artistic bric-a-brac scattered through

---

* Such a sum would easily have been enough for him to live on, maintain a studio, and pay several assistants, for a year.

his huge studio, leaving only a few handfuls of change in his cash-box for any looters to find.

The French invasion duly took place in the summer of 1499. Louis XII was assured of the support of Venice, which had now reverted to its role as Milan's traditional enemy, and the French king knew that he could also count on the support of Pope Alexander VI, who had switched his allegiance and sent his son Cesare Borgia to join the French. Ludovico Sforza fled, and in September the French army entered Milan.

As a trusted long-term employee of Ludovico Sforza—and aspiring to be his military engineer, no less—Leonardo must have been in some danger. Yet in his notebooks he remained as secretive as ever, with no mention of any perils he might have faced. Instead, there is a note written in someone else's hand: "Memorandum to Maestro Leonardo to discover as soon as possible information about the state of Florence, in particular how reverend father Girolamo [Savonarola] has organized the city's defenses." It appears that Leonardo was required to make contact with friends in Florence and gather information about the city's military readiness—in other words, to spy on his native city. There is no evidence that he acted upon this memorandum.

Leonardo would remain in Milan for three months after the French occupation. During this difficult time he almost certainly had his first meeting with Cesare Borgia, whose support for Louis XII was intended to gain French backing for the invasion of the Romagna that he had secretly planned with his father, the pope. Borgia had already gained permission from Louis XII to hire French troops for this operation, but he also required a military engineer—first to reinforce the fortresses that he captured, and then for such civil projects as he required in establishing his new state. Leonardo was the ideal choice for such a role, but he evidently prevaricated. Before he could be pressured into accepting Borgia's offer, or coerced into spying on Florence, he slipped out of Milan in December 1499, forced to abandon the *gran cavallo* with which he had intended to secure his fame throughout Italy. However, as we shall see, prior to leaving he appears to have given (or been obliged to give) some kind of assurance to Louis XII.

Leonardo left Milan with his young assistant Salai, who was now twenty years old, and the mathematical monk Pacioli. Accompanying them was a cart carrying some of Leonardo's unfinished paintings, folios of drawings, and sheafs of paper covered with designs and sketches, annotated in his mirror-writing code. This technique involved writing from right to left across the page, with the letters back to front. The apparently opaque text becomes transparently clear when it is read reflected in a mirror. This is a technique that is said to come more easily to left-handers, suggesting that Leonardo may well have had this trait. He had taken to using this simple but effective code to protect his ideas from being stolen. These represented, after all, just as much his intellectual capital as his talent for painting, and were equally original. But jotting down his thoughts in mirror-writing also meant that Leonardo could give free rein to wherever his observations and deductions might lead, without having to worry whether his ideas contradicted the current orthodoxy. Such ideas were liable to stray into the realms of heresy, which could have dangerous consequences. If this secrecy had been necessary while he had been living in the secluded quarters of the Corte Vecchia, how much more so was it now that he was traveling from place to place with nothing but his reputation and letters of recommendation to protect him.

Together Leonardo and his little troupe of followers set out east across the plains of the Po basin, stopping off briefly at Mantua before traveling on to Venice, which was now under such threat from the expanding Ottoman Empire that at night the distant fires of the Turkish soldiers in the foothills of the Dolomite Alps could be made out from the top of the Campanile at San Marco. Leonardo was immediately hired by the authorities as a military engineer and resorted to his old standby, suggesting that the authorities flood the Isonzo valley to halt the Turkish advance. In between times he pursued further investigations on an aquatic theme, designing a diving suit made of watertight leather, with wineskins filled with air for breathing and glass goggles.* He also produced devices for ramming enemy ships, and a recipe for the

---

* This suit was recently constructed for a television program, and was found to be entirely practical for limited periods of submersion in water around ten feet deep.

manufacture of "Greek Fire," which burned on water and could be poured in the path of enemy ships to set them alight.*

Paradoxically, in the midst of all this, Leonardo was becoming increasingly pacifist. He had given up eating meat because of his horror at the slaughter of animals, and contemporary anecdotes speak of him buying caged birds in the marketplace and setting them free. He was also exhibiting a growing dissatisfaction with painting: he no longer wished to be just an artist. Yet, ironically, the only other way of obtaining the prestige he sought, as well as finding the time to pursue the scientific researches that increasingly obsessed him, was by working as a military engineer. However, this growing internal conflict did not seem to affect him at this time: it was either repressed or ignored altogether. For Leonardo, now forty-eight years old and homeless, this was a time of action, rather than reflection.

In April 1500 news reached Leonardo that following a briefly successful attempt to retake Milan, Ludovico Sforza had eventually been captured by the French. On the back cover of his notebook, Leonardo jotted down, "The Duke has lost his state, possessions, and liberty; and he did not complete any of his projects." This last remark is a characteristically oblique reference to the *gran cavallo,* whose fate after the retaking of Milan by French troops would be described by the contemporary memoirist Saba da Castiglione: "I recall with sadness and disgust how this noble and ingenious work was used as a target by Gascon crossbowmen." According to Vasari, the French soldiers "smashed it to pieces."

Any hopes Leonardo might have had of returning to Milan and the easygoing employment of Ludovico Sforza were now dashed, and by the end of April 1500 he had returned home to Florence, still accompanied by Salai and Luca Pacioli. The city had once more undergone a violent change: the Borgia pope, Alexander VI, had excommunicated Savonarola in 1497, and a year later the people of Florence had overthrown him and seen him burned at the stake. Yet the Medici had not

---

* The closely guarded secret of "Greek Fire" almost certainly originated in the Middle East prior to the seventh century. Its ingredients remain a mystery, but it is likely to have been manufactured from distilled crude oil, which produced a primitive form of petroleum. Leonardo must have either learned or deduced its ingredients.

been returned to power, and Florence was now ruled by a republican government. Leonardo was renowned in his homeland as the creator of *The Last Supper* and the *gran cavallo*, and quickly obtained a commission from the Servite friars of Santissima Annunziata to paint an altarpiece for their church. According to Vasari, he was soon back to his old habits: "He kept them waiting a long time without even starting anything." Eventually he did manage to produce a full-sized cartoon of *The Virgin and Child and St. Anne*. As Vasari goes on to say:

> This work not only won the astonished admiration of all the artists, but when it was finished for two days it attracted to the room where it was exhibited a crowd of men and women, young and old, who flocked there . . . to gaze in amazement at the marvels he had created.

The following year Leonardo started another major painting, *The Madonna of the Yarnwinder*, but this too would remain unfinished.* He was now sharing his living quarters with Luca Pacioli and, according to a report by Fra Pietro Novellara, a leading church figure who was in Florence at the time: "Leonardo's life is extremely irregular and haphazard, and he seems to live from day to day . . . In short, his mathematical experiments have distracted him so much from painting that he cannot abide the paintbrush."

Such agitation seems to speak of more than mere reluctance to paint. Leonardo was now getting on in years, with the prospect of old age looming, and still he appeared to feel that his achievements were nothing when set against his enormous, yet curiously imprecise, ambitions. Judging from his notebooks, he continued to follow wherever the instincts of his exceptional mind led him. His intellect would focus his entire vision on a particular investigation—into mathematics, hydraulics, war machines, or whatever—achieving great progress in a period of intense concentration. And then his interest was liable to switch elsewhere: even on the same page, architecture could give way to anatomy,

---

* The original of this work has been lost, but copies have survived. Only the copies are completed paintings.

grotesque faces could grow alongside the intricate cogs of machinery, cartoon phallic graffiti alongside an uncannily precise and prophetic drawing of a bicycle—sequences of superb scientific investigation, artistic observation, and invention seemingly guided by whimsy. He wanted to discover all there was to know about every single thing that held his attention. Yet during these first years of his return to Florence, his agitation appears to have reached new heights. Nowhere else is his lifestyle described as "extremely irregular and haphazard"—Leonardo was no bohemian. During this period Novellara also mentions Leonardo having some mysterious "obligations to his majesty the King of France"— possibly some assurance that he had given when leaving (or to get him out of) Milan. Perhaps this was the source of his anxiety. Meanwhile Cesare Borgia, under the protection of the King of France, had launched into his campaigns to overrun the Romagna, and soon his army was posing a very real threat to Florence. As a result, in June 1502 Machiavelli and Bishop Soderini were dispatched for their fateful meeting with Borgia, which took place in the darkened palace at Urbino. On Machiavelli's return, a message must have been delivered to Leonardo, suggesting that, either for the good of Florence or because of the "obligations" he had to Louis XII, he should take up the post of military engineer to Borgia. In July 1502 Leonardo therefore left Florence to join his new employer.

2

Machiavelli: A Surprise Appointment

T HE SPECTACULAR FALL of Savonarola in 1498 had been Machiavelli's lucky break. At the surprisingly early age of twenty-nine he had been voted into a senior post in the new republican government. Unlike the other city-states of Italy, Florence prided itself on being a republic, and had at least a modicum of democracy. The city was ruled by the *gonfaloniere*,* who presided over an eight-man council known as the Signoria. These, and all other senior posts in the various chanceries and committees that administered the city's affairs and advised the Signoria, were appointed by a system of balloting, which was open to all guild members. Owing to its complexity, this system of voting had long been open to corruption, which was how the Medici family had wrested control of the city from the other leading families more than sixty years previously. But now the Medici had been ousted, and the city had reverted to its old, more open ways. The manner in which the ballots were run meant that each of the various districts throughout the city had its say in who was appointed. Even so, powerful backers were required for anyone to obtain a senior post. And Machiavelli must certainly have had his important supporters, for he was appointed secretary to the Second Chancery, which administered the internal affairs of the Florentine Republic. Prior to this there is no mention in the records of Machiavelli even serving in a minor post. He appears to have risen from nowhere.

* Literally "standard-bearer," and thus leader.

Niccolò Machiavelli was born on May 3, 1469, in Florence, in the Santo Spirito district of Oltrarno, across the river from the main center of the city. His father, Bernardo, was the illegitimate scion of an old Florentine family; he had gone bankrupt and was thus officially barred from practicing his profession as a lawyer. Bernardo lived off the income from his small estate in the country and continued to practice his profession "under the counter" at cut-price rates. Money was short in the Machiavelli household, and Niccolò would later recall, "I was born poor, and I learned to know want before enjoyment."

Picture of Bandini hanged, by Leonardo.

Despite this austerity, Machiavelli grew up in a rich intellectual atmosphere. His father had a library of books, largely by classical authors, and saw to it that his son was tutored, probably by impecunious scholars, sons of Benardo's friends. Yet Machiavelli's first profound lesson was not learned from books. In 1478, when he was nine years old, Florence was convulsed by the Pazzi conspiracy, the failed attempt to overthrow the Medici, which had been covertly backed by Pope Sixtus IV. During the course of these bloody events, Lorenzo the Magnificent was lucky to escape with his life, while his brother Giuliano was frenziedly stabbed to death in the cathedral. Pazzi sympathizers were then hunted down by a baying mob, who castrated them and tore them limb from limb. Machiavelli would later recall in his *Florentine Histories* how "the streets were filled with the parts of men." The following year news reached Lorenzo the Magnificent that the sole escaped assassin, Bandini, had managed to reach faraway Constantinople. Lorenzo sent word to the sultan, and Bandini was shipped back to Florence in chains to be publicly hanged—the occasion when Leonardo was in the crowd and sketched Bandini's body dangling on the end of the rope. Here was history—politics in all its rawness—being enacted before the young Machiavelli's eyes.

Machiavelli's education and his reading in his father's library were based heavily on the ancient Roman classics. We know from his later writings and letters that he was well versed in Livy and Virgil, and that he particularly enjoyed reading from *De Rerum Natura* by Lucretius. Where Leonardo had been drawn by the scientific, universal approach of Lucretius' poem, Machiavelli was most impressed by his unflinching vision of humanity, seeing it at the mercy of its own cruelties and the whim of fate. But the underlying lesson drawn from Lucretius by both Leonardo and Machiavelli was that the truth derives from our experience, rather than from any previous authority or divine revelation.

Machiavelli's father may have been under a cloud professionally, but he seems to have been popular and retained a wide circle of friends. The closest of these was the humanist Bartolomeo Scala, who in 1464 became head of the First Chancery, the senior civil servant in the city's administration, a post he would retain for more than thirty years, lasting through some of the most turbulent upheavals in the city's history. Young Niccolò Machiavelli began writing poetry, and Scala seems to have taken the tyro poet under his wing; he may have been the one who brought Machiavelli to the attention of Lorenzo the Magnificent, who was a highly accomplished poet himself. There is a possibility that Machiavelli was sent on a scholarship by Lorenzo to study law at the University of Pisa, which he had recently founded. At any rate, Machiavelli was certainly known to Lorenzo and his circle of humanist scholars and poets, for around this time he wrote a poem, a "pastorale," which was dedicated to Giuliano de' Medici, the youngest son of Lorenzo the Magnificent, in the hope of gaining either his friendship or his patronage.* This poem, along with two others by Machiavelli, appeared in a manuscript of Carnival poems also containing works by Lorenzo himself and by Poliziano, the leading Florentine poet of the period, all of which were illustrated with drawings by Botticelli. This was exalted company, and Machiavelli would precociously come to regard himself as a poet of similar renown, fit to be noticed by his great contemporaries, such as the poet Ludovico Ariosto. Years later, when Machiavelli was writing his long poetic parody *The Ass,* he wrote to a friend in Rome, where he knew Ariosto was then living:

> I have just been reading Ariosto's *Orlando Furioso;* and truly the whole poem is really fine and many passages are sublime. If he is there with you, pass on my regards and tell him my only complaint is that while he mentions so many other poets he leaves me out like a right prick. What he has done to me in his *Orlando,* I shall not do to him in my *Ass.*

This mix of high poetic praise and coarse vernacular hints at the range and complexity of Machiavelli's character. The face in his portraits, even when serious, appears to have the ghost of a smile—both weak and yet knowing, sly and yet somehow sympathetic. His lean appearance speaks of austerity, yet he is known to have been the life and soul of the party amongst his boisterous young friends, who looked up to him as their leader. In a wordplay on his name he was fondly nicknamed "Il Macchia," which had connotations of macho manliness, as well as meaning a blot or a blemish, suggesting that even in these early years he was also something of a roguish black sheep. All the evidence points to there being a streak of subversive perversity at the heart of Machiavelli's sympathetic character.

In April 1492, as Machiavelli was approaching his twenty-fourth birthday, Lorenzo the Magnificent lay on his deathbed. Machiavelli would later write in his history of Florence that Lorenzo "had been loved by fortune and by God in the highest degree"; but now his life was ending:

* Giuliano was named after Lorenzo's brother, who had been assassinated in the Pazzi conspiracy.

the heavens gave evidence that great calamities would take place after his death. Amongst many omens, the church of Santa Reparta was struck by a lightning bolt of such ferocity that its pinnacle was almost completely destroyed, much to the wonder and terror of the people.

The Renaissance may have seen the rebirth of a more rational humanist outlook amongst the intellectual elite, but the undercurrent of superstitions from the previous medieval era remained strong. In troubled times, such superstitions could come to the fore with the power of collective mania. The Renaissance also had a few reborn irrationalities of its own: the fall of Constantinople to the Ottomans in 1453, which had resulted in the flight of so much ancient Greek learning to the West, also saw a revival of such ancient superstitions as astrology, alchemy, and soothsaying.

With Lorenzo the Magnificent gone, Italy plunged once more into an era of instability. Ludovico Sforza began dreaming up his grandiose schemes in Milan, while in Rome the new pope, Alexander VI, embarked upon his machinations to establish a Borgia kingdom. Paradoxically, these were also the years of one of the Renaissance's greatest triumphs. In 1492 Columbus discovered a route westwards around half the globe to "the islands beyond the Ganges" and declared that he had "reached the mainland of Asia." This erroneous assumption would persist until 1502, when the Florentine Amerigo Vespucci made his second voyage across the Atlantic to South America, on an expedition financed by Lorenzo di Pierfrancesco de' Medici, a cousin of Lorenzo the Magnificent. Together with Leonardo, Vespucci had learned astronomy from the great mapmaker Toscanelli, which he had put to good use in becoming an expert navigator. As a result, he realized when taking observations of the stars on the South American coast that the world was much larger than had previously been thought, and that what Columbus had discovered was not a new route to Asia. On his return, Vespucci wrote to Lorenzo di Pierfrancesco de' Medici in Florence: "We arrived at a new land which, for many reasons that are enumerated in what follows, we observed to be a continent . . . I noted there the wonders of God and of nature." When news of this momentous discovery reached Florence, the authorities ordered a public celebration, and crowds gathered outside the Palazzo Vespucci, where a celebratory bonfire was lit that burned for three days. It was Amerigo Vespucci's navigational discovery that caused the new continent to be named America, after the latinized version of his name.

The Palazzo Vespucci was in the Santo Spirito quarter of Oltrarno, close to where Machiavelli lived, and he knew the family well. Agostino Vespucci, a relative of Amerigo, was one of Machiavelli's closest friends, and would become his loyal long-term assistant in the Florentine administration. Machiavelli would have heard of Amerigo's momentous discovery almost as soon as anyone in Florence, and he would allude to this brave exploit in his later writings, where he refers to "the dangers which await men who search out seas and lands unknown."

The Renaissance was emerging from the shadow of the classical past that had provided its impetus, and was now beginning to demonstrate original achievements. In Milan, Leonardo would observe in his notebook: "It is the rays of the sun reflected from the earth which cause the moon to shine," and would later jot down in code his momentous conclusion: "The sun does not move." Meanwhile in a large warehouse off the Piazza del Duomo in Florence, Michelangelo would begin chiseling into the eighteen-foot-high block of Carrara marble that would eventually become his *David*. An age was coming into its own: the modern world was being born.

Yet, as in ancient Greece, such achievements frequently occur when the civilization that produced them is under threat. The Italian city-states, like the Greek city-states before them, were weak and divided; and following the death of Lorenzo the Magnificent, Machiavelli would write that "Italy faced hard times . . . beneath stars hostile to her good." Such auguries were all too soon fulfilled, so that Machiavelli would "tell of so many mountain passes and so many marshes, filled with blood and dead men [when] . . . Italy in turmoil opened her gates to the Gauls [French] and the barbarians rushed in." Ludovico Sforza, who in the view of Machiavelli was the "prime mover of Italy's distress," had invited Charles VIII to cross the Alps to pursue his claim to the throne of

Naples. On his way south with his vast French army, Charles VIII passed through the Duchy of Milan and then entered Florentine territory. The city was in turmoil, and its ruler, Piero de' Medici, son of Lorenzo the Magnificent, rode in haste to meet Charles VIII, abjectly promising him money and territory as long as he spared Florence. When the Florentines heard of this they rose in revolt, and chased Piero de' Medici and his brother Giovanni from the city, signaling the end of Medici rule. Although Machiavelli had been a friend of the Medici, he could not refrain from observing that the city had now got rid of "the yoke that for sixty years had been crushing you."

As Charles VIII marched south from Milan he "liberated" Pisa, Florence's gateway to the sea, and then marched unopposed into Florence itself, his troops parading through the streets in an intimidating show of strength. Days later, the dwarfish stunted figure of Charles VIII sat on his throne above the people of Florence, who had been summoned to assemble in the Piazza della Signoria. He announced that they would be expected to pay 15,000 florins* towards the upkeep of his army—never had the city seen such humiliation.

When the French left Florence to continue south to Naples, the citizens turned in their distress to the fiery sermons of the fundamentalist preacher Savonarola. Already these had foretold with uncanny accuracy the events that were now unfolding in Italy: his prophecy that both the pope and Lorenzo the Magnificent would die in 1492 had proved correct, and the people were "persuaded by him that he spoke with God." Even Machiavelli, who was hardly sympathetic to such superstition, could not help recognizing how Savonarola's writing "showed his learning, his prudence and his intellectual powers." For some years now the citizens of Florence had suffered from a succession of epidemics and bad harvests, which made them particularly receptive to Savonarola's brand of religion. The days of Lorenzo the Magnificent's glorious festivals, with artistic entertainments fashioned by the likes of Botticelli and Leonardo da Vinci, were long since over: now was the time of repentance, with choirs of children dressed in white passing through the streets singing hymns

* Prior to the austere times of Savonarola, a merchant would have spent around 200 florins a year maintaining a household containing his large family and servants.

and collecting alms. In 1497 this collective self-mortification reached a peak when Savonarola demanded that the citizens of Florence make a "bonfire of the vanities," casting paintings, priceless books of classical learning, poems by the likes of Poliziano and Lorenzo the Magnificent, together with all manner of luxuries and finery, into a fire in the Piazza della Signoria. The spirit of the Renaissance itself was going up in flames: this too played its part in Machiavelli's political schooling.

In the midst of these turbulent times, Machiavelli's natural level-headedness ensured that he neither was swept up in the collective religious hysteria, nor became an embittered opponent longing for "the good old days" of the Medici. Machiavelli was not a religious man, and he developed a shrewd eye, observing how Savonarola operated, how amidst the fire and brimstone of his sermons he was also preaching populist reform. Under Savonarola's puritan rule, Florence began to take on more and more the appearance of a genuine republic.

Yet by now Savonarola had turned on the corruption and vices of the Church itself: "O prostitute Church, thou hast displayed thy foulness to the whole world, and stinkest up to Heaven." Out of natural curiosity, Machiavelli attended some of Savonarola's sermons, reporting to a friend in Rome how Savonarola was attacking the new pope, Alexander VI, "savaging him, saying such things about him as could only be said of the wickedest man you can think of." But Alexander VI was a powerful enemy, imbued with all the ruthlessness and cunning of a Borgia; he would not be mocked by a mere renegade priest, and soon began engineering Savonarola's downfall. This task was made easier by the fact that the fickle population of Florence started to tire of Savonarola's fundamentalist repression. Even so, his fall was both speedy and spectacular. Instead of the bonfire of the vanities, a year later Savonarola himself was on the fire in the Piazza della Signoria, burning at the stake. In the years to come, Machiavelli would draw his own conclusions with regard to these events:

Savonarola was unarmed, and thus he was destroyed along with his reforms while they were still new, as soon as the people ceased to believe in him and he had no way of rallying those who believed in him or forcing the disbeliever to heed his word.

Standing amidst the crowd, Machiavelli had observed how events could be determined by the character of a leader; but even the most inspirational of leaders was nothing, unless he had the means to combat his enemies and retain power. In the end, only the force of arms could do this.

Yet now it was Machiavelli's turn to step out of the crowd. Although many of Savonarola's reforms were swept away, the republican tenor of the government he had established remained largely intact. In May 1498 a new administration was voted into office, and the inexperienced twenty-nine-year-old Machiavelli was elected secretary to the Second Chancery, with the handsome annual salary of 192 florins.

The precise identity of Machiavelli's support remained obscured by the secrecy of the ballot, but he was probably backed by the clique that had formed around his father's close friend, the humanist Bartolomeo Scala, who had until recently been long-term head of the First Chancery. It also seems highly likely that Machiavelli received the support of a Medici faction headed by Lorenzo di Pierfrancesco de' Medici, whose wealth had now begun to rival that of the main Medici line. Lorenzo di Pierfrancesco may have been a cousin of Lorenzo the Magnificent, but he in fact headed the moderate Medici faction, which had no wish to see the return of Lorenzo's inept son Piero de' Medici. This faction dissociated themselves from the Medici who had fled into exile, and understood the mood of the people of Florence to such an extent that they even changed their name from Medici to Popolano ("Men of the People"). Machiavelli had powerful backers whose political allegiance was, at least for the time being, with the new Florence.

Evidence of the power of Machiavelli's backers can be seen in the fact that within a month he was appointed secretary to the Ten of War,* the committee most directly responsible for the administration of foreign

---

* Officially, "The Ten of Liberty and Peace," but at the time it was popularly, and more aptly, known by this title.

relations and military affairs. This was a post of considerable responsibility, for it was a testing time in Florentine foreign affairs. The situation in Italy was dire indeed. Three years previously Pope Alexander VI had succeeded in putting together the Holy League, which had helped drive Charles VIII and the French army out of Italy, but this unity had quickly fallen apart. Meanwhile Florence had gone to war to retake Pisa and regain access to the sea, which was essential to the city's prosperity, especially to such foreign traders as Lorenzo di Pierfrancesco de' Popolano (formerly Medici) and his attempts to gain access to the riches of the New World. However, the war against Pisa had not gone well: the Pisans were determined to hold on to their independence.

Then the news came through that Charles VIII had died in France and had been succeeded by Louis XII, who immediately announced his intentions by declaring himself King of France and Duke of Milan. Ludovico Sforza's precedent of inviting the French into Italy had now rebounded on him, and Italy tensed for another French invasion. It was known that Louis XII wished for a divorce, so that he could marry the widow of Charles VIII in a move to unite his kingdom. Pope Alexander VI seized the opportunity, offering the necessary papal annulment, but at a price: the pope would "sell him spiritual favors in exchange for temporal powers." This was one of Alexander VI's first steps towards establishing a Borgia kingdom: his aim was to secure Louis XII's powerful backing for this enterprise.

At the time, Florence was more concerned with the war against Pisa, and Machiavelli was requested to produce a state paper on the situation. Hardly had he delivered this document than he was dispatched in May 1499 on his first mission, to meet Jacopo IV d'Appiano, the lord of Piombino, a small seaside town seventy miles southwest of Florence. Jacopo was one of Florence's mercenary commanders fighting the war against Pisa and was demanding that he and his troops be paid more, a demand that was out of the question, according to Machiavelli's masters. Machiavelli arrived at Jacopo's camp outside Pisa to find himself confronted by a rough-and-ready soldier, who according to Machiavelli "spoke well, judged ill, and acted worse." Machiavelli succeeded in persuading Jacopo to drop his demands, in return for certain vague promises. As a result of this success, Machiavelli was dispatched in July on a rather more difficult and important mission to Caterina Sforza, Countess of Imola and Forli, which lay fifty miles across the Apennine mountains to the east of Florence in the Romagna.

Caterina Sforza was the illegitimate niece of Ludovico Sforza, the Duke of Milan, and was one of the more colorful characters of this colorful period. In her youth she had been renowned equally for her beauty and her spirited nature, both of which she still retained at the age of thirty-six. She had already lost three husbands, all of whom had fallen victim to the dangers of life amongst the warring statelets of the Romagna. This was the region that Machiavelli described as "a breeding ground for all the worst crimes, the slightest incident liable to give rise to outbreaks of murder and rape [resulting from] the wickedness of the ruling lords." Caterina had demonstrated her character to the full when dealing with the conspirators who had murdered her vicious and tyrannical first husband, whose lands and title she had succeeded in retaining. After being captured by the conspirators, she had persuaded them to allow her to enter the *rocca* at Forli, claiming that she would persuade its occupants to hand over this virtually impregnable fortress. The conspirators, suspicious of her motives, had retained her children as hostages. No sooner had she entered the *rocca* than she appeared on the battlements and rained down her defiance on the conspirators, vowing that she would avenge the murder of her husband. The conspirators at once threatened to murder her children, whereupon she dared them to go ahead, raising her skirts and dramatically exposing her nakedness, declaring defiantly that she still had the equipment to make more children. Realizing they had been outwitted, the conspirators fled into exile, leaving her children unharmed.

By the time of Machiavelli's visit in the summer of 1499, Caterina's army was commanded by her son Ottaviano, who had proved himself a skillful *condottiere* in the service of Florence. But now Caterina's uncle Ludovico Sforza was under threat from the French in Milan, and her son's contract with Florence had expired. When Machiavelli arrived at Caterina's court, he found that the Milanese envoy had beaten him to it, and Caterina's army was already preparing to leave for Milan. Nonetheless,

Caterina listened as Machiavelli put his case, and he even managed to establish a certain rapport with her, although she did tartly inform him that "she always liked what Florentines said, and disliked what they did." After a week of painstaking negotiations, Machiavelli managed to persuade Caterina to accept Florence's offer, despite having to confess to her that the city's hard-pressed exchequer could only afford to pay her a reduced amount. Then, just before signing the agreement, Caterina suddenly demanded that Florence should give a written assurance that the city would come to her aid whenever her territory was under threat, an assurance that Machiavelli simply could not give. Caterina appeared to be prevaricating, and before returning to Florence empty-handed, Machiavelli wrote to the Signoria of his exasperation, informing them how "I manifested my feelings in both words and gestures."

But in fact this was no last-minute whim on Caterina's behalf: she foresaw that she might soon be in a desperate situation. Any new French invasion would leave her small territory highly vulnerable, in need of all the allies she could muster. And her forebodings would indeed be confirmed just six months later. In October 1499 Louis XII marched into Milan, with Cesare Borgia at his side. Louis XII then loaned Borgia some 6,000 French troops, as part payment for his divorce, which had duly been granted by Borgia's father, Alexander VI. In November Borgia launched his first foray into the Romagna, heading straight towards Imola and Forli. After a brief siege the formidable walls of the *rocca* at Forli were breached by the continuous pounding of the French batteries, and Caterina was taken prisoner by Borgia.

The Signoria in Florence watched these developments with foreboding. The city now faced a potential threat in the east from Borgia, while at the same time it was waging war against Pisa to the west. Just three months previously the conflict with Pisa had descended into farce, provoking widespread unrest amongst the hard-pressed citizens of Florence who were forced to pay for this war. In August the pro-Florentine forces, led by the mercenary commander Paolo Vitelli, had begun a prolonged bombardment of Pisa's besieged walls. After several days, this had opened up a forty-yard breach, and a letter from the Ten of War, almost certainly composed by Machiavelli, had then expressly ordered Vitelli to take the city at once. After some hesitation, Vitelli's mercenaries, joined by some enthusiastic young volunteers from Florence, had apparently taken matters into their own hands and charged, carrying all before them. But before they could take the defenseless city, they had been ordered back by Vitelli. Yet the soldiers had appeared unwilling to obey, so Paolo Vitelli and his brother Vitellozzo had rushed into the fray and begun driving them back with their own arms. When news of this reached Florence, there was such an outcry that the Signoria panicked and called a secret meeting to decide what to do. Subsequent letters show that Machiavelli was present at this meeting. Unlike the dithering members of the Signoria, he was convinced that Vitelli's actions were not just incompetent, but showed evidence of treachery.* The Signoria were eventually convinced, not least by the young Machiavelli, that the only way to resolve the situation was to take direct action, and commissioners were dispatched to lure the Vitelli brothers from their men and take them prisoner. In late September Paolo was captured, but his brother Vitellozzo managed to escape (indicatively, heading towards Pisa). Paolo Vitelli was then brought to Florence, where he faced a mockery of an inquiry: in quick succession he denied treason, was subjected to a vicious bout of torture, and was beheaded.

The Signoria would subsequently redeem themselves when the city was threatened in November by Borgia's advance into the Romagna. In a skillful move, they approached the French in Milan and hired an army of Swiss and French soldiers to join the other Florentine mercenaries at the siege of Pisa. For the time being, this neutralized the threat from Borgia and his French mercenaries, who would not attack Florence while it too was employing French mercenaries hired from Louis XII. In February 1500 Borgia returned to consult his father in Rome, and for the moment the threat from the east appeared to be over.

Three months later Machiavelli's father died. Machiavelli had been

---

* Machiavelli would be proved right. Papers that were found by the advancing French army in Milanese territory showed that Vitelli had secretly agreed to prolong the war, as part of a plan for stirring up unrest in Florence against the government, with the ultimate aim of getting Piero de' Medici restored to power. It is unlikely that Machiavelli had this evidence to hand at the time, but his acumen speaks for itself.

fond of his father, and over the years they had developed a jocular, respectful, almost brotherly intimacy. Bernardo Machiavelli was buried in the family tomb at the church of Santa Croce, and Machiavelli attended the funeral service. His irreverent attitude towards religion was a private matter, kept for his circle of friends. He believed in going through the motions, attending church at the main religious festivals; any other course would have resulted in serious censure, and would have cost him his job in the government. However, a measure of his feelings towards his father and religion can be gauged from an incident that took place some four years later. A monk from Santa Croce informed him that a number of bodies from other families had surreptitiously been buried in the Machiavelli family tomb, and suggested that he should have them removed. To this Machiavelli merely replied: "Let them be, for my father was a great lover of conversation, and the more there are to keep him company, the better pleased he will be."

In June 1500 Machiavelli was a member of the three-man delegation dispatched from Florence to liaise with the French and Swiss mercenaries in the field before Pisa. After heavy French bombardment, the Pisans indicated that they were willing to surrender, but only on condition that the city was not occupied for another month. Machiavelli recommended that this offer be accepted, but he was overruled. The unruly Swiss mercenaries then refused to risk their lives storming the city and took matters into their own hands. Claiming that they had not been paid, they seized the senior member of the Florentine delegation and demanded a 1,300-ducat ransom for his return.* Machiavelli bravely attempted to intervene, but instead the Florentine delegate ordered him back to Florence to sort things out, which he duly did.

The Signoria soon realized that the only way to obtain their long-term aim of retaking Pisa was to send a delegation to Louis XII to resolve the situation, and Machiavelli was chosen as one of the two-man envoy. By now Louis XII had returned to France, and on July 18, 1500, the Florentine delegation set out posthaste on the journey north

---

* At this time the ducat was worth approximately 10 percent more than the florin, so this ransom would probably have amounted to around seven times the delegates' annual wage.

across the Alps. Machiavelli was to spend six long months on this mission, which involved all the usual rigors of early-sixteenth-century diplomacy. Besides the mental strain of having to remain fully alert during all the interminable bickering and deceit of such negotiations, there was also the rigor of traveling long distances, often as fast as possible, on horseback. Machiavelli appeared to enjoy both these elements of his work. He was physically fit: his portraits indicate a tall, lean, though not overly sturdy frame; while the clarity and incisiveness of his writings suggest an exceptionally sharp mind. His letters, in particular, reveal his warmth, wit, and self-awareness. On longer missions he would soon develop the habit of traveling with "his saddlebag stuffed with books." During the endless boring hours of inactivity that were inevitable on any such mission, Machiavelli would spend much of his time reading, usually Dante and Petrarch, though on his mission to France he is known to have taken Caesar's *Commentaries*. These would have provided an instructive text for Machiavelli, who would have been well aware that Caesar's clear, incisive description of his military campaigns always masked his ulterior political motives.

By way of entertainment, Machiavelli would also spend time writing witty letters, which had his friends in Florence "dying of laughter." He delighted in protraying himself as the fall guy, making himself appear ridiculous by describing the scrapes into which he had got himself. The most disgraceful of these would take place some years later, while on a mission to Verona, and gives a deep insight into how "Il Macchia" saw himself amongst his informal circle of intellectual friends:

> Bloody hell, Luigi!* How is it that Fortune hands it all to you on a platter, when I'm lucky to get even crumbs. While you get a feast of fucking, I'm in the midst of a famine out here. . . . I was randy as hell, when I came upon an old woman who launders my shirts; she lived in a dim basement. . . . she asked me to come in because she wanted to sell me a shirt. . . .

* This letter was addressed to Machiavelli's close friend, Luigi Guicciardini, brother of the famous historian Francesco Guicciardini.

[51]

So, naive prick that I am, I went inside. Here I made out in the gloom a woman cowering in the corner, affecting modesty, covering her body and her face with a towel. . . . The ribald old woman took me by the hand and led me over to her, saying, "This is the shirt I want to sell you, but I'd like you to try it on first and then pay for it." As you know, I am really a shy fellow, so I was terrified when the old woman left the room and closed the door, leaving me alone in the dark.

Having built up the situation with masterly detail, Machiavelli hastens to the denouement, describing it in lurid detail for the benefit of friends:

Anyway, to cut a long story short, I fucked her one. Although her thighs were flabby and her cunt damp—and her breath stank a bit—because I was so hopelessly horny I set to with a will. When I'd finished I decided to have a look at the merchandise, and took a piece of burning wood from the hearth to light the lamp. . . . Ugh! She was so ugly I almost dropped dead on the spot. The edges of her eyebrows were alive with nits. Her dribbly eyes had a huge squint, and one was larger than the other. . . . one of her nostrils was split, so you could see her snot. . . . Her mouth was twisted, and because she was toothless she couldn't help dribbling; while on top of that she had a wispy moustache. "What's the matter, sir?" she asked, but when she opened her mouth her breath stank so much that my stomach turned over: my guts started to revolt, and then they did revolt—so that I threw up all over her. . . .

And so on. This exaggerated tale should not be mistaken for reality—the writer was certainly sniggering to himself as he played to the crowd for all he was worth. Machiavelli was lonely, homesick, amongst foreigners, and wished to cheer himself up, just as much as he wished to amuse the distant friends he missed so much. On the other hand, this grotesque anecdote must have received at least some inspiration from the seedy low-life incidents in which Machiavelli doubtless became embroiled in the roadside inns and stables through which he passed on his travels abroad.

This letter also reveals a trait in Machiavelli's character that would later come to inform his finest writing. He was not afraid to imagine the worst—either of himself, or of others. In public, and in personal life, a man could be prey to his basest instincts. Machiavelli would become adept at seeing through cant and hypocrisy, in behavior as well as in negotiation. It was necessary to recognize the heart of the matter: what was at stake was often as distasteful or brutal as it was obvious, no matter how it was disguised by polite obfuscation.

Having dealt with a rough-and-ready character in Jacopo IV d'Appiano, a tough wily countess in Caterina Sforza, and obdurate mercenary commanders at Pisa, Machiavelli now faced dealing with the most powerful man in Europe, in the form of Louis XII, and he knew that the fate of Florence hung in the balance. One false move, and his undefended native city could be abandoned to the wolves. France, the pope, Cesare Borgia—to say nothing of the other Italian powers—all regarded rich but militarily weak Florence as fair game. Machiavelli could not afford to indulge in such niceties as stage fright or modesty: he was the big man, "Il Macchia," and it all depended upon him. (His fellow commissioner would soon drop out with illness, which may well have been partly diplomatic: he did not wish to be blamed if anything went wrong.)

But Machiavelli was quickly put in his place. Florence was small fry at the French court. France was entering into negotiations with Spain: together these two most powerful nations in Europe intended to conquer and divide between them the kingdom of Naples. It had taken Machiavelli and his fellow commissioner eight days to ride across the Alps to the French court, yet it would be another thirteen days before they were finally granted an audience with the king. Machiavelli refused to be overawed (he would later say of Louis XII that his "haughtiness masks his indecision"), but was forced to concede the reality of the situation in his report back to Florence: "The French are blinded by their own power, and only consider those who are armed or ready to give them money to be worthy of their esteem." And when it came down to the brass tacks of negotiation, the French simply turned the tables on Florence, refusing to accept that the Swiss mercenaries had not fulfilled their duties. As Machiavelli reported to the Signoria: "The King complains about having to pay the Swiss 38,000 ducats . . . which he says you ought to have paid, and he threatens to make Pisa and its surrounding territory into an independent state."

And that was it. While the Signoria in Florence dithered over whether to raise the money from its already hard-pressed citizens, Machiavelli hung about the court, unable to obtain any further audiences with the king. Instead, he did his best to ingratiate himself with Georges d'Amboise, Cardinal of Rouen, the king's powerful chief counselor and foreign minister. Summer passed into autumn, and still the Signoria prevaricated: no money was forthcoming from Florence. Meanwhile the French court moved from Nevers to Montargis, from Nantes to Tours: France was suffering from the plague and the court was constantly on the move in an attempt to avoid the contagion.

By now word had reached France that in September Cesare Borgia had launched a second campaign to extend his territory in the Romagna, taking Pesaro and then, on October 30, Rimini. Both of these cities were on the Adriatic coast, just seventy miles east across the mountains from Florence. The Signoria in Florence also learned that Borgia now had in mind restoring Piero de' Medici to power in the city. In a panic, they immediately dispatched word to Machiavelli that they would send the required money to France. Only if Florence was under French protection was it safe from the designs of Borgia and his father, Pope Alexander VI. Machiavelli was instructed to insist that Louis XII make clear to the pope that Florence was under French protection. Machiavelli's reply was hardly reassuring: "Concerning the matters which may arise in Italy, the King holds the Pope in higher esteem than any other Italian power."

Despite this, on November 4 Machiavelli managed to obtain a copy of a letter signed by Louis XII warning Borgia not to make any foray into Florentine territory. Machiavelli was now so short of money that he could no longer afford to send his messages to Florence by express courier, and begged to be allowed to return home. But the Signoria insisted that Machiavelli remain in France until he had a written agreement, signed by Louis XII, that guaranteed French protection for Florence. Inevitably, this took further time. November dragged by while Machiavelli remained kicking his heels, impatient to return. It was around this time that he had a highly significant exchange with the king's right-hand man, Cardinal d'Amboise.

Machiavelli and d'Amboise had become fairly close, largely it seems because Machiavelli felt no compunction about giving him the benefit of his fledgling—but nonetheless astute—political wisdom. Unbuttoning himself in the privacy of his dispatches to Florence, Machiavelli would describe Louis XII as "having long ears and short belief, in that he listened to everyone but only believed what he could lay his hands on"; however, in conversation with d'Amboise he put it more diplomatically, suggesting that if Louis XII wished to succeed in his aim of dominating Italy, he should pay attention to the lessons of history. If a king wished to rule a nation whose customs and culture were different from his own, he should cultivate the friendship of those who were naturally sympathetic towards him—such as, in this case, Florence. What he should not do is increase the power of those he could not trust, such as Alexander VI and the Church, "for by this policy he was making himself weak." Likewise he should not repeat the error of Ludovico Sforza of Milan, who had caused his own ruin by inviting in a powerful foreign nation, namely the French. Now Louis XII was making the same mistake by inviting into Italy the only foreign power to rival France, namely Spain, so that they could share the kingdom of Naples. Years later, Machiavelli would recall the cardinal's reaction:

> The Cardinal of Rouen said to me that the Italians knew nothing of war, but I answered that the French knew nothing of politics. For if they knew anything they would not let the Church attain such strength. Events in Italy [would] show how the greatness of the Church and of Spain were caused by France, and this [would be] the ruin of France's cause.

Machiavelli would go on to conclude:

From this it is possible to deduce a general rule, which almost always applies: whoever is responsible for allowing another to become powerful only ruins himself, for this power is brought into being either by ingenuity or by force, and both of these work against the power which allows it.

Although Machiavelli's conclusions are in fact seen with hindsight, the tenor of his reply to d'Amboise suggests that he was already beginning to think along such lines. All this was indicative of his increasing competence in and grasp of politics, in both practice and theory. This was to be the strength of his analysis: even at this early stage he always sought to understand the underlying principles of what was taking place. As such, he showed that he had the mind of a philosopher: he wished to invest the flesh and blood of politics and historical events with the bones of a science. To do this, it was necessary to look upon the world with an unflinching eye, to observe what actually happened, rather than what one wished or hoped would happen. And for this, Machiavelli's irreverent, unsentimental temperament was ideally suited.

Machiavelli did not get back from France until January 14, 1501. He found Florence in a parlous state: the exchequer was empty, the city had no armed force it could call upon, and Borgia, who "was turning the Romagna upside down," looked poised to make a move into Florentine territory, despite the efforts of Louis XII to restrain him. When the Signoria dispatched an envoy to meet Borgia and discover his intentions,* Borgia blustered and uttered vague threats: he claimed that he felt unable to trust Florence, whose western borders threatened his territory in the Romagna. He would feel more able to trust Florence if there was a change of government and the Medici were reinstated. This was now accompanied by direct pressure on the Signoria from the pope to hire Borgia as a *condottiere* to "defend" their territory. This meant that Borgia would be able to maintain an armed presence on Florentine

---

* Not to be confused with the mission to Borgia undertaken by Machiavelli and Bishop Soderini, which would take place the following year.

[56]

territory—paid for by the Signoria—which could influence the government. In this way he could gain power over Florence, without actually disobeying Louis XII.

These "suggestions" were soon backed by action. In early May 1501 Borgia and his army crossed into Florentine territory, heading directly for Florence. The city descended into chaos as citizens panicked, with many fleeing south into the countryside. On May 14 Borgia halted at Campi, ten miles north of Florence. Next day the Signoria capitulated, agreeing to an "alliance of friendship" with Borgia, according to which he agreed "in the event of danger" to make available to the Signoria 300 of his foot soldiers, so long as he was paid 36,000 ducats a year for three years. This was simple extortion, but at least it meant that the danger was over for the time being. Borgia and his soldiers skirted round Florence, heading southwest for the coast, where he took control of Piombino, ousting Jacopo d'Appiano. Alexander VI sent ships, and Borgia transported his men back to Rome, where he reported to his father. Florence remained independent, but it was now threatened on three sides by Borgia's territory.

Machiavelli was now thirty-two years old and the head of his family. His mother had died some years previously, and he appears to have lived alone with his younger brother Totto in the modest family home in Oltrarno. Machiavelli's opinion of such a bachelor set-up is suggested by a remark he let drop many years later in one of his plays: "they don't have women at home and they live like beasts." It was time he got married, and arrangements were duly made. Around August 1501 Machiavelli was married to Marietta Corsini, a young woman from a respectable family who brought with her a modest dowry. This appears to have tidied up Machiavelli's domestic arrangements, and to have curbed his sexual adventures at an opportune moment. Syphilis had arrived in Europe, probably from the New World, and had reached Naples by 1494. A year later it had been spread through Italy by the retreating French army of Charles VIII—thus becoming known in Italy as "the French disease." Machiavelli's sexual adventures, such as those of which he liked to boast to his friends in exaggerated terms, now took on an even larger imaginary element.

Taxes and the threat of invasion from Borgia had left the citizens of Florence impoverished, fearful, and rebellious, their unrest barely contained by the authorities. Outside in the Tuscan countryside the situation was not so easily contained, and disturbances now broke out in a number of towns. Trouble had been brewing for some time in Pistoia, just twenty miles northwest of Florence, with armed conflict breaking out between rival political factions. As a result, less than two months after his marriage Machiavelli was sent to Pistoia with orders to try and resolve the situation. He eventually managed to negotiate an uneasy truce.

By the end of 1501 intelligence began reaching Florence that Borgia was planning a third campaign into the Romagna, to complete his conquest of the region. And then what? The taking of Florence seemed the next logical step. The Signoria once again appealed to Louis XII, who with surprising haste agreed, in April 1502, to send 6,000 cavalry for the defense of the city, for a payment of 40,000 ducats for the next three years.

But before any French troops could arrive, disaster struck. On June 4 the southern town of Arezzo rose in revolt. One of Borgia's commanders, Vitellozzo Vitelli, who was camped in the Romagna just across the border, immediately moved in and occupied Arezzo, where he was welcomed by its inhabitants, who had almost certainly been working in collaboration with him. Vitellozzo then began moving through the prosperous region of the Val di Chiana, where town after town readily capitulated. News then reached Florence that Piero de' Medici was in Arezzo. It looked as if the days of republican rule in Florence were numbered. As the contemporary Florentine diarist Luca Landucci commented in his vernacular style: "The Florentines had been caught with their breeches down and their arse in a bucket, while all around were laughing at them."

Then news reached Florence that Borgia had left Rome on June 10 with an army of 7,000 men. It looked as if he was marching directly northeast to take Camerino, followed by a march to the coast to take Sinigallia. As a precaution he had sent ahead to his ally Guidobaldo, Duke of Urbino, asking permission to cross his territory in the unlikely event of this being necessary, and asking Guidobaldo if he could send a thousand soldiers to help out Vitellozzo in the nearby Val di Chiana. At the same time, Borgia sent word to Florence that he wished to meet a delegation empowered to negotiate for the republic in order to discuss matters of extreme importance.

On June 22 a two-man delegation departed posthaste from Florence. This consisted of Francesco Soderini, who was Bishop of Volterra as well as head of an important political faction in Florence, together with the young man who was now recognized as the city's most gifted diplomatic negotiator, Niccolò Machiavelli. They had only reached Pontasieve, less than ten miles down the road, when they received the news that Borgia had treacherously switched tactics, speedily marching sixty miles north towards unguarded Urbino. Duke Guidobaldo had fled for his life into the mountains, and the city had fallen without resistance. Urbino lay little more than twenty miles from the recently conquered Val di Chiana, and unless the French troops promised by Louis XII arrived at once, there was nothing to stop Borgia marching west towards undefended Florence.

No sooner had Soderini and Machiavelli arrived in Urbino than they were hustled into the dark and deserted ducal palace, where they were confronted by Borgia, his bearded features illuminated by a single flickering candle. Borgia at once launched into the offensive, accusing Florence of having reneged on the agreement it had sent him at Campi the previous summer, in order to prevent him from marching on the city. Borgia was in fact quite correct here: the agreement between Borgia and Florence had contained several promises, on both sides, which neither had any intention of keeping. For a start, Florence had entertained no intention whatsoever of acquiescing to Borgia's demand for a restoration of the Medici, for if Piero de' Medici had been restored to power, he would have been little more than a Borgia puppet—Borgia would thus have taken the city by subterfuge. Similarly, Florence had had little intention of paying the 36,000 ducats demanded by Borgia, for this had been diverted into the 40,000-ducat payment to Louis XII. Yet still Borgia insisted: "I am not pleased with your government. How can I trust you, how can I be sure you will not attack me? You must change your government and pledge to support me—for I have no intention of letting this state of affairs continue."

The precise dialogue in this conversation was recorded via a subsequent report sent to the Signoria in Florence.* From this it is always clear when Borgia is speaking, but the replies to his questions could have come from either of the two-man delegation. Machiavelli probably knew more about the details of Borgia's allegations, for his post in the administration ensured that he had been present when all decisions had been taken regarding Borgia, as well as when all communications to him had been written. On the other hand, Bishop Soderini was the senior member of the delegation, and thus most of the replies were probably made by him. Such were Borgia's bullying tactics that he would have allowed them little opportunity to consult each other during this confrontation. So it was probably Soderini who replied to Borgia's demand that Florence should change its government, insisting defiantly: "Florence has the government it deserves, and no other power throughout Italy keeps better faith with its people." Soderini went on to suggest that if Borgia wanted friendly dealings with Florence, he should first convince his subordinate Vitellozzo to withdraw from Florentine territory.

Borgia replied that Vitellozzo had acted on his own account—though he added that, given its behavior, he had not been displeased to see Florence receive such a lesson. He even hinted that Vitellozzo was working in conjunction with French wishes.

The Florentine delegation, again probably in the person of Soderini, reminded Borgia that it was Florence that had the support of the powerful Louis XII. To which Borgia replied menacingly: "I know better than you what the French king has in mind." If they were relying upon France, he warned them, "you will be deceived."

It may have been at this stage that Machiavelli sensed Borgia was bluffing. On the other hand, there was no denying the likelihood of what Borgia was saying.

* As a matter of protocol this report was addressed to the Ten of War, the council headed by Machiavelli, but it was of course intended for the *gonfaloniere* and his ruling Signoria, who would have taken any decisions in such important matters.

Soderini and Machiavelli left this meeting chastened, immediately retiring to their quarters to write their dispatch to Florence. Later the next day they managed to strike up a conversation with Borgia's commanders Giulio and Paolo Orsini. Confidentially they assured Soderini and Machiavelli that Vitellozzo's invasion of Florentine territory and his occupation of the Val di Chiana had the backing of France, and Borgia could now easily make a move on Florence itself. If the city called upon Louis XII, he might provide troops, but they would be sent too late to rescue the city. Borgia had an army of 25,000 men poised to invade: the campaign would be over in days, well before anyone could intervene. Machiavelli certainly realized that this "chance" meeting had been organized by Borgia to further his bluff, whatever it was, and in his dispatch to Florence he reckoned that Borgia in fact had only 16,000 men at his disposal. Even so, the situation looked grim.

At the third hour of the night,* Borgia once again summoned the Florentine delegation for a meeting in the darkened ducal palace. This time Borgia angrily demanded that the Florentines reply to his demands: was Florence to comply with his wishes, or not? Previously he had told them: "Make your decision quickly. I cannot keep my army here for long because this is mountain country and my men will soon run out of provisions. Let me tell you frankly, there can be no middle course—if you do not want me as a friend, you will find me your enemy." However, this time Borgia's threats culminated in a definite ultimatum: the Signoria had just four days to make up its mind.

Later events make it clear that other things must have been discussed at this meeting that were not included in the subsequent report. Did Machiavelli and Soderini, acting according to some plan prearranged with the Signoria, offer to Borgia as a show of goodwill the services of the most accomplished military engineer in Florence, namely Leonardo da Vinci? Or was it Borgia who insisted that Leonardo fulfill an under-

---

* According to the prevailing clock in Italy, this meant three hours after the ringing of the Angelus bell at sunset, or in some cases at six in the evening. Soderini and Machiavelli arrived in Urbino just after the longest day of the year, so this second meeting probably took place around midnight.

standing that had been given to him in the company of Louis XII in Milan two years previously? One of these must have taken place.

After this second meeting, with its ominous ultimatum, Soderini and Machiavelli finished their dispatch and sent it posthaste to Florence. The report was written in Machiavelli's hand, but signed by Soderini. According to Machiavelli's biographer Roberto Ridolfi, this signature looks "like an error or a forgery": either Soderini's hand was shaking or Machiavelli forged Soderini's signature in the haste of the moment.

In order to save precious time, it was decided that Machiavelli too should ride as quickly as possible back to Florence, so that he could answer at first hand any questions put to him by the Signoria, as well as deliver verbally any information that had not been included in the official dispatch. We know that Machiavelli felt there was an element of bluff in Borgia's threats. If Vitellozzo had acted of his own accord in the Val di Chiana, as Borgia claimed, this indicated that Borgia was not in full control of his own troops. It also meant that this invasion had not been carried out with the prior collusion of Louis XII. Borgia probably could not rely upon the support of Louis XII, as he claimed. On the other hand, could Florence rely upon the support of the French king? The evidence suggests that such was the drift of Machiavelli's thoughts as he sped on horseback the seventy miles across the Apennine mountains back to Florence, hurriedly snatching something to eat and changing horses at the remote staging-post inns on the way, desperate to waste as little time as possible as he carried word of Borgia's four-day ultimatum. And, as later evidence will confirm, we know that he also took with him Cesare Borgia's message to Leonardo da Vinci, informing him that he was now in Borgia's employ, and passing on his employer's first instructions.

3

The Pope and His Bastard

MACHIAVELLI'S ASSESSMENT OF the situation was closer to the truth than he realized. Borgia was certainly bluffing—but what Machiavelli and Soderini were not aware of was the extent of his bluff. What Borgia knew, and Machiavelli and Soderini did not, was that Louis XII had already dispatched troops to defend Florence. Borgia was aware that if only he could bully the Florentines into forming an alliance with him before the French troops arrived, his problems would be solved. The French would remain his allies, the size of the forces at his disposal would be considerably bolstered, and his covert project of ruling over a territory that spanned central Italy from coast to coast would be a step closer to realization.

Borgia was a man of considerable guile, daring, and psychological acumen. However, his reputation as a fearsome military commander was based more on his ability to move at speed and catch his enemy by surprise, often by means of treachery, than on any valor in battle. On the other hand, his reputation in other fields was richly deserved, and owed little to exaggeration. His behavior was often that of an inhuman monster, in both his depravities and his pursuit of his vast ambitions: he would stop at nothing. Yet he was also, like Leonardo and Machiavelli in their own very separate ways, a superb exemplar of the Renaissance man. Charismatic and handsome in his youthful prime, highly intelligent and well versed in the classics, he would cut a superb figure in the courts of Italy and France, when he put his mind to it. Here was a man who could be as magnetic in his charm as he could be terrifying in his evil.

The Borgias were Spanish, making them outsiders amongst the chauvinist Italians. Their enemies referred to them disparagingly as *Marrani*—the name given to the Spanish Jews who had publicly converted to Christianity, but privately continued to worship as Jews. For their part, the Borgias behaved as if they had never left Spain, retaining their Spanish culture and familial closeness, secretively speaking Catalan or Valencian dialect amongst themselves. Cesare Borgia, who would always sign himself "Cesar" (the Spanish version of his name), was born near Rome in September 1475. He was the first illegitimate son of Cardinal Rodrigo Borgia by his striking redheaded mistress Vannozza de' Cattanei. Cardinal Borgia had enjoyed several previous mistresses, and had already fathered a son and a number of daughters, but the strong-willed Vannozza ensured that her children would be the most deeply beloved by their father, and amongst his chief beneficiaries. As the second of Cardinal Borgia's sons, Cesare was from the start educated for entry into the Church. At an early age he began learning Latin from the master of the Borgia household, Lorenz Beheim, who was an expert classical scholar and an accomplished astrologist, accommodating the Borgia penchant for superstition. By the time Cesare was six, his father had prevailed upon Pope Sixtus IV to grant the boy a "dispensation" from his illegitimacy, thus enabling him to hold ecclesiastical offices. Thereupon Cardinal Borgia began obtaining a string of lucrative benefices for his son, who had not yet even taken holy orders. Despite this, by the age of fifteen Cesare had risen to become bishop-elect of Pamplona, the capital of the Spanish kingdom of Navarre. (The pope himself was forced to intercede to prevent a serious uprising by the indignant citizens of Pamplona, who deemed this appointment an insult to themselves and their kingdom.)

At the same time, Cardinal Rodrigo Borgia continued to ensure that his own career prospered, and by now he had risen to become vice-chancellor, making him one of the most powerful figures in Rome. This position enabled him to amass a fortune, and he soon began to live the life of a Renaissance prince, rather than a man of the cloth, equipping his palazzo with sumptuous furnishings and works of art, all very much in the Spanish style. Later, the sixty-year-old cardinal would even take on a new teenage mistress, the celebrated aristocratic beauty Giulia Farnese, who had recently married into the powerful Orsini family.

Although Cardinal Borgia may have lived a louche life, he made sure that he always attended the consistory, when the cardinals met to discuss the business of the Church. A man of intelligence and cunning, he quickly gained an expert knowledge of the financial dealings of the Church, and of the power politics involved in its operations. He also closely observed Sixtus IV's attempt to advance his political power in Italy, watching as the pope backed the Pazzis' unsuccessful attempt to assassinate Lorenzo the Magnificent and dislodge the Medici from Florence. Cardinal Borgia, for his part, looked to increase his influence in Spain, acquiring the archbishopric of Valencia, and later creating the dukedom of Gandia for his oldest son, Pedro Luis Borgia. When Pedro Luis died in 1488, Cardinal Borgia had the title transferred to Cesare's younger brother, the twelve-year-old Juan Borgia, who was his second son by Vannozza.

On reaching the age of seventeen, Cesare Borgia was sent by his father to the University of Pisa, which had recently been established by Lorenzo the Magnificent. The cardinal had learned that Lorenzo's second son, Giovanni, who was the same age as Cesare and was also being groomed for the highest echelons of the Church, was going to study at Pisa.* He wrote to Lorenzo that he was sending his own son to Pisa as a "pledge of the great love" he felt for the Medici, so that he could be under Lorenzo's "wing and protection."

It is possible that Machiavelli was an impecunious scholar at Pisa during this period; there are indications that he first encountered Giovanni de' Medici around this time, though there is no hint of his having encountered Cesare Borgia at this stage. By now Cesare had blossomed into a striking figure. One contemporary source even described him as "the handsomest man in Italy," and there was no hint of his priestly status, in either his behavior or his appearance. He dressed with peacock flamboyance in the latest fashionable attire, wore

---

* Lorenzo the Magnificent had used his influence to persuade Pope Innocent VIII to appoint Giovanni a cardinal at the age of fourteen, an unprecedented appointment even in such corrupt times.

his dark hair long about his shoulders, and sported a red-tinged beard, holding the eye of the crowd wherever he went. At Pisa he studied canon and civil law, quickly becoming noted for his diligence and brilliance; even the contemporary historian Paolo Giovio, who despised the Borgias, conceded that at the public disputation Cesare was required to undergo for his laureate, his examiners were dazzled by his "ardent mind" and with the way "he discussed learnedly the questions put to him both in canon and civil law."

But a year later in 1492 drastic changes took place that would transform Italy and alter Cesare's life forever. In April, Lorenzo the Magnificent died in Florence, and with that the uneasy political stability of the Italian states lost its most skilled protector. Then in July Pope Innocent VIII died, and on August 5 the cardinals embarked upon their secret conclave to elect his successor. Cardinal Borgia was a superlative operator in the kind of horse-trading that attended a papal election, where the opposing cabals bargained amongst themselves for support of their rival candidates. At the previous election in 1484, Borgia had been blocked by the powerful faction led by Cardinal Giuliano della Rovere, who had forced him to accept Innocent VIII as a compromise choice. This time Cardinal Borgia was sixty-one and realized that it would probably be his last chance to succeed to the papal throne. Once again he found himself blocked by his determined enemy Cardinal della Rovere, and for five days the intense discussions continued, with no sign of resolving the deadlock. Eventually it emerged that the balance was held by Cardinal Ascanio Sforza, brother of Ludovico "Il Moro" Sforza, the ruler of Milan.

According to the legendary story recorded by the contemporary diarist Stefano Infessura, on the night of August 10, four mules laden with treasure were observed leaving Cardinal Borgia's palazzo for that of Cardinal Sforza. More reliably reported is the fact that during these days the withdrawals from the Spannocchi Bank in Rome, where Cardinal Borgia deposited his money, were so massive that the bank itself almost went under. On the morning of August 11, as summer lightning flashed amongst the dark storm clouds above the hills of Rome, it emerged that—to widespread astonishment—Cardinal Ascanio Sforza had decided to cast his vote (and those of his faction) for Cardinal Borgia, who was consequently elected as the new pope and took on the name Alexander VI. Prior to his election the new pope had boasted somewhat exaggeratedly that during his years as vice-chancellor he had accumulated sufficient sacks of gold coins, pearls, jewels, and gold plate to fill the Sistine Chapel. A considerable portion of his personal treasure had been used to ensure his election, but the prize was worth it: the pope's annual income during this period was around 300,000 ducats, and the selling of rich benefices could amount to even more than this sum. Previous conclaves had been known to be corrupt, with money used to influence voting, but this occasion is generally reckoned to have been the first time in history when the papacy was simply bought outright.

During the tense days of the conclave Cesare had been in Siena, overseeing the training of the horse he was entering for the Palio, the most celebrated horse race in Italy. After his father's election, he was ordered not to attend the papal coronation, but instead to retire to the family fortress, some sixty miles north of Rome amidst the wooded hills at Spoleto. Alexander VI considered it impolitic to parade his family publicly on such an occasion. Yet within months, much to the outrage of all Rome, he moved Cesare, and later Cesare's younger sister Lucrezia, to live with him in the new Vatican quarter of Trastevere, which had grown up across the Tiber from the main city. Previous popes had been known to have children, but had never before publicly cohabited with them. Almost as controversial was Cesare's blatantly secular lifestyle, as recorded by his friend the ambassador from Ferrara:

> The day before yesterday I went to find Cesare at his house in Trastevere. He was on the point of going out for the hunt; he was wearing a worldly garment of silk and had his sword at his side. . . . He possesses marked genius and a charming personality. He has the manners of a son of a great prince; above all he is lively and merry and fond of society. [He] has never had any inclination for the priesthood.

Cesare was now appointed Archbishop of Valencia, with a stipend of 16,000 ducats—the post that his father had been obliged to vacate on becoming pope. During the first year of his reign Alexander VI appointed no fewer than eleven new cardinals, including Alessandro Farnese, the brother of his new mistress, Giulia, who now became known mockingly as "the bride of Christ" when she produced Alexander VI's daughter in the year of his accession. All Alexander VI's new appointments to the cardinalate were either Borgia relatives or very close and trustworthy friends, thus nullifying the power of Cardinal della Rovere and his faction in the consistory. Meanwhile the generous Cardinal Sforza had been rewarded with the vacant post of vice-chancellor. Prior to Alexander VI's reign simony had hardly been unknown, but this was taking it to new heights. As the contemporary Neapolitan poet Jacopo Sanazzaro wrote satirically of the new pope: "Alexander sells the keys, the altars, Christ himself—he has the right to sell them, he had bought them first."

Alexander VI soon showed that he was not even above using his young daughter Lucrezia to extend his political influence, though there his heart was in conflict with his ambitions. He loved Lucrezia dearly, and was loath to let her depart from his side. After betrothing the infant Lucrezia first to a Spanish nobleman, then changing his mind to betroth her to the better-connected Spanish Don Gaspare Aversa, Count of Procida, he would eventually decide to marry her at the age of thirteen to Giovanni Sforza, a cousin of Ludovico "Il Moro," thus consolidating his alliance with Milan.

In the summer of 1493, Alexander decided to bestow upon the eighteen-year-old Cesare the rank of cardinal, despite the fact that his son had still not even been formally ordained into the Church. When Cardinal della Rovere heard of this appointment he let out "a loud exclamation" and fell into such an apoplectic rage that he was forced to retire to his bed. The news reached the new young cardinal Cesare Borgia himself while he was on holiday with his mother, Vannozza, in the countryside north of Rome. At the time he was in the midst of an angry dispute with the governors of Siena, where his horse had just been disqualified from winning the famous Palio (after the jockey had been instructed by Cesare to throw himself from his horse in the last stretch, thus lightening its load as it galloped across the notoriously slippery sanded cobbles of the square around which the race was run). Instead the race had been awarded to Francesco Gonzaga, the Marquis of Mantua, the noted soldier who would later take command of the forces of the Holy League against Charles VIII. Cesare's angry letters to Gonzaga threatened serious political consequences, which were quite contrary to Alexander VI's diplomatic strategy. Already Cesare was showing signs that he was not entirely beholden to his father's every wish.

However, Alexander VI's first years as pope were not wholly devoted to simony and the pursuit of political power. He was also a man of considerable intellect and ability. One of his first acts had been to restore a semblance of civil order to the streets of Rome, which was now beginning to rival Florence as the leading city of the Renaissance. Even so, Rome remained in many aspects a medieval city: amidst the splendor of the derelict ruins of ancient Rome, and the magnificent fortified palazzi of the cardinals and leading families of the Roman nobility, the streets themselves remained squalid and dangerous. The large annual influx of pilgrims from all over Christendom had generated a booming tourist industry, with all the customary accoutrements that this entailed. Taverns and bordellos flourished; side streets were infested with robbers, cutthroats, and kidnappers, while the policing authorities had been bribed into a state of total ineffectuality. On becoming pope, Alexander VI had immediately strengthened the papal guards, as well as the effectiveness of the various policing authorities. A thorough and widespread search was launched for a long list of known gang leaders and murderers. When these were tracked down they were summarily hanged, their bodies left as a rotting example on the gallows lining the bridge across the Tiber leading to the papal fortress of Castel Sant' Angelo, from whose dungeons rose the wails of the many incarcerated lesser criminals.

On his accession, the new pope had promised a thorough reform of the papal finances, a subject close to his heart; and, to the astonishment of many, these reforms were rapidly implemented. Then in 1494 Alexander VI issued a papal bull that has arguably had more effect on the world than any before or since. With Spain's discovery of the New World, and Portugese explorations reaching beyond the Azores, around Africa, and into the Indian Ocean, the prospect of a conflict between these two powerful Christian nations grew ever more likely. This problem was resolved by Alexander VI's bull, which drew a line from north to south through the middle of the Atlantic 100 leagues west of the Cape Verde Islands. All new lands discovered to the west of this line would belong to Spain, all those to the east to Portugal.*

Alexander VI's action in this potentially ruinous dispute was much appreciated by both sides, though perhaps more so by the Spanish, to whom the independent papal adjudication had seemingly awarded the lion's share. As a recognition of this favor, King Ferdinand of Spain was prepared to overlook his contempt for the pope's son, Juan Borgia, the upstart Duke of Gandia. Ferdinand announced that he was now prepared to receive Gandia at court, and even permitted Gandia's betrothal to his royal cousin Maria Enriquez. Around this time Alexander VI also managed to secure a prestigious royal fiancée for his son Jofre, who became engaged to Sancia, the illegitimate daughter of Alfonso, son of the King of Naples. Immediate Borgia power would cease to exist when Alexander VI was no longer pope, but with his sons married into two royal families, it was evident that Alexander VI had greater, more permanent ambitions for the Borgia family. In pursuit of this aim, the new pope's increasing web of influence now extended the length of Italy, and beyond—from the Sforzas in Milan to the Medici in Florence, from the King of Naples to the King of Spain.

Yet in 1494 Alexander VI's plans fell apart, when Ludovico Sforza invited Charles VIII into Italy to claim the throne of Naples. The uncouth French king was viewed with horror by the sophisticated Italians; according to Guicciardini: "His limbs were so proportioned that he seemed more like a monster than a man." As his army swept south, it

---

* This line would later be moved to 370 leagues west of the Azores. Although it was intended that the New World should be Spanish, this new demarcation meant that when Brazil was discovered, it lay east of the new line and thus fell to the Portuguese. A lasting legacy of this can be seen in the fact that Portuguese is spoken in Brazil, whereas throughout the rest of South America the official language remains Spanish.

soon began to upset the precarious balance of Italian politics. When Pisa was taken, it became liberated from Florence. Amidst the upheavals, Piero de' Medici fled Florence, which itself suffered the humiliation of being occupied by the French army. Before Charles VIII would withdraw his army, he insisted that the Signoria sign a treaty of friendship, binding Florence to support the French cause.

Yet all this was a minor humiliation compared with what was to follow. To reach Naples, Charles VIII and his army needed to cross papal territory. Alexander VI summoned the few forces at his disposal—mainly drawn from the armies of the leading Roman families, such as the Orsini and the Colonna. After a desperate appeal to his Neapolitan allies, Alexander VI received further reinforcements, but these were hardly sufficient to resist the 60,000-strong French war machine that was soon on its way south.

Prior to the arrival of the French, battles in Italy had been largely choreographed affairs, conducted by rival *condottiere* with no wish to inflict injury upon their mercenary opponents, who might next season be their allies. When one side was maneuvered into an indefensible position (that is, one from which it could not readily flee), defeat would be conceded—and the two opposing commanders would come to a mutually satisfactory agreement. The massive medieval French army knew no such niceties. Battles were fought with bloodthirsty vigor, and would frequently end in the slaughter of all those who did not make good their escape. Such was the way war was fought in northern Europe—and the French army had been well practiced in this pursuit, the Hundred Years' War against the English having only petered to a halt some decades previously. At the same time, the French army was importing a new weapon into Italy—namely, the large mobile cannon. The Italians had smaller cannons hauled by lumbering oxen, whose ammunition consisted of small stone cannonballs, which usually shattered against the solid walls of the local fortresses. The vast French cannons were mounted so that they could be hauled speedily across country by teams of horses, and fired huge iron cannonballs capable of gouging holes in even the most formidable fortress walls. As Charles VIII marched south, one by one the fortresses standing in his path capitulated, often without a shot being fired, such was the terror that spread before the French army.

News now reached Alexander VI in Rome that Cardinal Ascanio Sforza had persuaded his Colonna allies to defect and seize the coastal ports of Ostia and Civitavecchia in the name of the French. Rome was now cut off from its supplies. As Charles VIII moved towards Rome, the Orsini forces too defected to the French.

Alexander VI realized that armed resistance would be useless and sent his few remaining forces south to Naples. On December 14, 1494, Charles VIII and his army marched unopposed into Rome. His forces were so vast that it took from three o'clock in the afternoon until nine o'clock at night for the columns of French foot soldiers, Swiss mercenaries, and squadrons of cavalry to pass through the streets. The seemingly endless procession was followed by the rolling thunder of the thirty-six mounted cannons rumbling across the cobbles dragged by lines of cart horses. The watching crowds gaped in terror at the sight of the eight-foot cannons, each weighing 6,000 pounds, their brass barrels glimmering in the light of the flares, their dark mouths large enough to contain the head of a man.

But still Alexander VI refused to submit to any public capitulation. Together with his son Cardinal Cesare Borgia, he fled through the secret tunnel from the Vatican into the massive ancient fortress of Castel Sant' Angelo. By now the city streets were in turmoil. Charles VIII set up public gallows to deter his men from looting, but still the French and Swiss soldiers attempted to swarm the walls of the barricaded palazzi in search of booty. Even the residence of Cesare's mother, Vannozza, was not immune: Swiss mercenaries managed to break in and ransack it, making off with 800 ducats. By now the French king had been joined by Alexander VI's sworn enemy Cardinal Giovanni della Rovere, who encouraged Charles VIII to demand that the pope submit to a council for the reform of the papacy. In the words of the contemporary historian Guicciardini, for Alexander VI the idea of submitting to reform was "an unspeakably terrible thought." Alexander VI obstinately stood his ground, but della Rovere and his supporting cardinals "constantly pressed the King to remove from the See a pope full of such great vices and abominations and to elect another." Eventually Charles VIII's patience ran out, and he lined up his cannons before the walls of the Castel Sant' Angelo; but before a shot could be fired, a large thirty-foot section of the ancient walls simply collapsed of its own accord, carrying away the soldiers who had been guarding its battlements and burying them in a heap of rubble. Hardly had the large dust cloud settled than Alexander VI agreed to meet Charles VIII.

Guicciardini succinctly summed up the Italian contempt for the French king: "Not only did he lack all knowledge of the arts, but he barely knew how to read and write. He was greedy to rule but quite incapable of it, because allowing himself to be continually influenced. . . ." Such a man proved easily charmed by the sophisticated avuncular display put on by Alexander VI. When Charles VIII went on his knees and made to kiss the pope's feet, Alexander VI graciously raised him to his feet. Even so, the pope was forced to make some concessions. When Charles VIII departed with his army for Naples on January 28, 1495, he insisted on having Cardinal Cesare Borgia riding at his side, as a friendly companion (and hostage), along with a train of nineteen mules carrying treasures and rich tapestries.

Two days later the French army reached Velletri, where the king and his traveling companion were to be the guests of the local bishop, none other than Cardinal Giuliano della Rovere. This would have been humiliation indeed for the proud young Cardinal Borgia, who could not abide even the slightest personal insult. However, it was not to be. According to Alexander VI's master of ceremonies, Johannes Burchard: "On January 30 news arrived that Cardinal Cesare Borgia had eluded the grasp of the French king and escaped from Velletri disguised as a groom from the royal stables, and that he had traveled so swiftly that he slept that night in Rome." Next day, he quietly slipped out of the city at first light. To add insult to injury, Borgia had also managed to arrange for half the treasure train of mules to be "stolen"; and the boxes carried by the remaining mules were found to be empty.

When Charles VIII realized that he had been tricked, he flew into a rage, shouting: "All these Italians are filthy curs and none is worse than their Holy Father!" Cardinal Borgia would lie low in the family fortress at Spoleto for two months, before venturing back to Rome. Yet within days of his return he would assert his presence in characteristic fashion. A detachment of the Swiss soldiers occupying Rome for Charles VIII was set upon in St. Peter's Square by several hundred heavily armed Spaniards; in the course of the ensuing melee, twenty-four Swiss were murdered and many more managed to escape only with severe wounds. Cesare Borgia was not one to forget an insult: it was Swiss soldiers who had ransacked his mother's house and stolen her money.

Meanwhile, after leaving Velletri, Charles VIII and his army had continued towards Naples. On hearing this news, King Alfonso II of Naples, who had only succeeded to the throne the previous year, quickly decided to abdicate and entered a monastery; soon afterwards the new king, his son Ferrante II, fled by sea for Sicily. On February 22, Charles VIII and the French army entered Naples in triumph and quickly proceeded to make themselves at home. Several sources speak of Charles VIII's vast sexual appetite and his enthusiasm for the women of Naples. He is said to have had a book drawn up with pictures of his favorites, which he would leaf through and slaver over in anticipation of their favors. Others confirm his obsession with copulation, but claim that he insisted upon novelty, and would never have the same woman twice. What was referred to as Charles VIII's favorite hobby soon became the subject of all manner of scandalous gossip throughout Naples. At the same time, his soldiery began earning for themselves a similarly tarnished reputation, as one eyewitness reported:

> The French were clownish, dirty and dissolute people; they were always to be found in sin and venereal acts. . . . They violated the women, with no respect whatsoever, then they robbed them and took the rings from their fingers, and if any woman resisted they cut off her fingers to have the rings.

Just a few months earlier, syphilis had reached Naples and was now rife amongst its citizens. The disease soon began to spread through the French army.

The French victory in Naples was viewed with alarm throughout

Italy, which it appeared would soon be overrun by the all-conquering invaders. Using his diplomatic powers to the utmost, Alexander VI quickly began trying to put together a Holy League to oppose the French. By now Ludovico "Il Moro" Sforza had realized the enormity of what he had done in inviting the French into Italy and, as Machiavelli put it, "had become afraid of falling into the ditch which he himself had dug." He was soon persuaded to join the Pope's Holy League, as was Venice, along with Siena and Mantua and several other minor Italian states. The League even received outside support from Spain, which soon succumbed to Alexander VI's persuasive arguments: the French had no business in Naples, which had for so long had close ties with Spain. Only Florence obstinately resisted joining the League. Much to the vexation of Alexander VI, the renegade priest Savonarola urged the Signoria to stand by the treaty it had signed with Charles VIII, rightly suspecting that the pope favored the return of the Medici. The Holy League was signed in Venice, and it was now that Alexander VI decided that his thirteen-year-old daughter Lucrezia should break off her second engagement and instead marry Giovanni Sforza, who as Lord of Pesaro on the northern Adriatic coast was allied to both Milan and Venice. This marriage would seal the Holy League. Despite recent setbacks, Alexander VI continued to believe in using his family to advance his political aims.

In May 1495 Charles VIII decided to march north from Naples and return to France, before he could be cut off by the forces of the Holy League. Alexander VI and Cardinal Cesare Borgia quickly absented themselves from Rome to avoid any embarrassing meeting with the French king, and when the French army pressed into northern Italy it was met by the combined forces of the Holy League under the Marquis of Mantua on the banks of the River Taro at Fornovo. The Italian army proved no match for Charles VIII. As Machiavelli described it, the French "marched onward over the belly of their foes, so that to those who beheld it the river appeared like a stream of blood, filled with fallen men and arms and horses cut down by the Gallic sword." Even so, the Italians managed to capture the French baggage train, which contained all the booty that the French had accumulated in Italy. Charles

VIII refused to turn back to recover this; he was now more determined than ever to return home as swiftly as possible.

But this was not all that Charles VIII would leave behind. As the French army marched north through Italy, it spread syphilis in its trail, leaving the disease in each region and city through which it passed, before carrying it across the Alps and into France. Once the disease had taken root in Rome, it would then be carried to every corner of Christendom by pilgrims returning home.

When the French left Italy, the Holy League soon began to disintegrate, and Alexander VI found himself once more facing open opposition on his own doorstep in the form of the powerful Orsini and Colonna families, whose fortresses controlled the main roads north and south of Rome. The Orsini remained obstinately favorable to France, to the point where they even flew the French flag from their battlements. They knew that Charles VIII was planning to return and wished to take full advantage of this.

In 1496 Alexander VI summoned his young son Juan, Duke of Gandia, back from Spain, and appointed him *gonfaloniere* of the papal forces. The handsome, profligate Gandia had long been Alexander's favorite, and his older brother Cesare could only look on in envy. As a cardinal, Cesare could not be appointed to any such military post. In October 1496 the young and inexperienced Gandia led the papal forces in their campaign against the Orsini. Within three months it had ended in disaster, with Gandia fleeing ignominiously back to Rome, whereupon Alexander VI was forced to make a humiliating peace with his enemies.

Alexander now withdrew to the Borgia apartments in the Vatican to ponder the future. It soon became clear that he had decided upon a change of strategy. The first indication that the pope was planning to break his alliance with Ludovico "Il Moro" Sforza in Milan came at Easter 1497, when Lucrezia's husband, Giovanni Sforza, suddenly fled back to his castle at Pesaro on the Adriatic coast, although some doubted that Giovanni's flight was entirely due to his getting wind of any switching of alliances by the pope. As soon as it became known that Giovanni Sforza had left his wife, Lucrezia, behind, word spread that the real reason for his flight might well have been his fear of Cardinal Cesare Borgia. This was perhaps the first hint of Cesare's feelings for his sister, and Rome was swept by rumors of incest. The Borgias had many enemies, and these rumors did not seem to have any basis in fact. On the other hand, as we shall see, Cesare was always particularly touchy with regard to any man in a relationship with his sister.

But the gossips of Rome soon had something else to occupy them. Two months after the flight of Giovanni Sforza, the body of Cesare's younger brother, the Duke of Gandia, was found floating in the Tiber. In the words of the pope's master of ceremonies, Johannes Burchard:

> When the Pope heard that the Duke was dead and thrown into the river like dung, he fell into a paroxysm of grief, and such was the anguish and bitterness in his heart that he locked himself away in his room and wailed with abandon.

The soldiers of Alexander VI's Spanish guard were ordered to scour the city in search of the culprits. Gandia had many obvious enemies, and his habit of cuckolding important figures had earned him much hatred. The Orsini, the Colonnas, and many others barricaded themselves in their palazzi as the pope's notorious Spanish soldiers roamed the streets. But no culprit was found, and the finger of suspicion was soon beginning to point at the envious Cesare, especially in the light of new rumors that began to spread. Gandia was said to have become unnaturally close to his sister Lucrezia, after she had been deserted by her husband. There might thus have been more than one reason for Cesare's envy. But as before, nothing could be proved. Then Alexander VI suddenly called off his soldiers, as if he now knew who was responsible for the murder of his favorite son—though if he did know the truth, he would not admit it publicly. It is possible he could not even admit it to himself. However, although Cesare appears the most obvious suspect, it remains just as likely that Gandia was murdered by the Orsini, agents of a jealous husband, or even by assassins hired by Giovanni Sforza, who had also heard the rumors of his wife Lucrezia's behavior.

Whatever the truth, it now became clear that Alexander VI had plans of his own for Lucrezia, who was sent away to the chaste atmosphere of the ancient convent of San Sisto, on the southern edge of the city, while her father began making preparations for her divorce from Giovanni Sforza. Pressure was put on Sforza to swear that the marriage had not been consummated, on account of his being impotent. Sforza, whose previous marriage had ended in his wife's death during childbirth, indignantly denied this charge, even going so far as to claim that "the Pope had taken her from him for no other purpose than to sleep with her himself." The gossips had a field day: many had remarked on the strength of the pope's feelings for his daughter, despite the fact that he insisted on using her to further his political ambitions.

By now rumors of the pope's scandalous behavior had begun to spread far and wide. Although these were in fact founded on mere gossip, things took a more serious turn when Savonarola began alluding to such matters in his sermons to the people of Florence. Savonarola railed on about the iniquities of the Church, and of the pope in particular, "saying how his opponent serves under the Devil himself," as Machiavelli recorded, "and trying to set all against the Supreme Pontiff." Alexander VI ordered the Florentine church authorities to take immediate action, but to little avail. When all other attempts to silence the rebellious priest had failed, he took the drastic step of excommunicating Savonarola, thus preventing him from preaching. But to the pope's astonishment and anger, this made little difference. Savonarola merely passed on his sermons to fellow priests, who delivered them in his stead. Such outright defiance could not be tolerated, and Alexander VI now brought to bear all his influence on the more conservative element amongst the Church authorities in Florence. As a result, Savonarola's downfall was soon engineered, and in May 1498 he paid the price for opposing the pope by being burned at the stake. Yet this did not bring about quite the outcome that Alexander VI had foreseen. He had quietly been hoping that his allies, the Medici, would now be restored as rulers of Florence. Instead, a new republican government, which included the young unknown Machiavelli, was voted into power. As a result, Florence would retain its pact with the French, who were able to supply mercenary troops to aid the city in its attempt to recapture the vital port of Pisa.

By this time news had come through that in April Charles VIII had died in France and had been succeeded by his cousin, the thirty-two-year-old Louis XII. This left Charles VIII's former queen, Anne of Brittany, a highly eligible widow, and anyone who married her could lay claim to Brittany, thus splitting off this valuable province from France. So in order to secure his kingdom Louis XII decided that he must divorce his wife, Jeanne, and marry Anne of Brittany. But for this he would require the assent of the pope. Alexander's position was further strengthened when he learned that Louis wished the pope to make his ambitious chief counselor, Georges d'Amboise, a cardinal.

If Louis XII was to be granted his divorce, and d'Amboise his red hat, it was evident that the French king would have to make considerable concessions to the pope. Alexander VI was determined to take full advantage of this opportunity, and demanded that the French king should from now on support him in his political endeavors. For a start, he would require French money and French troops to be put at his disposal in Rome. Alexander VI had come to the realization that if he was to render himself secure, and pursue his new aims, this could only be achieved with the aid of powerful military backing.

4

Cesare Rising

FOLLOWING THE MURDER of the Duke of Gandia, Alexander VI had been faced with little choice but to consider appointing his oldest son, Cesare, as *gonfaloniere* of the papal forces—there was no one else he could trust. First of all Cesare would have to renounce his cardinalate, but this meant that the pope would then be able to marry off his son in order to advance his political aims. From this time on, it was Cesare who was to be the object of all Alexander's ambitions. And only now did the full details of the pope's change of policy become apparent: he had set his eye on the kingdom of Naples.

After the departure of Charles VIII and the French army, King Ferrante II had reconquered Naples with the aid of the Spanish. Alexander VI decided that Cesare should marry Ferrante II's daughter Carlotta, thus putting him in line to take over the throne. To pave the way, Alexander VI proposed to marry off his daughter Lucrezia—who was now publicly declared a virgin—into the royal family of Naples. Unfortunately, Ferrante II refused to allow any of his legitimate offspring to marry the illegitimate Lucrezia, and instead offered his own illegitimate son Alfonso, Duke of Bisceglie. In July 1498 the marriage took place in Rome, under the watchful eye of the pope. However, it was clear that the Neapolitan royal family was reluctant to allow the eighteen-year-old Carlotta to marry Cesare Borgia. Yet Alexander VI felt sure that he could overcome this difficulty. For some time Carlotta had been living at the French court, and Alexander VI made it clear that he would only grant Louis XII his wishes, concerning his divorce and the granting of a cardinal's hat to d'Amboise, if Louis XII was willing to support Cesare in his bid to marry Carlotta. Louis XII and Alexander VI entered into a secret agreement, whereby Louis would support Carlotta's marriage, as long as she agreed, and at the same time Alexander would be compensated with further soldiers and money for the papal forces, while their prospective young commander, Cesare Borgia, traveled to France to claim his bride.

On December 1, 1498, Cesare made a spectacular triumphal entry into Chinon, on the Loire, where Louis XII was holding court. Both Cesare and his father had been determined to impress the French court, and had spared nothing. Cesare was preceded by dozens of liveried attendants, seventy mules bearing chests of gifts, and sixteen chargers led by grooms in the Borgia colors of gold, crimson, and yellow. As Cesare ascended towards the castle, he was seen by the crowd to be wearing colorful silks and a collar emblazoned with diamonds, estimated to be worth all of 30,000 ducats. But as Machiavelli would learn when he visited Louis XII two years later, the powerful and sophisticated French held the Italians in little regard. Cesare Borgia in all his finery may have cut a striking figure for the crowd, but the king and his nobles merely joked amongst themselves and laughed down their long sleeves, considering all this pomp a little too much. Cesare, for his part, soon began to feel overawed by his surroundings: this was the first time he had visited a foreign country, and the first time he had not been under his father's protection.

As Alexander VI and Cesare had already learned, the man who had the power to influence the king was his counselor d'Amboise, who was more than charmed when Cesare presented him with his red hat, confirming him as Cardinal of Rouen. In return, the king confirmed Cesare's appointment as Duke of Valentinois.* As Cesare began to accustom himself to the ways of the French court, his confidence grew, and he was soon impressing Louis XII with his bearded good looks, his powerful physique, his fine intellect, and his wit. As a gesture of his esteem, Louis XII made Cesare a member of the exclusive and

---

* From now on this would be the title by which Cesare Borgia would be known, and in Italy he would be known as "Il Valentino," the popular Italian version of this title.

prestigious Order of St. Michael. There was only one snag: the young Carlotta refused point-blank to marry Cesare. This was put down to a combination of teenage recalcitrance, the fact that she had fallen in love with someone else, and her family's disregard for the illegitimate Cesare. But there may possibly have been another reason for Carlotta's rejection. When the twenty-three-year-old Cesare had been leaving Rome, the Mantuan ambassador had noted: "He is well enough in countenance at present, although he has his face blotched beneath the skin as is usual with the great pox." Cesare's libertine behavior had led him to catch syphilis, which would one day cause him to wear a mask. Fortunately for him, this initial disfigurement seems to have cleared up on his long journey to the French court, as was usually the case with this early stage of the disease. Even so, it is possible that his prospective bride gained news of these unattractive symptoms.

Louis XII had said that he would not compel Carlotta to marry against her will, and he remained as good as his word. In March the wedding was called off. The self-confident Cesare now revealed the other side of his character, and was plunged into black despair. He risked returning to Italy in disgrace as a laughingstock. But by this stage Louis XII had become more than impressed by Cesare: he liked him and regarded him as a friend. As a result, he went out of his way to find Cesare a new bride—eventually coming up with the attractive sixteen-year-old Charlotte d'Albret, who was related to the new Queen of France and was also the younger sister of the King of Navarre, the kingdom that straddled the northern Pyrenees between France and Spain. The marriage between Cesare and Charlotte duly took place on May 12, 1499, at Blois.

Alexander VI professed himself delighted with Cesare's new bride. This marriage would link the Borgia family to France, as well as reinforcing its ties with Spain. On the other hand, it put an end to Alexander VI's project to establish Cesare on the throne of Naples. The Pope would now have to rethink his plans for a permanent Borgia power base.

By this time Louis XII was preparing for his invasion of Italy, during which he intended to depose Ludovico "Il Moro" Sforza from the dukedom of Milan, claiming it as his own. Cesare was given command of a squadron of heavy cavalry in the invading French army, and in early August 1499 he left Charlotte to join the long march south.

When news of the imminent invasion, and Cesare's role in it, reached Rome, it was greeted with consternation amongst the pro-Sforza faction. Cardinal Ascanio Sforza, who had regained favor after his disloyalty during the invasion of Charles VIII by helping the pope put together the Holy League, now precipitately fled Rome, quickly followed by his allies, the Colonna. The Orsini, who had remained so loyal to France, saw no reason to follow suit—for the time being. Meanwhile, Lucrezia's new husband, the Duke of Bisceglie, belatedly realized that Alexander VI had abandoned any wish to remain friendly towards Naples and fled from the city in terror, leaving his six-months-pregnant wife distraught.

In the late summer of 1499 the French army marched into Italy, once again sweeping all before it. City after city capitulated, and after an uprising in Milan, Ludovico "Il Moro" Sforza retreated from the city, which soon fell. On October 6, 1499, Louis XII led the triumphal procession into Milan, with Cardinal d'Amboise and Cesare Borgia in his train. Cesare shared with Louis XII an interest in the arts, and the following day he accompanied the king on a visit to the monastery of Santa Marie delle Grazie, to view the celebrated fresco of *The Last Supper* by Leonardo da Vinci. Louis XII was so impressed that, according to Vasari, he "wanted to remove it to his kingdom . . . but as the painting was done on a wall his majesty failed to have his way." Later, Cesare met Leonardo himself, almost certainly in his studio in the Corte Vecchia (Old Court). In the ballroom he would have seen Leonardo's vast clay model for the *gran cavallo* (great horse), and later Leonardo must have shown Borgia some of his sketches of ambitious civil and military engineering projects—some of which had already been realized, such as the irrigation canals outside the city.

It it difficult to know who might have initiated this viewing. Had Borgia already heard of Leonardo's fame as an engineer? Or would Leonardo have shown his drawings to the powerful young soldier by way of advertising his wares—just as he had done to his former employer

Ludovico Sforza? Either way, Borgia would have been deeply interested. He would soon be needing a military engineer on his next project.

The pope's plans for his son had changed. Instead of inheriting the kingdom of Naples, the plan now was for Cesare to carve out his own kingdom, in the Romagna, with the aid of the troops that Louis XII had promised. Rather than lead these troops directly to Rome, Borgia would launch a surprise attack down the Via Emilia, the old Roman road that led straight as an arrow into the heart of the Romagna.

The Romagna, including The Marches (Le Marche), stretched from Ferrara in the north down to Urbino, and on south to Ancona on the Adriatic coast. Strictly speaking, this was all part of the papal territories, but the various small city-states that occupied this region were now more or less independent, ruled for the most part by families and petty tyrants, who paid little regard to their frequently changing papal masters. This was a region of remote valleys and woodlands, described by Machiavelli as:

> a breeding ground for all the worst crimes, with the slightest incident liable to give rise to outbreaks of widespread murder and rape. This arose because of the wickedness of the ruling lords, and not, as was commonly held, on account of the brutal nature of their subjects. For because these lords were poor, but chose to live as if they were rich, they had to resort to innumerable cruelties, which were inflicted in all manner of ways. . . . These people were impoverished, but were subjected to no consistent application of law, so they would seek to redress their injuries on others even worse off than themselves.

It was the Romagna that produced the men for the mercenary armies of the *condottiere*, who were hired by cities such as Florence to fight their wars for them. And amongst their rulers were such characters as Caterina Sforza, Countess of Imola and Forli, who had contemptuously raised her skirts to her husband's murderers, and who proved such a tricky negotiator for Machiavelli on his early diplomatic mission.

On November 9, 1499, Borgia rode out of Milan with a French

force consisting of 1,800 cavalry, 4,000 mainly Gascon and Swiss infantry, and a sizable force of mobile artillery, which included several of the new large horse-drawn siege cannons that had inspired terror throughout Italy. His initial objective was the taking of Imola and Forli. This was Borgia's first military campaign, but he had at his side several experienced commanders, including the mercenary Vitellozzo Vitelli, who was particularly keen to avenge the death of his brother Paolo at the hands of Florence. And, in his eyes, Caterina Sforza was an ally of Florence. Imola soon fell, and Forli had surrendered by mid-December. Borgia rode into Forli in the midst of a violent rainstorm, to find that Caterina Sforza, together with her many supporters, had taken refuge in the notorious *rocca*, a fortress that was reputed to be impregnable. In an attempt to resolve the situation, Borgia rode out before the fortress, clad in full armor, and his attendant heralds blew a fanfare summoning Caterina to a parley. The countess duly appeared on the battlements, a tall, striking red-headed figure now thirty-six years old. When Borgia promised her, in the name of the pope, safe passage and compensation for her lost lands, she called defiantly down to him that she did not trust the pope any more than she believed his son. In fact, Caterina was being far more devious than she appeared. She knew that French notions of chivalry did not countenance involving women in war, and hoped this might for a while deter the French troops under Borgia's command. She was playing for time: just days previously she had dispatched a courier to Rome with a message for the pope. This message, allegedly offering her surrender, was placed in a cane tube which also contained cloth that had been wrapped around the cadaver of a plague victim. However, her plot to kill the pope was betrayed, and Alexander VI soon communicated to his son what had happened.

Borgia now ordered his cannons, skillfully positioned on the heights overlooking the *rocca* by his expert artilleryman Vitellozzo, to begin a continuous barrage lasting day and night. By January 12, 1500, a large breach had been opened in the walls, enabling the German and Swiss soldiers to storm the *rocca*. Caterina and her 2,000 supporters retreated to separate refuges within the fortress, though amidst the confusion they were unable to raise all the drawbridges in time. Caterina herself made it into the narrow confines of the central keep with hundreds of defenders, where in a last-ditch attempt to thwart her attackers she ordered the magazine to be torched. But the detonations and smoke only caused mayhem amongst her men, who were already crammed together within the walls, and she was eventually forced to surrender. Despite the power of the French siege guns, this had not been the inevitable outcome, as Machiavelli would astutely note when he later wrote *The Art of War*: "This castle, which all said was impregnable, fell because of two mistakes: first, it contained too many different refuges; and second, each refuge was not in control of its own drawbridge." Borgia must by this stage have realized that if he was to retain the territory he had conquered, he would need to rectify such defects, and this could only be done by an expert military engineer of the caliber of Leonardo.

The fiery Caterina now became the prisoner of the twenty-four-year-old Cesare Borgia. This inevitably led to all manner of salacious gossip. According to the contemporary Venetian diarist Marino Sanuto, "Duke Valentino [Borgia] . . . was keeping the said lady, who is a most beautiful woman . . . day and night in his room; with whom, in the opinion of all, he is taking his pleasure." Some sources claimed that he raped her; others, noting her notorious appetite for younger men, suggested that force may not have been necessary. Either way, these two inflammatory characters were to spend quite some time in each other's close company, until suddenly Borgia's campaign was halted in its tracks. On January 26, 1500, news came through that Ludovico "Il Moro" Sforza had mustered 9,000 largely Swiss troops and was marching to retake Milan. The French military commander of the city immediately summoned all his troops, and Borgia was left with little more than a skeleton force. All he could do was post garrisons to maintain the towns he had taken, leaving in charge his trusted Spanish commander Ramiro de Lorqua.* He then returned to Rome to consult his father, bringing

---

* Ramiro de Lorqua was in fact his Spanish name. In Italy, and in histories of this period, he is often referred to as Signor Rimino, Remiro, and other variations, as well as Lorca, de Orco, d'Orco, and so on.

with him Caterina, who was bound eventually for a dungeon in Castel Sant' Angelo.*

Cesare Borgia was given a triumphal welcome back in Rome by Alexander VI. The brash, edgy young man who had left for France on his first solo mission now returned a conquering hero. Even his clothes had changed: instead of the gaudy, colorful silks and bejeweled medallions he had worn on his arrival at the French court just fifteen months previously, he was now strikingly dressed overall in black, offset by the gold collar of the Order of St. Michael, which he had been granted by Louis XII. He appeared to have gained a sinister self-possession, confidently aware of the drama of his presence. Cesare was greeted effusively by his father, who now evidently regarded him as his pride and joy.

Soon news would arrive from France that Borgia's wife, Charlotte, was pregnant. The Borgia line was guaranteed. Cesare at once sent for his wife to join him in Rome, but she replied that her physical condition prevented her from making such a long and arduous journey. In fact, Louis XII had forbidden her to travel. Charlotte's presence in France could be used to rein in any political moves that Borgia might be contemplating, without first consulting Louis XII himself. Charlotte would eventually give birth to a daughter, named Louise, who would be brought up at the French court: the future of the Borgias was being held hostage.

News now reached Rome that the army of Louis XII had defeated Ludovico "Il Moro" Sforza of Milan, who had been carried off to France in chains. Cesare was overjoyed at the victory of his friend and backer Louis XII, and soon recovered from the absence of his wife by embarking upon an affair with one of Rome's most beautiful courtesans, the Florentine-born Famietta. The top courtesans in Rome were noted for their intellect and sophistication as well as their beauty, while their liaisons with rich cardinals and scions of the leading aristocratic Roman families enabled them to amass fortunes and live in considerable luxury.

* She would later be released, under pressure from the chivalrous Louis XII, and would die six years later in Florence. All she would say of her time in the hands of the Borgias was: "If I could write of anything, I would stupefy the world."

Indeed, the home of one of Famietta's colleagues was so magnificently furnished that when she was visited by the Spanish ambassador, it was said that he would spit in the face of a servant rather than besmirch her luxurious carpets.

Despite Cesare's happiness, he remained a troubled character—especially where Lucrezia was concerned. By now her husband, Alfonso, Duke of Bisceglie, had returned to live with his wife and their newborn child. Alexander VI and Cesare appeared to welcome this development, and Alfonso was even invited to take part—as representative of his father, the King of Naples—in Cesare's triumphal entry into the city after his successful campaign in the Romagna. However, on the evening of June 15 Alfonso was attacked on the steps leading up from the piazza to St. Peter's by a group of masked men with daggers. According to Burchard: "He was gravely wounded in his head, right arm and leg, while his assailants escaped down the steps." Alfonso managed to stagger into the Vatican, and was carried up to the papal apartments, where a shocked Alexander VI ensured that his personal physician gave all possible medical assistance to his son-in-law. When Lucrezia saw her husband covered in blood, she collapsed.

Next day, word of this sensational assassination attempt spread quickly through Rome, and Alfonso's close friend Raphael Brandolinus, the Florentine-born humanist scholar, wrote in a letter: "Who hired these assassins remains unknown. However, I dare not write down the names of those who are suspected of this deed, as it is dangerous to commit such things to paper." The Pope himself was strongly suspected by many: his strategy was now linked to France, and the Borgias had no need, or wish, for any ties with Naples. But the chief suspect was certainly Cesare, whose attitude towards anyone who loved his sister remained deeply conflicted. For days, Alfonso's life hung in the balance, and he was lovingly nursed night and day by Lucrezia.

Over the coming weeks his condition slowly improved, but an atmosphere of fear attended his recovery. Alexander VI ensured that the door to Alfonso's room remained guarded at all times; meanwhile Cesare issued the apparently conflicting order that no one was to bear arms within the precincts of the Vatican. By mid-August Alfonso was able to walk unsteadily about his room and look down over the enclosed sunlit garden below the Borgia apartments. On the afternoon of August 18 he was being entertained by his favorite hunchbacked dwarf, laughing with Lucrezia, together with several Neapolitan dignitaries. Suddenly the door burst open and in rushed the Spanish commander of Borgia's personal guard, Don Michele.* He was followed by a gang of armed men. The Neapolitan dignitaries— who included Alfonso's uncle, the ambassador—were bundled from the room, together with the hunchback and the two physicians in attendance on Alfonso. Brandolinus described how Lucrezia, "stupefied by the suddenness and violence of the act, shrieked at Don Michele, demanding how he dared commit such an offense before their eyes and in the presence of Alfonso."

Don Michele appeared to heed these words, taken aback by the sheer violence of Lucrezia's remonstrations, and protested that he had no knowledge of the purpose behind what he was doing, but was merely acting as he had been told, because "he had to live by the orders of another, but that they, if they wished, might go to the Pope, and it would be easy to obtain the release of the wanted men."

Lucrezia immediately rushed down the corridor to see Alexander VI, but when she returned she learned that Don Michele had strangled Alfonso. Upon hearing this news, Lucrezia, "terrified by this most cruel deed, oppressed by fear, beside [herself] with grief, filled the palace with [her] shrieking, lamenting and wailing."

This time there was no doubt in most people's minds about who was responsible for such an outrage: all the evidence pointed at Cesare. Despite this, Alexander VI's behavior towards his daughter prompted other suspicions. Lucrezia was inconsolable, yet in the words of her biographer Maria Bellonci: "Her tears soon got on the Pope's nerves, for he was congenitally incapable of understanding why anybody who was twenty years old and had all her future before her could be

---

* Also known as Miguel da Corella, or more usually by the Italians as Michelotto. I have chosen not to use the latter because of its comparative similarity (especially to English ears) to the names of several other commanders employed by Borgia. When writing about this character, Machiavelli and Guicciardini also called him Don Michele.

so upset." With some irritation, Alexander VI allowed Lucrezia to retire to the seclusion of her estate at Nepi, twenty miles north of Rome.

The timeliness of Bisceglie's death now became apparent. Just five days after this event, news reached Rome that Louis XII was to press his claim to the throne of Naples, and in recognition of Alexander VI's support for this claim he was sending a force of 2,300 French militia to enable Cesare to launch a second campaign of conquest in the Romagna.

On October 2, 1500, Cesare Borgia—accompanied by his commanders Vitellozzo and Don Michele, as well as Paolo and Giulio Orsini—left Rome to head his army of 7,700 mixed Spanish, Italian, and Swiss troops, heading for Umbria. En route Cesare made a brief detour to Nepi, to visit the grief-stricken Lucrezia. There are no reliable details of what precisely took place at this meeting between brother and sister, but its miraculous results were plain for all to see. Cesare and Lucrezia were reconciled, and within a few months Lucrezia had happily returned to Rome to be with her father (who already had plans for yet another strategic marriage for her).

After joining up with the 2,300 French troops sent by Louis XII, Cesare set out across the Apennines into the Romagna, heading for the Adriatic coast. Upon hearing this news, Giovanni Sforza, Lucrezia's divorced first husband, who was back in residence at his ducal palace in the seaside town of Pesaro, quickly understood the immediate object of Cesare's campaign and fled. Cesare marched into Pesaro unopposed and now took up residence in the ducal palace where Lucrezia had lived during the two years she had been Countess of Pesaro. Here he received emissaries from various interested parties in the region, who were understandably anxious to learn his future plans. Amongst these was Pandolfo Collenuccio, the emissary from Ferrara, whose territory lay along the northern border of the Romagna, some two days' march up the coast. The fifty-six-year-old Collenuccio, a poet and historian of some distinction, quickly discovered Cesare's qualities, understanding him to be "a brave and powerful character, capable of largesse of spirit, who prefers to deal with plainspeaking men. . . . He is filled with aspiration and has a longing for greatness and renown." But he then noted Cesare's darker side, reporting news of the ulcer that Cesare was suffering from in his groin (a recurrent symptom of his syphilis), and how he was known to be "hard in revenge." He also described how Cesare was in the habit of conducting his business by night, receiving emissaries as he sat in the dark, with candlelight behind him illuminating their faces and his own face in shadow.

Cesare's campaign now advanced sixty miles northwest to besiege the small town of Faenza, and after this fell he continued up the Via Emilia towards Bologna. Cesare knew that he could not take Bologna, as it was under the protection of Louis XII, but by menacing the city with his troops he managed to cow its ruler Giovanni Bentivoglio into agreeing to hand over Castel Bolognese, the city's outpost that stood amongst Borgia's towns along the Via Emilia. This agreement was negotiated by his commander Paolo Orsini, and was sealed by a marriage between Bentivoglio's son Ermes and a daughter of Giulio Orsini's. The Romagna's northwestern border was thus protected by Bologna.

A month later, in May 1501, Alexander VI bestowed on Cesare the title Duke of the Romagna "in his own name." This last phrase signified the pope's intentions loud and clear. The papal territories that Cesare had subdued were now his own dukedom, hereditary possessions of the Borgia family, and would no longer pass to the next pope on Alexander VI's death.

When Cesare Borgia had launched his second campaign into the Romagna, Machiavelli had been in the midst of his mission to the court of Louis XII. Machiavelli had immediately recognized the danger that Borgia posed to Florence. It was in part his emphasis on this danger in his dispatches back to the city that encouraged the ruling Signoria to pay Louis XII the money he was owed for providing mercenaries in the war against Pisa, at the same time securing from Louis a letter warning Cesare not to invade Florentine territory.

Yet soon after Machiavelli returned to Florence early in 1501 the situation took a turn for the worse. The Borgia city of Forli was just four miles from the Florentine oupost of Castrocaro, and by this stage Borgia's possessions in the Romagna lined the length of Florence's eastern border. Worse still, the Signoria learned that Borgia had signed an agreement with Florence's enemy Siena, which lay on its border to the south. It was now that Borgia sent his menacing messages to the Signoria; these were backed by menacing action, when he dispatched his commander Liverotto da Fermo with 200 cavalry to bolster Pisa in its continuing struggle to remain free from Florence. There followed a demand that the Signoria take Borgia on as Florence's *condottiere*. As such, he would then be able to move his army into Florentine territory, and thus influence the city's affairs, perhaps even enabling him to reinstate Piero de' Medici in a puppet government. The Signoria knew that Piero de' Medici had recently gone to Rome to consult the pope, and news now came through that he was waiting at Bologna, poised to return. The Signoria dithered: the exchequer was bankrupt after paying Louis XII and could not afford to pay for any protection. The city was, to all intents and purposes, defenseless.

Without waiting for any full reply to his demands, Borgia and his troops swooped southwest from Bologna into Florentine territory, only halting at Campi, just ten miles from the city walls of Florence. According to the Florentine diarist Biagio Buonaccorsi: "At this time the city found itself in the greatest disorder and with practically no men under arms. Many of the citizens were overcome with fear and fled. . . . The place was in the grip of apprehension and mayhem." These events must have been witnessed by Machiavelli and Leonardo, who were both resident in the city during this period. Leonardo may even have begun to wonder if he had made a mistake in returning home, when the city was evidently in such a vulnerable and unstable state. On May 14, Borgia sent a list of his demands to the Signoria, and a day later they capitulated, signing an agreement that promised 36,000 ducats (which they had not got). To the surprise of the Signoria, Borgia made no move, and for three fraught days the defenseless city awaited its fate. Then, without warning, Borgia and his troops suddenly decamped, marching southwest towards the coast. What the Signoria did not know was that by now Alexander VI had sent a message warning

Cesare that Louis XII had ordered d' Aubigny,* the commander of the French troops in Italy, to march south immediately and drive him from Florentine territory.

When Cesare reached the coast, he laid siege to the strategic port of Piombino, which soon fell into his hands. He then returned to Rome. His second campaign in the Romagna had been a territorial success, but it appeared to have ended in a gross tactical blunder. His swoop across Florentine territory had not resulted in the city's falling into his hands. Worse still, both Florence and Louis XII were now fully alerted to his intentions, and would be able to take measures to thwart his plans. On the other hand, with the taking of Piombino, Cesare now had Florentine territory virtually encircled. Most important of all, he had discovered for himself Florence's weakness and the abject state of its government.

But Florence's vulnerability was as nothing compared to that of Naples. The French had concluded an agreement with Spain that Naples should be partitioned between them, and d'Aubigny now led the French army south to conquer Naples. Encouraged by Alexander VI, Cesare joined the French forces, along with his commanders Vitellozzo and Baglioni, together with 400 of his troops, all clad in the smart new scarlet and yellow colors of the Duke of the Romagna.† In return for the pope's support, Louis XII had promised further troops, which Cesare would need if he was to launch a third campaign to complete his conquest of the Romagna. The progress of d'Aubigny's French army down through Italy bore ominous similarities to that of Charles VIII just seven years previously, and overcame Naples with similar ease.

---

* In fact, d'Aubigny was a Scotsman, Bernard Stewart, third Lord of Aubigny, a title highlighting the "Auld Alliance" between France and Scotland, which would last for two and a half centuries (1295–1560). As a result, the invading army of Charles VIII, as well as the various invading armies of Louis XII, all contained regiments of kilted warriors. Similarly, Johannes Burchard recorded that there was a sizable contingent of *Scottese* amongst the troops that took part in Borgia's triumphal entry into Rome at the end of his first Romagna campaign.

† It was no coincidence that these were also the traditional Spanish colors.

Having fulfilled his obligations, Cesare returned to Rome in mid-September to find the city celebrating the betrothal of Lucrezia to Alfonso d'Este, the son of the Duke of Ferrara. With this, Alexander VI had secured the alliance of Ferrara, the territory that lay directly to the north of the Romagna, thus securing a buffer between Cesare's new dukedom and powerful Venice.

The betrothal was being celebrated in the absence of the prospective bridegroom, who remained in Ferrara, but this did little to dampen the enthusiasm of the seventy-year-old Alexander VI and his twenty-six-year-old son. As a Ferrara envoy noted disapprovingly of the prospective bride, "Whenever she is at the Pope's palace, the entire night, until two or three o'clock, is spent dancing and at play."

That autumn the Borgias would excel themselves, building upon the already solid foundations of their infamous legend. The Borgia household in the Vatican now included an unexplained three-year-old male child called Giovanni, widely referred to as the "Infans Romanus." Many suspected that this child was an illegitimate offspring of Lucrezia and Alexander VI's beloved Spanish manservant Perotto (whose body ended up in the Tiber, almost certainly dispatched by Cesare). The pope now issued a public bull legitimizing this child, declaring him to be the offspring of Cesare and an unmarried woman; at the same time Alexander VI issued a private bull naming himself as the father. Both of these bulls were almost certainly untruthful, although Lucrezia was probably the mother. Under the circumstances, one can hardly blame the anonymous contemporary correspondent who wrote, "Cesare murdered his brother, slept with his sister, spent the treasure of the Church, and was the terror of his father Alexander." Rumors of incest between Alexander VI, Cesare, and Lucrezia seem only too understandable. Although it is difficult to ascertain the truth, further notorious events during the coming autumn would seem to suggest at the very least an element of unconscious incestuous feelings between father, son, and daughter.

October 1501 would see a scandalous event worthy of the ancient Roman emperors, which was described by the pope's master of ceremonies:

On Sunday evening, October 30, Don Cesare Borgia gave a supper in his apartment in the apostolic palace, with fifty decent prostitutes or courtesans in attendance, who after the meal danced with the servants and others, first fully dressed and then naked. . . . Chestnuts were strewn about, which the prostitutes, naked and on their hands and knees, had to pick up [with their vaginas]. . . . The Pope, Don Cesare and Donna Lucrezia were all present to watch. Finally prizes were offered to those men who fucked these prostitutes the greatest number of times.

The Borgias enjoyed sex as a spectator sport, which seemed to act as a form of bonding. Burchard recorded another incident that took place on November 11: Alexander VI and Lucrezia were looking out of a window and noticed two mares with winter wood strapped to their backs being led by a peasant through the gate beside the Vatican. When the mares reached St. Peter's Square, the Vatican guards were ordered to cut their straps, throw off the wood and

lead the mares into the courtyard immediately inside the palace gate. Four stallions were then freed from . . . the palace stables. They immediately ran to the mares, over whom they proceeded to fight furiously and noisily amongst themselves, biting and kicking in their efforts to mount them and seriously wounding them with their hoofs. The Pope and Donna Lucrezia, laughing with evident satisfaction, watched all that was happening from a window above the palace gate.

Such family entertainment for father and daughter appears as harmless fun compared to the way Cesare chose to entertain his sister, when he used an enclosed courtyard of condemned men as target practice with his crossbow. On the occasion when a Roman satirist alluded to Cesare's depraved behavior, he had his tongue cut out and nailed to his severed hand.

The following month the bells of Rome chimed for Lucrezia's wedding. In the manner of the time, this too was celebrated by proxy, with the bridegroom remaining at home in Ferrara. At the wedding ball (held in the same hall where Lucrezia had celebrated her marriage to Bisceglie three years previously) the pope gazed down benevolently from his throne, flanked on one side by his cardinals and on the other by his children. According to an eyewitness: "Alexander asked Cesare to lead the dance with Donna Lucrezia, which he did very gracefully. His Holiness was in continual laughter."

On January 6, 1502, Lucrezia bade farewell to a distraught Alexander VI (who had a premonition that this was the last time he would see his beloved daughter).* Later, amidst falling snow, she set out from Rome for her new home in Ferrara, with Cesare riding at her side. They were accompanied by a train of more than 600 horses and pack mules, carrying Lucrezia's dowry of 100,000 ducats,† guarded by 500 armed men of the papal guard. A few miles down the road Cesare too took his leave of Lucrezia, entrusting her to the protection of his loyal commander Ramiro de Lorqua.

As Lucrezia's procession made its way through the Romagna, Cesare had arranged for her to be cheered through the cities of his new domain. Not to be outdone, Guidobaldo, the thirty-year-old Duke of Urbino, laid on a grand ball for Lucrezia amidst the splendors of his ducal palace. Unlike the rougher northern cities of the Romagna that belonged to Cesare, Urbino was both independent and highly civilized. Guidobaldo's father, Federigo da Montefeltro, had made such a fortune as a *condottiere*—employed on occasion by Milan, Florence, the pope, and others—that on his retirement he had transformed Urbino into one of the wonders of the Renaissance. Here Raphael had first learned how to paint, and the ducal palace contained the finest works of art, together with a library that rivaled the one created by the Medici in Florence.

Back in Rome, Cesare consulted his father as he planned his strategy for his third campaign into the Romagna. His intention was to complete his conquest of the entire region for his new dukedom, as well as to make sure that this time he managed to cow Florence into complying

---

* This premonition would prove correct.
† A laborer's annual wage at this period was fifteen ducats.

with his wishes. As soon as he was master of the situation, he would demand that Florence send him a delegation authorized to negotiate on behalf of the Signoria. This would be the delegation for which Machiavelli would be chosen—the first occasion on which Borgia the warrior would attempt to browbeat Machiavelli the philosopher, the outcome of which would involve the hiring of Leonardo the artist.

Part 2

In the Romagna

5

Treachery and Bluff

B Y EARLY JUNE 1502 Cesare Borgia was in Rome putting the final touches to his invasion plans with his commanders already assembled in the field: Lorqua at Cesena, Vitellozzo and Baglioni close to the southwestern Romagna near the Tuscan border.

Just as Machiavelli had foreseen, there had been increasing tension between the French and the Spanish regarding their joint takeover of Naples. Louis XII now had great need of Borgia support—in the form of the pope's diplomatic strength, and the potential backing of Borgia and his commanders. Borgia was determined to take advantage of this, especially with regard to Florence, where the cost of the seemingly endless war against Pisa, and the increasingly heavy tax burden imposed by the Signoria on the cities of the republic, had already provoked widespread unrest. Then on June 4 the Florentine city of Arezzo in southern Tuscany rose in revolt, its citizens surging through the streets calling openly for the restoration of the Medici. In preparation for Borgia's campaign, his commander Vitellozzo just happened to have a force of 3,500 men across the border. Seizing the opportunity, Vitellozzo moved towards Arezzo, where the citizens threw open the gates and welcomed him into the city. It is not certain how much all this was stage-managed by Vitellozzo, with Borgia's foreknowledge. Yet the sheer speed of events, as well as Vitellozzo's hastily executed opportunism, certainly took Borgia by surprise. If he had been in full control, this move would presumably have taken place when it would have produced the maximum effect—that is, when Borgia had left Rome and was already launching his invasion of the southern Romagna. As it was, it took place before Borgia had even left Rome. Then news reached him that Piero de' Medici was in Arezzo, accompanied by Borgia's commander Baglioni, while Vitellozzo was moving west into the Val di Chiana, encountering virtually no resistance from the towns in his path. Events were moving fast, but under whose control? Vitellozzo was intent upon wreaking revenge on the Florentines for the "murder" (as he saw it) of his brother Paolo three years previously, after his treachery at the siege of Pisa. Indeed, when Borgia disclaimed all involvement in Vitellozzo's "invasion," he insisted that this alone was surely what had prompted his commander's action.

On June 10 Borgia belatedly left Rome with his other commanders: Liverotto da Fermo, Paolo and Giulio Orsini, and 7,000 men. They struck north up the Via Flaminia, the ancient Roman road that led towards the Romagna, with the apparent aim of taking Camerino and then moving on to the coast to take Sinigallia.* As a courtesy, Borgia sent ahead to Guidobaldo, Duke of Urbino, for permission to cross his territory, while at the same time Vitellozzo asked Guidobaldo to send 1,000 of his soldiers to assist him in the taking of the Val di Chiana. Originally apprehensive of Borgia's troop movements so close to his territory, on learning that Borgia and his forces had struck east off the Via Flaminia in the direction of Camerino, Guidobaldo sent his greetings to Cesare, and on June 20 he left Urbino for a summer-evening dinner party with his friends in the nearby countryside. The gentle strains of lute music beneath the stars were suddenly interrupted by the arrival of a series of breathless messengers. Cesare's attack on Camerino had been a blind. His troops had suddenly sprung up as if from nowhere, and were at this very moment advancing southwards from San Marino, east from the coast, and northwards from the Via Flaminia, all converging on the city of Urbino, which it was expected they would reach by morning.

Guidobaldo fled, riding for the safety of the mountains as fast as his

---

* Now spelled "Senigallia." In Borgia's time it usually appeared in documents as "Sinigallia," but also as "Sinigaglia" and other variations.

horse could carry him. His next few days would be spent desperately eluding the Borgia patrols that had been sent looking for him: negotiating a zigzag course along the frontier paths of the high Apennines, relying on isolated peasant dwellings for hospitality, finally venturing down into the Po valley. Eight days later, having covered nearly 200 miles, he reached the safety of the city of Mantua, which was ruled by his wife's family, arriving in a distressed state, "having escaped with only my life, and the doublet and shirt I stood up in."

As expected, the outriders of Borgia's forces were within sight of Urbino early on June 21, and reported no resistance. Later that day, after having covered forty miles in just over twenty-four hours, Borgia rode into Urbino unopposed, accompanied only by his personal guard. The taking of Urbino, and the treacherous manner in which he had done it, was to cause widespread outrage. The Montefeltro family of Urbino were held in high regard throughout Italy. Guidobaldo's *condottiere* father had run successful campaigns for all the major powers, and his transformation of remote Urbino into a Renaissance city was widely admired. The Montefeltro family was connected both culturally and by marriage to leading figures throughout the land. Guidobaldo's father had been created a duke by Pope Sixtus IV; Guidobaldo's wife was a Gonzaga; he himself was close to the powerful Cardinal Giuliano della Rovere, and was a friend of Leonardo da Vinci's mathematical colleague Luca Pacioli.

Dismissively, Borgia excused his treacherous actions by insisting that Guidobaldo himself was the treacherous one. Borgia claimed he had intercepted evidence that Guidobaldo had sent assistance to defend Camerino against Borgia's threatened attack, and this may well have been true. Either way, it made no difference. The thirty-year-old Guidobaldo was weak, both physically and psychologically: such an inexperienced politician would have found it difficult to stand up to Cesare Borgia, whatever the circumstances.

The fact is, Borgia was bound to take Urbino if he intended to establish the Romagna as a viable and defensible territory. Geographically, Urbino held the key to the region. At a stroke it could cut off the northern Romagna from the southern Marches, as well as severing the Romagna's links to Rome down the Via Flaminia. It also controlled the passes across the Apennines, linking the Adriatic to Tuscany. Florence's links to the west coast had already been cut by the loss of Pisa and the taking of Piombino. Its routes across the Apennines to the Adriatic were now similarly cut, a severe loss for a city whose wealth was so largely dependent upon trade.

No sooner had Borgia taken Urbino than he set about systematically pillaging the city, sending its valuables north by mule train to Cesena, which he had designated as the capital of his new dukedom. By the end of this operation he would have removed 150,000 ducats' worth* of artworks, as well as most of the famous library and quantities of salable jewels and treasure. Part of this would be used to pay for his campaign, but part was also intended to finance the establishment of his administration. Ironically, Borgia's pillaging of Urbino indicated that he intended his Romagna dukedom to be much more than simply a territorial conquest. He wished to establish his rule on a permanent basis: this was to be a civilized Italian power.

After Borgia's first campaign in the Romagna, he had left his trusted commander Lorqua in charge of his conquered territory, and since then, an administration of sorts had begun to be established. Borgia's rule had for the most part replaced petty tyrannies that were loathed by the populace, and his takeover had been widely welcomed. Yet as Machiavelli has made clear, this was a lawless region, "a breeding ground for all the worst crimes," and Lorqua's rule had required harsh measures to impose its authority. If Borgia was to establish even a modicum of peaceful civilian life in his new dukedom, this would require money, and what was Urbino's loss was intended to be the Romagna's gain.

As we have seen, prior to Borgia's lightning move on Urbino he had sent word to the Signoria in Florence that he wanted a meeting: they must dispatch at once someone who was authorized to discuss a "matter of great importance." As a result, Bishop Soderini and Machiavelli had found themselves hastily riding over the mountains (along much the

---

* In other words, almost a thousand times more than the annual wage of a senior civil servant such as Machiavelli.

same tracks that the fleeing Guidobaldo had taken), arriving at Urbino on the evening of June 24. Thereupon they were hastily ushered into the ducal palace, where Borgia was waiting for them. This time he had Florence at his mercy and, in Machiavelli's words, the city "was quaking heart and soul in suspense at the prospect of him joining forces with Vitellozzo, and together with him inflicting great woe upon its citizens." Borgia launched into an angry tirade against the hapless Florentine delegation. Soderini held his nerve, but was definitely perturbed. Machiavelli may well have been perturbed too, but over and above this he was also impressed, and would convey this in his dispatch back to Florence:

> This lord is truly splendid and magnificent, and in war there is no enterprise so great that it does not seem small to him; in the pursuit of glory and territory he is unceasing and knows neither danger nor fatigue. He arrives at a place before anyone is aware that he has left the place he was at before. He is beloved by his soldiers and he has in his service the best men in Italy. All this makes him victorious and formidable, particularly in the light of his constant good fortune.

The news that Borgia had suddenly taken Urbino, the arrival at night fatigued after the long, hard ride over the mountains, no sooner out of the saddle than hustled into the palace, the armed guards and the locking of the doors behind them, and then Borgia's dramatic candlelit appearance at the head of the darkened hall—all this must have played its part in lowering Machiavelli's defenses. Machiavelli was thirty-three years old, and had already met several important figures, yet this powerful first impression would remain with him for the rest of his life, affecting all his subsequent thinking about Borgia.

Later during this encounter in Urbino, Machiavelli's diplomatic skills would lead him to suspect there was an element of bluff in Borgia's bombast. But this could no longer disturb the ideal image of a forceful, unscrupulous conqueror, which had so impressed itself upon his mind.

Yet unknown to Soderini and Machiavelli, during the previous days

Borgia's situation had undergone a drastic transformation. Louis XII, who was about to establish his court at Asti in northern Italy, had not been so completely distracted by his quarrel with Spain as he appeared. He had watched Cesare's third campaign in the Romagna and was well aware of what he was up to. But this was not all. As a result of Borgia's treacherous seizure of Urbino, his enemies in the region had taken flight and were now on their way to put their case to Louis XII, who was said to be particularly annoyed at Borgia's blatant move into Arezzo in Florentine territory. However, this move by Vitellozzo was not entirely Borgia's doing, and Borgia was now fully aware that his commander was at best only partially under his control. As if this were not bad enough, Borgia had then got wind of a plot against him, which was being hatched amongst his commanders Vitellozzo, Baglioni, and Liverotto da Fermo. Many of their castles and domains lay along the western and southern borders of Borgia's Romagna dukedom, and they had now come to realize their vulnerability in the light of Borgia's continuing expansionist intentions. Only by turning against him were they likely to survive. Even Paolo and Giulio Orsini, who were with Borgia at Urbino, were rumored to have been approached to join the plot. At the moment, they were assisting Borgia in his intimidation of the Florentine delegation, by "confidentially" informing Soderini and Machiavelli that Vitellozzo's capture of Arezzo had the covert backing of Louis XII, which meant that Borgia could now easily make a move on Florence itself, if he so chose. Yet for how much longer would the Orsini keep up the pretense of supporting Borgia? They were the last of the powerful aristocratic Roman families to hold on to their lands and castles. Alexander VI had picked off the other leading families one by one, as the occasion arose, ending up by seizing the castles and lands of the Colonna family only a few months previously, when they had made the mistake of siding with Naples against the French and the Spanish. The Orsini had evidently begun to wonder how soon it would be before they too were picked off and their lands became part of the increasing Borgia domain.

Borgia realized that his only hope with regard to the Florentine delegation lay in attempting a colossal bluff. Indeed, this was to be one far greater than that suspected by Machiavelli—who had merely deduced that Vitellozzo was probably beyond Borgia's control, and suspected that Louis XII's support for Borgia was not quite as strong and unquestioning as Borgia liked to pretend. In pursuance of his bluff, Borgia knew that he would have to terrify the Florentine delegation into submitting to his wishes, and the only way he could do this was by issuing them an ultimatum. If they did not give in to his demands and ally themselves with him forthwith, he would take the city by force and impose his will that way. Having issued his ultimatum, Borgia gave them four days to come up with an answer.

It was a considerable gamble. Borgia knew that this was the minimum time he could give the Signoria in Florence to receive his message and send him back a binding and authoritative reply. Meanwhile he just hoped that it would be at least four days before any of Louis XII's troops arrived to defend Florence. If Florence could be browbeaten into an alliance with him before the French troops arrived, any move by Louis XII would be defused: they would all be allies together. At the same time Borgia would have outwitted his treacherous commanders. With both Florence and France as his allies, Vitellozzo and his cronies would not dare move against him. Vitellozzo could even be forced to hand back Arezzo and any other conquests he had made in Florentine territory, so that Borgia might well be seen as the city's savior.

Machiavelli had been impressed, and even fearful, when Borgia had angrily issued his ultimatum. So far at least, Borgia's bluff had succeeded. It was in a state of some apprehension that Machiavelli had set off without delay to receive the Signoria's answer to Borgia's ultimatum. And by way of a gesture to placate Borgia's wrath, it seems that the Florentine delegation had offered him the services of Leonardo da Vinci, as an expert military engineer.

For Soderini and Machiavelli to have made this offer, they must have come to some arrangement with Leonardo beforehand. He was to be a bargaining counter to save the city. It is unclear whether Leonardo would have been talked into this or simply ordered by the Signoria to comply. There is also the possibility that he volunteered—he was finding it difficult to gain employment on his return to Florence, and as we have seen from the letters by the well-connected priest Fra Pietro

Novellara to Isabella d'Este, his behavior was showing uncharacteristic signs of bohemian instability. Did the Signoria know about Leonardo's "obligations to his majesty the King of France," which were also mentioned by Novellara? Were these obligations in some way linked to Borgia's previous offer of employment when he had arrived with Louis XII in Milan? Borgia had certainly always had plans for the Romagna, and now that it had become his new dukedom these plans had become more developed—to the point where they required the services of an expert engineer. Borgia wished to strengthen the fortifications of many of the castles that he had taken, and had plans for certain engineering projects similar to those that Leonardo had undertaken on the canals around Milan. For instance, it is known that Borgia wished to excavate a navigable canal linking the strategically located city of Cesena, which was now the capital of his new dukedom, to Porto Cesenatico some ten miles to the east on the Adriatic coast. This was intended both to be a trade link and to enable the Romagna to receive military reinforcement by sea. Borgia had long-term plans for a hereditary family dukedom, and Leonardo was just the man he needed to lay the foundations of such a project.

When Machiavelli set out on June 29 and rode hell-for-leather back to Florence, he also carried a note from Borgia to Leonardo, giving him his first instructions in his new role. This note has never been found, but as we shall see, the evidence for its existence is overwhelming. Leonardo, it seems, had no choice in the matter.

6

Obeying Orders

L EONARDO DA VINCI was fifty years old when he left Florence in
early July 1502 to begin working for Cesare Borgia. At the time
of Leonardo's departure, Borgia was in Urbino, but instead of
taking the direct route to report for duty, Leonardo set off in a westerly
direction towards the Borgia-held city of Piombino, indicating that he
had already received his orders from Borgia. Evidently he was to make
a tour of inspection of the fortifications held by Borgia, detailing their
state of repair and suggesting possible improvements, making his way
around the southern border of Tuscany towards the Romagna, where
he would then report to his new employer at Urbino.

In a fresh notebook, Leonardo lists the things he must pack to take
with him: "boots," "boxes in the custom house," et cetera. These include
an apparent reference to glasses ("a support for spectacles"), which
suggests that his eyesight was beginning to feel the effects of late middle
age. However, he had not yet become the bearded sage of his later years,
and his face probably still resembled that of the clean-shaven middle-
aged self-portrait that appeared in the Vitruvian man, with its curly
center-parted shoulder-length hair.

His journey can be traced from the jottings made in his notebook,
which only covered his leisure time, for these pages contain nothing
more than the occasional characteristically oblique reference to what he
was actually doing: making annotated sketches of fortifications, as well
as possible military and civil projects, for Borgia. At the outset, Leonardo
journeyed southwest across Tuscany towards the coast, his mind

ever-alive to the possibilities and details of what he saw. He notes, "Method for draining the marsh of Piombino"; he jots down a schematic sketch of how the waves break on the shore; elsewhere he observes stormy weather, "The waves of the sea at Piombino; all foaming water . . . how it leaps up into the air." He next traveled inland, remarking on "the bell of Siena, that is, the way it moves and the place where its clapper is attached," accompanied by a sketch of the bell's shape. Then he reached Arezzo, where he met Vitellozzo and drew a map of the region. This map was probably intended for the commander, as the names on it are not in Leonardo's customary mirror-writing, and it evidently was not included amongst the reports he was making for Borgia. Possibly in return for this favor, Vitellozzo appears to have promised Leonardo that he would send him a manuscript of Archimedes that Leonardo knew to be at San Sepolcro, less than twenty miles east in the mountains, which was soon to be taken by Vitellozzo's troops. Leonardo would have been informed of the existence of this valuable manuscript by his mathematical companion Luca Pacioli, a native of San Sepolcro, from whom Leonardo had parted when he left Florence.

But there is evidence that Leonardo's visit to Arezzo, and his encounter with Vitellozzo, was not quite as trouble-free as is suggested by these few facts. Leonardo would have been aware that by the very nature of his employment he was acting as an informal spy, gathering information that might well prove useful to Florence, if he returned to the city or an opportunity arose for him to pass it on. Borgia would certainly have been aware of this too, but would not have been particularly concerned. Nor indeed would Vitellozzo.

Yet Vitellozzo may well have been concerned on another count. Borgia had sent Leonardo on a tour of the fortifications supposedly under his command, in the expectation that Leonardo would report to him details of all that he had seen. Vitellozzo would not have welcomed Leonardo in this capacity: he would have wanted neither the state of his defenses nor the disposition of his troops passed on to Borgia. Consequently, Leonardo could well have been in considerable danger while acting in pursuance of his mission, and at the same time inadvertently acting as a spy for Borgia. Vitellozzo was probably as obstructive as he could be to Leonardo, without actually threatening him, or his life. To do so would only have alerted Borgia to his treachery (which he was not yet aware Borgia had uncovered). His promise to Leonardo that he would obtain for him the Archimedes manuscript may well have been intended as a show of goodwill, an indication that his apparent obstructiveness was in fact due to the dangers of the campaign rather than any aggression on his behalf. Had Vitellozzo suspected that Borgia knew about his treachery, Leonardo would at best have been taken hostage.

Leonardo may have been scrutinizing all he saw, with his usual profound eye, but his understanding of what was actually taking place, with regard to his own situation, was dangerously blinkered. At any rate, after leaving Vitellozzo he passed on into the high Apennines, where he noted the lie of the mountains for use in later maps. He also made studies of the mountain valleys and the Romanesque five-arched bridge over the upper Arno at Buriano. Years later, this landscape and the bridge would appear as the mysterious background to the *Mona Lisa*.

Three sketches by Leonardo da Vinci, thought to be of Cesare Borgia.

Sometime late in July, Leonardo eventually reached Urbino. By now Borgia's campaign had achieved yet another characteristic triumph. After several weeks of siege by the Orsini brothers, the seventy-year-old ruler of Camerino, Giulio Varano, had finally negotiated a surrender, giving Borgia's troops possession of the town, at the same time allowing himself and his two sons safe passage to neutral territory. But no sooner had the city been occupied than Varano and his sons were seized: the old man was dispatched to a dungeon in a nearby castle, where he would soon die, and his two sons were murdered on the spot. All this had been carried out by the Orsini brothers, but they had been acting on Borgia's strict orders. Such was the employer whom Leonardo would now join.

As ever, there is no direct mention of this significant encounter in Leonardo's notebooks. At one point he makes a cryptic reference to Borgia's looting of Urbino: "Many treasures and great wealth will be entrusted to quadrupeds who will carry them to various places." He also mentions: "Stairs of the [palace of the] Count of Urbino," beside which is a rough sketch—possibly the very stairs up which Machiavelli and Bishop Soderini were hustled in the dark on the way to their first dramatic meeting with Borgia. The nearest Leonardo comes to any explicit comment on his meeting (or meetings) with Borgia is a page containing three red-chalk sketches, which are widely thought to be of Borgia. If such is the case, this is no longer the brilliant young student who was "the handsomest man in Italy." Instead we see a full-bearded, heavy-lidded man who is past the first flush of youth and now thickening into middle age. His features have a certain coarseness, he is tired and clearly preoccupied: a worried man. Yet it is still possible to read into his features a latent power and intelligence. Campaigning and debauchery have taken their toll, as indeed syphilis may have been doing as well.

Leonardo's sketches are very much a first, intent psychological probing of this larger-than-life figure—part hero, part degenerate, a brave but treacherous monster, with winning ways and great charm, yet capable of extreme viciousness. Although Leonardo cannot have known (just as Machiavelli had not known a month previously), Borgia was now at one of the most crucial junctures of his life. Unwittingly, Leonardo may even have sketched him at the very time when he was pondering the fateful decision he was about to make.

These detailed sketches would seem to have been in preparation for a full-scale portrait of the new Duke of the Romagna. But this was not to be. Just days after Leonardo's arrival in Urbino, Borgia vanished. "Where is Valentino?" Leonardo's notebook observations break off to ask, with uncharacteristic directness.* He must have been as shocked as all the others at Urbino by Borgia's sudden disappearance.

* This is in fact the sole time that Leonardo mentions Borgia in his notebooks.

7

"Either Caesar or nothing"

BORGIA HAD DECIDED upon a desperate gamble: he would ride north to confront Louis XII at his court, and persuade him not to listen to all his enemies who had gathered there. He would win his friend the French king to his cause. During the last week in July 1502, Borgia slipped away from Urbino, disguised as a Knight of St. John, with a guard consisting of just three of his most trusted lieutenants. Within twenty-four hours, stopping only to change horses, they had covered more than eighty miles and reached Forli, where Borgia secretly sent ahead to Louis XII, informing the French king that he wished to meet him.

This was not going to be an easy meeting. Louis XII had already received so many of Borgia's enemies. Guidobaldo, Duke of Urbino, and a surviving heir to the deposed Lord of Camerino had both requested French help in getting themselves reinstated in what they saw as their rightful domains. Giovanni Sforza, Lucrezia's disgraced former husband and deposed Lord of Pesaro, had also received a sympathetic hearing. Louis XII was said to have told these petitioners that he would in principle be willing to hire them French troops, which they could use to reconquer their domains, but only if they had sufficient funds to pay for them.

And this was not all. On July 8, the very day after Louis XII had arrived at Asti, he had ordered a French contingent to march south to protect Florence from any Borgia invasion. At the same time he had ordered Borgia to withdraw Vitellozzo's troops from Arezzo, and pull back Baglioni's forces from the Val di Chiana. Having no alternative, Borgia sent word to Vitellozzo and Baglioni, ordering them to withdraw. But would they even listen to his commands?

Even so, for a moment it looked as if Borgia might have succeeded in his bluffing game with Florence. Unaware of French troop movements, the Signoria in Florence had dithered beyond Borgia's four-day deadline. Finally, on July 10 they had sent word that they were willing to accept most of Borgia's demands, but suggested that negotiations should be held under the joint auspices of the French king and the pope—in the forlorn hope that this might just prevent Borgia from invading at once.

When Borgia received this reply in Urbino, he was furious. This time his bluff had been called, if inadvertently: he knew that by now French troops would be in Florence. Such was his fury that the remaining Florentine delegate in Urbino, Bishop Soderini, eventually became so terrified that on July 20 he simply fled for his life. Then word had reached Borgia that French troops had arrived before Arezzo, intent on driving Vitellozzo and Baglioni from Florentine territory by force, if necessary. Borgia once again ordered Vitellozzo and Baglioni to withdraw, threatening that if they did not he would send his own troops to occupy Città di Castello, the town of which Vitellozzo himself was lord. This was a reckless last resort to make them conform to the wishes of Louis XII. Vitellozzo was almost certainly the leader of the conspiracy against Borgia, and such a threat to Città di Castello would only confirm amongst the conspirators that he intended to absorb into his new dukedom the cities they ruled. Now there could be no hope of any reconciliation with Vitellozzo, and at a stroke Borgia finally lost any shred of loyalty that remained amongst the other leading commanders in the conspiracy. But it was paramount that he be seen to be conforming with the wishes of Louis XII. All Borgia's hopes rested on this.

Such was the man whom Leonardo had sketched at Urbino: tense and preoccupied, racking his brains and desperate—a lion at bay. Yet despite the urgency of the situation, Borgia now chose to divert from his mission to Louis XII, taking a detour of 100 miles north to call on his beloved sister Lucrezia at Ferrara. Soon after her marriage she had become pregnant by her new husband, Alfonso d'Este, the son of the Duke of Ferrara; but in July Cesare had learned that his sister's pregnancy was undergoing difficulties. He had immediately sent her a long affectionate and supportive letter, signing this "from your brother who loves you as himself." Despite all his pressing difficulties he had then set about dispatching his own personal physician, the Spanish bishop and medical expert Gaspare Torella, to Ferrara to attend Lucrezia.*

Borgia himself arrived at Ferrara on July 28. According to Maria Bellonci, Cesare and Lucrezia "spent the whole night conversing in the incomprehensible dialect of Valencia." During the course of this long conversation, Cesare is said to have promised Lucrezia that he would make the mysterious "Infans Romanus," whose upbringing had been "entrusted" to her, his successor to the dukedom of the Romagna. This was family business of the utmost secrecy—yet even now that we know so many of these secrets, the identity of the "Infans Romanus" (his actual parentage) remains as obscure as ever. Cesare then left at dawn, whereupon the heavily pregnant Lucrezia was so overcome after this intense and exhausting encounter that she suffered a serious relapse, from which she would take some time to recover.

Borgia now continued on his way to see Louis XII, whose court had by this stage moved to Milan. Here the French king had been joined by further sworn enemies of the Borgias, such as Alexander VI's old rival Cardinal Giuliano della Rovere; Francesco Gonzaga, Marquis of Mantua; and the son of Bentivoglio of Bologna. Even more ominous was the presence of Cardinal Giambattista Orsini, who was said to have recently fled from Rome to warn Louis XII against the pope and his son. The only good news for Cesare was that Vitellozzo and Baglioni had finally succumbed to his threats and withdrawn from Arezzo and the Val di Chiana.

---

* Torella was an unusual choice for Borgia as his personal physician. Although he was one of the most skilled doctors in the papal service in Rome, he did not believe in the treatment of syphilis. As this was a sexually transmitted disease, it did not deserve to be cured, on theological grounds: "Ought one to work against the will of God, who has punished them by the very means in which they have sinned?"

Louis XII was waiting for Borgia, and knew precisely when he would arrive in Milan. However, he chose to keep this secret until August 5, the very day of Borgia's arrival; only then was he heard to whisper the news into the ear of his city governor, in such a way that he knew it would be overheard. The news spread like wildfire, but even more astonishing for Borgia's enemies was the way the French king greeted his surprise guest. According to one of the Marquis of Mantua's retinue:

> His Most Christian Majesty welcomed and embraced him with great joy and led him to the Castle, where he had him lodge in the chamber nearest his own, and he himself ordered the supper, choosing diverse dishes, and that evening three or four times he went to his room dressed in shirt sleeves, when it was time to go to bed. And he ordered yesterday that he should dress in his own shirts, tunic and robes, for Duke Valentino brought no baggage wagons with him, only horses. In short—he could not have done more for a son or a brother.

Borgia's enemies had overlooked the fact that Louis XII genuinely liked Cesare. He had not forgotten the young man who had so beguiled him at his court in Chinon, to whom he had even given a royal bride from his wife's family. Through the coming days Borgia reveled in his popularity at court, and exercised all his considerable charm on Louis XII. Here was a powerful personality, a bold and witty friend for the king: a true companion. He had chosen to come to his friend, to acknowledge his allegiance and thus place his fate in the king's hands. Louis XII was touched.

Borgia's enemies began to melt away from the court—but not before Louis XII had engineered an astonishing reconciliation between Cesare and his long-term enemy Francesco Gonzaga, Marquis of Mantua. Prior to Borgia's arrival, Gonzaga had openly declared to the Venetian ambassador that if Borgia showed his face in Milan, he would challenge "that bastard son of a priest" to a duel and rid Italy of his malignant presence. Yet just days later Louis XII persuaded Gonzaga to effect a public settlement with Borgia and, as an open and lasting mark of this new friendship, Gonzaga agreed to the betrothal of his three-year-old son Federigo to Borgia's two-year-old daughter Louise.

How had Gonzaga been persuaded to undergo such an astonishing volte-face? Mantua stood on the border of Milan, and was under guarantee of protection by French troops; but Louis XII was determined to use all the forces he could muster in order to reassert the French claims against encroachment by Spain in Naples. He had no wish to intervene in any dispute between Borgia's expanding Romagna and the threatened Mantua. But with this strategic bethrothal, everyone got what they wanted: Louis XII freed himself from his obligation to Mantua; Gonzaga defused any threat from Borgia; and Borgia had yet another ally to protect his northern border—along with Ferrara, into whose ruling family Lucrezia had married; and Bologna, whose ruler, Bentivoglio, had signed a pact with Borgia after conceding to him Castel Bolognese the previous year. Yet Borgia was aware that Bologna had suddenly become a weak link in this defensive chain. Bentivoglio had married his son Ermes to an Orsini, as part of the peace pact, but now the Orsini were switching sides; Bentivoglio could no longer be trusted as an ally, yet he remained under the protection of Louis XII.

Cesare would stay on for almost a month at the court of Louis XII as it moved about northern Italy. During this time a secret agreement was drawn up between them. According to this, Borgia promised to relinquish his attempts on Florence, and in return Louis XII would relinquish his protection of Bologna. Borgia was to be left free to deal with his treacherous commanders as he saw fit, while Louis XII would provide him with sufficient troops to make up for their loss. In return, when the French king made his move against the Spanish in Naples, Borgia agreed to provide him with as many papal troops as he could muster, while Alexander VI would guarantee him free passage through the papal territories.

Borgia had achieved all that he wanted, and more. Meanwhile, Machiavelli's earlier assessment of the French situation in Italy had been vindicated. Louis XII was making the mistake of increasing the power of those he could not trust, namely Alexander VI and Cesare Borgia.

Similarly, he was now suffering from the disadvantage he had brought upon himself by inviting another foreign power—namely Spain—into Italy. Here indeed was proof of Machiavelli's assertion "that the French knew nothing of politics."

On September 2 Borgia took his leave of Louis XII at Genoa, parting with the words, "Sacred Majesty, I render infinite thanks for the great benefit I have received from you. . . . When the time comes I will present myself to you at the head of ten thousand men." Now Borgia had to work out how he would outwit his treacherous commanders, who had scattered and taken up various strategic positions at the edges of his territory. Once again, despite the urgency of the situation, he broke off his journey to call in and see Lucrezia at Ferrara, arriving there on the night of September 7.

After Cesare had left on his previous visit, Lucrezia's condition had turned from bad to worse. With the onset of September she had entered into the seventh month of her pregnancy, but had then undergone a crisis. Her physicians and attendants had despaired for her life. On September 5 she had been racked by spasms and had subsequently given birth to a stillborn child. She was too ill to receive Cesare when he arrived in the night, two days later. Next morning he found her still at death's door, and when her temperature rose alarmingly, the assembled physicians concurred that she should be bled. As one of them later reported to her father-in-law, Ercole d'Este, Duke of Ferrara:

> Today at the twentieth hour [i.e., around two in the afternoon] we bled Madonna [Lucrezia] on the right foot. It was exceedingly difficult to accomplish it, and we could not have done it but for the Duke of Romagna, who held her foot. Her Majesty spent two hours with the Duke, who made her laugh and cheered her greatly.

During the following night she had a relapse, and next morning the priest was called so that she could be given the last rites. Her attendants prepared for the worst, but the physicians now began to detect signs of recovery. Either way, Cesare seems to have decided that he could not afford to linger any further at Ferrara, and some hours later he suddenly rode off into the night. Lucrezia would eventually recover, and several years later she would intercede to save Cesare's life, but would never again set eyes on her brother.

8

"A new science"

BACK IN FLORENCE during the late summer of 1502, Machiavelli was embroiled in sorting out the difficult political situation in Arezzo and the Val di Chiana. When Louis XII's force of 4,000 hardened Swiss troops accompanied by artillery had arrived outside Arezzo, Vitellozzo and Baglioni had soon withdrawn from Florentine territory, leaving the rebellious citizens under a French occupying force.

Florence had been rescued from its perilous situation more by luck than judgment. Despite this, Machiavelli's role, along with that of Bishop Soderini, in dealing with Borgia and apparently saving the city, was deeply appreciated by the administration. From now on Machiavelli would regularly be chosen for important missions to represent the city, a task he enjoyed to such an extent that his trusted friend and assistant Agostino Vespucci would write to him, referring to "that spirit of yours, so eager for riding, wandering and roaming about."

Machiavelli was now dispatched by the Signoria to sort out the situation in Arezzo. It was not the first time that he had dealt with the aftermath of a rebellion: the situation he had faced at Pistoia the previous year had been very similar, and he would end up advising much the same measures. After assessing the circumstances at first hand, Machiavelli set off back to Florence, leaving behind as the Florentine representative Piero Soderini (brother of Bishop Francesco Soderini). Once back at the Chancery, Machiavelli wrote to Soderini asking him to do his best to persuade the French commander to remain in Arezzo, as Florentine troops could not be spared from the siege of Pisa, where the Pisans had recently launched a new offensive. Machiavelli would pay a number of visits to Arezzo during August and September, and advised the Signoria that if Florence was to retain Arezzo after the French left, the city would have to be dealt with severely. The Signoria agreed, but their measures were half-hearted. Machiavelli was instructed to write to Soderini, ordering him to round up and send back to Florence under armed guard all the local men

> whom you think either by intelligence or courage or wickedness or wealth are capable of acquiring a following; and you should err on the side of sending twenty more rather than one less, without concern for the total number or for the possibility that the city may be so emptied of its men.

A year later Machiavelli would summarize his thoughts on this matter in a short treatise entitled *How to Deal with the Rebellious Citizens of the Val di Chiana*. This is the first work in which he displays both his ambitions as a thinker and the growing originality of his thought. His intention was to compare contemporary events with similar events that had taken place many centuries earlier in ancient Rome. In doing so, he wished to derive the general principles and rules that underlay all human behavior, for "the world was always inhabited, as it is now, by men who always had the same passions." In the words of his biographer Pasquale Villari: "Urged on by genius, great powers of analysis, and a restless fancy, he attempted to create a new science."

Despite Machiavelli's undeniable originality, his thinking was very much in the Renaissance mold. The rebirth of classical knowledge had prompted many contemporary thinkers to cast aside the fatalistic, essentially spiritual outlook of the medieval era in favor of a humanistic world view. This saw human beings as having power over their own fate: no longer did the events of the world unfold according to a divine destiny whose workings humanity could never discover. Instead, events happened for a reason: they had a cause, and they had an effect. If we could discover how this causal structure operated, we had the key to political events, and even to history itself.

In Machiavelli's view, the way to discover this causal structure was by a close study of similar events taking place at different times in history. Such a task had the positive effect of allowing Machiavelli to put the considerable expertise he had gained in the course of his political and diplomatic duties on a scientific footing, by discovering general rules. But it also encouraged him to indulge in his love of maxims and principles. At best, these generalizations produced genuine insight; at other times they were to be applied beyond their proper scope; and at worst they were self-evident or simply empty of real content. Yet such distortions were perhaps inevitable at the outset of such an ambitious enterprise—the creation of an entirely new way for humanity to think about itself and assess the value of a society's actions. The "Know thyself" that had characterized the thinking of the ancient Greeks, and the philosophy of Socrates, was now to be extended beyond individual action to the realm of collective political action.

Evidence of Machiavelli's involvement in this profound endeavor can be seen quite clearly even in this early work on the treatment of the rebels of the Val di Chiana, in which he criticizes the Signoria of Florence for its ineffective action. "The Romans knew that half measures were to be avoided, and that peoples must either be conquered by kindness or reduced to impotence. . . . History is the teacher of our actions, and especially of our rulers. . . ." He pointed out that the Aretini (inhabitants of Arezzo) had always been rebellious, and would remain so—because the Signoria had failed to treat them as the Romans would have done:

> In fact, you have not benefited the Aretini, but on the contrary have harassed them by summoning them to Florence, stripping them of honors, selling their possessions; neither are you in safety from them, for you have left their walls standing, and allowed five-sixths of the inhabitants to remain in the city, without sending others to keep them in subjection. And thus Arezzo will ever be ready to break into fresh rebellion, which is a thing of no slight importance, with Cesare Borgia at hand, seeking to form a strong state by getting Tuscany itself into his power.

Tellingly, Machiavelli then goes on to point out how "the Borgia neither use half measures nor halt half way in their undertakings. . . . Among other qualities of greatness possessed by the Pope and the Pope's son, they likewise have that of knowing how to seize and profit by opportunities, which is well confirmed by our experience of what they have already done." Machiavelli's manuscript broke off at this point, but he had little need to remind anyone that Borgia had certainly learned lessons from ancient Rome: his motto "Either Caesar or nothing" was much more than bravado or a simple conceit. Like Machiavelli, the warrior had drawn his conclusions about the lessons to be learned from history.

There were in fact good reasons for the Signoria's ineffectual policy with regard to Arezzo. First, the republic was in a parlous state. The war with Pisa dragged on; yet another contingent of French troops would now have to be paid for, which meant further taxes for an already disgruntled citizenry; and despite the suppression of Arezzo, the country-side beyond the city walls of Florence remained in a state of dangerous ferment. The latter state of affairs also meant that, as with the rich farmlands of the Val di Chiana, agricultural supply lines were frequently disrupted, leaving Florence itself increasingly short of basic goods.

Yet underlying such events was an even more profound malaise. This lay in the democratic mechanics of the republic's government—most notably in the election of the chief of state, the *gonfaloniere*, and his ruling Signoria, both of which remained in office for just two months. Initially, this had been intended to prevent any individual from establishing himself in power, yet its very impracticality had soon led to covert understandings between the powerful leading families, along with creeping corruption. When the elections and the government were manipulated, as in the time of the Medici, the brief term of the *gonfaloniere*'s office was little problem: the power behind the throne dictated the republic's policy. But following the reforms instituted in the Savonarola period, the government had returned to a more ineffectual democratic mode. In the words of Roberto Ridolfi:

Their curious way of electing the Signoria by lot for very short periods regularly brought to power men without experience or ability, and removed them from office before they gained any experience of public affairs.

As a result there was no continuity of government, and no lasting responsibility for actions taken in office—the government simply muddled through, with no long-term goal. Less evident side effects meant that state secrets soon became widely disseminated, while the *gonfaloniere* and Signoria, as offices, accumulated no lasting tradition of precedent. Something had to be done, but instead of attempting overall reform, it was typically decided to shelve any such notion by simply electing a *gonfaloniere* for life—in the hope that he would then gradually introduce the necessary reforms. The new post was strictly defined: he had to be over fifty years old, and neither he nor his sons could engage in any trade, but in return he would be paid the princely annual salary of 1,200 florins (more than six times the wage of a senior civil servant such as Machiavelli). And if he exceeded his powers, the *gonfaloniere* could be deposed by a three-fourths majority vote in a committee formed of the Signoria and the leading city councils.

However, the choice of a suitable man to fulfill this role presented a considerable problem. Memories of the Medici (deposed only eight years previously) and of Savonarola (burned at the stake just four years previously) were still all too clear in the minds of the citizenry, who had no wish to see history repeat itself. The leading families favored a strong ruler drawn from amongst their ranks, while the populace favored a popular leader who would redress the injustices they suffered. Inevitably, a compromise figure was eventually chosen. On September 20, 1502, Piero Soderini was elected from amongst no fewer than 236 candidates, and thus became *gonfaloniere* for life. Soderini was a member of one of the lesser leading families, which had a tradition of public office. He had served the republic in a number of roles, including a two-month spell as *gonfaloniere*, ending up more recently as the city's representative at Arezzo. He was known to be a reliable rather than an ambitious man. On the other hand, he was undoubtedly a man of modest abilities, with little in the way of personal charisma or leadership qualities.

The man chosen to write on behalf of the Signoria to Piero Soderini in Arezzo, and inform him of his new post, was his colleague Machiavelli. The choice of Soderini was a stroke of good fortune for Machiavelli, as he was by now a good friend of the family, having worked alongside Bishop Francesco and Piero Soderini, impressing them both with his acumen and abilities. Unlike some others in the administration, the Soderini brothers also had a more human side that warmed to Machiavelli personally. Although he was now married and approaching middle age, Machiavelli retained his maverick side. He was still "Il Macchia" the disgraceful joker, who did not appeal to all tastes, and who

> with his flaunted vices and hidden virtues, with his bold and jesting manner, with an intelligence that at first encounter shocked the mediocre and made him appear to them presumptuous or eccentric, had qualities which made him unpopular with the majority and greatly loved by those few who knew him well and appreciated his courtesy, his humor and his talent.

By now the situation in the Romagna had once again taken a turn for the worse. The Signoria was well aware of Cesare Borgia's new pact with Louis XII, and the French king's warning to him not to venture into Florentine territory. But they had also heard of the treachery of Borgia's commanders, who made up a considerable force on their own account—and, worse still, their units were at large in central Italy. Now that they were no longer under Borgia's command, even theoretically, they were free to attack Florence if they so chose. And this was more than a mere possibility. Vitellozzo still wished to avenge the murder of his brother Paolo by the Signoria, and his foray with Baglioni into Arezzo and the Val di Chiana could well be repeated. At the same time, it was known that Baglioni was still in contact with Piero de' Medici, who would stop at nothing to have himself and his family reinstated.

It was at this time that Cesare Borgia wrote to Florence, requesting that the Signoria send to his court an emissary of sufficient authority to continue the negotiations, which had been broken off so inconclusively at Urbino. Borgia insisted that during this difficult period it was necessary that Florence should be kept informed of his intentions. On this point the Signoria readily agreed, and it was quickly decided that the ideal man to act as the official Florentine commissioner to the Borgia court was Machiavelli. It is likely that he was also instructed to make contact with the other Florentine who held a post at Borgia's court, namely his chief engineer, Leonardo da Vinci, in the hope that he might be able to furnish more precise details of Borgia's intentions. On October 6, 1502, Machiavelli set out from Florence for the Romagna.

9

Leonardo at Work

WHEN BORGIA SUDDENLY vanished on his hectic mission to Louis XII at Asti, Leonardo was left to his own devices. He would certainly have received further instructions from Borgia, but his notebooks reveal little indication of any urgency in this regard. On July 30, 1502, immediately after Borgia's disappearance, he observes simply, "the dovecote at Urbino." He then set off on his tour of inspection, noting the occasional local custom as he passed through the countryside: "At the foot of the Apennines, the shepherds make peculiar large cavities in the mountains in the form of a horn, in which they place a real horn. This small horn then combines with the shape of the cavity to form a huge horn which makes a very loud noise." However, this ingenious method of communication was a rarity, and when Leonardo saw how clumsily the local carts were designed, with all the weight placed on the two small wheels at the front, thus making them inefficient and difficult to pull, in his exasperation he could not help exclaiming that the Romagna was "the chief realm of all idiocy."

After two days' traveling Leonardo reached the coast, and recorded that he was "in the library at Pesaro." What he found there, what he read, was not recorded. From here he made his way up the coast, where a leisurely week later he had traveled the twenty miles to Rimini. Here he was intrigued by a musical fountain, and possibly by the idea of creating a work of similar ingenuity for Borgia—to adorn the new capital city, or maybe simply to entertain his new employer as he had amused Ludovico of Milan with his ingenious devices. With reference to such a project, Leonardo suggested to himself: "Make harmonies from the different cascades of water like you saw at the fountain in Rimini on the 8th day of August 1502."

Two days later he was at the capital of the Romagna, Cesena, where the locals were celebrating the Feast of San Lorenzo, which coincided with the local grape harvest, and he sketched the special hook that the locals used to carry the bunches of grapes. Although by now Borgia was deeply immersed in trying to charm Louis XII at his court in northern Italy, he had not completely put Leonardo from his mind. In his hasty departure from Urbino, Borgia had either forgotten or simply not had time to issue Leonardo with his personal letter of recommendation, or passport, instructing his military commanders to allow Leonardo free passage throughout the territory of his dukedom. This he now proceeded to write, dating the document August 18 at Pavia, prior to dispatching it by courier to Leonardo at Cesena. It is worth looking at this document in some detail, because it is highly revealing:

> To all our lieutenants, castellans, captains, *condottieri*, officials, soldiers and subjects who are presented with this document: Our most excellent and most dearly beloved friend, the architect and general engineer Leonardo da Vinci, the bearer of this pass, has been commissioned to inspect the buildings and fortresses of our states, so that we may maintain them according to their needs and on his advice. Furthermore we order and command the following: All will allow him free passage, exempt from any public tax or charge either to himself or his companions, and will welcome him in a friendly fashion, and allow him to inspect, measure and examine anything he wishes. And to this effect, you will provide him with any men he requires and give him any help, assistance and favors he asks. It is our wish that for any work to be carried out within our states, beforehand each engineer be required to consult with him and conform to his judgment. Let no man presume to act otherwise unless he wishes to incur our wrath.

The explicit and forceful wording of this pass suggests that some of those whom Leonardo had previously encountered had chosen not to "welcome him in a friendly fashion" or seen fit to "give him any aid, assistance and favor he asks." Leonardo had been acting as Borgia's spy, albeit in an unwilling capacity, and during his visit to Arezzo, Vitellozzo had presumably not allowed him the complete freedom to inspect and report on anything he wished. The reference to "companions" in Borgia's document indicates that Leonardo did not travel alone, and may well have brought with him from Florence as his servant the rascally Salai. It has also been suggested that there is some significance in Borgia's choice of words to characterize Leonardo: *"nostro . . . dilectissimo familiare"* (our . . . most dearly beloved friend), which is much more than the normal or required term of familiarity, implying that Borgia regarded him on a personal level as his close friend.

It seems likely that in Leonardo's presence Borgia had not always been as preoccupied as he appeared in Leonardo's sketches. They must have conversed. The tough soldier had once been a brilliant scholar, yet his character suggests he was no pedant. He was not the type of person to make Leonardo feel inferior about his lack of a classical education. On the contrary, the intellectual in Borgia must have been intrigued by Leonardo's multifarious genius and the cornucopia of ideas that spilled from his fertile mind. Likewise, Leonardo must have welcomed this intelligent employer, who took his projects seriously and wished to put them into immediate practice. It is likely that they quickly warmed to each other. And the final lines of Borgia's passport for Leonardo make it abundantly clear that he required each of his commanders and citizens to treat Leonardo with a similar favor and respect "unless he wishes to incur our wrath." This was no idle threat where Borgia was concerned: a man was liable to have his tongue cut out and nailed to his severed hand for such discourtesy.

On receiving his passport by courier from Borgia, Leonardo left Cesena for the coast, where he recorded in his notebook: "At Porto Cesenatico, on the 6th of September, 1502, at the fifteenth hour [i.e., 9 a.m.]." He quickly set about making plans for the defense of the port, observing "the way in which bastions ought to project beyond the walls of earth in order to defend the outer dykes, so that they are not vulnerable to artillery fire." And it looks as if he immediately inaugurated work on dredging the inner harbor and the canal that linked this to the sea, for he observed: "The diggers of the ditches form a pyramid." It is hardly surprising that work began so early on this project, for it was intended that the canal should eventually extend ten miles inland to Cesena, a major engineering feat.

Leonardo's "nodding donkey" digger head.

However, it must soon have become clear to Leonardo that such a project was beyond the capacity of the limited manpower available. He appears to have given considerable thought to this matter, as is indicated by various drawings that he made in his notebook that covers this period. There is a sketch of a large machine for removing the earth excavated by diggers in a canal, as well as a pump and then what appears to be a large-scale automatic digging machine. There is also a clear sketch of the head of a mechanical digger, which bears an uncanny resemblance to a modern-day "nodding donkey" oil-head pump, where Leonardo's pulley-assisted seesaw motion clearly anticipates the modern mechanism by some 400 years.

These drawings are undeniably small and mostly vague, and the purpose of what they depict is at first obscure. However, when compared with the remarkably similar drawings made in a later notebook, their purpose becomes evident. The later sketches are not only larger and more detailed, but also more fully realized. In the earth-moving machine it is clear that the central drum is at least twenty feet tall, and it has also been realigned to make the machine more efficient. This later drawing was made in conjunction with an even more ambitious project in which Leonardo would become involved just a year later. It has been suggested that he may even have begun constructing some of these huge excavating machines at Cesenatico in the late summer of 1502, and the fact that the drawing of the later earth-moving machine was modified implies that there may be some truth in this view, though it should be said that no physical evidence has yet been found of any such machine.

In September, when Borgia returned from his visit to Louis XII in northern Italy, he took up residence at Imola and pressed ahead with his plans for his new dukedom, sending orders to Leonardo to set about designing a new university building in Cesena, as well as a new palace of justice for his capital. In the midst of all this Leonardo still found time for further futuristic speculation: it was probably while traveling across the flat, windy countryside between Cesenatico and Cesena that he had the idea of constructing a mill driven by wind power, fifty years before this was first put into practice in Holland.

While Leonardo was transforming the defenses and infrastructure of the Romagna, Borgia's administration was also taking effect. Immediately after Borgia's first campaign of conquest in the Romagna, his loyal Spanish commander Ramiro de Lorqua had been left in charge of the makeshift military government of the region when Borgia returned to Rome. This regime was later established on a more permanent basis at Cesena, where Lorqua was designated "governor and deputy" of the Romagna, in effect taking complete control of the day-to-day running of the province during Borgia's absences on campaign or in Rome. Lorqua was a stout fifty-year-old: a fearsome character with a black beard, he habitually struck an aggressive pose, his chin raised, his right hand thrust into his belt, as he surveyed those about him. He was Borgia's toughest enforcer, and proved a highly effective (if merciless) ruler of the Romagna, crushing all dissent and doing his best to stamp out the traditional lawlessness of the region—a necessary prerequisite if Borgia was to rule over his conquered territories in anything but name. Machiavelli would later characterize Lorqua as "a cruel and impetuous man, who was allowed by Borgia to rule in the most dictatorial fashion," while Villari, echoing several contemporary sources, went even further, stating that Lorqua committed "the most unheard of cruelty in [his] post."

Then suddenly and unexpectedly, on August 14, 1502, Borgia dismissed Lorqua from his post, demoting him to military governor, with his headquarters in Rimini—far from the center of power in the Romagna. It looked as if this was a test of Lorqua's loyalty. Lorqua had been a colleague of Vitellozzo, the Orsini, and others whom Borgia now knew were involved in a plot against him, though because Lorqua was Spanish he had never been completely accepted by Borgia's Italian commanders. Despite Lorqua's apparent loyalty, Borgia may well have had his suspicions. The order demoting Lorqua had come through while Borgia was away in northern Italy with Louis XII, so there would have been no confrontation—or demands by Lorqua for an explanation. It also removed Lorqua from any strategic center of power in case he was planning to overthrow Borgia. And if he did not obey his order to take up his post in Rimini, Borgia would have understood at once where Lorqua's loyalties lay. He would then have waited for the troops promised by Louis XII before he set off back to the Romagna.

In place of Lorqua, Borgia would later appoint Antonio di Sansavino. The very opposite of Lorqua, Sansavino was renowned for his "mild character and popular manners," as well as his virtue and dislike of corruption. Machiavelli, who was not given to flattery, would describe

Sansavino admiringly as "a most learned man of the highest repute." Borgia created for Sansavino the new post of "President of the Romagna," a position that combined the head of the administration with that of chief justice. Here, if anyone, was the man who could lay the foundations of a just and efficient administration and reconcile the lawless citizens of the Romagna to their new government. And this is precisely what he did. Sansavino—in consultation with Borgia—would over the coming months establish a cohesive government that united the Romagna in a way that had not been seen since the disintegration of the Roman Empire. Each of the main cities and its surrounding commune retained its traditional privileges and form of taxation, while its administration remained in largely local hands. At the same time, Sansavino also established a central administration and a Rota, a supreme court of appeal, which moved on a regular circuit of the seven main Romagna cities—Fano, Pesaro, Rimini, Cesena, Faenza, Forlì, and Imola. Sansavino presided over the Rota, but it also had seven judges, each appointed by one of the seven communes. However, the territory remained under the protection of four military governors and the garrisons under their command. Chief of these governors was Lorqua at Rimini, and the other three were also Spanish, thus ensuring their absolute loyalty to Borgia. These governors were allowed considerable autonomy, but were under orders not to interfere with the civil administration unless directly instructed to do so by Borgia himself.

The contemporary historian Francesco Guicciardini, who was no admirer of Borgia, conceded that where the Romagna was concerned, Borgia "had placed in the government of those peoples, men who had governed them with so great justice and integrity, that he was greatly loved by them." Only the ever-observant Machiavelli would have his reservations about Borgia's rule in the Romagna, remarking on how Borgia himself had a tendency to allow his unruly French and Spanish soldiery to indulge in lawless behavior that would not have been tolerated in the citizens they were meant to be protecting.

While Sansavino was busy installing his administration, Leonardo passed through the territory applying his military and engineering expertise to the Romagna's defenses. One of his first recommendations, ironically echoing an earlier suggestion of Borgia's chief artillery expert, Vitellozzo, was for Borgia to order powerful cannons of the new French caliber, so that he would not have to rely upon those hired out to him by Louis XII. Borgia immediately placed orders with the foundry at Brescia, in northern Italy, which was one of the few places in Italy capable of attempting such work. This foundry would have been recommended to him by Leonardo, who had toured the workshops of northern Italy in the course of his preparations for casting the *gran cavallo*.

By the time Leonardo took up employment with Borgia, he had become arguably the greatest military technician in Italy—in theory, at least. During his employment by Ludovico "Il Moro" Sforza in Milan he may have busied himself with all manner of artistic, experimental, and mathematical pursuits, but he had not neglected to continue his studies of military engineering. The main textbook that Leonardo consulted on this subject is known to have been *On the Military Arts (De re militaria)* by Roberto Valturio, which was written around 1460 and was circulated in manuscript before its publication in 1472.

Evidence of Leonardo's confidence in his advanced military knowledge can be seen from the detailed letter he had written to Sforza as early as 1482. In this he had derided "those men who claim to be skilled inventors of war machines" who in fact produced "machines which are no different from those used by anyone else." He then claimed that he would "reveal his secrets" to Sforza, and proceeded to list a vast array of ingenious military techniques, machines, and equipment. These included how to drain the moat of a castle during a siege, how to destroy "any citadel or fortress, even if it is built on a rock," details of various mortars, sea vessels, and "tunnels dug without noise and following torturous routes," as well as "fire-throwing engines, of beautiful and practical design" and fiendish traps "not in common use."

All this confirms that Leonardo had read *On the Military Arts* before he went to Milan, which meant that he must by then have begun to teach himself Latin, as an Italian version of this work was not published until after he arrived in the city. Yet most interesting of all is the nature of this work. Its author, Roberto Valturio, had been employed half a

Valturio's artillery dragon on rollers.

century previously by the notorious Lord of Rimini, Sigismondo Malatesta, widely known as "the wolf of Rimini." Malatesta was a tough and skilled *condottiere* who was capable of heinous treachery; he poisoned his wife, and even planned to assassinate Pope Pius II (who pronounced him "canonized in Hell" after the plot was discovered). Malatesta, possibly with the assistance of Valturio, is said to have invented the exploding shell, a description of which is included in *On the Military Arts*.

This was the first work printed in Italy that described and illustrated the new weapons coming into use during the fifteenth century. Nevertheless, strictly speaking, *On the Military Arts* is hardly an original work. Many of the military devices and practices that it describes would have been known to Archimedes; others date from Roman times, while still others are medieval adaptations of these classical methods. However, *On the Military Arts* does also include some Arabic weapons—though on examination these are really little more than exotic versions of equipment already known in Europe. One such weapon is a fantastic machine shaped like a dragon on rollers, which fires projectiles from its mouth. Other weapons described by Valturio include a variety of battering rams (one in the shape of a tortoise),* fortified galleys, catapults, and so on. Many of these are illustrated in some detail by woodcuts, said to be by the Veronese artist Matteo de' Pasti. One glance at these pages and it is immediately clear where Leonardo received his inspiration for the ingenious machines that began to cover the pages of his notebooks in Milan. He even drew copies of some of Valturio's machines in his notebooks, before developing more advanced versions of his own.

This does not in any way detract from Leonardo's originality, whose superior quality is immediately clear from any comparison. The woodcuts in *The Art of War* have a distinctly medieval quaintness to them, whereas Leonardo's cornucopia of inventiveness is recognizably the work of a Renaissance artist, as well as a mathemically informed Renaissance mind. However, Valturio's work does show what fired Leonardo's imagination: out of such prosaic beginnings he would create a technological poetry the like of which had never been seen before. Whereas Valturio drew imaginative pictures of such things as a partly submersible boat, an armor-protected vehicle of sorts, even a diving apparatus (which would have been lethal), Leonardo's notebooks depict intricate working drawings of flying machines, tanks, diving equipment, even a bicycle, all conceived with mathematical precision, many of which would not become a reality for centuries to come, and a good proportion of which have since been found to work.

---

* Others depict a ram's skull used at the battering end, echoing the original of this weapon. By the medieval era this "ram's head" was cast in metal.

The nature of warfare was now beginning to change as never before. The impregnable fortresses of the medieval era, some of whose walls were more than twenty feet thick, had been able to withstand sieges almost indefinitely. Yet even these were now vulnerable to the powerful new heavy artillery. In consequence, Borgia had ordered inadequate fortresses, such as the one he had captured at Castel Bolognese, simply to be razed to the ground. Others were to be adapted to the new weaponry, and this was where Leonardo came in. He ensured that, wherever possible, the fortresses of the Romagna had corner forts that were rounded, or walls that were sharply cornered, to lessen the effect of direct hits by causing the artillery to bounce off at an angle.

Yet Leonardo's work for Borgia was not entirely devoted to his master's long-term engineering requirements, and there is evidence that he accompanied Borgia on some active military campaigning. Leonardo's friend the mathematician Luca Pacioli describes an event that was almost certainly recounted to him by Leonardo a year or so later:

> One day Cesare Valentino, Duke of Romagna and present Lord of Piombino, found himself and his army at a river which was 24 paces wide, and could find no bridge, nor any material to make one except for a stack of wood all cut to a length of 16 paces. And from this wood, using neither iron nor rope nor any other construction, his noble engineer [Leonardo] made a bridge sufficiently strong for the army to pass over.

Possibly as a gesture of gratitude for this, or some similar exploit, Borgia rewarded Leonardo with a personal gift. Borgia had uncanny psychological insight into those around him and had evidently noticed Leonardo's weakness for fine clothes. Amongst a list of clothes to be deposited "in a crate at the monastery," Leonardo recorded, "one cape in the French style, which belonged to Duke Valentino."

There is also evidence that Leonardo may have been present at the taking of Fossombrone, a small town some ten miles southwest of Urbino, on October 11. In a later notebook, he remarks on the design for a fortress: "Be sure that the escape tunnel does not lead to the keep of the fort's commander, lest the fortress be captured by treachery, as happened at Fossombrone." Borgia was not present at the taking of Fossombrone, which was conducted by two of his most loyal and brutal Spanish commanders, Ugo de Moncada and Don Michele, the strangler of Lucrezia's second husband, Bisceglie. Fossombrone had revolted against Borgia's rule, but Don Michele and Moncada managed to trick their way into the central keep of the town's fortress, and then their soldiers proceeded to pillage the town and massacre its inhabitants. If Leonardo was present, this must have left a searing impression. It was presumably this, or some similar scene, that led him to describe warfare as the "most brutal madness."

All this raises the seemingly insoluble problem of Leonardo's attitude towards his role as a military engineer working for Borgia. Amongst the collection of riddles that he wrote in his notebooks—some intended as public entertainment for the courts, others as purely private and guarded expressions of his more unorthodox opinions—is one that reads:

> One who by himself is gentle and gives no offense will become terrible and ferocious when he is in bad company, and will most cruelly take the lives of many men, and would kill even more if he were not prevented by bodies without a soul, which have emerged from dark caves in the earth, namely metal suits of armor.

The answer to this riddle, as hinted in the last phrase, is "swords and spears." Significantly, Leonardo goes on to characterize these as weapons "which of themselves do harm to no one." If this was intended as a justification for his activities as an inventor of weapons and armaments, it hardly bears reasonable examination. Yes, logically speaking, a sword is not a weapon of murder until it is used as such by a human being, but this logic does not apply to Leonardo's military inventions. The cornucopia of lethal and original weapons that he sketches in his notebooks are not neutral, passive objects like a sword or a spear. These pages are covered with such things as exploding cannonballs, a scuttling tank spitting fire, and so forth: they are weapons in action. Alongside these gruesome weapons, there is a glimpse of his fascination with the catastrophes of nature: tornadoes, floods, deluges overwhelming the world. At least in the private pages of his notebooks he seems to succumb to a pressing fear-fascination with such scenes of violence and catastrophe, whether they are acts of nature or man-made. This double-edged preoccupation evidently fulfilled some deep need in his psychology. Leonardo may have believed in mathematical reasoning, seeing it as the "supreme certainty" that underlay all the elements of his work, but in his notebooks such certainty had gone far beyond the restraints of logic.

Leonardo's situation in this instance curiously echoes the contemporary duality of mathematical reasoning and logic in the Renaissance era. Although the central activity of both was deductive, their histories were in disparate states of development. Mathematics had recently begun to make strides—prompted to a large extent by the introduction of Indo-Arabic concepts such as zero and negative numbers, and in the practical field by Pacioli's dissemination of double-entry bookkeeping and the rediscovery of Archimedes' mechanics. Mathematics was on the brink of a great age of advancement. Meanwhile logic was in a sterile stasis, remaining in virtually the same state as it had been since its inception by Aristotle in fourth-century BC Greece. The syllogism remained supreme:

> Murder is committed by human beings.
> A sword is not a human being.
> Therefore, a sword cannot commit murder.

Mathematical science enabled Leonardo to enlarge his imagination, to extend the human body into an instrument of superhuman capability, able to travel under water, burrow through earth, excavate canals, and possibly even fly through the air. He wished to see everything, to understand everything, to imagine everything, no matter what contradictions this might involve. Logic limits by insisting upon consistency. If enlarging his vision involved self-contradiction, then so be it. At this stage, we can do little other than view Leonardo as just such a self-contradictory enigma: the pacifist military engineer; the vegetarian animal-lover who invented chariots with whirling blades for scything men and horses in two; the pensive mathematician drawn to visions of apocalyptic chaos. We must see him as he was seen by his companions in the Romagna, even as he was seen by the sly, perceptive eye of Borgia: the curiously dandified military engineer, drawing about him the smart French cloak given to him by his master as the chill mists of autumn drew in; standing beneath the thick castellated wall of yet another town fortress, holding up his quadrant to measure its height, perhaps donning his thick-rimmed round spectacle-lens holders in order to record his observations more precisely; pacing out the lengths of the moat and inner courtyards, making compass observations of the direction of the silhouetted town across the fields; occasionally stopping to make a tiny drawing or jot down a reminder—*"Finestre da Cesena"* (windows at Cesena)—in the little bound notebook that he kept hanging on a thong secured to his belt.* Yet had anyone peeked over his shoulder as Leonardo was writing in his notebook on this occasion in Cesena, all they would have seen in a tiny, seemingly impenetrable script was: "*ɒnɘꙅɘϽ ɒb ɘɿƚꙅɘni˥.*"

What a figure he must have presented to Borgia's brutal Spanish officers, to the hard, heartless mercenaries under their command, to the rough peasants and simple townsfolk of the Romagna. Leonardo was already famous as the artist who had painted a miraculous picture that made Christ and his saints look like living people, as alive as if they still breathed and walked the earth, while they sat at the Last Supper. Yet now he chose instead to draw tiny cartoon figures laboring and heaving at huge, intricate machines capable of wreaking death and destruction. He was a solitary, seemingly gentle figure, but there was something inflexible in the way he went about his business, lost in deep meditation, occasionally sketching obscure facets of the world about him, his thoughts encoded in a curious secret script. So much about him so

* Notebook L, at the Institut de France in Paris, which contains most of what Leonardo wrote whilst journeying through the Romagna in the latter half of 1502, measures just four by two-and-three-quarter inches, around the size of the palm of his hand.

utterly elusive—just as much to those in early-sixteenth-century Italy as to us today. And even, one suspects, to himself. There was something about him that resembled his riddle of the suit of armor, that body without a soul, which protected against the blameless swords and lances that had become murderous weapons in the hands of men.

Yet this impenetrable suit of armor, this vegetarian warmonger, could pen—in his reverse mirror-script—the following profound and apparently heartfelt credo, in which he addresses himself to humanity at large:

> And you, man, who will discover in the work I have done the wonderful works of Nature herself. If you judge that it would be a wicked act to destroy it, reflect that the most wicked act of all is to take the life of a man. For if his external form appears to be such a marvelously subtle construction, realize that this is nothing compared with the soul which dwells within this structure; for that, whatever it may be, is a thing divine. Leave it then to dwell within its handiwork, in its own good will, and as it so pleases, and let not your rage or malice destroy such a life—for in truth, he who does not value it, does not himself deserve to have it.

Such was the man who served, with no apparent show of unwillingness (even in the privacy of his notebooks), as military engineer to the ruthless murderer Cesare Borgia, a monster whose name would enter history as a byword for infamy.

10

Borgia at Bay

WHEN BORGIA RETURNED in September 1502 from his visit to Louis XII in northern Italy he established his headquarters at Imola and began assembling his troops. He was now resolved to take Bologna, which Louis XII had announced was no longer under his protection. Alexander VI sent word from Rome confirming suspicions that Bentivoglio of Bologna had joined the Orsini in their plot against Borgia. Such a betrayal was perhaps to be expected; Borgia had made a mistake in allowing Paolo Orsini to negotiate the treaty with Bologna, and to seal this by marrying his niece to Bentivoglio's son Ermes, thus creating a family loyalty that circumvented both Orsini's and Bentivoglio's loyalties to him. However, in order to rectify this state of affairs, Alexander VI would now set in motion events that would give Cesare the excuse to invade the city and depose Bentivoglio.

Nominally at least Bologna remained a papal state, and Alexander VI summoned Bentivoglio to Rome, accusing him of despotic and corrupt rule of the papal fiefdom, a situation that he was ordered to rectify within a fortnight or the pope would take immediate action on this matter. The ground was now prepared for Borgia to invade, but to Alexander VI's consternation he made no move. In truth, the seventy-one-year-old Alexander was becoming increasingly vexed by his twenty-seven-year-old son's behavior. When Cesare had ridden off without his father's leave to visit Louis XII, Alexander had initially been furious at his son's hot-headed decision. The pope's anger had quickly descended into deeper anguish: Cesare's impulsive action was threatening to upset all Alexander's most carefully laid diplomatic plans, which relied upon his position as pope, and on his ability to play off the balance of power between the French (whom he instinctively distrusted) and his fellow Spanish (whom he also distrusted, but to whom he instinctively felt closer).

When Alexander learned that Cardinal Orsini, the head of the Orsini family, had slipped out of Rome and arrived ahead of Cesare at Louis XII's court in northern Italy, he feared the worst. In his covert strategy against the last of the powerful aristocratic Roman families, Alexander VI had publicly maintained friendly relations with Cardinal Orsini, as long as the Orsini family remained under French protection. In this way he could keep an eye on the cardinal, and possibly even take him hostage should the need arise. Now Cardinal Orsini had outwitted him and was liable to encourage Louis XII to take Cesare hostage. Cesare's precipitate action would be the ruin of the Borgia cause, which had taken so much time and effort, marriages, murder, and money to establish. The pope was too old, and his dissipations had left him too tired, for him to begin scheming all over again: this was the Borgias' last chance to establish a permanent power base that would outlast Alexander VI's occupancy of St. Peter's throne.

Yet despite their differences, Alexander and his wayward son nonetheless had the selfsame project in mind, and although they now appeared to be going about this in their separate ways, they both ultimately relied upon the same source: native Borgia instinct. But where Alexander believed in the treachery and patient unrelenting schemes of an old man, Cesare believed in the treachery and decisive action of youth. And this time his colossal gamble paid off: Louis XII was charmed, Cardinal Orsini slunk away, and in Rome a highly relieved Alexander VI could only marvel at his son's audacious success. The Borgia strategy remained intact.

Not long after Cesare had returned to the Romagna, Alexander VI sent word to Imola, insisting upon a secret meeting with his son to discuss future strategy. The pretext for their meeting would be the installation of the four-year-old Giovanni Borgia (the "Infans Romanus" of enigmatic pedigree) as Lord of Camerino, the initial step in lining him up as heir to Cesare Borgia and the dukedom of the Romagna. This ceremony was to take place in early September. Cesare slipped out of Imola, Alexander VI vanished from Rome; they met at Camerino, in The Marches, a hundred miles northeast of Rome and close to the southern border of the newly expanded Romagna dukedom. None but father and son were privy to the details of their sequestered conversations, conducted in the Catalan dialect, and no record of these conversations remains. The enormity of what was decided at this meeting would only gradually become apparent as events unfolded over the ensuing months.

It was when Alexander VI returned to Rome that he summoned Bentivoglio from Bologna and set in motion the plan for Borgia's seizure of the city. Irritated at Cesare's lack of immediate action, Alexander now took matters into his own hands, and in an astute move ordered Paolo and Giulio Orsini to report to Borgia for the march against Bentivoglio in Bologna. As commanders in the papal employ, they were bound to join Borgia, in his official capacity as *gonfaloniere* of the papal forces. Prior to this, the Orsinis' treacherous machinations had been conducted in secret: they had not actually declared themselves and still remained unsure of how much Borgia actually knew, or even suspected, of their plot. Now at last they would be forced into the open, along with any other of Borgia's commanders who were in on the plot. Either they joined Borgia for his planned march on Bologna or they deserted him.

Unbeknown to Alexander VI, Borgia's apparent hesitation had been because he had decided to call off the march against Bologna, for fear of entering a trap of his own making. If he moved against Bologna in the north, even if he was accompanied by Vitellozzo, Baglioni, and the others, he would leave the whole of the southern Romagna unguarded. This would be exposed to attack from any forces that Vitellozzo and the others had left behind on the pretext that they were guarding their domains and castles, which were concentrated in Umbria and up alongside the Florentine border. So Borgia had decided to sit tight and see what ensued. The longer nothing happened, the sooner the French troops promised him by Louis XII would arrive to strengthen his own limited force. At present he had just 5,000 foot soldiers at his disposal, and these were mainly scattered in garrisons guarding cities throughout the Romagna. Louis XII had promised to send him 2,500 Gascon foot soldiers and 1,000 cavalry, yet even with these Borgia knew that he would be heavily outnumbered. According to his calculations, if Vitellozzo and Baglioni combined with the Orsini and others, they could muster a force of more than 9,000 foot soldiers and 1,000 cavalry.

The Orsini and their forces were garrisoned in their family castles north of Rome, while Gianpaolo Baglioni was at Perugia, and Vitellozzo had retired to his lordship at Città di Castello, where he had been laid low by a bout of syphilis. However, Alexander VI's dispatch from Rome ordering Paolo and Giulio Orsini to report to Borgia for the march on Bologna soon brought matters to a head. In late September Cardinal Orsini summoned a meeting at La Magione, his castle by the shores of Lake Trasimeno, which happened to be tactically situated halfway between Rome and Imola.

During the first days of October, Borgia's enemies from far and wide gathered at La Magione. They made an unsavory crew, many of whom would be acutely characterized by Machiavelli in his later writings. The senior member of the Orsini clan, Cardinal Giambattista Orsini, was "a man of a thousand tricks." He was also notorious for his louche ways—during his earlier period of friendship with Alexander VI, their dinner parties had included debauched scenes reminiscent of ancient Rome. Others present at La Magione included Borgia's treacherous commanders Giulio and Paolo Orsini, the latter characterized as "vain, weak, credulous and mentally unstable." Their close colleague Vitellozzo was carried in on a stretcher, his venereal condition causing him to moan with pain. Along with him came his protégé, the "criminal and nefarious" Liverotto, Lord of Fermo, a classic small-town despot of the unruly Romagna-Marches region who was already notorious throughout Italy for his "infinite treacheries and cruelties." Most notable amongst these was the manner in which he came by his title: having invited his relatives and friends to a large banquet, he had them all murdered, including his kindly uncle, the Lord of Fermo, who had adopted him when he was orphaned as a child and had brought him up as his son. To secure his position Liverotto then murdered the two remaining infants who had a claim to Fermo—one thrown from a high window, the other having its throat slit while being cradled in its mother's arms.

Also present was the unappetizing Gianpaolo Baglioni, perceptively described by Machiavelli as "a man of vicious heart . . . and great cowardice." Baglioni was notorious throughout Italy for "having committed incest with his sister, and killing his cousins and nephews in order to become ruler of Perugia." Others who attended La Magione included Ermes, son of Giovanni Bentivoglio of Bologna, who was now married to an Orsini; Guidobaldo of Urbino also sent along a representative.

It soon transpired that the brains behind this meeting was Pandolfo Petrucci, the brutal tyrant of Siena, who had realized the vulnerability of his Tuscan city-state if a stand was not made by Vitellozzo, the Orsini, and the others whose domains stood along the southeastern border of Florentine territory. The seventy-seven-year-old Petrucci was a wily and ruthless character, who had married into the powerful Borghese family and later murdered his father-in-law in order to retain power. At La Magione, Petrucci would demonstrate his intelligence and strategic skills, news of which was soon relayed to Imola by Borgia's spies. Borgia duly took note of this problematic character, factoring him into his future plans.

In order to try and bolster their position, the plotters had also made covert approaches to both Venice and Florence, the two established major states of the region, both of which had good reason to oppose Borgia and his expansionist policies in the Romagna. It looked as if this time Cesare Borgia had met his match in all the areas in which he so prided himself: villainy, treachery, and military brute force.

The proceedings at La Magione were opened by Baglioni, who dramatically revealed that he had intercepted a secret communication between Alexander VI and Borgia. This ordered Borgia to summon Giulio and Paolo Orsini, Liverotto da Fermo, and Baglioni himself to a meeting at Imola, where Borgia was to lure them into a trap and seize them. Several of those present leaped at once to their feet, violently condemning Borgia's treachery; Vitellozzo and Bentivoglio even went so far as to swear they would murder him at the first opportunity. Baglioni appealed for an immediate and concerted invasion of Borgia's dukedom "in order not to be devoured by the dragon one by one." But this first meeting eventually broke up indecisively, as those present were unwilling to commit themselves to any hasty course of action. They would consult amongst themselves before holding a second meeting.

As the discussions at La Magione continued, Venice and Florence looked on warily, assessing the news relayed to them by their various paid informants. Venice had been unwilling to commit itself to any anti-Borgia move, for fear of making an enemy of Louis XII. Florence too was noncommittal; although the city had no love for Borgia, it was under no illusions about the likes of Vitellozzo and Baglioni, who had already invaded its territory. Similarly, several others present at La Magione had their own separate dreams of expanding their territory at the expense of Florence, while secretly entertaining avaricious ideas concerning the division of a reconquered Romagna. This was the main problem. All those present had their own separate agendas, as well as not fully trusting their fellow conspirators; at the same time, they were all secretly afraid of confronting a man of Borgia's evident power and vindictiveness. As a result, the group had no obvious leader, or even a straightforward plan. Some were for launching an immediate all-out attack, while Borgia was vulnerable—a move that could in all likelihood succeed. Although none of them trusted one another, they were all united in their distrust of Borgia. Was he really as vulnerable as he appeared, or was this yet another of his notorious deceptions? Others counseled a more prudent approach, suggesting that they should oust him from the Romagna city by city. Through the first week of October the conspirators debated, frequently plotting amongst themselves against those they did not trust.

Sensing that this would happen, Borgia decided to act. He sent an undercover message to Paolo Orsini, offering him lavish terms as well as the favors and protection of his father, the pope, if Orsini chose to return as one of Borgia's commanders in the field. Borgia's instincts had quickly singled out Paolo Orsini as the weakest and most indecisive amongst the conspirators. Paolo, and to a lesser extent his brother Giulio, had already begun to have misgivings about moving against Borgia whilst he had the support of Louis XII, to whom the Orsini had for so long remained loyal. Borgia also made it plain that this offer could include any others who might be persuaded to return to his service.

When word of Borgia's offer became known at La Magione, a number of the conspirators expressed themselves in favor of a rapprochement. Baglioni was violently opposed: he knew Borgia well enough to understand that he could never be trusted. The meeting broke up in disarray, with Ermes Bentivoglio and the Duke of Urbino's representative riding off in high dudgeon—only to be stopped in their tracks by some amazing news. When word of the meeting at La Magione had spread through The Marches and the Romagna, this had inspired a revolt at San Leo, fifteen miles north of Urbino, where on October 7 the rebels had tricked their way into taking the reputedly impregnable clifftop fortress in a ruse worthy of Borgia himself. Machiavelli, to whom these events were related at first hand by Borgia, described what happened:

> The castellan was strengthening the fortress and had brought there some carpenters. So the conspirators arranged that some beams that were being dragged into the castle should be left on the bridge, which, being thus encumbered, could not be raised by the garrison. On this opportunity, the conspirators, fully armed, rushed over the bridge into the castle.

In light of this news, a miraculous change of heart took place amongst the conspirators, who quickly reassembled at La Magione, signed an accord on October 9, and sprang into action. They would launch a two-pronged attack on Borgia. Ermes Bentivoglio would strike north towards Imola in the heart of the Romagna, while Vitellozzo and the Orsini would march directly northeast into Urbino territory to support the rebels.

When news of the meeting at La Magione had first reached Alexander VI in Rome, he had once again sensed that all his plans for a permanent Borgia heritage might yet come to nothing—at which he was said to have been thrown into a paroxysm of anger. The Venetian ambassador, Antonio Giustinian, described him "raging like a bear" and cursing the perfidy of the Orsini. His son Cesare, on the other hand, continued to bide his time. After assessing the situation from his headquarters at Imola, he sent messages urging his loyal Spanish commanders to exercise caution and retreat as soon as possible to concentrate his few forces at Imola.

By October 11 the conspirators were on the March: Vitellozzo's cavalry was within striking distance east of Urbino, with Baglioni's forces advancing from the south. The city's garrison was commanded by two of Borgia's most notorious Spanish henchmen—Ugo de Moncada and the strangler Don Michele. Under orders from Borgia, they reluctantly beat a tactical retreat, and when news spread throughout the countryside that Urbino had been occupied by the anti-Borgia conspirators, the citizens of Fossombrone, just ten miles to the east, rose in spontaneous revolt. This proved too great a provocation for Moncada and Don Michele, who disobeyed Borgia's orders and diverted to Fossombrone. Having tricked their way into the fortress through the secret passage of the emergency exit, their hardened Spanish troops proceeded to pillage the town and massacre its citizenry, who were for the most part peasants armed only with sticks and farming implements.

As already mentioned, Leonardo's notebook indicates that he was probably present at Fossombrone during this massacre, and he may indeed have witnessed the revolt from its outset. The improvements to the fortress at San Leo would certainly have been carried out under his instructions, probably even under his supervision. This would account for his being amongst Don Michele's retreating forces at Fossombrone. But Leonardo was not out of danger yet. Upon hearing what had taken place at Fossombrone, Vitellozzo and Orsini now joined up with Baglioni, making a combined force of 12,000 men. They then marched swiftly towards the coast, with the aim of cutting off Don Michele and Moncada as they made their way north to join up with Borgia. On October 15 they surprised Don Michele's troops at the tiny village of Calmazzo, where the Spanish were heavily outnumbered and routed. Don Michele just managed to escape with his life, and Moncada was taken prisoner, while the survivors beat a hasty retreat to barricade themselves at Fano on the Adriatic coast. Once again, Leonardo must have been lucky to survive; but the lethal melee he had witnessed would make a deep and lasting impression, which would have a transforming effect upon both the man and his art.

Three days later Duke Guidobaldo of Urbino re-entered his city in triumph, a popular leader cheered through the streets by his loyal citizenry. By this time Giovanni Bentivoglio of Bologna and his son Ermes were making their way southeast down the Via Emilia towards Imola. Bentivoglio dispatched a vanguard of 2,300 troops, which took Castel San Pietro, just seven miles up the road from Borgia's headquarters. Borgia still had a line of communication open to Lorqua with his garrison at Rimini, but this was more than a day's march away. He was now virtually under siege.

In early October the conspirators had sent word to Florence, urging the republic to join them in the final defeat of Borgia. The response of Gonfaloniere Soderini and the Signoria was for once both decisive and unexpected. In the words of Machiavelli, who would certainly have been present at their deliberations:

> The Florentines, because of their hatred of [Vitellozzo] Vitelli and the Orsini for various reasons, not merely did not join them but sent Niccolò Machiavelli, their secretary, to offer the Duke [Borgia] asylum and aid against these new enemies of his.

II

Machiavelli's Mission

MACHIAVELLI HAD ARRIVED at Imola as early as October 7, 1502, at the very outset of the crisis. Borgia seems to have been reassured by Machiavelli's presence, even though he must have known—as indeed Machiavelli would have known—that Florence's offer of asylum or assistance was largely meaningless under the circumstances. At any rate, unlike during their previous encounter, this time Borgia immediately set out to charm Machiavelli, greeting him like a true friend and appearing to take him into his confidence. To Machiavelli's surprise, and admiration, Borgia seemed not in the least disturbed by the threatening situation that he faced. He referred to the conspirators dismissively as a "collection of no-hopers and bankrupts." As long as he had the backing of his father the pope and of his friend Louis XII, "the ground was on fire under their feet, and they would never have enough water to put it out." Next day he confidentially showed Machiavelli a document in which Louis XII promised Borgia his full assistance. This time Machiavelli's diplomatic experience was able to confirm that Borgia was not bluffing. As a result of his mission to the French court two years previously, he was able to recognize that the official signatures on the royal document were genuine. Louis XII had promised Borgia 300 lances.* But

---

* A lance was a military unit dating back to feudal times when barons and knights would rally with their retinue to support their liege-lord. By the turn of the sixteenth century in Italy, a lance was usually made up of one mounted and heavily armed man-at-arms, accompanied by a few attendant foot soldiers and some light cavalrymen. The 300 lances sent by Louis XII consisted of around 2,500 soldiers.

would this, combined with the limited forces Borgia had at his disposal, be enough to withstand the onslaught of the vastly superior forces of the conspirators?

Borgia continued to press Machiavelli to agree to an alliance with Florence, but despite the Signoria's generous offer of "asylum and aid," it remained unwilling to commit the republic to any formal agreement. Consequently Machiavelli had been well briefed and prepared for this eventuality. He had been dispatched to Borgia's court at Imola as a mere envoy, without specific powers, rather than as an official ambassador, who might have been pressured into making concessions in the republic's name. In the words of the Borgia historian E.R. Chamberlin: "The Signoria sent Niccolò Machiavelli with strict instructions to admit nothing, promise nothing, concede nothing. He was to observe Borgia until the situation cleared."

During the ensuing days of October, messengers bringing news of one disaster after another reached Borgia: the San Leo revolt, the conspirators' two-pronged invasion, Guidobaldo's triumphant re-entry into Urbino, then the defeat of Don Michele at Calmazzo. But these messengers reported to Borgia directly, and the contents of their dispatches were not revealed. Machiavelli did his best to discover what was going on, but as he reported back to the Signoria his efforts met with limited success, "for at this court, things which are meant to be kept hidden are never even alluded to, and are cloaked in the most commendable secrecy."

Borgia placed a high premium on secrecy and intelligence. Machiavelli was well aware that no matter what precautions he took, his dispatches and letters home were liable to be opened and read, with some simply being intercepted and destroyed. As a result, when he wrote back to his masters in Florence, which he did on an almost daily basis, he sometimes adopted a guarded or oblique tone, and was averse to naming sources who had provided him with information. He also wrote just as frequently to his friends, as they did to him; in these gossipy letters Machiavelli and his friends often resorted to the slang or code words they used amongst themselves, particularly when retailing any juicy gossip or ribaldries. These included references to such apparent irrelevancies as "onions," "a cloak," "the hat . . . of several colors," "black satin," and the like. "Onions" seems to have referred to previously sent letters; the other more obscure remarks are best left to salacious speculation.

Machiavelli used his diplomatic skills to the utmost, and cultivated friendships with many influential contacts at Borgia's court, not least being one he referred to as "the chief man who is closest to this Lord"— almost certainly a reference to Agapito Geraldini, Borgia's private secretary. Machiavelli's personal relationship with Borgia was certainly pursued in order to glean the slightest hint of information from this most secretive of men; Borgia likewise encouraged Machiavelli's friendship for his own purposes. Even so, these two disparate characters seem to have developed a mutual respect. Borgia appreciated Machiavelli's intellectual qualities, and appears to have warmed to the roguish element in the wily Florentine envoy's character. Machiavelli, for his part, developed a growing admiration for Borgia's uncanny competence in handling the ever-increasing difficulties of his situation, and for his ability to make rapid, yet shrewd decisions. The man who sought to philosophize about politics was beginning to see in this unscrupulous man of action a solution to the problems that faced any political leader. But perhaps most of all, at this early stage, Machiavelli admired Borgia's sheer resilience of character.

When Borgia learned of the superior forces that his adversaries had at their disposal, he laughed contemptuously, pointing out to Machiavelli that "when they claim to have: 'A force of six hundred men-at-arms, on paper'—it means just that, on paper. In other words, nothing." What kind of men were these conspirators and their forces, compared with himself and the hardened Spanish warriors he had fighting for him? Despite the conspirators' apparently overwhelming numbers, "the more I know of them, the less I respect them." And what of their leaders? "This Vitellozzo has such a great reputation, but I can't say that I've ever seen him performing any actual acts of bravery: he's always excusing himself because he has the French disease. All he's good for is pillaging defenseless places, and robbing those who run away from him, and this kind of treachery."

What Machiavelli did not know—and would not know until Borgia revealed it to him several weeks later—was that Borgia had got wind of the plot against him as early as June, and since then had been biding his time, carefully preparing the ground. Significantly, it was only the cities of The Marches, such as Urbino and Fossombrone, that had risen in revolt against Borgia. The cities of the Romagna had remained loyal to him. They had no wish to see the return of the petty tyrants who had ruled them so mercilessly. Of necessity, in order to hang on to his conquests after his first two campaigns, Borgia's initial government under Lorqua had been almost as merciless as those that it replaced, with few effective institutions, and rough justice summarily dispensed. But now that Lorqua had been replaced by the respected and humane Sansavino, who was in the process of establishing a just and uncorrupt administration, Borgia's rule was gaining the respect of the local population. It looked as if Borgia was here to stay, and meant to stand by his promises that his new dukedom would become a power of which Italy could be proud.

All this meant that during the darkest days of the conpirators' invasion, with Borgia under virtual siege in Imola, and Don Michele returned after his defeat at Calmazzo, Borgia had been able to dispatch Don Michele into the Romagna hinterland to recruit a thousand local men as reinforcements. The men of the Romagna had been quick to rally to Borgia's cause; on top of this, many of them had already served as mercenaries and required little training. Borgia had also been able to send word to his military governor Lorqua at Rimini, instructing him to make a tour of inspection of the Romagna towns, ensuring that their fortresses and defenses were well maintained and fully prepared.

A fact that the conspirators had overlooked was that Borgia had vast sums of money at his disposal, which they did not. Hence his reference to them as "bankrupts." As prearranged, Alexander VI sent 18,000 ducats from Rome, so that Borgia could afford to pay and equip his new recruits; this influx of cash also enabled him to send word to Milan to hire an extra 500 Gascon and 1,500 Swiss infantry. These were tough troops indeed, feared throughout Italy even more than Borgia's brutal Spanish warriors.

As hints of these developments leaked out, Machiavelli was suitably impressed. Even more so when he learned of Borgia's military organization: his teams of fast couriers, his communication links, and his efficient network of spies, who constantly supplied him with intelligence. As Machiavelli wrote back to the Signoria in Florence: "He has spent, in the two weeks since I have been here, as much money for couriers and special messengers as anyone else would have spent in two years." Even under a state of near siege in Imola, Borgia had been able to send, and receive, important messages from as far afield as Rome and Milan, while at the same time keeping in contact with Florence through Machiavelli. Meanwhile, through his sister Lucrezia's court in Ferrara, he learned of events in Venice—this arrangement having been secretly set up during his fleeting visits to Lucrezia on his way to and from seeing Louis XII. Venice continued to watch and wait: its main preoccupation remained the prospect of an invasion from the ever-expanding Ottoman Empire. Even so, Borgia knew that Venice was extremely wary of his project in the Romagna. Despite the Venetian ambassador's reassurances to Alexander VI in Rome, Borgia knew that he needed to keep a close eye on any developments in Venice. Ferrara, which shared a fifty-mile border with Venice, was ideally placed as a source of information. As Machiavelli had astutely observed, Borgia's strategy depended to a great extent upon springing surprises on his enemies, and he did his best to make sure that they could not do the same to him.

Despite all this, if the conspirators had launched a concerted all-out attack they could well have driven Borgia out of the Romagna, and might even have defeated him, had they managed to corner his troops and force him to make a stand. But towards the end of October news reached Imola that the French forces, backed by heavy cavalry, were already on their way from Milan. Borgia's moves to divide the conspirators had caused them to dither, and now their time was running out. Machiavelli continued to watch from the sidelines, with growing admiration. Here was a new kind of soldier—the warrior ruler who used guile rather than force, who achieved his aims by means of intellect and unscrupulousness. He was utterly without principle, save his one guiding principle—the achievement and maintenance of his own power, by any means available.

12

The Ghost

Leonardo's map of Imola.

WHILE BORGIA SCHEMED, and Machiavelli spied, a ghostly presence hovered in the background. None of Borgia's known orders, or Machiavelli's dispatches to Florence, make any explicit mention of Leonardo da Vinci. Even Leonardo's own notebooks make it difficult to discern what he was doing. Yet we know that he was in Imola during this dangerous time. Presumably he had made it back to Borgia's headquarters with Don Michele and his troops fleeing from the rout at Calmazzo. The confirming evidence placing Leonardo at Imola during this period is a map that he made of the city. This is a work of astonishing technical achievement and precision; it is also a work of some beauty, which is heightened by the delicate wash coloring of the snaking blue course of the nearby River Santerno, the pale green of the surrounding fields, and even the red clusters of houses within the city. Leonardo's map depicts every street, every parcel of land and its buildings, as well as the entire city ramparts, together with their fortified gates, main fortress, and surrounding moat. These are all seen as if from the heavens, or a bird's-eye view, just as we expect of a map today. At the time, this was something of an innovation.

Map-making was undergoing a period of technical advance, largely due to the discoveries being made in the New World and the Indian Ocean. The crew list for all exploring ships now regularly included a skilled map-maker who did his best to record the routes taken, geographical positions, and precise linear details of the coastlines that were followed. In medieval times, maps tended to depict landscape features by means of simple drawings—mountains might be depicted as their peaks appeared from ground level, or as a series of humps; castles would be depicted with their battlements, rather than in overview plan. Leonardo's map is very much an example of the new Renaissance style, and, as such, one of its finest early examples.

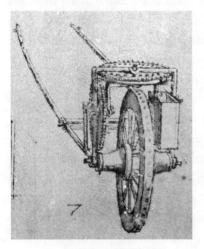

Leonardo's hodometer.

We know from surviving preliminary sketches that Leonardo determined the lengths of the streets and other dimensions by painstakingly measuring the distances involved and jotting them down. For this he would have used assistants, though he certainly oversaw the entire project himself. Distances were measured by simply pacing them out on the ground, or by the use of cords knotted at regular lengths, or with the aid of a hodometer, an instrument that measured distances by running a wheel across the ground. This hodometer was Leonardo's own invention, and probably followed one of the three designs he drew in his notebooks during his period in Milan. The most advanced of these made use of a vertical rotating wheel (as in a wheelbarrow) whose notches clicked forward a cogged wheel set horizontally above it. This upper wheel rotated once every ten *braccia*,* and according to Leonardo, after covering a mile it "makes the ear hear the sound of a little stone falling into a basin made to serve it."

Leonardo's map of Imola is centered on the main crossroads near the old marketplace, and from here, lines run out in the eight main compass directions (north, northeast, east, et cetera) across outlines of the surrounding fields and terrain, to the circular border of the map. Alongside the map Leonardo included the directions and distances to nearby towns. "Imola, as regards Bologna, is five points from the west towards northwest, at a distance of 20 miles. Castel San Pietro lies exactly northwest of Imola, at a distance of 7 miles." This, as well as the city's defensive details, indicates that the inspiration for this innovative and aesthetic work of technology was an order from Borgia. Imola was under siege, with Bentivoglio's forces camped northeast up the Via Emilia at Castel San Pietro. Borgia needed an accurate map of the city's defenses if he was to resist attack or perhaps withstand a serious siege.

Interestingly, the directions at the side of the map ("Bologna . . . 20 miles" and so on) are all in the mirror-writing customarily used by Leonardo for his private notes. This suggests that the surviving map, which is now in the Royal Collection at Windsor Castle, is a beautified copy of a more functional original that he drew up for Borgia, which

---

* *Braccio* means arm; *braccia* are thus distances measured in terms of an arm's length, usually reckoned in this period to be *around* sixty modern centimeters (almost two feet). The inexactitude was a medieval hangover, where the value of a measure of distance was liable to vary considerably from place to place. Thus a *braccio* in Milan was 59.5 cm, whilst that in Venice was 68.3 cm. Leonardo probably had in mind Florentine *braccia*, which are usually reckoned to have been between 59.9 cm and 60.4 cm long.

would also have included directions and distances, but not in Leonardo's personal code. The fact that the fortress, which occupies the southwestern corner of Imola, is altered in accord with suggestions that Leonardo proposed to Borgia, rather than as it was in reality at the time, supports the conjecture that this is an aestheticized version of a functional original.

Medieval maps, with their drawings of mountains, castles, and even fanciful animals such as dragons, possessed their own quaint but nonetheless recognizable aesthetic quality—a beauty that the more precise and practical early Renaissance maps frequently lacked. It may be that this copy of the original military map for Borgia was an attempt to explore how some element of that medieval aesthetic quality could be retained. As such, it certainly succeeds in a way that many ensuing similarly precise maps do not. Precision quickly gave way to the formulaic; the reality of the terrain was adapted to the purpose of the map, rather than simply portrayed. Specific features—such as roads, towns, mountain contours, and so forth—were emphasized at the expense of a natural bird's-eye verisimilitude. Not until the advent of satellite photography do we find maps whose precision and color regain that element of charm and beauty. Here too, though in a much more subtle way, it seems Leonardo was once again far ahead of his time.

Yet Leonardo's work was not entirely devoted to meditatively pacing out the streets and confining walls, then beautifying his heaven's-eye view of Imola and its environs. Machiavelli, in his dispatch back to Florence on October 9, 1502, observed: "The Duke [Borgia] has so much artillery and in such good order that he alone possesses almost as much as all the rest of Italy put together." Presumably, the new large-caliber cannons that Borgia had ordered had arrived from the foundry at Brescia. As Borgia's chief military engineer, Leonardo would have been responsible for the "good order" of this powerful weaponry, which so impressed Machiavelli.

There is good evidence that during this period Leonardo may also have been engaged in other military work for Borgia. According to several reliable sources, some months later at the siege of Ceri, Borgia "made use of new inventions of singular ingenuity . . . including mortars capable of firing multiple explosive projectiles, mobile precision artillery and large-scale catapults . . . such as found in the notebooks of Leonardo da Vinci." Furthermore, we know that amongst Borgia's siege engines was "a huge machine held to be capable of carrying up to 300 men up to the ramparts." The initial stage of the construction of this "huge machine" was carried out in Rome some time early in the following new year by Leonardo, but was completed under the supervision of Borgia himself after Leonardo had left his employ. This indicates that Leonardo must earlier have had discussions with Borgia about such military inventions, and must have revealed to him detailed plans showing how to build them. The only time when such discussions could realistically have taken place was during these autumn months at Imola, when Leonardo must have drawn up detailed plans from ideas that he had previously sketched in his notebooks during his years with Ludovico Sforza in Milan. These earlier notebooks depict several machines that fit the above descriptions, though none of the more detailed construction drawings he supplied to Borgia have survived.

Despite Machiavelli's remark about Borgia's quantity of artillery, which he must have seen for himself, we do not know for certain that he met his fellow Florentine, who probably spent much of his time busying himself in Borgia's arsenal. Indeed, there is no concrete evidence that Machiavelli and Leonardo met during the time when they were known to have been together in Imola: from around mid-October to early December 1502. As already mentioned, Machiavelli's regular and extensive dispatches made no mention of Leonardo. Ironically, this very lack of evidence would seem to confirm that they did meet, and get to know each other closely, at this time.

Imola was by any measure a small town indeed—the city within the walls depicted by Leonardo's map is considerably less than a mile long and less than half a mile wide. Even at his measuring pace, Leonardo could have strode all around the walls in less than an hour. Likewise, Borgia's court was no great affair, making it certain that Machiavelli would soon have come into contact with his fellow Florentine. More, he would probably have sought Leonardo out, as they had almost certainly met previously—when Machiavelli returned to Florence from

Urbino carrying Borgia's first instructions to Leonardo. For Machiavelli, Leonardo would have been a good source of information about what the secretive Borgia had in mind, what was happening around him, who was coming and going, and so forth. Yet for Machiavelli to have mentioned such a source by name would have placed Leonardo in some danger when his dispatches to Florence were intercepted and opened.

Machiavelli's dispatch for November 1 mentions that he had a conversation with Agapito Geraldini, Cesare Borgia's private secretary, and that he confirmed the truth of what he had been told in this conversation by talking "to another who is well acquainted with this Lord's secrets." Two days later Machiavelli mentions in his dispatch how he had a "lengthy conversation" with "one of the first secretaries, who confirmed everything I wrote in my other letters." These dispatches make free use of the names of people at Borgia's court, which makes the fact that he does not mention the name of the first secretary or the person who knows Borgia's secrets rather more significant. It appears that he has no intention of giving away the name of someone who may have been a major and regular source of information. This mysterious "friend" or "chief secretary" is mentioned again in later dispatches.

On October 14 Machiavelli's close friend and loyal assistant at the Chancery, Agostino Vespucci, wrote to him reassuringly:

> I am sure, by God, that you are held in great honor there, you whom the duke himself and all the courtiers favor, so that they heap praise on you as a prudent man, surround and flatter you. That is a pleasure, since I love you dearly.

Agostino was in fact much more concerned about events in Florence. He felt it his duty to warn Machiavelli about what was happening at the Chancery, and about Marcello Adriani, Agostino's unpopular colleague who was meant to be looking after Machiavelli's office:

> I do not want to keep secret from you certain things which may end up by preventing you from finishing your work. Dear Niccolò, even if these things creep and crawl about out of

sight, they'll soon be out in the open. You know what men are, with all their lies and secrets, their rivalries and hatreds, you know what they're like, those whom you depend on at present. Therefore, because you're so prudent, you must look after yourself and us too, and help us overcome our difficulties. Write to Marcello and wake him up, prod him, rouse him, push him and goad him into getting on with things and taking on his responsibility for your work as he's meant to be doing. Get him to start dictating some letters, not to ignore the whole business as if it were none of his concern and was beneath him. Since you left he's done nothing but sit on his arse as if he's in a trance, so lazy and slothful he has become.

Agostino insists upon his loyalty to Machiavelli: "I wish you were back with us so that you would be the only one in charge of us here at the Chancery." Nonetheless he then goes on to tell Machiavelli how his other great friend and assistant, Biagio Buonaccorsi, has been deeply upset by what they all see as Machiavelli's desertion of them in their time of need: "Biagio hates you for leaving us, and is always rabbiting on, insulting you, damning and blinding you to hell. He's in complete despair and doesn't know what to do." There may have been an element of joshing in such remarks, but they cannot have made for reassuring reading. With friends like this, Machiavelli hardly needed enemies.

Just days later, Biagio wrote Machiavelli a long letter full of gossip, much of it disguised in the (fairly transparent) personal code that Machiavelli and his cronies used amongst themselves, especially when writing about women and other men's wives: "I think I can console her, because when they needed to send to Livorno for someone to show how to make sparrows sprout new feathers, I suggested her and said that she sprouted feathers so well that she bumped Sir Antonio right out of bed with one of her re-sproutings." With regard to the situation at the Chancery, Biagio solemnly assured Machiavelli: "I carry messages up to the *gonfaloniere* every day, and I always put in a good word for you like the true friend that I am."

The fact is, they were all fearful that without Machiavelli to look after them, they were liable to lose their jobs. As Biagio wrote: "The new *gonfaloniere* [Soderini] is starting a reorganization of the city administration, because he wants to reduce the salary budget for the Chancery." Machiavelli too was worried on this score. Even though he had the trust of Soderini, he was not immune from the bitter backbiting and factional infighting that characterized the workings of the Florentine administration. When you were absent, you had to rely upon your friends to support your cause—which can hardly have been reassuring for Machiavelli, considering the duplicitous way his friends were behaving.

As previously on Machiavelli's missions from Florence, the Signoria made few provisions for keeping their envoy in funds, and Machiavelli was soon forced to start dipping into his own pocket to support himself at Borgia's court. On top of this, communications with Florence remained unreliable, and not only due to interception by Borgia's agents. As Biagio wrote to Machiavelli on November 15: "The Signoria felt you weren't sending us enough dispatches, because the one you said you sent on the 5th never arrived, and perhaps you didn't even write it at all. That arsehole Totti [the official Florentine courier] took over a week to get here."

However, all these misunderstandings and carpings were as nothing compared to the difficulties Machiavelli was now having over his new young wife, Marietta. Earlier in the summer she had given birth to their first child, a daughter named Primerana, and she was not pleased when in early October she learned that her husband was deserting her and her months-old infant to set out on yet another of his missions, this time to the court of Cesare Borgia at Imola. Somewhat disingenuously, Machiavelli seems to have assured her when he set out from Florence on October 4 that he would be back in a week. When he did not return, Marietta began sending to the Chancery for news of her husband. She felt both resentful and hurt at being abandoned in this fashion; she missed him deeply and was at the same time concerned about him. Too angry to write directly to her husband, she began writing to Biagio and his colleagues, who passed on the news in their letters to Machiavelli. Typical is Biagio's letter of October 18:

Madonna Marietta sent me a letter by way of her brother in which she asked when you will be back. She says she won't write to you, and she is making a great song and dance about it all. She's angry because you promised her you wouldn't be away more than 8 days. So in the devil's name, come back. . . .

Initially at least Machiavelli appears to have paid little attention to this matter, and reverted to his usual self, judging from a passage in the letter he received a week or so later from his Chancery assistant and pal Bartolomeo Ruffini:

Your letters to Biagio and the rest of us go down a treat. All the jokes and witticisms you make in them have us falling about with laughter. . . . All's well with your lady wife. She often sends messages to us here, asking for news about you and when you're coming back.

Despite such reassurances, as the days turned into weeks with still no sign of her husband returning, Marietta became increasingly agitated. While Machiavelli was being forced to spend what little money he had, just to maintain appearances and his upkeep at Borgia's court, Marietta seems to have had even less money to support herself and her infant daughter at home. Machiavelli had not yet even managed to pay her the dowry she was owed according to the wedding contract; she was relying upon her family for everyday support, and soon she moved into the house of her brother-in-law so as not to be left penniless and on her own. Stuck across the mountains on the other side of Italy, Machiavelli could do nothing, and in the end his friends too became increasingly annoyed with him over Marietta's constant badgering for news. As Biagio put it:

Madonna Marietta is cursing God at her fate. She claims that she has been robbed of everything—her virtue, her possessions— right down to her last shred of dignity. For your own good, organize for her to receive the rightful dowry she's owed, like any other woman. Or we'll never hear the end of it.

But by now Machiavelli himself was running out of money and begging the Signoria to send him some or allow him to come home. He also appealed directly to the *gonfaloniere*, but as Soderini eventually wrote back to him:

> My very dear Niccolò,
> I am very pleased with the dispatches you have sent us. I will refrain from informing you about the state of your private affairs because I am sure you receive news of this every day and know that all is well. I wish to tell you that you must not leave your post. When the time is right I will bear your plight in mind and recall you. But for the time being stay where you are. If you need anything at all, please let me know.
> Farewell
> Piero Soderini, *gonfaloniere*, from the palace.

No money, no recall: one can only imagine Machiavelli's exasperation at such treatment. As a result, he was now forced to ask his friends to send him cash, as well as cloth so that he could keep up appearances and remain appropriately dressed for a representative of the republic at a foreign court. Far from feeling sorry for his friend, Biagio had by now lost all patience with him—although he did manage to send Machiavelli money, at the same time telling him what he could do with it: "Shove it up your arse, because we're sending you money and cloth and what you asked for, even though Madonna Marietta is desperate. . . . The *gonfaloniere* told me again this evening that he will be recalling you soon."

Significantly, the "what you asked for" mentioned by Biagio included a copy of Plutarch's *Lives*, the classical work of biography that compares great men of ancient Greece with similar figures of ancient Rome. Machiavelli's classical education had instilled in him a high regard for ancient Rome, when Italy was great and united under a forceful leader— a Caesar, no less. And here he was, with Cesare Borgia, whose motto "Caesar or nothing" harked back to Rome's greatness. Ideas were beginning to crystallize in Machiavelli's mind. Partly through wish-fulfilment, partly through classical exemplar, partly through the decisive behavior of the man he saw before him at Imola, Machiavelli was beginning to make comparisons between Borgia and his great Italian predecessors. He was beginning to see in Borgia the one contemporary who might finally unite Italy, rid it of its foreign oppressors, and make it great once more.

13

Borgia Negotiates

DESPITE ALL MACHIAVELLI's distractions, during these difficult months he continued doing his best to discover what Borgia was up to, attempting to analyze precisely how he was dealing with the difficult situation. On October 23, 1502, Machiavelli succeeded in gaining a long audience with Borgia, during which Borgia continued to wax indignant about the treachery of the Orsini clan, who were still putting out feelers concerning a reconciliation. As he put it to Machiavelli:

> Now they are playing the part of friends, and write me kind letters. . . . Today Signor Paolo [Orsini] is to come to see me, tomorrow the Cardinal [Giambattista Orsini], and thus they think to bamboozle me at their pleasure. But I, on the other hand, am only dallying with them, I listen to everything and I take my own time.

As Borgia rightly surmised, the conspirators were in increasing disarray. Vitellozzo was incapable of taking to the field on account of his syphilis, and the Duke of Urbino was confined to his couch by a severe flare-up of congenital gout. Paolo Orsini had long been noted for his fickleness and vanity, and by now his weakness was plain for all to see—even amongst his own soldiers he had become known as "Madonna Paolo." He continued to act as go-between, ineptly disguising himself as a mere messenger as he scurried between Borgia and his fellow conspirators.

The Orsini were by this stage mainly concerned with protecting their own family territories, which remained as vulnerable as ever to Borgia's expansionist plans for the Romagna and Alexander VI's policy in Rome.

Machiavelli watched the comings and goings at Borgia's court, but was at a loss to discover what precisely was happening, reporting in his October 27 dispatch back to Florence: "It is impossible to discern what the Duke has in mind. . . . I cannot see how he can pardon such treachery, nor how the Orsini can lay to rest their fears over what he will do to them." Yet early in November news began to leak out that Borgia had signed an agreement with the Orsini. By November 10 Machiavelli had secretly managed to get hold of a copy of this agreement and immediately relayed its contents back to Florence. Borgia had sworn a pact with the Orsini and Vitellozzo, in which they agreed to defend each other against attack. The Orsini and Vitellozzo agreed to revert to their former alliance with the papal forces under Borgia's command. For his part, Borgia promised to continue his payments to the Orsini and Vitellozzo for their military services, and he also sought to allay any lingering fears they might have:

> None of them would be required to report to him in person any more than they wished. On the other hand, they promised to restore to him the dukedom of Urbino, Camerino, and any other territory which they had recently occupied. They also agreed to aid him in all his campaigns, and not to engage in any war or take up other military employment without his permission.

Upon hearing that he had been betrayed by his friends, the hapless Duke Guidobaldo of Urbino fled his capital in great anguish and fear for his life. Hearing that Borgia's men had been sent to look for him, he tried to escape in disguise on a mule, but only managed to reach Castel Durante (modern Urbania) some seven miles down the road before suffering a nervous collapse. Fortunately he was taken in by some loyal subjects and managed to evade Borgia's clutches for the time being.

As part of the new agreement with the Orsini, Alexander VI let it be known that Cardinal Orsini was free to return to Rome. The pope also graciously intimated that there was no compulsion whatsoever in this friendly offer. The cardinal cautiously decided to accept: much of his wealth, possessions, and financial assets remained at his palazzo and bank in Rome.

Following the agreement, Vitellozzo wrote a conciliatory letter to Borgia, expressing how delighted he was that they were once again friends. Yet all was not quite as it seemed. On November 24 Machiavelli conveyed to Florence the ominous reaction of Borgia's secretary Agapito to Vitellozzo's letter: "He stabbed us in the back, and thinks he can heal such a wound with mere words."

Bentivolgio of Bologna, who had not been part of this agreement, sent a similarly ingratiating letter to Borgia, who negotiated a separate, forgiving agreement with the lord of this strategically placed city, which guarded the northern approaches to the Romagna. To cement the agreement, Bentivoglio undertook to provide for Borgia, for the coming year, 200 men-at-arms and 200 light cavalry; for his part, Borgia promised to provide half such a force to defend the city of Bologna at any time necessary during the next eight years, on payment of 12,000 ducats a year. This treaty was to be guaranteed by the pope, the King of France, the Signoria of Florence, and Cardinal Orsini. As Machiavelli would observe, this agreement was much more generous than the abject surrender that Borgia had imposed upon Bologna the previous year. Yet Machiavelli recognized the truth of the situation: despite Louis XII's assurances to Borgia that Bologna was no longer under his protection, the French king would probably not have allowed Borgia to keep the city if he had taken it—owing to its strategic defensive position with regard to Milan, Lombardy, and other northern Italian territory that the French now occupied. By means of this new generous treaty with Bentivoglio, Borgia had not only provided himself with cash and extra forces, but had also skillfully cemented his friendship with Louis XII; at the same time he reassured Florence, treating the republic as if it were already his ally, and simultaneously reinstated Cardinal Orsini as one of the leading powers of the Church. (Even so, Orsini, who had now returned to Rome, is said to have remonstrated loudly with the Bolognese ambassador in the presence of the pope, denouncing his disloyalty for making a separate agreement with Borgia.)

In another skillful move, Borgia now dealt with Guidolbaldo of Urbino. Friendless and homeless, Guidobaldo had sent word to Florence, Venice, and Sinigallia in the hope that one of them might grant him asylum. Florence and Venice had regretfully turned down his request. Guidobaldo was an intelligent, cultured, and popular young man, but the risk of antagonizing Borgia was too great.* The small town of Sinigallia, on the coastal strip of territory that still remained independent of Borgia, sent an even quicker reply refusing Guidobaldo. Then, in a surprising move, he was offered asylum by Vitellozzo, though it quickly became clear that this was under secret instructions from Borgia himself. The price of asylum was an agreement that Guidobaldo would quit his hiding place in Urbino territory and travel at once to the Vitellozzo domain of Città di Castello. Guidobaldo had no alternative but to submit to Borgia's wishes. However, despite his forlorn farewell to Urbino, and his advice to his citizens to bow to the inevitable, several castles in Urbino territory (including San Leo) remained loyal to him.

Borgia understood that the citizens of Urbino retained an affection for Guidobaldo, and now set about a charm offensive to win them over to his cause. His first move was to dispatch as his representative Antonio di Sansavino, whose efficient and understanding rule as *presidente* of the Romagna had made the population increasingly favorable to Borgia. The permanent institutions of government were already being set in place: an indication of Borgia's intention to establish a permanent and law-abiding dukedom in the previously lawless Romagna. Even so, Borgia knew that the people remained wary of him, fearing that all this might be just a façade, and that he was liable at any time to revert to the previous vicious tyranny of his Spanish commander Lorqua and his brutal Spanish deputies.

---

* The superb portrait by the Venetian artist Jacopo de' Barbari of the mathematician Luca Pacioli demonstrating his geometrical apparatus also depicts a fashionably dressed young man with frizzy shoulder-length auburn hair standing at his side, in the manner of a pupil. This is widely thought to be a portrait of Guidobaldo.

On December 6 Paolo Orsini accompanied Sansavino through the city gates and into the palace at Urbino, from which two proclamations were then issued in Borgia's name. The first of these granted a pardon to all the citizens of Urbino who during recent events had defied the authority of the Duke of the Romagna. The second guaranteed the civil rights of the people of Urbino, which were not to be transgressed by any of Borgia's soldiers occupying the city, on pain of death to any offender. These proclamations were backed by an edict, purportedly from Guidobaldo in exile at Vitellozzo's lordship of Città di Castello, in which the former Duke of Urbino formally surrendered his city to Borgia. Sansavino then set about establishing a provincial administration, making sure to adhere as closely as possible to local custom, and to listen to the advice given to him by leading citizens, at the same time ensuring that he conformed, as humanely as possible, to Borgia's wishes. As the contemporary Romagna chronicler Andrea Bernardi remarked admiringly of Sansavino: "Rarely, if ever, has the Italian temperament produced the like of such a man."

Despite such benevolence on Borgia's behalf, Machiavelli could not help sensing that all was not well with him: there was a distinct sense of unease about the court. In fact, Machiavelli was becoming increasingly dissatisfied with his role at Imola. The stress of continuing to try to discover Borgia's every move, combined with the pressure from his friends over Marietta back in Florence, may well have contributed to the bout of fever to which he now succumbed. But still Gonfaloniere Soderini refused to allow him to return home. Physical conditions at Imola had been deteriorating for some time. As early as mid-November, Machiavelli had reported:

> All the cities in this region of the Romagna are short of victuals and supplies, and when the next expected batch of foreign soldiers arrives things are liable to get worse, unless this Lord [Borgia] manages to secure supplies from elsewhere. I inform your lordships [that is, the Signoria] of this development so that you can take precautions against any cross-border raids into Florentine territory.

On top of this, the mild autumn weather of October had long since given way to the mud and cold rains of November in the Romagna. Now the weather had taken a further seasonal turn, and each morning the fields and wayside woods beyond the city walls were white with the first heavy frosts of winter.

Yet it was more than just the physical conditions that were deteriorating. Machiavelli's dispatches for late November and early December began to speak of Borgia's "evil moods," and the "sinister" remarks he had begun to let drop about the former conspirators, with whom he was now supposed to be reconciled. Borgia's attitude towards Machiavelli too had changed for the worse. He no longer took the Florentine envoy into his confidence, boasting in his presence of how confident he felt. Instead he avoided all company, Machiavelli's included. On November 22, Machiavelli reported back to Florence:

I have made no attempt to see the Duke, because I have nothing new to report to him, and he quickly becomes irritated by stale news. As I have already informed you, nobody speaks with him except three or four of his ministers and some foreigners, all of whom only report to him on matters of importance. Now-adays he does not leave his antechamber until around eleven or twelve o'clock at night, sometimes even later. Consequently it is impossible to see him without having been granted an audience by appointment. And when he is informed that a man has nothing but words to bring him, he refuses to speak to him.

Machiavelli was beginning to despair: his mission seemed to be serving no purpose whatsoever, and he was wasting both his own money and that which the Signoria had begrudgingly begun sending him. On December 6 he begged the Signoria to recall him "so as to relieve the government of their expense and me of all this painful waste of time, since for the last twelve days I have been feeling very ill, and if I go on like this I shall only return home in my coffin."

Machiavelli *was* ill, and certainly did not have enough money to hire a servant to look after him. Such assistance would have been in short supply in Imola, where many of the inhabitants would have been pressed into attendance on the army, or put to work for Borgia. We can only speculate, but there is a strong possibility that during Machiavelli's illness Leonardo would have looked after him. As fellow Florentines in a foreign court amidst foreign soldiers, they would surely have been drawn together, and as fellow intellectuals they would have been a rarity at Imola. Borgia would have been one of the few others to have shared such interests. We know that Borgia was drawn to Machiavelli by his intellect, but what they discussed were largely political matters of the moment. We can only wonder about Borgia's conversations with Leonardo, as the artist sat sketching him. Likewise we can only imagine what Machiavelli and Leonardo might have talked about as they sat together on rickety chairs of an autumn evening before a fire in some drafty corner of Borgia's court, dining off scraps and nuts, washed down with watered wine. As winter came on, they would have wrapped themselves in their cloaks against the whining wind that rattled the windows and penetrated the corridors of Borgia's palazzo residence, much as it does today.

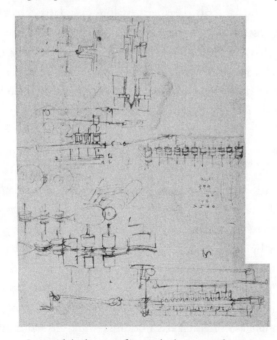

Leonardo's drawing for a calculating machine.

Amongst Leonardo's many tasks, he had been set to work by Borgia to design improvements for the fortress of Imola, whose massive walls had been completed just two decades earlier by the formidable Caterina Sforza. These walls and the wide surrounding moat had proved insufficient to keep out Borgia himself just three years previously on his first Romagna campaign. In Leonardo's notebooks of autumn 1502 there are some vague sketches relating to fortifications, and notes about making fortress walls curved wherever possible to reduce the impact of cannonballs: "Percussion is less strong the more oblique it is." It may well be that this was the occasion when he reminded himself: "Be sure that the escape tunnel does not lead to the keep ... lest the fortress be captured by treachery, as ... at Fossombrone." He would certainly have used his hodometer in the course of this work, and during the evenings there is a possibility that he began thinking about extending the use of this ingenious mechanical measuring device, whose interlocking vertical and horizontal cogged wheels notched up the distances. These wheels could justly be described as an analog calculating machine, which could—at a stretch—be seen as a primitive early computer. This would not have been the first time that Leonardo had turned his mind to constructing a calculating device. We now know of some extraordinary drawings that he made in Milan at around the same time as he drew his first three hodometer designs.

For almost 500 years these drawings were lost, until in February 1967 they were accidentally discovered by American researchers working in the National Gallery of Madrid. These hitherto unknown sheets from Leonardo's notebooks are now known as the *Codex Madrid*. They contain a drawing of thirteen interconnected cogged wheels, each of which has digits registering the numbers one to nine. The machine could be operated by a handle, and as the first wheel passed beyond nine, it registered the first digit on the next wheel through tens, hundreds, thousands, and so on. This machine would thus have been capable of adding and possibly, with a few simple modifications, of subtracting. The mechanisms of Leonardo's hodometer and his calculating machine are distinctly similar, and whilst constructing his hodometer he may well have seen how to overcome the difficulties inherent in his drawing of a calculating machine.*

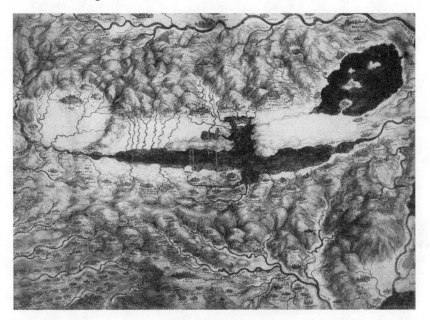

Map of Val di Chiana.

We know that during this period in Imola, Leonardo also drew a number of maps, quite apart from his beautiful and exact town plan of Imola. At least one of these maps related to his travels during his previous months working for Borgia—this is a colored map of the Val di Chiana, which is aligned with north to the left. The distances relating to the central features of the map were probably taken down during July, when he traveled through Arezzo on his long, sweeping journey to report to Borgia at Urbino. The distances from Arezzo to the river are a fair approximation to reality, while other distances in the outer regions are much less exact and appear to be a deliberate

---

* Leonardo's drawing of a calculating machine was seen in 1968 by Dr. Roberto Guatelli, who noticed its resemblance to a drawing in the *Codex Atlanticus*. Putting these two drawings together, he managed to construct what he claimed to be Leonardo's adding machine, which was found to work. This was exhibited, until it too was lost, and is now thought to be somewhere in the IBM archives.

foreshortening. In the bottom right-hand corner (that is, southwest) the map even shows a small section of the sea along the west coast of Italy, thus enabling the position of the region to be "placed" in Italy as a whole.

The names on this map are not in Leonardo's usual mirror-writing, but in easily legible script. Traces of sealing wax found on the back of this map indicate that it was at some stage fixed to a wall or board, possibly for presentation at a meeting or council of war. Leonardo almost certainly made it for Borgia, which raises some interesting questions. Why was Leonardo asked to make a map of this particular region? Was it intended for use as a campaign map? If so, it looks as if Borgia may at one stage seriously have thought of launching an attack on Vitellozzo and Baglioni while they were occupying the Val di Chiana against his orders, just as he threatened. This plan could well have been abandoned because Borgia had insufficient military forces at his disposal, since the promised French troops from Louis XII did not arrive in time. Such a bold surprise move would have made sense for a number of reasons. At a stroke, Borgia could have eliminated two of the most power-ful conspirators, before they even knew that he had discovered their plot. By liberating the Val di Chiana he would have demonstrated that he was Florence's ally, thus facilitating the agreement with Florence that he so desired. On the other hand, if he had lingered on in the Val di Chiana, this might also have cowed Florence into an agreement with him. Such an unexpected strike could only have been to Borgia's advantage and would have been typical of his strategic thinking.

Interestingly, Leonardo's map also has relevance to a scheme for the diversion of the Arno, which Leonardo and Machiavelli would later attempt. During their period together in Imola, Leonardo may well have shown this map to Machiavelli, sowing the seeds of this very idea. As we have seen, Leonardo had already worked out a project for diverting the Arno into a navigable canal, thus giving Florence direct access to the sea. As part of this project he had suggested damming the upper waters of the Arno, writing in his notebook: "Sluices should be constructed in the Val di Chiana at Arezzo, so that when the Arno lacks water during the summer months the canal will not run dry." These sluices were probably intended to turn the marshy Lago di Chiana into an actual lake (or reservoir), much as it appears on Leonardo's map.

Machiavelli would certainly have been intrigued by such an imaginative scheme, which would at a stroke have transformed the geography of Tuscany as well as the fortunes of Florence, and he may well have questioned Leonardo about the details, in order to assess its plausibility. Yet for the time being Machiavelli's most pressing concern remained gathering information about Borgia from the man he referred to in his dispatches as his "friend." Leonardo may have been ideally placed for providing such information, but we should not jump to any conclusions here. Even if only to cover his tracks, Machiavelli's "friend" is likely to have included a compendium of other sources, not least Machiavelli himself. Years later he would advise a young ambassador who was setting out on a mission for Florence:

> examine and consider the consequences of all you can, and give your judgment on it as you write about it. Yet because putting your own judgment into your own mouth would be offensive, try using in your letters the following method. Tell them what is happening, and who is involved, and what their intentions are, then write: "With regards to what I have written, prudent men here who know about these things say that the outcome will be such and such."

Examples of this method are not difficult to spot in Machiavelli's dispatches from Imola to the Signoria. As, for instance, when he writes: "I think I should tell you about a conversation that I had a few days ago with that friend I wrote to you about, who said to me: . . ." And here he writes at considerable length his detailed and expert assessment of the situation, retailing his own opinions as "the words of this friend."

Machiavelli's understanding of the devious ways of the world, and his active participation in these ways, was beginning to deepen. This was a formative period, one that would mold his entire philosophy and later outlook on life. In the words of his great biographer Pasquale Villari, Machiavelli now invested in the drama unfolding before his eyes all the ardor of one seeking for truth in a scientific spirit and method. At times he seemed to be an anatomist dissecting a corpse, and feeling sure of discovering in it the germ of an unknown disease. He had an unequaled gift of faithful and graphic narrative, and his style attains to a vigor and origin-ality. . . . In these letters we see Machiavelli's political doctrines grow into shape under our eyes, we note his rigorness [*sic*] of method, and also find the greatest eloquence of which he was capable.

It is surely no accident that Machiavelli was beginning to apply to politics the very method that made Leonardo into one of the first genuine scientists of the modern age. As Leonardo put it in his notebook:

My intention is first to consult experience before I proceed any further, and then by means of reasoning to show why such experience is bound to operate in such a way.

For this is the true rule by which anyone who wishes to analyze the effects of nature must proceed; for although nature begins with the cause and ends with the experience, we must follow the opposite course, namely (as I have said before) to begin with the experience and by means of it investigate the cause.

Yet in the midst of all this formative experience, Machiavelli was ill and in despair, begging the Signoria to recall him to Florence:

Besides realizing that I can be of no possible use to you here, I am reduced to a terrible physical state by a bout of heavy fever . . . from which I have not yet recovered. At the same time, this is no way for me to look after my domestic problems in Florence, so that I am losing out on all fronts.

As if this were not bad enough, he was also running out of money and unable to find messengers willing to takes his dispatches to Florence:

I offered a reward of two ducats, but no one was willing to take my dispatch because of the extremely bad turn of the weather. For the last four days it has snowed without cease and because of this no one is willing to try and cross the passes over the Apennines.

Then suddenly on December 10, in the midst of a snowstorm, Borgia and his troops began moving out of Imola. Accompanying him were his Spanish troops and his artillery, as well the contingent of men recruited from the Romagna, and the Swiss and Gascon troops he had been sent by Louis XII. In all, Borgia now had under his command throughout the Romagna as many as 12,000 men. These consisted of 3,000 French heavy cavalry, 2,000 light cavalry, and some 7,000 infantrymen. His ordnance consisted of twenty cannons, ranging from the powerful French-caliber cannons to smaller, more maneuverable artillery. Machiavelli could only watch as Borgia and his men disappeared into the flurrying snow, heading southeast down the Via Emilia in the direction of Cesena, leaving behind the famished city of Imola, where—according to Machiavelli—Borgia's troops had by now "devoured everything down to the very stones."

14

A Definitive Move

MACHIAVELLI WAS AT a loss. Was Borgia moving his large force in order to join up with the army of Louis XII on its much-predicted march down Italy to reassert French claims in Naples? Or was he intending to drive along the coast towards Sinigallia and Ancona, occupying the last unconquered territory of the Romagna-Marches? Or was he possibly planning a surprise move against Venice? If previous form was anything to judge by, there was no telling what Borgia might do.

Machiavelli was not the only one at a loss. In Rome, Alexander VI was becoming increasingly agitated by his son's behavior. Evidently, none of Borgia's movements were in accord with the secret strategy they had agreed upon at Camerino in September. Alexander VI was particularly keen to retain Venice as an ally, both to safeguard against any moves on Borgia's new dukedom and for the protection of the papacy. Consequently, he made a point of cultivating the Venetian ambassador Guistinian, frequently confiding in him views that were not passed on to the rest of his court. As Giustinian wrote in his dispatch to Venice on November 24, 1502, reporting the pope's latest confidence: "Borgia's first move will be against Sinigallia, to prevent it from attempting to aid those remaining loyal to the Duke of Urbino." In reality, this was little more than what the pope hoped would happen. By now Borgia had become completely unpredictable, and Alexander VI could no longer even be sure they were working towards the same goal. The pope had his own assessment of the political situation, which he confided to Giustinian on December 2:

Up till now, the main safety for the Papacy and Venice has been in the jealous rivalry between France and Spain. If they were not distracted by this, Italy would be finished. And don't imagine that Venice will be immune from all this—you would be drawn into it too. The Papacy and Venice are both old, and we must consider our posterity. The only hope for the Papacy is with Venice, which is everlasting. For the love of God, we must unite to secure the salvation of Italy.

According to Giustinian, Alexander VI spoke these words with such feeling that it was "as if they came from his heart rather than his mouth."

On top of all this uncertainty, Borgia's third campaign in the Romagna was proving a huge drain on the papal coffers. Borgia may have ransacked the considerable treasures of Urbino, and supplemented his war chest with other sundry plunder and pillage, but according to Giustinian his campaign was still costing Alexander VI the vast sum of 1,000 ducats a day. This is confirmed by information that Machiavelli managed to glean from Borgia's treasurer, Alessandro Spannocchi: during October and November Borgia had run through more than 60,000 ducats. Borgia then sent to his father for further cash, but according to Giustinian's dispatch of December 17, "the Pope is most unwilling to send him any more money, because it seems to him that he is simply throwing it away. Yet he does not know how to say no to the Duke [Borgia]." The same dispatch mentions how Alexander VI had busied himself all day personally counting out 14,000 ducats to send to his son.

News had by this time reached Rome that Borgia had left Imola, but when Alexander VI heard that he had halted with his troops just two days' march down the road at Cesena, and showed no signs of making any further move, the pope's fears and uncertainties over his son's intentions spilled over. He flew into a rage, shouting: "What the devil is he doing? Why is he staying there? We told him to move on at once." For Sinigallia—or so the pope hoped. According to Giustinian, the pope in his anguish began screeching in Spanish, repeatedly calling his son "Bastard son of a whore!"

Alexander VI was now almost seventy-two years old, but remained as vigorous as ever. In order to distract himself from his worries he threw himself with gusto into his "customary diversions," frequently staying up all night feasting and being entertained by courtesans, for "without them there was no feast worth having." The sun would often be up before he retired. His days too were often occupied with similarly degenerate spectacles. Alexander VI's master of ceremonies, Johannes Burchard, described how on Christmas Day, of all days:

> After dinner thirty actors took part in a masquerade in the piazza before St. Peter's. Many of them were wearing long large noses in the form of penises, all virile and erect. . . . The Pope watched from a window.

Alexander VI's reinstated friend Cardinal Orsini was a regular companion at the banquets and entertainments that took place during this period, and often joined in gambling with Alexander, both of them staking hundreds of ducats on the throw of dice or the turn of a card. However, despite their "friendship," it is difficult to see how Cardinal Orsini and Alexander VI had so quickly become reconciled, especially in the light of the long-standing distrust between the Borgia family and the Orsini clan, with its recent escalation into open antagonizm. Less than three months previously Cardinal Orsini had been conniving with his fellow conspirators at La Magione to murder Cesare, whilst Alexander VI had been raging in Rome for the cardinal's blood. And now they appeared to be utterly reconciled. According to Burchard, Alexander VI "had told the Cardinal that he would resign the papacy in his favor, on condition that he undertook to protect and defend the Duke [Borgia]." Although Alexander VI was aging, it is impossible to believe that he seriously considered stepping down from the papacy at this time, and equally impossible to believe that he contemplated handing over this office to Cardinal Orsini. Likewise, it is hardly likely that Orsini would have believed a word of this offer. Both of them were notorious for their treachery, and neither was known for his gullibility. The only explanation for Cardinal Orsini going along with Alexander VI's unlikely offer was that he had in mind some treacherous scheme of his own, which might in turn have brought about the same object—namely, his taking over the papacy, though certainly not acting as Cesare Borgia's defender afterwards. Borgia's dukedom would have been seen as the spoils of such a coup. So it seems likely that neither Alexander VI nor Cardinal Orsini trusted each other an inch, yet for the time being it suited their purposes to keep a close eye on each other. The cardinal observed carefully when the pope gave vent to public displays of anger and bewilderment at the behavior of his son. The pope's frustration seemed genuine enough, and Cardinal Orsini remained perplexed: he too was just as keen to know what Cesare Borgia was up to in the Romagna.

On December 12 Cesare Borgia and his large contingent reached Cesena. Here he took up residence at the capital of his Romagna dukedom. However, this showed all the signs of being a temporary visit. Borgia ordered his 12,000 men to remain camped outside the city walls, with the French contingent establishing themselves alongside the Via Emilia on the way to Rimini. Soldiers were ordered not to molest any of the inhabitants on pain of severe reprisal: the civic rights of the citizens in the new dukedom of the Romagna were now sacrosanct. Such respect had certainly been appreciated by the citizens of Imola, who had grown used to the just administration of Sansavino. Nonetheless, a lingering suspicion of Borgia remained: the citizens retained the grimmest memories of the time less than two years previously when Lorqua had been left in command, along with his ruthless Spanish soldiers, who had terrorized the region.

Machiavelli caught up with Borgia on December 14, possibly traveling to Cesena with Leonardo and other noncombatant members of the duke's court. Here he gradually recovered from his illness, at the same time continuing to do his best to glean any scraps of information about Borgia's intentions. But no one seemed to know what was going on.

Then suddenly, late on December 20, Machiavelli witnessed a wholly unexpected development, which he reported to the Signoria in a dispatch hurriedly written at ten o'clock that night: "When I was at court this evening, the French officers unexpectedly arrived in a body to see the Duke. . . . Whilst they were waiting in the antechamber they began talking amongst themselves, and I could see from their gestures and manner that they were angry." Evidently something important was afoot. After the French officers left their meeting with Borgia, Machiavelli went to call on the Baron de Bierra, one of the French officers whose friendship he had cultivated during the previous weeks. De Bierra told Machiavelli: "In two days we will be leaving here and will return to the duchy of Milan. Those are the orders we have just received." As Machiavelli continued in his dispatch: "This event came completely out of the blue and the entire court is turned upside down. . . . No one really knows what is happening and everyone has a different explanation."

The most likely explanation seemed to be that Louis XII was summoning his heavy cavalry in preparation for the march on Naples. But next morning during Machiavelli's conversations with his confidants amongst Borgia's entourage, a different story began to emerge. It appeared that Borgia himself had ordered the French cavalry back to Milan. As Machiavelli later reported: "The Duke no longer has sufficient funds to pay the French." But it soon emerged that this was not the sole reason for the French withdrawal. The French commanders had taken to following their own initiative, and were at times barely under Borgia's control; it appeared that Borgia considered these men no longer necessary for whatever it was he had in mind.

On December 22 the French contingent of 450 lances (consisting of more than 3,000 crack troops) left Cesena for the long march north to Milan. Whatever the explanation for their withdrawal, it was plain for all to see that Borgia had lost his toughest troops, which made up the main battle force of his army. News of Borgia's sudden weakness spread far and wide, soon reaching the camps of the former conspirators Vitellozzo and the Orsini brothers. In Rome, Alexander VI was plainly becoming frightened, though Cardinal Orsini appeared less concerned; meanwhile Giustinian reported back to Venice: "The suspicions that the Duke can do anything of great moment have ceased."

Despite this serious weakening of Borgia's forces, the ever-watchful Machiavelli noted (and reported to the Signoria) that 600 newly recruited Romagna infantrymen had recently arrived at Cesena from their training ground in the rugged hills of the Val di Lamone some forty miles to the west, and that 1,000 Swiss infantry were reportedly just over a day's march away at Faenza. Even so, Machiavelli wrote: "It is said that the Duke is due to march south in the direction of Pesaro. On the other hand, he is now down to less than half his forces and two-thirds of his reputation." Yet whatever was to be made of all these comings and goings, the least concerned person appeared to be Borgia himself.

On the very night that the French troops departed from Cesena, Borgia attended a ball thrown for him by five of the leading citizens of his capital city. This event was recorded by a local chronicler who remarked that Borgia appeared in the best of spirits, frequently dancing with a local beauty called Cleofe Marescotti "with whom he was greatly taken, and it seems that his feelings were returned." The fact that Cleofe was married to one of his hosts does not seem to have concerned him, or her.

Yet beneath this glittering occasion, events were taking a dark turn. Borgia had summoned his fearsome military commander Ramiro de Lorqua from Pesaro, and Lorqua had arrived that very evening. On Borgia's orders, he was seized and flung into a dungeon in the castle. This came as a shock to everybody: Lorqua was one of Borgia's oldest and most trusted friends. The stocky fifty-year-old Spaniard had been a familiar sight around Borgia since his university days—a dark-bearded, silent figure, who habitually adopted a scornful, arrogant pose with his hand stuck in his belt.

There is evidence that during the next three days Lorqua was interrogated and tortured, for it later became clear that he had revealed some surprising information to Borgia. Lorqua had secretly been in league with Liverotto da Fermo, when the latter had conspired against Borgia, along with Vitellozzo, the Orsini brothers, and others.

At first light on the morning of December 25, Lorqua was discovered in the main square of Cesena beneath the walls of the castle, wrapped in his finest brocade cloak, his kid-gloved hands at his side. His body was decapitated, his head stuck on a lance. Beside him was the blood-spattered wooden execution block and blade. As Machiavelli hurriedly reported to the Signoria in Florence:

This morning Lorqua was discovered with his body cut in two on the piazza where he still lies, and all the people have been able to see him. No one is sure of the reason for his death, except that it so pleased the Duke, who by so doing demonstrated that he can make and unmake men as he wishes, according to their deserts.*

Years later, Machiavelli would state the reason for Lorqua's demise:

Because Borgia knew that the severities of his past rule had made many people hate him, he was determined to purge these people's minds and win them over entirely to his cause by showing that any cruelty which had taken place was none of his doing, but had come about entirely through the brutal nature of the man he had left in command.

Machiavelli concluded that Borgia's policy had been successful: "The ferocity of this spectacle caused these people at the time to be gratified and awe-struck."

Machiavelli's suggested reason for Lorqua's death fits well with the political philosophy that was developing in his mind during his time in the Romagna. He was beginning to see Borgia's amoral and pragmatic methods as the paradigm of how to achieve and hold on to power. The discovery of Lorqua's treachery with Vitellozzo and the others would seem to have been a further contributory motive for Borgia's action. Yet there was also a third, more secret factor contributing to Lorqua's gruesome end, and on a deeper psychological level this may have been the most compelling of all. Just eleven months previously Lorqua had been placed in charge of the military escort accompanying Lucrezia Borgia on her journey from Rome to her new home in Bologna, where her new husband was waiting for her. Apparently sometime during the course of this journey there occurred an incident "affecting the honor of Madonna Lucrezia," for which Lorqua was responsible. What precisely took place is unclear, but a number of contemporary chroniclers picked up rumors of this incident and claimed that it was the true reason for Lorqua's brutal execution. Knowing Cesare's behavior towards anyone

* Some have suggested that Lorqua's body being "cut in two" meant that it was severed laterally, as if prior to quartering, and that the block and blade laid out beside him would have been seen as indication that he was a traitor.

sexually involved with Lucrezia, even in wedlock, any rumor of this sort concerning Lorqua would certainly have placed him in danger from her brother and his jealous regard for her "honor."

Despite Machiavelli's continuing pleas to be relieved of his post, the Signoria insisted this was impossible: in the present political situation it was imperative for Florence to have an envoy at Borgia's court, and he was the best person to fulfill this task. By way of encouragement, Machiavelli now received another letter from Gonfaloniere Soderini himself, accompanied by twenty-five ducats to cover his expenses, and sixteen *bracchia* (around ten yards) of finest Florentine black damask for use as diplomatic gifts in the course of his duties. At the same time, he still received the occasional witty notes from his friends. Along with the letter from Soderini and the fine black cloth, there was a letter from Machiavelli's old pal Buonaccorsi, signing himself "Brother Biagio" and joshing him: "If I know you, you'll end up filching a doublet for yourself out of this cloth, you nasty rascal."

Although Machiavelli's dispatches detailed all the facts he could discover concerning the recent sensational events, the Signoria persisted in demanding that he provide them with even more information. They wanted Machiavelli to try to discover all he could about what Borgia was thinking, his future intentions, when and where he might make his next move, and so on. Exasperatedly, Machiavelli wrote on December 26, explaining to them that Borgia was:

> a highly secretive man, and I am convinced that no one but he alone knows what his next move will be. His chief secretaries have told me that he only reveals something when he orders it to be done. He does not do anything unless he is forced to do it, and only then does he act, never otherwise. This is why I can send your lordships no further information at present.

At around this time the former conspirators Vitellozzo and the Orsini brothers sent an offer to Borgia from where they were encamped to the south in Urbino territory. According to Machiavelli's later description:

Liverotto da Fermo was sent to deliver the offer, which suggested to Borgia that if he wished to launch a campaign into Tuscany, they were ready to join him. If not, they would besiege Sinigallia. The Duke replied that he would not begin a war in Tuscany because the Florentines were his friends, but he would be very pleased if they marched against Sinigallia.

As if in confirmation of Machiavelli's dispatch on December 26, warning of Borgia's unpredictability, later that very day he suddenly moved out of Cesena, proceeding southeast down the Via Emilia. Yet this time he did not even take his remaining troops with him. Instead, he was accompanied only by his personal corps of men-at-arms. The main body of his forces had been ordered to fan out into the country-side and proceed south in small detachments. To any passing observer, it would now have appeared as if Borgia remained in command only of a sorely depleted force.

Just eight miles south of Cesena, Borgia crossed a small river called the Rubicone. As Latin scholars, Borgia and Machiavelli would both have been mindful of the symbolism of this event: 1,500 years previously Julius Caesar had crossed the Rubicone, thus committing himself irrevocably to march on Rome and install himself as ruler of the Roman world. Both Borgia and Machiavelli, in their own very different ways, must have understood that momentous events were now taking place, and there was no going back for Borgia, no matter what it was that he had in mind.*

Two days later, on December 28, Borgia reached Pesaro on the coast. Here, according to Machiavelli's later description:

> The Duke received a dispatch that the town of Sinigallia had surrendered to Liverotto da Fermo's forces, but that the castle itself had not consented to surrender, because the castellan

---

* The Rubicone is known to have changed its course since the classical era. The river that Caesar in fact crossed was probably several miles to the north of the present Rubicone.

was bent upon surrendering only to the Duke himself in person, and to no one else. In consequence, the Duke was urged to come to the city as soon as possible.

The small seaside town of Sinigallia was a fiefdom of the della Rovere family, who remained bitter rivals of the Borgias. (It was Cardinal della Rovere who had almost succeeded in blocking Cardinal Rodrigo Borgia's ascension to the papacy as Alexander VI.) The present ruler of Sinigallia was nominally the twelve-year-old Francesco della Rovere, whose mother was the sister of Guidobaldo of Urbino, and thus no friend of the Borgias. Francesco della Rovere was under the protection of the Genoese *condottiere* Andrea Dorea, who in fact ruled Sinigallia in Francesco's name during this period.* As soon as it had become evident that Sinigallia was in danger, Dorea had sent Francesco to safety with his mother, who had traveled across the mountains on a donkey disguised as a monk. Although Sinigallia had fallen, Dorea had continued to hold out against Liverotto da Fermo's troops and remained in the fortress; he was the "castellan" who refused to surrender the keys to his castle, except to Borgia in person.

On December 29, a day after leaving Pesaro on his way to Sinigallia, Borgia reached Fano. Next day he sent word to his commanders at Sinigallia. These included Vitellozzo and the Orsini brothers, as well as Liverotto da Fermo, but not Baglioni, who despite the rapprochement with Borgia had remained suspicious of his intentions and had returned to Perugia. Borgia informed his commanders that he would join them at Sinigallia the next day, December 31. Prior to this, all troops apart from Liverotto's garrison were to be withdrawn from the town, leaving room for Borgia's forces to be garrisoned there. At the same time, all the gates were to be locked, except the southern gate through which Borgia would lead his troops. Vitellozzo and the others were to move their troops down the coast and into the hills, in preparation for a march south to take Ancona.

---

* Andrea Dorea would later achieve historical renown as a naval commander who fought against the Ottoman navy and Barbary pirates. The Italian liner that sank off Nantucket in 1956 was named after him.

According to Machiavelli: "That same day Borgia also ordered all his scattered contingents, who amounted to more than 2,000 cavalry and 10,000 infantry, to report at daybreak next morning at the Metauro River, five miles south of Fano." That evening Borgia held a meeting with his ever-loyal Don Michele and seven of his other Spanish, Swiss, Gascon, and Italian commanders, issuing them with secret instructions. But that very evening an ebullient Borgia could not refrain from hinting at his intentions to Machiavelli, who seemingly did not grasp the full import of what he was being told.

Back in Rome, Alexander VI had been moody and depressed over Christmas, apparently preoccupied by his worries over what his son was up to—though he had given away little of what he was thinking to the ambassadors who now thronged the papal court. Word had earlier reached Rome from the Romagna that Borgia was joining forces with Liverotto da Fermo and his other commanders, causing alarm throughout central Italy. Was Borgia planning to march on Florence? Or Siena? Or perhaps Perugia? Or even to march on Naples with Louis XII? The rumors continued to fly around Rome. Then, on December 30, Alexander VI's mood underwent a transformation: Borgia had evidently at last informed his father of his plans. Alexander VI became more voluble, expressing his intention to set up a fast courier service to Sinigallia in order to keep in close contact with his son; and in his patent relief he joyfully invited his old friend Cardinal Orsini that night to one of the private dinner parties they so enjoyed together.

Although the precise contents of Borgia's message to his father remained a mystery, the next day Alexander VI happily told his court: "We are all awaiting [Borgia's] return for Carnival. No one can celebrate the way he does. He will do a thousand follies and throw away several thousands of ducats."*

---

* Carnival was the lengthy period of feasting and festivities that traditionally preceded the forty-day fast of Lent. Carnival began on December 26 and lasted until Shrove Tuesday (Mardi Gras). Alexander VI's remark thus suggests that he may even have been expecting his son back in Rome as early as the first weeks of January 1503.

15

"An action worthy of a Roman"

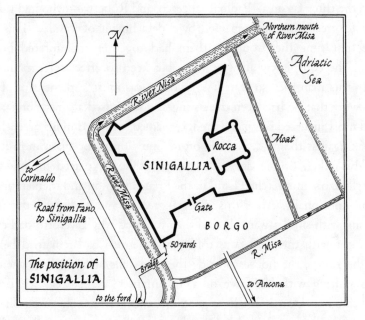

Map of Sinigallia.

IN THE WINTER dawn of December 31, 1502, Cesare Borgia rode out of Fano along the Via Emilia towards Sinigallia, which was just fifteen miles down the coast. Preceding him marched the Swiss contingent, their polished breastplates and pikes glinting in the pale early sunlight, and behind them came the cavalry. Although Borgia was not riding into battle, more than one observer noted that he was fully armed, as well as wearing chain-mail body armor and a breastplate. He was surrounded by his personal bodyguard, all fully armed and clad in their colorful red and yellow livery. Outside town on the banks of the Metauro River, Borgia was joined by the rest of his forces: in total he now had almost 15,000 men.

In the words of Machiavelli, who would ride down this same road just a few hours later: "Riding south towards Sinigallia, the mountains sweep down to your right, with the foothills so close to the shore that there is sometimes only a short distance between them and the sea." A mile or so before Borgia reached Sinigallia, he was met by Vitellozzo and the three Orsini—Paolo, Francesco, and Roberto—who had ridden out to greet him, accompanied by a detachment of cavalry. This was the first time the group of them had together encountered Borgia since the conspiracy; all were wary, but keen to effect a reconciliation with this man they so feared. Vitellozzo was most apprehensive of all, knowing that he had been the strongest voice raised against Borgia, and had most incurred Borgia's hatred. Unarmed, wrapped in his green-lined cloak against the cold, he rode on his mule up to Borgia, cap in hand. To his relief, Borgia descended from his horse, placed his hand on Vitellozzo's outstretched hand in the French fashion and then embraced him emotionally. After this, Borgia greeted and embraced the three Orsini with similar warmth, and then inquired why Liverotto da Fermo was not with them. He was told that Liverotto had remained behind at the Borgo, the houses outside the city walls at Sinigallia, where he was waiting with his force of 1,000 infantry and 150 cavalry. Borgia indicated to Don Michele to ride off and collect him. According to Machiavelli, who was still in Fano, but would later hear Borgia's firsthand description of these events: "Borgia winked knowingly at Don Michele" before he rode off on his errand.

When Liverotto da Fermo had joined them, Borgia and his five reconciled commanders started towards Sinigallia, all relieved at how easily their reconciliation had been effected, now talking amongst themselves as in the old days. It was just after midday when they reached Sinigallia.

At this time Sinigallia was to all intents and purposes an island, with one side bordered by the sea, two sides bordered by a curve of the Misa River on its way to the sea, and the other side bordered by an artificial channel dug from the river to the sea to complete the moat. The Borgo stood before the city walls, within the moat to the south. Borgia's advance guard of heavy cavalry rode across the wooden bridge that led from the Fano road across the moat to the Borgo. Once across the bridge, the cavalry executed a skilled prearranged maneuver, splitting into twin columns that wheeled round to face each other, leaving a guarded passage leading directly to the city gate, through which the main body of Borgia's forces could now pass. This maneuver also effectively sealed off Liverotto da Fermo's men in the Borgo, at the same time severing any means of communication between them and the main body of Vitellozzo's troops camped along the shore and in the foothills to the south.

A thousand Swiss and Gascon infantry then marched across the wooden bridge, between the lines of cavalry, through the city gate and into Sinigallia. Borgia, together with Vitellozzo, Liverotto da Fermo, and the three Orsini followed, with Liverotto's escort and Borgia's personal guard of liveried men-at-arms bringing up the rear. As these passed into the inner walled town, the gates swung closed behind them.

By now Vitellozzo, Liverotto da Fermo, and the Orsini had begun to have their suspicions about the events unfolding around them. Apprehensively they rode alongside Borgia, who led them through the streets to the arched gateway of a palazzo, which (according to several sources) Don Michele had already selected for Borgia as his head-quarters.* Here Vitellozzo and the others attempted to take their leave of Borgia, but he bade them dismount, giving them his word that they were perfectly safe. In a friendly fashion he explained that he wished to confer with them on some urgent business. Feeling that they had no

---

* Don Michele would certainly not have had time to select a house for Borgia's head-quarters whilst on his errand to pick up Liverotto da Fermo. This means that Don Michele must have visited Sinigallia and made contact with Vitellozzo and the others sometime during the previous days. He was presumably also instructed to observe whether Vitellozzo and the others were obeying Borgia's orders about withdrawing their troops from Sinigallia. There can be no doubt that Don Michele did select this house, as its layout was vital to Borgia's plans.

alternative, they dismounted and followed Borgia through the gateway and into the inner courtyard of the palazzo. Here he led them up the main stairway and into the salon, where he sat down with them. According to a contemporary account:

> Having remained a while with them, [Borgia] said that for necessities of nature he must withdraw but would soon return. Hardly had he left the room than there entered the men deputed for the work, who bound their hands behind their backs and took them prisoner.

Several accounts mention Paolo Orsini crying out in a shrill voice, reminding Borgia that he had given his word. But by now Borgia was out in the courtyard, where he mounted his horse and ordered the officer in charge of Liverotto da Fermo's escort to withdraw and join their main force in the Borgo. As the troops made their way through the narrow streets, without warning they were surrounded and cut down by Borgia's men. Borgia then ordered his men to ride out of the gate into the Borgo. Here they were to strip and disarm the rest of Liverotto da Fermo's soldiers, who were by now heavily outnumbered by Borgia's forces, which had continued marching across the wooden bridge over the moat into the Borgo.

Throughout these events the Genoese *condottiere* Andrea Dorea had been standing above Sinigallia on the high ramparts of the *rocca*. Observing what had taken place, he decided it was time to surrender to Borgia. As we shall see, Borgia almost certainly interrogated Dorea after accepting his surrender. Borgia then dispatched his heavy cavalry into the hinterland to disarm the forces of Vitellozzo and the Orsini, which were camped in the hills and along the coast. Unaware of what had taken place, and separated into isolated detachments, they were quickly deceived and offered little or no resistance.

Meanwhile in the streets and alleyways of the Borgo things soon got out of control as Borgia's troops ran amok, plundering and killing anyone they suspected of being sympathetic to Livoretto da Fermo or the della Rovere family. In no time the Borgo was being sacked, amidst scenes of bedlam. Later in the afternoon Borgia himself rode out of the gate in full armor, accompanied by armed cavalry from his personal bodyguard, and began attempting to restrain his men amidst the chaos.

It was at this stage that Machiavelli arrived from Fano. Crossing the bridge into the Borgo, he found himself confronted by the mayhem. Borgia caught sight of him and called him over, triumphantly informing him that he had fulfilled his plan, taking Vitellozzo, Liverotto, and the three Orsini as his prisoners. Interestingly, he then told Machiavelli: "This is what I wanted to tell Bishop Soderini, when you both came to see me at Urbino, but I never trusted the secret to anyone." This revenge had been incubating in Borgia's mind since June. Even as he galloped across Italy to see Louis XII, even as his spies sent reports of the conspirators' meeting at La Magione, throughout his cat-and-mouse dealings with Paolo Orsini, and even as he negotiated his treaty with the conspirators—a treaty guaranteed by Louis XII, the pope, Cardinal Orsini, and the Signoria of Florence—he had been biding his time, waiting for the precise moment. This secret must have been passed on by Borgia to Alexander VI during their clandestine meeting at Camerino—accounting for the pope's growing impatience and exasperation at his son's behavior, as well as his seemingly contradictory willingness to continue supplying his son with money.

Machiavelli was aghast, and more than a little terrified, by the blood-curdling scene that greeted him in the Borgo before the walls of Sinigallia. Upon learning from Borgia what had happened, Machiavelli rode quickly past the throng and through the gate into the walled city. No sooner had he been allotted his quarters than he sat down to pen a dispatch to the Signoria in Florence. His agitation is evident as he hurriedly passes on what is happening, and what he has learned from Borgia:

> The town is still being sacked and it is now an hour before sunset.* I am extremely worried. I am not even sure that I will be able to find a messenger to relay this message to you. I will write to you at length later.

---

* Machiavelli in fact wrote "the twenty-third hour"—that is, one hour before the Angelus bell marking the end of the day. Several sources have mistakenly taken this for eleven o'clock at night.

With regard to the fate of Vitellozzo, Liverotto da Fermo, and the three Orsini, he adds: "My opinion is that these prisoners will not be alive tomorrow morning."

Two hours after sunset Borgia sent for Machiavelli, greeting him:

in most excellent cheer, expressing his great satisfaction at his triumph. . . . He reminded me how, the previous day at Fano, he had dropped a hint about what was to happen, yet without revealing everything. . . . He had wise and affectionate words to say about Florence, offering his friendship. . . . He wished you to know that in destroying his mortal enemies he had also destroyed the enemies of Florence and France, and by so doing he had uprooted an evil that had threatened to spread throughout Italy.

That same night, almost certainly after this meeting with Borgia, Machiavelli wrote his promised longer dispatch to the Signoria. This would never reach its destination, either because it was intercepted by Borgia's agents or more likely because the messenger destroyed it, not wishing to be caught with an incriminating document. News of such happenings, and details of how they had come about, were dangerous.

Machiavelli's premonition about the fate of Borgia's prisoners was to prove at least partially correct. In the early hours of the morning Vitellozzo and Liverotto da Ferma would meet a grisly end. Machiavelli later heard how the two of them were tied back-to-back on a bench:

They both behaved in a manner wholly unworthy of their past exploits. Vitellozzo begged that he be allowed to see the Pope, so that His Holiness could give him plenary indulgence for his sins. Liverotto wept, blaming Vitellozzo for all the injuries done to the Duke.

As was the Spanish custom of the period, they were garrotted, using a loop of cord or lyre string around the neck, with a lynch-pin inserted and then twisted, tightening the string until the victim choked to death. The executions were carried out by Don Michele, the expert strangler, and were said by some sources to have taken place in the presence of Borgia himself. This would certainly have been characteristic.

Later that same night Borgia wrote a letter explaining what had happened and giving justification for his actions. This letter was addressed to the ruling Doge of Venice, and similar letters would later be sent to Perugia and other cities, evidently to allay any fears that might have been raised in these quarters. He would also send word to Alexander VI in Rome, informing him of recent events, though there would have been less need for justification in this instance. The copy of his letter to Perugia, which, later came to light in the archives of that city, denounced Vitellozzo, the Orsini, and the others in no uncertain terms, reminding his correspondents of their earlier

> perfidious rebellion and atrocious treason ... against His Holiness the Pope and ourselves. So atrocious was this baseness, that neither the beneficent clemency of his [Holiness] ... nor our renewed indulgence to them, weaned them from the slough of their first vile designs, in which they still persisted. And as soon as they learned the departure of [my] French troops on their return [to Louis XII] ... they, feigning an urgent desire to aid in our attack on Sinigallia, mustered a third only of their infantry, and concealed the remainder. . . .

But Borgia had been "distinctly forewarned of all," as he put it in his letter. Yet how had he learned this information? Borgia certainly did not trust Vitellozzo and the others, and it is now clear that even after they had signed the treaty with him, he continued with his plan to destroy them. But this is not the same as being "distinctly forewarned" of their intentions. In fact, this only happened after he arrested Lorqua. Not only did Lorqua reveal that he had been in on the former conspiracy with Vitellozzo, the Orsini, and the rest, but he also revealed that there was an ongoing plot to assassinate Borgia. The evidence for this was later disclosed by Alexander VI in conversation with Giustinian, who reported in his dispatch to Venice that the pope

> began by saying that when Lorqua knew that he was already under sentence of death he told the Duke [Borgia] that he wished to let him understand something for his own good. He had plotted with the Orsini to take the territory of Cesena [that is, the Romagna], but this had come to nothing when the treaty was signed between the Orsini and the Pope [and Borgia]. Despite this, Vitellozzo had still vowed to kill the Duke, and Liverotto da Fermo was in on the plot too (he mentioned no other names). Seeing the best way to achieve his aim, Vitellozzo had conspired with a crossbowman that when Borgia was out riding, he should kill him.

After hearing this confession, Borgia had taken the precaution of wearing a suit of chain-mail both day and night until he managed to seize Vitellozzo at Sinigallia. And before Vitellozzo was put to death, he admitted under interrogation the truth of Lorqua's confession, adding that Liverotto da Fermo was also in on the plot.

But even this was not the whole story. Apparently Andrea Dorea, the castellan at Sinigallia, had been instrumental in the conspirators' plot too: it was he who had stated that he would only surrender the fortress to Borgia personally, the ruse intended to lure Borgia to Sinigallia and his death. Borgia mentioned in his letter to Perugia that "the castellan, seeing the plot defeated, quickly surrendered the fortress." Borgia would not have known of Dorea's part in the plot, but he must have had his suspicions and interrogated Dorea after he surrendered, in this way learning of his implication.

On January 3, 1503, Alexander VI in Rome received a secret message from Borgia announcing that he had succeeded in his plan, and had taken captive Vitellozzo, Liverotto, and the three Orsini at Sinigallia. The pope immediately sent a highly selective version of this message to his friend Cardinal Orsini, informing him of the good news that the Orsini, with the later assistance of Borgia, had at last succeeded in taking Sinigallia. Cardinal Orsini hurried to congratulate Alexander VI.

The Cardinal had walked straight into the trap: he was seized the moment he entered the Vatican and then removed under armed escort to the dungeons of the Castel Sant' Angelo. Alexander VI at once ordered the seizure of the cardinal's palazzo, having it ransacked of all its treasures; at the same time, the cardinal's mother and various other women were evicted with nothing but the clothes they stood up in, doubtless on the pope's orders. These women were forced to wander the streets of Rome, begging friends to assist them—but none dared, as Alexander VI began to purge the city of all Orsini sympathizers. Others too felt the force of the pope's vengeful wrath. The Medici family feared for their lives, bishops were hauled from their beds, and the Bishop of Chiusi was even said to have died of fear, as Alexander's agents attacked and pillaged their palazzi. According to Giustinian's dispatch on January 6: "The Pope has become obsessed with seizing all the gold he can find." He added that this was not all, for the pope had promised ominously: "What has happened so far is nothing compared with what is planned for the future."

In the midst of all this the pope still insisted upon joining in the Carnival events that filled the calendar for January and February. He spent afternoons at the horse races, went to the theater, and attended the grand balls accompanied by his flock of loyal cardinals (most of whom he had personally appointed, for considerable sums). This entourage presented quite a picture at such events, with "some in their red cardinal's robes, while others were decked out in fancy dress, all accompanied by the sort of companions who most pleased His Holiness, some of whom lay reclining at his feet."

Meanwhile Alexander VI's erstwhile boon companion Cardinal Orsini lay languishing in the dungeons of Castel Sant' Angelo. When news of what had happened reached the Orsini clan and their powerful allies outside Rome, an immediate offer of 26,000 ducats was made to Alexander VI for his release. At the same time the cardinal's mother sent one of her friends for an audience with the pope, where he was offered a large pearl that it was known he had long coveted, as long as he pardoned the cardinal for whatever sins the pope evidently believed him to have committed. Alexander VI gratefully accepted the pearl, but no pardon was forthcoming.

When Cardinal Orsini had been in the dungeons for more than a month, with still no sign of his release, rumors began to circulate about his condition. Giustinian reported somewhat sardonically that the middle-aged cardinal was showing "symptoms of derangement," leaving the Venetian Signoria "to judge for themselves the cause of such a malady." He later reported that most were now of the opinion that "his drink had already been poisoned by the Pope." Despite such rumors, the pope insisted upon "ordering that he be attended by the finest physicians, who were to give him their best attention." Yet all this was to no avail, for the cardinal soon developed a high fever, and on February 22, 1503, he died. Two days later the same physicians were summoned by Alexander VI to declare that Cardinal Orsini had died of natural causes; whereupon the pope ordered that the cardinal be given a public funeral, with all the due honors usually granted to such a distinguished senior cardinal.

Meanwhile Cesare Borgia had quickly departed from Sinigallia on January 1, 1503, taking with him all his forces and carrying in his train the three captive Orsini. It was several days before the courier dispatched by Alexander VI from Rome finally caught up with Borgia, delivering the message that Cardinal Orsini had been seized. By now Borgia and his forces had advanced almost a hundred miles east across the mountains and reached Città della Pieve, where on January 14 the three Orsini were strangled "in the Spanish manner."* News of the completion of Borgia's revenge on his treacherous enemies quickly spread throughout Italy.

Although Machiavelli had plainly been terrified by Borgia's deeds

---

* On the other hand, Borgia's biographer Woodward points out that, according to Giustinian (*Dispacci*, vol. 1, pp. 356–7), the "Cavaliere Orsini" (seemingly Roberto) was set free "possibly on ground of services rendered," suggesting that he may have been the source who "distinctly forewarned" Borgia of the conspirators' plot to kill him. However, Machiavelli, who was on the spot, makes no mention of his figure. As Woodward comments (p. 295n): "The Cavaliere Orsini remains something of a mystery."

at Sinigallia, just over a week later he was writing to Florence expressing his admiration for Borgia: "The Duke's actions are accompanied by a unique good fortune, as well as a superhuman daring and confidence that he can achieve whatever he wants." As Machiavelli saw it, this was how true Italian heroes, such as the great figures of ancient Rome, would have dealt with the situation. Yet Machiavelli was not the only one to be so dazzled as to draw this comparison. When Louis XII heard of Borgia's feat, he declared it to be "an act worthy of a Roman hero." And the contemporary historian Paolo Giovio, no friend of the Borgias, famously referred to Cesare's feat at Sinigallia as "a most beautiful deception." Many in Italy, it seemed, were longing for a powerful figure to lead their country in a return to its former glories.

Part 3

Looking to the Future

16

"What has happened so far is nothing compared with what is planned for the future"

W HEN MACHIAVELLI HAD written that Borgia was capable of obtaining "whatever he wants," this had been no idle phrase. It seems likely that by this stage he may well have begun to suspect the true enormity of Borgia's plans. But for the time being Borgia was concerned with lesser, more immediate matters. He was determined to seize the territory that had belonged to those who had conspired against him, and it was evident that he intended to do this as swiftly as possible. Borgia left Sinigallia on January 1, 1503, marching his troops and artillery out of the city with all speed. According to Machiavelli, this operation had been carried out "in the worst possible weather, as unfavorable for making war as can be imagined." Winter had set in with a vengeance, and the conditions were heavy-going: by January 5 Borgia had only reached Guildo Tadino, some fifty miles away on the Via Flaminia heading south.

But Borgia was soon to be greeted with a succession of good news. On hearing of the murder of Liverotto da Fermo, the city of Fermo had immediately and gratefully surrendered to Borgia agents. The citizens of Fermo reckoned they were well rid of their tyrannical ruler, and were all for joining the "liberated" cities of the Romagna under Borgia's banner. His methods may have been cruel, but once he had achieved his aim, his rule appeared to be just. Next came the news that a deputation from Vitellozzo's Città di Castello had arrived to surrender their city to Borgia. They too were glad to see the end of their despotic lord. The reign of the last remaining petty tyrants of the Romagna was collapsing fast. The following day came envoys surrendering the keys to Perugia, informing Borgia that Baglioni had fled his city and taken refuge with Pandolfo Petrucci in Siena.

It soon became clear that Borgia's main aim was now to capture Petrucci, and eliminate once and for all the man who he was convinced had masterminded the conspiracy against him. During December Borgia had invited Petrucci to join him in Sinigallia, so that they could discuss future strategy for the region with his friends Vitellozzo, Liverotto, and the Orsini. But the cagey old man had not trusted Borgia. Now all of Petrucci's worst suspicions had been confirmed, and Borgia was on the march towards Siena.

On January 10, during Borgia's overnight stop at Torgiano, he summoned Machiavelli to his chamber and began unburdening himself at some length to the Florentine envoy. Later, Machiavelli would report on this conversation in one of his most vital dispatches back to Florence. Borgia had told him:

> You know how anxious I am to be friends with your Signoria, whose high esteem I regard as the greatest support for my dukedom. So I can be very frank with you. . . . You can see how things have turned out between me and my enemies—who are just as much your enemies too. They are either dead, my prisoners, fugitives, or if they are standing their ground they know that they await their fate at my hands. . . . Chief amongst these is Pandolfo Petrucci, who, owing to his cunning, his access to large amounts of money to hire mercenaries, and his hold on his city with its strategic position, represents a constant threat.

Borgia explained to Machiavelli his tactics with regard to Petrucci: "If possible I want to take him alive, and to this end the Pope is sending him reassuring messages, whilst undercover of these I am creeping up on him. . . . It is sweet to deceive such cunning men, who consider themselves to be masters of deception." However, Borgia was at great pains to stress that he had no designs on Siena itself, because where Tuscany was concerned, "Louis XII is in charge of the shop." Instead, Borgia's present campaign was intended merely "to rid these cities of their tyrants and return them to their rightful lord the Church." He had assured the French king that these cities were not intended to become part of his dukedom in the Romagna.

Unsurprisingly, Louis XII was not deceived when he received such assurances, and sent a series of forceful notes to Alexander VI instructing him to restrain his son. The pope himself was also not happy with Borgia's behavior. He wanted his son to campaign against his enemies the Orsini, and eliminate them once and for all, not pursue his own headstrong policy against Siena, which would be the ruin of all Alexander VI's plans. Meanwhile the remaining members of the Orsini clan, who had taken refuge in their strongholds north of Rome, presented a direct threat to the pope himself, who remained unprotected in the Vatican.

In Florence, the Signoria belatedly decided that the situation was becoming serious and that Borgia once again posed a distinct threat. One of the city's leading figures, Jacopo Salviati, was dispatched to Borgia's court with full ambassadorial powers to negotiate on Florence's behalf. When he arrived, he was to inform Machiavelli that he could at last return home.

On January 21, Machiavelli sent his final dispatch to the Signoria. Despite what Borgia had told him, he remained convinced that Borgia would press his luck as far as he could, taking Siena and perhaps even moving on Florence, unless he was somehow restrained by Louis XII, who unfortunately now appeared more concerned with overcoming the Spanish in Naples than with becoming involved in the affairs of Florence.

Meanwhile in Rome, Alexander VI angrily told his court and the assembled ambassadors:

We have done everything in our power to make [Borgia] give up the enterprise of Siena. . . . Nonetheless he is absolutely resolved to disregard us. . . . We promise you, that since we have sat in this chair [the papal throne], we have never heard of anything which causes us greater displeasure. And nonetheless we must have patience: he wills it thus, and it seems to him that he can do to us with impunity that which he is doing.

There is no doubt that Alexander VI was deeply frustrated and angered by his son's unwillingness to obey him, but it must be remembered that the pope frequently played up their disagreements so that Borgia could pursue policies that it was not in Alexander VI's interests to condone, but with which he covertly agreed. Alexander's insistence upon this occasion that "nonetheless we must be patient" hints that here too, despite his public anger, there may have been an element of collusion. The pope's secret meeting with his son at Camerino back in September would certainly have touched on policy to be pursued in central Italy after the elimination of the conspirators. In all likelihood, Alexander VI's real anger was caused by Borgia impulsively seizing the opportunity to take Siena, without first eliminating the Orsini, as they had probably agreed. When Borgia marched towards Tuscany with his forces—which were, after all, officially the papal forces—he was in fact leaving the pope dangerously exposed in Rome, vulnerable to the very real threat of Orsini revenge.

Regardless of any threat to his father, Borgia continued to press north, entering Sienese territory, giving his Spanish troops a free hand to lay waste the villages and towns in their path. This time there was no Machiavelli to record what happened, but word soon reached Alexander VI in Rome, and on January 23 Johannes Burchard recorded in his diary:

Word has reached us that during the last few days the Duke has seized the fortresses at Sarteano and Castel Piave, and also San Quirico. By the time they reached San Quirico all they found were two old men and nine aged women. The Duke's soldiers hung these unfortunates by their arms and lit a fire beneath their feet to make them reveal where the local treasures had been hidden. The poor women, knowing nothing, or in any case not revealing anything, died hideously. After having smashed everything in the village the soldiers burned it to the ground.

Borgia was now within twenty miles of Siena, yet despite such intimidation Petrucci stood his ground, encouraged by his loyal populace. Despite his faults, Petrucci was a native of Siena and a comparatively popular leader: his subjects much preferred the devil they knew to the Borgia whose legendary infamies had spread before him.

This left Borgia in something of a quandary. He realized that if he actually took Siena, this would completely transform the situation in central Italy. Such action would certainly incur the wrath of Louis XII, who might well take action. Yet as Borgia had hinted to Machiavelli, his main target was not so much Siena as its ruler, Pandolfo Petrucci. With this in mind, on January 27 Borgia sent an ultimatum to the people of Siena:

> We hereby swear to God that if, within twenty-four hours of receiving this letter, you have not already immediately driven out Pandolfo, we will regard each one of you like Pandolfo himself, and without delay we will proceed to exterminate all the towns, subjects, and goods that are yours, and also your city and all its citizens. For by so doing you will have declared yourself my enemies, and you will be utterly reduced to such a state of devastation and misery that you will never recover.

Under the circumstances, these would certainly have appeared to the citizens of Siena as no idle words. But as Machiavelli had perceptively noted at Urbino six months earlier, when Borgia appeared at his most fearsome he was often bluffing. And this was no exception. Not only could he not march on Siena, but word had now reached him that the Orsini had left their castles and assembled a force that was marching on his father in Rome. Borgia's bluff had to work quickly.

And so it did. By return messenger Petrucci asked for a guarantee of safe conduct if he left Siena. Surprisingly Borgia agreed, allowing Petrucci passage to the safety of the independent city-state of Lucca, some sixty miles to the north on the other side of Florentine territory. On January 28, Petrucci, accompanied by his fellow conspirator Baglioni, tearfully took his leave of Siena and fled in the direction of Lucca. But

Borgia had no intention of keeping to his guarantee and immediately sent a detachment of fifty fast cavalry to seek out Petrucci and bring him back, dead or alive. Not trusting Borgia, the aged but canny Petrucci took precautions, staying off the main highways and making his way by back paths through the rural terrain he knew so well, thus eluding his pursuers until he reached safety.

Having evicted Petrucci from Siena (but without actually occupying the city), Borgia now turned south, leading his troops towards Rome. The Orsini forces had proved disorganized and uncoordinated; even so, they had already managed to sever the vital route linking Rome to Ostia on the coast, the city's main source of supplies. Meanwhile a depleted and hastily assembled force marched south from the Orsini fortresses towards Rome, but were halted by the papal guard occupying the fortified bridge across the River Anio at Mentana, just ten miles northeast of the Eternal City. Alexander VI realized that this engagement was at best a holding operation, and soon the aging pope was manifesting his fear and anguish in histrionic scenes at court. Several witnesses describe how he wept and railed against the perfidious Orsini, at the same time raining down threats and curses on the head of his recalcitrant son. For once, it seemed there was no subterfuge: the division between the pope and the *gonfaloniere* of the papal forces appeared irreparable.

But Alexander VI had not counted on the irresolution of his enemies. As soon as word reached the Orsini that Borgia was heading south towards Rome, their forces took flight for the safety of their castles. Alexander VI miraculously recovered his composure; however, some other church dignitaries were less comforted by the news that Borgia was returning. According to Burchard's diary, during Borgia's absence the lothario Cardinal d'Este had succeeded in seducing not only Borgia's sister-in-law, but also his favorite Roman mistress. Mindful of Borgia's sensibilities concerning the women closest to him—whether family or otherwise—the cardinal at once fled the city in mortal terror.

To the pope's extreme irritation, Borgia halted his troops at Viterbo, some forty miles north of Rome. Inexplicably, he remained there for some ten days, during which time Alexander VI dispatched a succession of increasingly angry messages ordering him to attack the Orsini.

Such was the pope's irritation that he eventually even threatened his son with excommunication. Worse still, if Borgia did not obey his father's orders immediately, he would be stripped of his post as *gonfaloniere* of the papal forces, and the pope would take command of them himself. Borgia pointedly ignored these missives. Excommunication meant nothing to him; as for being deposed from his command, this was a threat that he knew his father would not—even could not—fulfill.

But why did Borgia not move against the Orsini? Now that Machiavelli had at last been relieved of his post and had returned to Florence, we no longer have his detailed and incisive dispatches analyzing the situation. Consequently, it is difficult to be sure of Borgia's thinking at this stage. Florentine ambassador Salviati's messages reveal little— he may have had authority to negotiate, and thus play an active role in Florence's relations with Borgia, but he was not an analyst of Machiavelli's caliber. Besides, Borgia neither knew Salviati nor respected him, as he had Machiavelli: the Florentine ambassador was not going to be taken into Borgia's confidence that easily.

As far as it is possible to discover, Borgia spent his time at Viterbo engaged in talks with representatives of the Colonna and Savelli, the aristocratic Roman families whose power had previously been broken by Alexander VI. He also made it plain to his father that he was unwilling to attack two of the most powerful Orsini strongholds. The first of these was Bracciano, the fortress of Giangiordano Orsini, whose behavior was so willful and unpredictable that he had even been labeled by the Orsini themselves as a "public madman." The uncharacteristically honorable reason Borgia gave for not attacking Giangiordano Orsini was that, like himself, he had been appointed by Louis XII to the Order of St. Michael, and one of the rules of this order was that no member should take up arms against another. The second fortress Borgia refused to attack was that at Pitigliano, the stronghold of Niccolò Orsini, who was in fact the mercenary commander of the Venetian army. Alexander VI was determined at all costs to crush the Orsini, the last remaining opposition to his power in Rome, once and for all; but Borgia realized that although this was now possible, it was inadvisable. In attacking Bracciano and Pitigliano he might have sealed the fate of the Orsini, but he would also have alienated Louis XII and Venice. He knew too that the eccentric Giangiordano had in fact opposed the Orsini joining the plot against him at La Magione. By showing that he had no ill will against Giangiordano, and was willing to negotiate with the Colonna and the Savelli, he sought to defuse the entire situation.

Despite Borgia's fearsome reputation, he was not in fact a great military commander in the field: as Machiavelli had astutely observed, he sought wherever possible to achieve his aims through shrewd strategy, sudden unexpected moves, or ruthless treachery. If he could at this stage defuse the Orsini opposition when they were ready to oppose him, it would leave him free to strike at them later when they least expected it. But this was just one of several options. A new alliance with the ancient aristocratic Roman families such as the Colonna, the Savelli, and the Orsini would restore their pride, and at the same time provide Borgia with support in a region that for the present lay beyond his Romagna domain. As Machiavelli had prophetically observed more than two months previously, in one of his missives to Florence summarizing the likely outcome of events for Borgia, "When the Pope dies, [Borgia] will still need to have some friends in Rome." This was but the first hint of the scope of Cesare's ambition after his father was no longer pope. The Romagna was secure, Siena was acquiescent, Florence was in the balance, and now he appeared to be making preparations for Rome. Alexander VI had almost certainly confirmed most of this with Borgia during their meeting at Camerino; it was only for the moment that their tactics differed. Even so, Alexander VI would definitely have known Borgia's ultimate aim. The idea of Rome becoming a permanent Borgia fiefdom would have been conceived by Alexander VI himself, almost certainly at the outset of his papacy, if not earlier. Contrary to the prevalent perception, Borgia family ambitions were just beginning to be realized. Only Machiavelli seems to have had an inkling of what was afoot: this must have come from his long conversations with Borgia, his psychological assessment of the man himself and the true extent of his ambitions, as well as certain clues that Borgia must have let drop.

Yet Borgia knew that before he could form any unlikely alliance with the ancient Roman families, he would first of all have to bring the Orsini to heel—and in order to do so, he would have to make a strong and decisive move against them. On February 19 he did just this, moving his troops en masse from Viterbo, marching thirty miles south to the small fortified hilltop town of Ceri, and laying siege to the stronghold of Giulio Orsini, brother of the late Cardinal Orsini. Owing to its position atop a sheer outcrop of rock, the imposing, thickly walled fortress at Ceri appeared to be utterly impregnable, and Borgia was aware that this siege would be closely watched by the other members of the Orsini clan in their various heavily fortified castles throughout the region. Having hurriedly deployed his troops in their siege positions, Borgia then made an unexpected but nonetheless characteristic move. On February 25 he departed for Rome, in time to join in the pre-Lenten Carnival—just as his father had predicted two months previously, though hardly under the circumstances His Holiness had expected.

Indeed, Alexander VI was outraged at Borgia's behavior, and immediately berated his son on his return to Rome: this was no time to be thinking of Carnival jollities. Relations between the pope and his son quickly became strained. Giustinian even sent a dispatch to Venice reporting a rumor that during one evening their relationship had deteriorated to the extent that the seventy-two-year-old pope had ended up brawling with his twenty-seven-year-old son. Despite this, it was difficult to discern precisely what was going on between them. Relations may have become volatile, and even violent on occasion, but Alexander VI and Cesare remained undeniably close. Above all else they were Borgias: outsiders, Spaniards, surrounded by others who were jealous of these foreigners and their ambitions. Others may have wanted them gone, but the Borgias were determined to remain; and for this Alexander VI and Cesare needed each other, and they knew it.

Cesare spent the next fortnight or so of Carnival enjoying himself, though according to Giustinian he was never seen without a mask. Such behavior was not unusual during Carnival, when the wearing of a mask was customary, facilitating much of the loose and licentious behavior that was a feature of the festival. It is also possible that by now Borgia was beginning to exhibit more permanent disfiguration arising from his syphilis, such as telltale blotches on his face—a good reason for not being seen unmasked. Giustinian remarks: "Every day he goes hunting, although he does not let himself be seen in the city." Another reason for this elusiveness would have been the secret military preparations Borgia was making at the time, as it was now that he began supervising the assembly of the "huge machine held to be capable of carrying up to 300 men up to the ramparts," which had been designed for him by Leonardo during his time at Imola.

Borgia is known to have returned to the siege of Ceri for a couple of days in mid-March, and it has been suggested that at around this time Leonardo's machine may well have been dragged the twenty miles northwest to Ceri. This seems unlikely for various reasons—the most convincing being that it would have been unsuitable for use here, as the cliffs below the walls at Ceri are well over 100 feet high. Leonardo's huge siege machine would have been held in reserve for use as a secret weapon against the other Orsini strongholds.

On the brief mid-March visit to Ceri Borgia was accompanied by his military engineers; but we know that these did not include his chief military engineer, Leonardo, for there is conclusive evidence that Leonardo was back in Florence by early March. Despite this, Borgia must have given his team of military engineers orders to assemble the other weapons that Leonardo had previously designed for him, using Leonardo's drawings for the purpose. These weapons were to be ready in two weeks' time, for use in what was expected to be the final stage of the siege. We know this weaponry included "mortars capable of firing multiple explosive projectiles, mobile precision artillery, and large-scale catapults," and if these were constructed according to the designs that appear in Leonardo's notebooks, they must have been highly effective. Indeed, according to Borgia's biographer Charles Yriarte: "At the siege of Ceri, Borgia used exceptional weapons which would instigate a new era in the history of warfare during the Renaissance."

All this weaponry cost a great deal of money, such that the maintenance and payment of the papal army, as well as the expensive siege of Ceri, were proving a huge drain on the Vatican exchequer. The disagreements that occurred between Alexander VI and Cesare during this period were almost certainly over strategic objectives, but they could well have been exacerbated by financial problems. Either way, such differences were certainly set aside when the pope embarked upon a concerted campaign to raise funds to pay for his son's military expenses.

In mid-March, Alexander VI began mapping out the first details of this financial strategy. By the end of the month Giustinian was reporting to Venice that the pope had issued a bull creating no fewer than eighty new positions at the papal court, costing each of those fortunate enough to be appointed the sum of 760 ducats—"so if you add it all up you can see how much he made," concluded Giustinian. Such a ploy may have raised more than 60,000 ducats, but this was not enough, apparently.

Alexander VI now resorted to his old habits. Within a fortnight Giustinian was reporting that on April 8 the Venetian Cardinal Michiel had suddenly been taken ill. Throughout the ensuing two days he was racked with such violent sickness that he finally died in the early hours of April 10. Before dawn, on orders from Alexander VI, the cardinal's palazzo was gutted of its entire content of valuables, which amounted to a huge quantity of gold plate, jewels, and precious stones, rumored to be worth more than 150,000 ducats. According to Giustinian, when he arrived to attend the papal court that morning, he found all the doors to the Vatican barred. The pope was unable to receive anyone because he was too busy counting the proceeds from the late cardinal's palazzo. When the pope finally summoned Giustinian three days later, the Venetian ambassador found His Holiness still personally engaged in this task, while the rest of the court looked on. But Alexander VI complained to Giustinian: "Look at it, there are only 23,382 ducats. Yet word has spread around the entire country that I've got hold of 80,000 to 100,000 ducats." The pope was convinced that Cardinal Michiel had been worth far more than this, and insisted to Giustinian that an immediate search should be carried out at all the cardinal's Venetian estates to discover where he had hidden the rest of his assets.

To make up for this unexpected shortfall, Alexander VI resorted to another of his old habits by appointing a number of new cardinals. In order to safeguard his loyal majority amongst the College of Cardinals, he chose to appoint five with Spanish and family connections. Unfortunately, loyal candidates for the cardinalate who were possessed of both sufficient spiritual and financial resources were now in short supply, so it was decided to dispense with the former requirement, and many were dismayed at the character of the new appointments. In a tactical move, designed to encourage Florence to favor the Borgia cause, the pope also made a cardinal of Machiavelli's colleague and friend Francesco Soderini, Bishop of Volterra and brother of Piero Soderini, the city's *gonfaloniere* for life. (This appointment to the cardinalate was almost certainly at Borgia's prompting.) In the event, nine new cardinals were appointed, for varying sums rising to 20,000 ducats. According to Giustinian, by this means Alexander VI managed to raise between 120,000 and 130,000 ducats, "thus demonstrating to the world that His Holiness was capable of expanding the Papal income at will."

At the end of March, Cesare Borgia had left Rome and returned to supervise the siege at Ceri. Leonardo's weaponry was now all in place, and a concentrated bombardment of the fortress began, during which 6,000 cannonballs are said to have been fired. Within the week Giulio Orsini had put out feelers, offering to surrender in return for safe conduct to Pitigliano. Borgia agreed, and on April 5 Ceri duly surrendered. To widespread surprise, Giulio Orsini was permitted to journey unmolested to Pitigliano. When news of these events spread, the other Orsini castles surrendered of their own accord, with the exception of Bracciano and Pitigliano, which had both been assured by Borgia that they were not under threat.

Louis XII himself now stepped in, ordering that a truce be declared between the Orsini and the Borgias. On April 11 a pact was signed in Rome, under the auspices of the French ambassador. Honor was restored, and the pope was once again free from threat in the Eternal City, but at some financial cost. A few days later, Giustinian reported how Alexander VI had confided to him that Cesare's siege of Ceri alone had cost as much as 40,000 ducats. Compared with the money the pope had just seized from Cardinal Michiel, and the vast sum he was planning to raise with the creation of his new cardinals, this was nothing. It looked as if Alexander VI had in mind an even greater project, to be realized sometime in the near future. This may also have accounted for the large troop-carrying siege engine designed by Leonardo, which Borgia had had constructed and was now under wraps in Rome.

17

Leonardo at Work

THE PRECISE DETAILS of Leonardo da Vinci's activities during late 1502 and early 1503 are difficult to discern. Nonetheless, there are hints and clues. We can be fairly certain that he was with Borgia when the latter was under virtual siege at Imola during the autumn of 1502. One of the first things that Machiavelli had noticed on his arrival in early October was that "The Duke has so much artillery and in such good order that he alone possesses almost as much as all the rest of Italy put together." This was certainly Leonardo's responsibility, as Borgia's chief military engineer. During the ensuing weeks of the siege Leonardo produced his beautifully detailed map of Imola and supervised the reinforcement of the fortress. At this time he almost certainly planned with Borgia the weapons that would later be used at the siege of Ceri, as well as the vast armored troop carrier capable of transporting 300 soldiers up to the wall of a besieged city.

All this makes it almost certain that Leonardo followed Borgia sometime after he unexpectedly marched out of Imola with his troops during the snowstorm on December 10. In this case he would have witnessed the tumultuous events that took place a few days later at Cesena, when Borgia's French troops suddenly departed for Milan and, in Machiavelli's words, "the entire court [was] turned upside down." Thus Leonardo would also have been present the following early morning when the sensational discovery was made in the main square of Lorqua's decapitated body with his head stuck on a lance.

Machiavelli, who was a practiced diplomat and was to an extent worldly wise in such matters, was certainly disturbed by this unexpected turn of events, to judge from the tenor of his dispatches back to Florence. We can only conjecture at the effect of such a gruesome deed upon the quiet and contemplative Leonardo. As ever, no mention was made of these events in his notebooks—his reactions to the disturbances of reality, whether quotidian or sensational, were put from his mind. Yet they registered, at least on some level: the evidence suggests that he was not an unfeeling person, only that he sought to overcome (or avoid) his feelings. As he wrote early on in his notebooks: "You can have no greater or lesser dominion than over yourself." And as he noted somewhat cryptically on another occasion: "Where there is the greatest feeling, there is the greatest martyrdom; a great martyr."

Leonardo's recent biographer Charles Nicholl has noted that on occasions when Leonardo was likely to have been deeply moved, a certain repetitive tic is noticeable in his notebook entries. Thus, when his recently widowed mother Caterina had traveled all the way to Milan to live with him when she was in her mid-sixties and near to death, the entry recording this moving event reads:

> On the 16th day of July.
> Caterina came on the 16th day
> Of July 1493.

The quasi-poetic form of this entry would seem to be no accident.

Another telltale quirk on such occasions can be the making of detailed lists to control the thoughts and divert the writer from concealed emotions. This would certainly seem to be the case when Leonardo came to record the death of his mother, which is simply marked by an entry headed "Funeral expenses for Caterina." This is followed by a list of all that was involved, complete with the cost, ranging from "For 4 priests and 4 clerks: 20 *soldi*" to "For Bearing the body: 8 *soldi*"; from "Bell, book and sponge: 2 *soldi*" to "Sweets and candles: 12 *soldi*." Only the expenses of those paid indicate the people who were present:

other mourners who attended, such as Leonardo himself, are not recorded.

The tiny notebook (Notebook L), which Leonardo is known to have kept attached to his belt to facilitate his jottings on the spot whilst he moved about in the Romagna, was not suitable for writing lists. Indeed, this was probably not used when he returned to his living quarters. His working drawings for Borgia depicting such things as weaponry, improvements to fortifications, and dredging machines are all lost. (Our knowledge of his machines and weaponry derives from descriptions and drawings that he made many years earlier in Milan.) All this suggests that amidst the comings and goings of his travels with Borgia, either Leonardo may have mislaid a larger personal notebook or this may have gone missing at a later date and might yet be discovered, as was the case with the *Codex Madrid*. There is certainly evidence that several of Leonardo's notebooks have not been found. In that case, Leonardo may well have resorted to making meticulous lists during this turbulent period with Borgia.

Another, more ingenious suggestion is that he distracted his feelings by painstakingly drawing and coloring the beautiful and meticulous copy of the map of Imola that he had made for Borgia. Besides being a work of art, this was also a work of consummate control. The messiness of the quotidian external world, where all manner of unmentionable deeds took place, was reduced to an almost abstract exactitude.

If Leonardo was disturbed by the tumult at Cesena created by the French departure and Lorqua's death, how much more deeply he must have been affected by the shocking murders at Sinigallia and their anarchic aftermath amongst Borgia's soldiers. Again, there is no concrete proof that Leonardo was actually at Sinigallia; however, he is most likely to have been amongst the support group that included Machiavelli, all of whom reached Sinigallia before nightfall. Even if Leonardo did not arrive amidst the thick of the murderous anarchy taking place in the Borgo, he would certainly have been told, in the most excited and graphic terms, of the events that unfolded that day and the following night— details of which were being recounted within days at the courts throughout Italy. By now Leonardo must have begun to rethink his entire attitude towards devoting his talents to military engineering.

Yet for the time being he had his obligations to Borgia to fulfill, and was forced to follow his master. Thus he must have been present at Città della Pieve when Borgia had the three Orsini strangled, and then he must have seen the village of San Quirico after the atrocities committed by Borgia's Spanish troops.

The evidence indicates that Leonardo left the main contingent of Borgia's troops at Buonconvento, fifteen miles short of Siena, sometime in late January 1503. Indicatively, this was less than a day's march beyond the devastated San Quirico. Leonardo could only have left on Borgia's orders, and it may well have been that Borgia recognized the effect all this was having on Leonardo—who, as far as we know, had never had firsthand experience of actual warfare before he joined Borgia on his Romagna campaign.

Leonardo headed southeast: on the later pages of his Notebook L he names a number of towns and the distances between them: "From Buonconvento to Casa Nova is 10 miles, from Casa Nova to Chiusi 9 miles ... Perugia ... Santa Maria degli Angeli, and then to Foligno." The very precision of these entries is psychologically revealing: here surely is evidence of "the greatest feelings" suffering "the greatest martyrdom." On a more realistic level, these entries indicate that Leonardo (together with the small military escort he would have been given) must have traveled by a roundabout route, skirting regions held by the Orsini, and then made his way from Foligno directly south down the Via Flaminia to Rome. Here Leonardo would have begun supervising the initial stages of the building of the large armored 300-man siege weapon.

By this stage Leonardo was certainly looking for a way out of his post as chief military engineer to Borgia. Just weeks earlier, when Machiavelli had been recalled to Florence, he had probably assured Leonardo that he would use his influence with the Signoria to find him alternative employment, so that he could be recalled. Yet this held out little prospect of success: Borgia was unlikely to agree to surrender such an important member of his staff, especially if he was planning further military action. And all the indications are that this was very much the case—judging from Alexander VI's remark concerning "what is planned for the future," and the fact that Leonardo had been set to work on a massive siege engine, which it quickly became clear was not intended for use at Ceri.

Yet just when Leonardo must have begun to despair, there arose an opportunity for him to take matters into his own hands. This came in the form of a totally unexpected offer of employment that would remove him from the clutches of Borgia, and indeed from Italy altogether. Surprisingly, this opportunity came to him through Alexander VI.

The pope was keen to resolve the difficulties between European Christendom and the expanding Ottoman Empire to the east, which had now become a major threat. Already its forces had threatened Venice, and had long since expanded across the Balkans to the southeastern shore of the Adriatic—less than fifty miles across the sea from the southern Italian mainland.* Mindful of the need to placate the Ottomans, in February 1503 Alexander VI showed Leonardo a letter from Sultan Bejazit II concerning a sensational project.

In the course of the peace negotiations between Venice and the Ottoman Empire, Sultan Bejazit II had sent an ambassadorial delegation to Rome in 1502 to meet Pope Alexander VI. Amongst other things, the Turkish ambassador carried a message informing the pope that the sultan was seeking an engineer who could build a bridge across the Golden Horn. This represented a considerable challenge: the Golden Horn is the wide inlet from the Bosporus that separates the ancient

---

* In 1480 the forces of Sultan Mehmet II had even crossed the Adriatic and unexpectedly occupied the city of Otranto on the heel of Italy, massacring 12,000 men and sawing the local bishop in half while he was still alive. But a year later, on the death of Mehmet II, the city had been abandoned by all but a token force, which had quickly been overrun. More recently, in 1501 the Turkish navy had taken advantage of Borgia's siege of Piombino to raid the nearby Tuscan coast, temporarily taking possession of the tiny island of Pianosa and later attacking the coast of Sardinia, before sailing west to attack the Balearic Islands, then on through the Strait of Gibraltar to attack the Canary Islands.

heart of Constantinople (Stamboul) from the northern Pera shore onto which the city had expanded. At this point, at its mouth into the Bosporus, the Golden Horn is 800 feet wide.

During the siege of Constantinople in 1453 Sultan Mehmet II had constructed a floating bridge consisting of ships roped together, but Bejazit II wished to build a permanent bridge under which galleys and masted ships could pass into the safe anchorage of the inner Golden Horn. No comparable structure had ever been attempted before, but Bejazit II was doubtless aware of the ambitious new architects and engineers who were now beginning to appear in Europe with the advent of the Renaissance. The great architectural advances being undertaken in Italy, especially in spans and arches, were largely related to the construction of ambitious domes and roofs for cathedrals. The 138-foot-span dome that crowned the cathedral at Florence, and the cupola atop Milan Cathedral, were achievements that outshone even the 100-foot dome of the Hagia Sophia in Constantinople. This had been erected in the late sixth century, but for centuries afterwards had remained an unsurpassed achievement owing to the fact that the techniques used in building it had been lost, along with so much other classical knowledge. Now that this knowledge was being resurrected in Italy, it could surely be used to create yet another marvel in Constantinople, in the form of the Pera bridge. Leonardo was one of the few engineers in Italy capable of contemplating such a task. His exceptional engineering abilities extended far beyond the military sphere, and this grand project would demonstrate his genius to the full.

One of the leaders in this field was Donato Bramante, who had been working in Milan during the period of Leonardo's residence in the city. Bramante had befriended the young Leonardo, who referred to the older master in his notebooks as Donino ("dear Donato") and would learn a great deal from him during the decade or so they were close friends. In 1487 the thirty-five-year-old Leonardo and Bramante both submitted plans for the addition of a dome to Milan Cathedral, an extremely bold and risky project, given the dilapidated state of this great Gothic structure. In his proposal Leonardo compared his work to that of a physician, who—according to the prevailing medical theory of the period—sought to establish a harmony in the body, restoring the balance between the different elements in the sick patient:

> The case of the invalid cathedral is similar. It also requires a doctor-architect who understands the edifice well, and knows the rules of good building from their origin . . . what are the causes that keep together an edifice and make it last, what is the nature of weight and of energy in force. . . . Health is a balance or concord of the elements which hold it together.

In the event, Leonardo's plan would be rejected, as would that of Bramante (who fifteen years later would go on to design the basilica of St. Peter's in Rome). But Leonardo's idea of harmony and interlocking balance between the separate elements would continue to be central to his notion of architecture and engineering. Just as the interlocking cogs transferred and magnified force from one part to another, driving his machines, so the opposing forces of the interlocking masonry held together and indeed strengthened the structure as a whole, giving it the apparent ability to defy gravity over a considerable span. This notion would spectacularly manifest itself in Leonardo's design for the Pera bridge across the Golden Horn.

Leonardo's sketch for the
Pera bridge at Constantinople.

Even so, Leonardo's design for the bridge was not entirely original; it was to a certain extent inspired by a pioneering structure that he had seen in autumn 1502. This was the Alidosi bridge in the foothills of the Apennine mountains at Castel del Rio, just twelve miles southwest of Imola. The bridge had been begun in 1499, and was on the main route linking Florence to Imola. Leonardo must have pondered its graceful single span across the narrow upper reach of the Santerno River, and conceived of a way of extending the principle upon which its span was based. Leonardo did most of his thinking upon the page, in words and drawings: "All our knowledge has its origins in our perceptions. . . . Science is the observation of things possible: prescience is the knowledge of things which it is possible to achieve." Yet there is no sketch or even comment on the Alidosi bridge that so impressed him: another omission that suggests there may well be a lost notebook from this period. However, we do have a sketch of the bridge that it inspired—namely, the Pera bridge. In Notebook L there is a tiny simple outline of a single-span bridge, both in plan and in elevation. This is no more than a thumbnail sketch (indeed, it is around the size of a thumbnail!), and might easily have been overlooked as some form of obscure doodle, but for the few lines of accompanying mirror-written text: "The bridge at Pera: 40 *braccia* wide, 70 *braccia* above the water, 600 *braccia* long; that is to say, 400 over the sea and 200 on the land, thus making its own supports."

Assuming a *braccio* to be equivalent to about two feet, this means a bridge spanning 800 feet of water, the precise distance between the two shores of the Golden Horn, proportions that would have been included in the sultan's original letter—which either has been lost or remains to be discovered in the Vatican archives. There is also a remark in another of Leonardo's notebooks that might possibly have relevance here: "Ask Bartolomeo the Turk about the flow and ebb of tide in the Black Sea." Bartolomeo Turco, as he is more usually known, was a renowned traveler of the period, who in 1502 published a book of sonnets about the Aegean islands, which also included detailed maps of the region.

However, from this point on Leonardo makes no further mention of the Pera bridge project, and it is generally agreed that he must have let it lapse, presumably on the grounds that, after mature consideration, he considered the bridge a feat beyond even his abilities. But Sultan Bejazit II was more persistent. In 1504 a group of Franciscan monks arrived in Rome from Constantinople bringing a message for Michelangelo, which—according to the artist's close friend and biographer Ascanio Condivi—said that the Sultan "wanted to employ him in building a bridge from Constantinople to Pera and other works." But Michelangelo too soon lost interest in the project. And so the matter rested for almost 450 years.

Then in 1952 an amazing discovery was made in the archives of the Topkapi Museum in Istanbul, by Franz Babinger, the great German scholar of Ottoman history. This was a letter, written in Turkish-Arabic script, which was described as: "A copy of a letter that the infidel named Linardo sent from Genoa. This letter was written on July 3." No year was given, but it was probably 1503, by which time Leonardo had returned to Florence. The mention of Genoa was no more than the equivalent of a postmark, meaning that the letter had arrived in Constantinople by sea from the port of Genoa.

Despite the introduction of occasional oriental turns of phrase, there can be little doubt that this letter translates (or perhaps paraphrases) an original in Italian by Leonardo. In content, and partly in manner, it bears a strong resemblance to the letter of introduction that Leonardo had written some twenty years previously to Ludovico "Il Moro" Sforza of Milan, in which he described in the most confident terms his wide variety of abilities. As before, Leonardo began by outlining his many original talents and accomplishments: for example, how he "can build a mill that does not require water, but is powered by wind alone." Such windmills, with sails, were already well developed in Holland, but not used in Italy—apparently because the weather was considered unsuitable. In a rare oversight, Leonardo does not seem to have realized that such windmills were already in wide use in the Aegean and would thus have been known to the Turks.

Leonardo continues his letter: "As well as this, by the will of

God—may He be praised to the highest—I have a way of extracting water from ships without using ropes or cables, but instead making use of a 'machine' that drives itself." Leonardo's notebooks contain drawings of several hydraulic machines, some dating from his earliest years in Milan, and there is no doubting his supreme ability and achievements in this department. However, this sentence from Leonardo's letter to the sultan is not quite all that it seems. The opening invocation to God was almost certainly inserted by the translators: Leonardo was in the habit of describing his talents in merely subjective terms. The letter to "Il Moro" is peppered with remarks such as "I know how . . . ," "I have methods for . . . ," "I have ways . . . ," "I will make . . .": God is not mentioned.

In Leonardo's earlier letter to "Il Moro" he had held back the main thrust of the letter—his wish to cast the great equestrian statue—until the end. In his 1503 letter to Sultan Bejazit II he adopted a similar ploy:

> I, your slave,* have learned of your intention to build a bridge from Stamboul to Galata [Pera], and that you have not been able to do this because you could not find a man capable of doing it. I, your slave, know how. I will make it rise in a curve . . . so that a ship can pass under it even when its sails are raised.

This description certainly matches the drawing Leonardo made in his notebook; but what follows is less clear. The following paragraph begins:

* This is usually translated as "your servant," which would have been the customary European way of addressing a master or prospective employer. However, Leonardo was not in the habit of adopting such a submissive tone. He was willing to flatter with praise—"Il Moro" had been addressed as "most illustrious Lord"—but he would not deign to belittle himself, simply ending his letter with his name. It thus becomes evident that in his letter to the sultan the term "your slave" was an insertion by the Turkish translators: an extreme obeisance that would have been customary at the Ottoman court. The German word used by Babinger in his translation from the Turkish is the unmistakable *Sklave*.

And I would erect a drawbridge so that when one wants one can pass on to the Anatolian coast. But as there is a constant current here, wearing away the shore, the bridge could be moved and made to turn in such a way that the water passed beneath it without causing any damage. All this could be produced at a low cost.

This reference to the Anatolian coast is surely wrong. The Anatolian shore is on the Asian side of the Bosporus itself, not the other side of the Golden Horn, which is merely an inlet of this much wider waterway. Some have argued that here Leonardo was suggesting that he could build a drawbridge across the Bosporus, a distance of more than a mile at this point.* On the other hand, the translators would certainly have spotted Leonardo's mistake. Or was it Leonardo's mistake? Even though Leonardo had never visited Constantinople, he had a good working knowledge of the region, as a result of his early studies in Florence with the great geographer Toscanelli. His notebooks make several references to the Black Sea, the Bosporus, the Sea of Marmara, the Dardanelles, and the Aegean, all part of this waterway where, as he remarks: "The Black Sea always flows continuously through into the Aegean." Admittedly, some of his comments on the region are speculative, or fanciful: "The Caspian flows through a subterranean cavern into the Black Sea." Even so, he certainly would not have mistaken the Golden Horn for the Bosporus. This error may well have been maliciously inserted by the Turkish translators in line with some court intrigue, so as to prevent the "infidel" from being appointed to an important post by the sultan. As Leonardo's French biographer Serge Bramly remarks: "The Sultan's secretaries probably made only a partial and perhaps slanted translation of the original."†

---

* The first bridge across the Bosporus was not completed until well over 450 years later, in 1973. It crossed the water three miles to the north, where the Bosporus is slightly narrower: even so, its span was 3,522 feet, and it was regarded as one of the great feats of twentieth-century engineering.
† Indeed, such is the detailed geographical information of the Levant in Leonardo's early notebooks that several scholars—including the redoubtable Jean Paul Richter—

Interestingly, Leonardo's letter to Sultan Bejazit II differs from his earlier letter to "Il Moro" in one highly significant way. No mention is made by Leonardo of his military engineering skills, of which he had previously been so proud. Leonardo had been shown the sultan's offer by Alexander VI in February 1503, but by the time he came to write to Constantinople in July he was no longer in Cesare Borgia's employ. His period of employment with Borgia and his firsthand experience of military matters appear to have cured him of any further ambitions as a military engineer.

On the other hand, he also makes no mention of his artistic skills in this letter, at least in the form it has come down to us. He would certainly have known that there would be ample opportunity for him to practice these skills in Constantinople, for he would not have been the first well-known Italian artist to take up residence in the Ottoman capital. In 1479, following an earlier peace treaty between Venice and the Ottoman Empire, as a token of goodwill Venice had exported a number of its artists to the court of Sultan Mehmet II. The finest of these had been Gentile Bellini, who was fifty years old and at the height of his powers. Bellini had remained in Constantinople for almost two years, during which he painted a portrait of the ill and aging Sultan Mehmet II (which now hangs in the National Gallery, London). When one day Bellini showed Mehmet II a painting that contained a depiction of John the Baptist's severed head, the Sultan insisted that it was inaccurate. Bellini disagreed, so in order to prove his point Mehmet II called over a nearby slave and had him beheaded on the spot, thus showing how he was indeed right. So

---

have been convinced that he actually traveled to the East, at least to Cyprus, and maybe as far as Armenia and Syria, with a period of employment by the Sultan of Egypt. This was said to have taken place around 1482, after he left Florence and before he took up residence in Milan. Leonardo's notebooks of this period contain a series of letters addressed to his friend "The Defterdar of Syria, lieutenant of the sacred Sultan of Babylon" in which he describes the travels he has undertaken since leaving Babylon: "Finding myself in this part of Armenia . . ." etcetera. These are almost certainly an imaginary exercise, with much of the geographical description adapted from several recognizable sources.

perhaps it was fortunate that Leonardo's letter was ignored: a man who had sickened of working for Borgia would have found such behavior all too familiar.

Yet evidence has recently come to light suggesting that there could have been an even more mysterious reason why Leonardo was interested in moving to Constantinople. The anthropologist Luigi Capasso of Chieta University in central Italy has carried out a study of the fingerprints detected on Leonardo's notebooks, and is convinced that he has identified the pattern of Leonardo's fingerprint: in particular, a clear image of Leonardo's left index fingerprint. Amongst the range of human fingerprints, some distinctive features are common to particular ethnic groups. According to Capasso: "The one we find in this fingertip applies to 60 percent of the Arabic population, which suggests the probability that his mother was of Middle Eastern origin."

This claim is not as outlandish as it might at first appear. Following the Black Death in the late fourteenth century, Italy suffered from a severe deficiency in servants and people to carry out menial tasks. As a result, during the ensuing century there were regular shipments of slaves, a good proportion of whom came from the Middle East. These were taken on by many families throughout Tuscany, even by the Medici. For example, it is known that the great fifteenth-century banker of the Medici family, Cosimo de' Medici, took a slave girl as a mistress when he was a younger man; and it is possible that the dark-complexioned Medici pope Clement VII was born to a slave girl in the Medici household. Slaves were also taken on by landowners, such as the da Vinci family. It is thus possible that Leonardo's mother, Caterina, was a slave of Middle Eastern origin, which would account for the pattern in Leonardo's fingerprint. Further evidence to support this speculation comes from the fact that Leonardo's mother was called Caterina, a name that was frequently bestowed upon slaves, especially those imported from Constantinople who did not have "Christian" names.

All this is at best unproven theory, but it would certainly add a compelling motive for Leonardo writing his letter to the sultan and wanting to live in Constantinople. Consider the vagaries of his life during the previous three years. First he had been forced to leave Milan on the fall of Ludovico Sforza. Then, after a brief period of wandering, he had found difficulty settling in his native Florence. Consequently he had "chosen" to enter the employment of Borgia—or simply been passed on to him by the Florentine authorities, or been obliged by some previous agreement. This had proved to be a traumatic mistake. Such experiences may well have left Leonardo disillusioned with his native Italy. Indeed, such disillusion would certainly become evident during his later years, causing him to move abroad. All this could easily have inspired in him the romantic notion of traveling to live in his "motherland" (the very land where he had imagined himself traveling during his younger years). As is evident, such a conclusion is speculation based upon speculation—yet there is sufficient grain of fact to suggest such an intriguing possibility.*

Leonardo would never travel to Constantinople to build his bridge; but this does not mean that the bridge was never built. In 1996 the Norwegian artist Vebjørn Sand, using a team of professional engineers, constructed a scaled-down version of Leonardo's bridge as a footbridge at Ås across the main E-18 highway between Oslo and Stockholm. Leonardo had intended to use granite, which is highly resilient under stress, and computer models showed that it would have been quite feasible to construct a full-sized bridge with this material. In the event, the Norwegian engineers used wood, and their scaled-down version has a 300-foot span—as against Leonardo's intended 800-foot span. According to the Norwegian engineers, Leonardo had "surmised that the classic keystone arch could be stretched narrow and substantially widened without losing integrity, by using a flared foothold or pier and the terrain to anchor each end of the span." It would be 300 years before Leonardo's "surmise" would become a generally accepted engineering principle.

Leonardo was almost certainly shown the letter from Sultan Bejazit II sometime early in 1503, around the time Alexander VI decided to

---

* To which there may well one day be a definitive answer, if it proves possible to subject these stains on Leonardo's manuscripts to DNA testing.

make Bishop Francesco Soderini a cardinal in an attempt to encourage Florence to form an alliance with Cesare Borgia. By now Machiavelli had been back in Florence for almost a month, and in response to Leonardo's pleas he may well have persuaded Gonfaloniere Piero Soderini to request the return of the military engineer whom Florence had loaned to Borgia more than half a year previously. Possibly as a means of further encouraging good relations with Florence, Cesare Borgia and Alexander VI must have agreed to allow Leonardo to return to his home city. His work on his war machines was complete, and there is no sign that Leonardo simply abandoned his work for Borgia and disappeared home. Such a move would certainly have incurred Borgia's anger: this would have been seen as a betrayal, and Leonardo was well aware what effect such action had on Borgia. At the very least, cavalry would have been dispatched to hunt him down and bring him back. There is no hint of this in any of the sources; even the better-informed ones, such as Burchard and Giustinian, contain no mention of Leonardo at this time, other than of his work on the huge siege machine in Rome. So we can only assume that Leonardo's parting with Borgia was undertaken with the blessing of both Cesare and the pope.

We know that Leonardo had arrived back in Florence by early March, for in his notebook he records a visit to his Florentine bank: "Saturday the 5th day of March I withdrew from Santa Maria Nuova 50 gold ducats, leaving 450. The same day I gave 5 of these to Salai, who had loaned this amount to me." This would seem to indicate that Leonardo had not yet been paid by Borgia, and had chosen not to wait around until such time as this occurred. It is also another clue that Leonardo might have been accompanied during his time in the Romagna by Salai, working as his assistant. At any rate, Leonardo was at last free from Borgia, a state for which he had almost certainly been longing for at least two months. And he had learned from his experience. Something within him had changed forever during his eight months working for Borgia. For a start, his regard for his military engineering skills, once his greatest pride and joy, would never be the same again. His development of such skills—born of pride and ambition, as well as the will to pursue his destiny as he saw fit—had been a grotesque error. Yet this change of attitude would only be the most immediate and evident indication of a more profound psychological change that had taken place as a result of his terrifying experiences with Borgia.

18

Machiavelli Uses His Influence

W HEN LEONARDO RETURNED to Florence in the early spring of 1503 he found the city in a parlous condition. Pisa continued to hold the mouth of the Arno, thus blocking Florence's main outlet to overseas trade. Now that Machiavelli had resumed his position as secretary to the Ten of War, the waging of the war against Pisa was officially his responsibility. By this stage the conflict had descended into stalemate, with the city in no fit state to hire an effective *condottiere* and his troops to rescue the situation. Yet what was to be done? With trade at a virtual standstill, the exchequer was empty. The population was already taxed to the hilt, and the poorer classes were becoming increasingly resentful at their reduced state, jealous of others who appeared able to continue with their comfortable lives just as they had always done.

Machiavelli recognized the hard question that had to be faced: if anything was to be done about the war, more money was required. Soon after his return he had been commissioned to prepare a report on the situation and what was to be done about it. This he duly produced, under the title "Words to be spoken on the provision of money . . ." As its title implies, this was intended to be given as a speech, probably by Gonfaloniere Soderini to the Signoria. In his report, Machiavelli opened by presenting the city's rulers with some home truths: "At present, you are incapable of defending your subjects." With laudable frankness, he went on to point out the city's vulnerable position amidst the treacherous bear-pit of contemporary Italian politics:

Beyond the borders of Tuscany, you stand between two or three powers, all seeking your ruin rather than your preservation. All around you Italy is ruled by the King of France, the Venetians, and the Pope together with his son the Duke. With regard to the King of France, you must be told the truth. And I am the one who is going to do this. . . . The only remedy is to build up your forces to sufficient strength so that in all his decisions he will have to pay as much attention to you as he does to the others in Italy. . . . As for the Venetians, they are only interested in threatening you in order to extract money, when that money would be better spent fighting against them rather than strengthening them. . . . And we all know how much trust can be placed in the Pope and his son the Duke. . . . Others grow wise by learning from the dangers of their neighbors, but you do not. You have no faith in yourselves, and you merely squander time and opportunities. . . .

Yet Machiavelli's aim was not to induce despair; instead he wished to stress the seriousness of the situation, so as to provoke the city into action. He now came to the crux of the matter: "Remember, one cannot always rely upon someone else's sword. One must be prepared to fight for one's own cause. And to be ready for this, one must have the means." In what would become a feature of Machiavelli's style, he now used historical precedent to reinforce his argument. In this instance, he chose the fall of Constantinople to the Turks—the greatest recent catastrophe to have struck Christendom, which had occurred just fifty years previously and remained a chilling reminder to subsequent generations of how seemingly eternal features of history could vanish overnight. Machiavelli recalled how the Byzantine emperor, faced with the danger of the ever-advancing Ottoman army, had appealed to the rich citizens of Constantinople to pay for the defense of the city, but they had laughed him to scorn. Later, when the Ottoman siege had begun, the affrighted citizens had rushed to the emperor, offering him their gold; but he had driven them away, telling them: "Go and die with your gold, since you would not live without it."

Machiavelli's criticism was particularly forceful: "You do not recognize your present weakness, and you do not take account of the uncertainty of Fortune." As shown by his previous observations on Borgia, Machiavelli was coming to see that a central role in events was always played by Fortune (in Italian, *fortuna*: fate, chance, luck). With Constantinople in mind as an example for Florence, Machiavelli drew the simple but effective lesson: "Fortune will not help those who do not help themselves." The conclusion was obvious: "Florence must arm itself. As one cannot rely upon the sword of others, so one must have one's own sword to hand, to take up when the enemy is approaching." He ended with a rallying cry: "Florentines, I do not believe that you desire your city to fall. You were born free, and have your liberty in your own hands."

The Signoria was persuaded, but the people were in no mood for further taxes. In an attempt to resolve the situation, Gonfaloniere Soderini summoned a meeting of the elected groups of representatives for each district of the city. In the midst of this, representative Luigi Manelli from the Scala district gave a speech berating the authorities, alleging that their taxes were "being used by the rich to crush the poor." Three days later his fellow representatives from the Scala district were summoned to the Palazzo della Signoria and asked if Manelli's sentiments reflected their feelings and those of their district. Several distanced themselves from Manelli's opinion, whereupon Soderini ordered that Manelli be arrested. After the customary judicial torture, he was tried and convicted— sentenced to be banned from holding public office for life and banished forthwith into exile for ten years. Such action would seem to expose Machiavelli's call for Florentines to defend their "liberty" as nothing but rhetoric. Yet this was far from being the case. Despite the many restrictions on their liberty, the citizens of Florence were proud of their somewhat ramshackle system of democracy. This may have remained open to corruption by powerful interested parties, and may also have had its own unspoken rules that one transgressed at one's peril, but it was by far the most libertarian rule amongst the major powers in Italy. Venice remained tightly controlled by its oligarchy, Milan and Lombardy were under French rule, Rome and the Romagna were ruled by the Borgia family, whilst the former kingdom of Naples was divided between Spain and France. In Florence, alone amongst the major Italian powers, the citizens at least had a say in how they were ruled. Manelli had been banished, rather than executed: for Soderini, his real crime had been fomenting revolution and undermining the city's will to defend itself.

Eventually Soderini ordered that a tithe should be gathered from all citizens for the protection of the city. To soften the blow, he extended this to all individual members of the Church who were resident in Florence. They had previously been exempt from such taxes, being answerable only to the pope. Accordingly, Soderini now sought permission from Alexander VI to collect the tithe from his priests in Florence. Such a move, requiring an agreement between Florence and Alexander VI, set immediate alarm bells ringing in Siena. By now Louis XII had exercised his power and forced Cesare Borgia to relinquish Siena, commanding that Pandolfo Petrucci be reinstated. In order to reassure Petrucci that Florence was not siding with Alexander VI in a further attempt to oust him, Machiavelli was dispatched in April to explain the Signoria's position. Louis XII's restoration of Petrucci was part of his attempt to create a league between Siena, Florence, and Bologna, which was designed to deter Borgia from any further territorial adventures in the region. Florence intended to remain within this alliance, under French protection. Machiavelli assured Petrucci that any agreement between Alexander VI and Florence was purely for tax purposes.

When Machiavelli returned from Siena to Florence, the Ten of War issued a decree enrolling several thousand young men in the army, and in May further foot soldiers and men-at-arms were recruited, much to the alarm of Pisa. In June this populous but poorly organized Florentine contingent marched west along the Arno valley towards Pisa. On June 19 news reached Machiavelli and the Ten of War that the Florentine forces had captured the strategic fortress of La Verruca, which stood to the east of Pisa overlooking the river from the hills to the north.

In appearance, this represented little more than a propaganda victory: the Florentine force was not sufficient to threaten the city itself, whose citizens remained safely behind their impregnable walls, confident in the knowledge that they could continue to be supplied by sea. Yet it soon became clear that this Florentine move was part of a secret plan that had probably been hatched by Machiavelli and Leonardo during their time together at Borgia's court in Imola the previous autumn. What they had come up with was a scheme that was daring, devastating, and innovative: to divert the Arno before it reached Pisa, turning its waters into a channel leading south towards the coast. As Pisa lay some five miles from the actual mouth of the river, this would drain the water from the course of the Arno as it passed through Pisa, effectively cutting the city's link to the sea and preventing it from being supplied by sea whilst besieged by the Florentine army.

A similar bold scheme had been tried before by Florence, at the siege of Lucca in 1434. On that occasion the great architect Filippo Brunelleschi, creator of the famous dome on Florence Cathedral, had been brought in to divert the River Sercio, so that it would wash away the ramparts of the city of Lucca, flooding it into submission. The defenders of Lucca had watched from the walls as the Florentines began excavating the dike to divert the river, and had quickly surmised what was afoot. Under cover of darkness, soldiers from Lucca had crept out of the city and demolished the dikes in such a way as to divert the river out over the plain and wash away the camp where the Florentine soldiers were sleeping. This fiasco would have made Gonfaloniere Soderini and the Signoria very wary of attempting anything similar against Pisa, but they must have been persuaded of the efficacy of Leonardo's scheme by Machiavelli's skilled advocacy. In order to avoid the same mistake, the Florentines needed to take the fortress of La Verruca, which stood overlooking the point at which the diversion was to be dug, thus enabling them to defend the excavation site. It would seem that, having been convinced of the scheme, Soderini contacted Alexander VI requesting the return of Leonardo. The pope, seeing it in his interest to show goodwill towards Florence, allowed Leonardo to return from Rome.

There is evidence that Leonardo presented the details of his scheme before Soderini and the Signoria. This comes in the form of a detailed map, drawn around this time by Leonardo, which depicts a bird's-eye view of the Arno as it flowed down between the mountains, then through Florence and on to the sea. The map has dried wax on the back, indicating that it was at one time fixed to a wall, as if for a presentation, and—unlike Leonardo's private maps—the place-names were not in mirror-writing. Also dating from around this time are a number of more sketchy maps showing how the Arno could be diverted south, just before Pisa, so that it would flow through a channel down to the Stagno di Livorno, a large marshy area near the coast, thus depriving Pisa of its river-route to the sea. More than one of the maps thought to date from this period depict both the Pisa diversion and the route that Leonardo had planned for a navigable canal linking Florence to the sea, which he had drawn up all those years earlier in Milan. The different maps show alternative routes both for the diversion and for the canal, indicating that these routes must have been a matter of some discussion. The combination of these two schemes, one to be attempted after the other, was probably what swayed the Signoria and convinced them to go ahead with the initial diversion.

A hint that the first part of this scheme had already been sanctioned by the Signoria can be seen in Leonardo's rapid arrival at La Verruca. News of its capture had only reached Florence on June 19, yet a report from the commanding officer at La Verruca, written on June 21, states that "Leonardo da Vinci was here in person, together with his assistants, and we showed him around the entire place. He seemed to be very pleased, and told us he had found ways of making the fortress impregnable." Leonardo's notebooks show a drawing of La Verruca and some sketches of its position in the Pisan hills. They also depict the Arno flowing past below: the site for the proposed diversion, where those digging the channel would be under the protection of the fortress.

Leonardo and his team returned to Florence, but five days later work began on repairing the fortress under a master builder, following Leonardo's instructions. Then on July 24 Leonardo was back, this time in his capacity as a hydraulics expert (*maestro d'acqua*). According to the official report back to the Signoria:

Leonardo, together with his team, and Alessandro degli Albizzi [a member of the Signoria] discussed the plan in great detail with the governor. Many objections were raised, but in the end it was decided to go ahead, either with the Arno diverted as it flows, or after it has been channeled off from its main course.

From the sound of this, no final plan had yet been agreed upon. Faced with the difficulties that now became evident when viewing the actual site, it even looks as if some were already beginning to have doubts about the scheme. Leonardo too must have had his misgivings, but not on account of the scheme's feasibility: he was always supremely confident of his technical abilities. Leonardo's misgivings would have been over the very nature of the scheme—that is, its military aspect. As a result of his experiences with Borgia, and having witnessed at first hand the true nature of warfare and its attendant activities, Leonardo was now determined to relinquish his career as a military engineer. However, it was probably only on account of the Arno diversion scheme that he had managed to gain release from Borgia's employ. He could console himself that although the scheme itself was undeniably military, when put into practice it was not liable to result in loss of life.

As ever, when Leonardo was working on one subject, his thoughts were liable to turn to a variety of associated topics. Either now or sometime during the following year when work on the Pisa diversion actually began, Leonardo's notebook becomes filled with speculations about water, swimming, a diving suit, and even "how by means of a machine many people may stay under water for some time." He quickly realized that such a machine could be used for military purposes "as a means of destruction under the sea, by piercing a hole in the bottom of a ship, and sinking it and drowning all the people in it." But now he has had enough of war and destruction, and vows, "I will not publish, nor divulge such things because of the evil nature of men."

The nightmare of working for Borgia may have been over, but the memories remained. By now Leonardo must have been aware of the danger he had been in, even whilst traveling to meet Borgia, passing through Arezzo, and meeting Vitellozzo, unwittingly acting as Borgia's spy. Then there had been the massacre he had witnessed at Fossombrone, after Don Michele's troops had tricked their way in through the secret passage; the sudden murder of Lorqua; to say nothing of the sheer horror of Sinigallia, and who knows what else—all had wreaked their effect, affording him a horrific insight into the truth of human nature. No longer would he be able to pen in private his fine sentiments about the preciousness of human life, whilst publicly making a mockery of all they stood for, by working on machines of destruction. Now he knew, through and through, what he had once only written: "the most wicked act of all is to take the life of a man. . . . He who does not value [life], does not himself deserve to have it."

Working on the details of the Florence canal, and the need for sluices to control the flow of water, must have prompted Leonardo to re-examine his map of the upper Arno, which he had drawn during his time with Borgia, as well as the sketches he had made of this region. And it was now that he began to see this craggy blue-remembered landscape with new eyes. Sometime during the spring of 1503 Leonardo rediscovered his delight in painting. Possibly this was related to his deeper understanding of the preciousness of human life, for by the summer he had started his preliminary sketches for what would become his most celebrated painting, that of the young woman who would be known as "Mona Lisa." The background had already begun forming in his mind: this, many would recognize as the landscape of the upper reaches of the Arno, the little arched bridge behind her left shoulder being identified as the Ponte Buriano outside Arezzo. Others would recognize the craggy outcrop behind Mona Lisa's right shoulder as La Verruca, whose site he had visited and sketched in July 1503, in preparation for the Pisa diversion.

But suddenly the entire diversion project was put on hold. In the kingdom of Naples the French had suffered a series of defeats at the hands of the Spanish, causing them to withdraw to the port of Gaeta. It looked as if Louis XII's guarantee of protection to Florence was now in jeopardy, and Florentine troops were withdrawn from Pisa to protect the city. In Rome, the changing fortunes of the French and the Spanish were reflected in the behavior of Alexander VI and Cesare Borgia. The pope secretly favored the Spanish, putting out feelers for an alliance between Spain, himself, and Venice. Cesare, on the other hand, continued to favor Louis XII. As Giustinian reported, "the two were in open conflict, both pursuing their own ends."

As a result of this conflict, even those amongst the inner circle of Borgia confidants now found themselves in danger. Jacopo da Santa Croce had long been a familiar of Alexander VI—indeed, he had been the loyal emissary who had been entrusted with escorting the unsuspecting Cardinal Orsini to the Vatican from his palazzo, on the day of his arrest. Despite this, in June 1503 Jacopo was arrested on orders of Borgia and flung into the Castel Sant' Angelo. Days later he was suddenly released, after payment of an undisclosed sum to the papal coffers. A week later, without warning, he was rearrested. At dawn on June 9 his executed body was found laid out on the bridge before Castel Sant' Angelo, in remarkably similar fashion to that in which Lorqua's body had been laid out in the public square at Cesena. This was evidently another public warning. Rumors flew: was Borgia trying to signal the fate of anyone who betrayed him? Word began to spread that Jacopo had secretly switched his alliance to the Orsini, but few people found this credible. More suspected that this was part of the growing conflict between the pope and his son.

At the same time, another mysterious series of events took place, involving Francesco Troches, the trusted Spaniard who had for many years acted for both Alexander VI and Cesare Borgia, delivering some of their most secret communications. The twists and turns of this affair baffled even Giustinian and the rest of the ambassadors to the papal court. In mid-May Troches had been dispatched from Rome on a covert mission carrying a message to Pandolfo Petrucci of Siena. Petrucci was baffled by this message, which reassured him that, despite his reinstatement, Borgia planned no further move against Siena. Petrucci swiftly passed on this message to Florence, which he now saw as his protector.

On May 19, the very day that Troches arrived in Siena, Borgia in Rome issued a warrant for his arrest, on the grounds that he had treacherously taken flight from Rome. As Troches traveled on his way from Siena back to Rome, a loyal messenger warned him of the danger, and he immediately took flight for the port of Civitavecchia, from where he traveled on a galley to Genoa. A papal galley soon set out in pursuit, with orders to detain Troches at all costs. He was evidently aware of the determination of his pursuers, and in the attempt to shake them off his trail, he took ship from Genoa to Sardinia, whence he doubled back to Corsica. Here, in the first week of June, the papal galley finally caught up with him. Troches was arrested and hauled back in chains to Ostia, the port of Rome. Arriving there on June 8, he was greeted by Borgia's notorious henchman Don Michele. At this point the story becomes less clear. Don Michele is said to have transported Troches to Rome, where that night he was brought before Borgia. He was then interrogated into the early hours, whilst Don Michele waited out of sight beyond the door. The topics under discussion in this interrogation are not known, but when it was over Don Michele came in and Borgia then stood outside the door, listening to the choking cries of his former confidant as he was garrotted by Don Michele, Borgia's undisputed master of this form of execution.

It was surely no accident that Troches was murdered on the very same day as Jacopo da Santa Croce's body was found on the Castel Sant' Angelo bridge. Even the pope appeared shocked, going to some lengths to assure a cardinal at his court that he had no part in Troches' murder. However, he would certainly have suspected the reason for it. As the fortunes of the French in Naples had begun to wane, Cesare had joined with his father in the secret negotiations with the Spanish: Troches had apparently passed on news of this to Louis XII.

Yet things soon became even more complex and devious, as Alexander VI began hedging his bets. Although the pope had by this time openly sided with Spain, even to the extent of allowing the Spanish to recruit soldiers in Rome, he covertly sent word to the French, who were now assembling an army in northern Italy. This army was intended to march south, join up with the French forces at present being besieged by the Spanish at Gaeta, and then inflict a final blow against the Spanish forces in the kingdom of Naples. Alexander VI offered to pay two-thirds of the cost of this army, on condition that when they defeated the Spanish, his son Cesare would be allowed to rule Naples, or at least Sicily. This was a bold offer, but Alexander VI knew that the French would be permanently overstretched if they tried to keep Naples; in return for the kingdom of Naples, Alexander was prepared to allow the French free rein to extend their territory in northern Italy. This appeared to be a reasonable deal—except for the fact that the pope was also conducting a secret dialogue with Venice, suggesting an alliance with the papal forces, with the aim of driving from Italy all foreign armies—that is, both the French and the Spanish.

Amidst all Alexander VI's treacherous diplomacy, it is possible to discern one single guiding aim: the furthering of the Borgia cause, whichever way events turned. Despite the evident conflict between the pope and his son, neither of them diverged from this common goal. For the time being, Alexander VI's double-dealing offers to the French, the Spanish, and the Venetians had the more immediate aim of keeping them all at bay, with their various armies retained in their separate territories. This suited Borgia, who was busy assembling his own army in Rome. By this stage he had 600 men-at-arms, together with 600 light cavalry and 4,000 tough foot soldiers, many of whom had been recruited from amongst the former mercenaries of the Romagna, whence further troops were due to join him soon. This was now very much a Borgia army: all were outfitted in the Borgia colors of quartered red and yellow, emblazoned with the name "Cesar." But this was intended to be more than just a vainglorious echo of ancient Roman power and grandeur. The core of Borgia's army consisted of the hardest fighting men on the peninsula: Spanish infantry, and the dreaded Stradiotes—Albanian light cavalry who had gained their spurs fighting the Ottoman army in the Balkans. According to the contemporary chronicler Francesco Matarazzo:

The Duke had by now become the leading commander in Italy. . . . He had the finest soldiery in his armies, for the most celebrated mercenaries served under him. The way he treated his soldiers, allowing them to take what they wanted from land through which they passed, meant that soldiers flocked to his banner. Besides, fortune smiled upon him and he had accumulated so much treasure and fine possessions that no one in Italy could match it, nor was there anywhere in Italy such a great body of soldiers, with such fine horses and cloth of gold uniforms, and their number seemed limitless.

One of the reasons Borgia was able to gather such a large force in Rome was that he had little need of heavy garrisons in the Romagna. He had continued his policy of gaining the confidence of the population by firm but just government. In the larger towns such as Imola, Urbino, and Cesena, the administration retained any talented locals who were willing to take an oath of allegiance to Borgia. These local administrations were headed by military prefects who answered directly to Borgia, but were for the most part free to rule as they saw fit. Similarly, in the clerical administration, preferment was given to local priests, and the outside purchase of offices was stopped. This was the first time in centuries that the people of the Romagna had seen the beginnings of a peaceful and efficient unified rule. What was more, this rule was to a certain extent in their own hands, and its citizens appreciated this—leaving Borgia to go about his other business in Rome, with his much-feared soldiery inflicting no further injuries upon the citizens of his ever-expanding dukedom.

In June, Borgia began to deploy his forces once more. Perugia was one of the ancient papal states, but—like its counterparts in the Romagna—it had over the years devolved to virtual independence, finally being taken over by the notorious Gianpaolo Baglioni. Although Baglioni had now fled, and after the events at Sinigallia a deputation had presented Borgia with the keys to the city, this had proved a somewhat ceremonial gesture, and the city had remained independent. But now Alexander VI sent word to Perugia that it must accept Borgia as its ruler. At the same time the pope made it clear that he was willing simply to buy off the rulers of Lucca and Siena with large sums of money, so that their territories could be added to Borgia's domain. Meanwhile Borgia dispatched north a force of 3,500 cavalry and 2,000 infantry, which took up positions, strategically encamped between Perugia and the border of Tuscany. The smokescreen for this maneuver was that this was Borgia's contingent making ready to join up with the French when they left Milan on the march south. As a result of such moves, Florence now found itself beleaguered, to all intents and purposes at Borgia's mercy. In the hope of retaining Borgia's friendship, the petty rulers of many northern Italian states were conspiring to let him have Florence—for this, they divined, was his aim. How wrong they were.

With all major players in Italy kept at bay by Alexander VI's diplomatic double-dealing—nay, treble-dealing—all that was now needed was for the French to march on Gaeta and for the outcome of their encounter with the Spanish to be decided. But to reach Gaeta the French had to march south, which meant that Borgia was unable to move on Florence for fear of attracting their attention, which might have been diverted from Gaeta to defend the city that they saw as their ally. Nothing could happen before the French were defeated (as seemed most likely) by the Spanish. With Spanish backing, Borgia would then be able to march on Florence, and indeed would have all of northern Italy at his feet.

It now became clear to many what Alexander VI had meant when, following the events at Sinigallia, he had boasted: "What has happened so far is nothing compared with what is planned for the future." Once Borgia had taken Florence and established himself in northern Italy, he would then, with Venetian help, drive the Spanish from Naples and eventually unite the whole of Italy under Borgia rule. There were a few far-sighted observers, Machiavelli amongst them, who had suspected all along that such were the Borgia aims. Yet even these perceptive commentators were in for a surprise. Indeed, the truth of what was being planned appears to have been beyond the imagination of all but Machiavelli. And what he guessed was the closest of the Borgia secrets, probably known only to the three innermost members of the family—namely, Alexander VI, Cesare, and Lucrezia.

Lucrezia, recognizing the successful unfolding of the early stages of the plan, had not been able to restrain herself from hinting at the ultimate Borgia secret to her confidant, the poet Ercole Strozzi, who would himself later allude to it in one of his poems, claiming of Cesare Borgia that he had "once expected the high grace of his father's throne." And Lucrezia was not the only one who found it difficult to keep this ultimate secret. Even Alexander VI, realizing that he was now getting old and would in all likelihood be dead in a few years' time, had asked the Venetians to protect his son with the words, "I will see to it that the Papacy shall belong either to him or to you." His intention was nothing less than that his son should succeed him as pope: the greatest institution in Christendom, the papacy itself, was to become a secularized hereditary possession of the Borgia family! In the words of the celebrated nineteenth-century authority on the Italian Renaissance, the Swiss scholar Jacob Burckhardt, speaking of Cesare Borgia:

> He, if anybody, could have secularized the States of the Church, and he would have been forced to do so in order to keep them. Unless we are much deceived, this is the real reason of the secret sympathy with which Machiavelli treats the great criminal; from Caesar, or from nobody, could it be hoped that he "would draw the steel from the wound," in other words, annihilate the Papacy—the source of all foreign intervention and all the divisions of Italy. The intriguers who thought to divine Caesar's aims, when holding out to him hopes of the kingdom of Tuscany, seem to have been dismissed with contempt.

Everything had been planned, down to the last detail: whichever way events turned out, Borgia would use them to his advantage. But, as he himself would later admit to Machiavelli, there was one eventuality that he had not foreseen.

By July the French army had at last been assembled: a force consisting of 1,200 men-at-arms, 1,400 light cavalry, and 8,000 infantry. On August 6 the news reached Rome that the French army had finally set off on the long march south to Naples. According to Giustinian, when the news was announced, "the Pope and the Duke were beside themselves with joy."

August 1503 proved to be the hottest and most parched high summer that Rome had experienced in living memory. All the firsthand commentators remark on how unbearable the heat became, and how it soon began to take its toll. Under normal circumstances the papal court would have moved out to one of the Borgia family retreats in the cooler countryside, but with the political situation so finely balanced, neither the pope nor Cesare was willing to leave the city. After the tolling midday bell had rung out over the rooftops, the sun would reduce the Eternal City to a heat-stunned silence; and at dusk the malaria mosquitoes would spread in from the low-lying waters of the Tiber and the undrained swamplands to the west of the city. The Vatican was particularly susceptible from both these quarters. Then there was a hint of worse news: rumors began to spread that the bubonic plague had broken out in the slums.

The southward march of the French army proceeded so slowly that it looked as if Gaeta might fall to the Spanish before they arrived. On hearing that the French had left Milan, the Spanish had launched a concerted onslaught. If Gaeta fell, the French would have no port from which they could be supplied, and their army would almost certainly turn on its heels and head back to Milan, with perhaps half of its number returning across the Alps to France. Yet if the French continued to march south, Borgia would soon be forced to join them, together with his army, in order to allay any suspicions held by Louis XII. It soon became clear that Borgia's entire enterprise hinged on whether or not Gaeta fell in time. The pope became increasingly agitated, yet Cesare appeared curiously insouciant, setting out each morning at first light for his hunting trips into the cool, misty countryside, returning only with the heat of the day. By now the presence of the plague had been confirmed, and daily the number of victims increased. Worse still, the disease was no longer confined to the sweltering, stinking slums: in the first week of August the pope's cousin, the vastly overweight Cardinal Juan Borgia-Lanzol, died soon after succumbing to the first symptoms. Giustinian reported that he had been poisoned by Borgia, but although this rumor quickly swept the city, it seems unlikely to have been true. The pope, mindful of his own corpulence, was heard to comment ominously: "This month is a bad one for fat people." Four of his recent predecessors on the papal throne had died at this time of year. No sooner had Alexander VI made his remark than an owl flew in through an open window and fell at his feet. The pope paled and exclaimed: "This is an evil, evil omen." His sole consolation was the birth, at around this time, of another illegitimate son to an unknown Roman woman. The infant would be christened Rodrigo, after his seventy-three-year-old father.

On Saturday evening, during the first week in August, the pope and Cesare went to dine with Cardinal Adriano da Corneto, one of Alexander VI's newly appointed cardinals, in his vineyard on the hillside of Monte Mario just a mile or so northeast of the Vatican. The party lasted into the night, before the pope and his son returned to their apartments in the Vatican. On August 7, two days after this party, Giustinian reported that he had been surprised to be received by the pope seated in his chamber wrapped about with shawls. The pope appeared depressed and said he was worried about the fever that was spreading through Rome. He also mentioned how he was anxious now that the French troops were approaching papal territory, every day increasing the need for some kind of definitive action by Cesare. Four days later Cardinal Adriano succumbed to a serious fever. This was August 11, the anniversary of Alexander VI's accession to the papal throne, a day usually celebrated with some gusto by the pope. But on this occasion he was overcome by apathy, and seemed to many to be showing his age. The next day, after breakfast, Alexander was seized by a fit of vomiting and was taken to his bed. That very day, Borgia was on the point of setting out to take command of his troops near Perugia, in preparation for joining up with the French army, when he too was struck down with similarly violent symptoms and was forced to take to his bed, on the floor above the papal apartments.

In an attempt to keep secret what was happening, the Vatican doors were locked, and all visitors and ambassadors were turned away, while Alexander VI and Cesare were attended only by their personal physicians. Even so, rumors soon began to leak out beyond the confines of the Vatican into the city itself.

On August 13 the pope's physicians decided to bleed him copiously, and this appeared to have a reviving effect on the vigorous elderly patient. According to Giustinian, who was able to question the doctors as they left the Vatican, that afternoon the pope was able to sit up in his bed and play cards. Upstairs, Cesare's fever was much worse, and his physicians decided upon more drastic measures. On August 15 he was removed from his bed and lowered into a large oil jar filled with ice and water. The shock caused the skin to peel from his body, and next day he was reported to be in a delirium.

Although he was apparently at death's door, he nonetheless remained conscious of the danger of the situation. Despite the attempts of the Borgia faction to maintain secrecy, news that the pope and Cesare had been struck down with fever soon began to spread beyond Rome. When members of the Orsini faction got wind of these rumors, several of them returned to Rome, hoping to take advantage of the situation. But already Borgia had sent orders summoning his troops from Perugia, together with messages of reassurance to his leading prefects in the Romagna. He was determined to forestall any attempts to foment unrest, or even an uprising, by agents of the Vitelli clan or followers of Guidobaldo of Urbino.

On August 17 the pope's condition began to deteriorate, and it appeared that he had not long to live. That evening Giustinian hurried back to his quarters and wrote in his dispatch, "The Vatican was in pandemonium. Everyone was seeking to save himself and his belongings, yet with the utmost secrecy." On the morning of August 18 the pope was able to receive the sacraments from his personal confessor. Johannes Burchard noted that at no time since he had been struck down with his illness had he made mention either of Cesare or of his beloved Lucrezia. Later he had a suffocation fit that rendered him unconscious, and he died that afternoon.

Upstairs, Borgia had begun to recover slightly, but was still helpless with exhaustion. Burchard described what happened when he heard of his father's death:

Borgia, who was sick, sent downstairs Don Michele with an escort of heavily armed men. These entered the Pope's apartment and secured all the doors behind them. Then one of them unsheathed his dagger and threatened Cardinal Casanova that he would slit his throat and throw him out of the window if he refused to hand over the keys to the Papal treasure. The terrified cardinal handed over the keys. Then Don Michele and his men went, one after the other, into the chamber behind the Pope's bed. They took all the money that was there and two caskets containing around 100,000 ducats.

They also removed gold, plate, and jewels estimated at around 300,000 ducats. But, according to Burchard, in his haste Don Michele did not think to search the locked chamber adjoining the pope's bedroom, and in this way missed all manner of jeweled miters, precious stones, rings, and vases, which would have been enough to fill several chests. Don Michele and his men disappeared upstairs, carrying their loot to Borgia. Those present in the pope's bedchamber quickly scurried about, pocketing all they could lay their hands on. Then the doors were ordered to be opened, and Alexander VI's death was ceremoniously announced to the world.

That night, his body was laid out in the main hall of the Vatican, the scene of so many of his famous debauched parties. Here it was left in the dark with just two candles burning beside the open coffin. No one spent the vigil in attendance on the pope, and Burchard remarked upon how empty the Vatican had now become, with just a few servants present.

Next morning the body was raised on its bier and ceremoniously carried across to St. Peter's, where a scuffle broke out when the Vatican guards attempted to seize the golden candlesticks being carried by the chanting monks accompanying the body. In the ensuing brawl the pope's body was unceremoniously dumped and abandoned. Burchard and some of the Vatican servants eventually dragged the open coffin inside the railings protecting the high altar, where they locked the iron grille door to prevent any of Alexander VI's enemies from desecrating his corpse.

When Burchard returned in the afternoon he found that the pope's body had become so decayed and bloated that it was barely recognizable as human. "The skin of his face was the color of black cloth, like that of the most black of Africans, and it was disfigured with purple blotches. His nose had swelled up and his tongue was so enormous that it filled his entire mouth and ballooned out between his wide open lips." Those present were of the opinion that they had never seen anything so ghastly in their lives.

Yet more was to come. It was decided that the pope should be buried at once, but by now the body had become so hideously swollen that it was as wide as it was long. As nobody dared to touch it, a rope was tied around one of its feet and a porter dragged it off the bier along the ground to the open grave. Burchard described what happened next:

> The six porters whose duty it was to bury him began making blasphemous jokes about the Pope and his grotesque appearance. The carpenters had made the coffin too narrow and too small, so they bent the mitre, wrapped the body in some old cloth and began stuffing it into the coffin anyhow, pummeling at it with their fists to make it fit.

By now all kinds of wild rumors had begun to circulate about what had happened to the pope and his son. The most persistent and widely believed of these stories told how Alexander VI and Cesare had in fact intended to murder the rich Cardinal Adriano da Corneto for his fortune, which was known to be held largely in the form of quickly disposable assets such as coins. The cardinal was to be poisoned at the dinner party he had given the previous week, but in the event, there had been a muddle over the poisoned flask of wine and they had all drunk from it. This appeared to be confirmed by the Venetian historian Paolo Giovio, who was in Rome at the time: when he visited the cardinal after he had fallen ill, Cardinal Adriano told him that he believed his illness was the result of poison slipped to him by one of the Borgias. Such was the story that quickly spread beyond the confines of Rome. Just four days after Alexander VI's death it had reached Florence; days later Milan and Venice; and weeks later the nineteen-year-old Martin Luther would even hear it whilst he was studying at the University of Erfurt in Germany. Soon all Christendom knew how the pope had died.

For Alexander VI and his son to have suffered such a fate might have been seen as poetic justice, but it was probably not the truth. The Borgias' chosen method of poisoning was "cantarella," whose secret method of preparation has been lost. This poison was known to have come in the form of a white powder with a pleasant taste, and was almost certainly an arsenic concoction that could be sprinkled over food or into wine without betraying its presence. This "eternity powder" was usually administered in a fatal dose, which killed the victim rapidly, within a day or two. However, it could also be administered in less lethal doses, as a "time poison" with a delayed action, and could take days, or even weeks, to kill its ingester. This delayed-action poison would appear to be the obvious explanation for what happened to the cardinal and the two Borgias. Unfortunately for this theory, most sources argue that the lesser doses of "cantarella" had to be administered on a regular basis, achieving a cumulative effect, for it to be lethal. Such could not have been the case in this instance.

As we have seen, Cardinal Adriano was not struck down until four days later, whilst Alexander VI and Borgia did not fall ill until a week after the party. All seem to have been afflicted by the same illness, suffering vomiting fits and recurrent bouts of worsening fever; and the final appearance of Alexander VI's body also provides a clue. The cardinal, the pope, and his son were almost certainly all bitten by infected mosquitoes on the night of the vineyard party. The disease incubated for several days, and then manifested as virulent malaria. Many others in the Vatican, including other cardinals, were similarly struck down during August 1503. Some have suggested that the appearance of Alexander VI's cadaver indicated plague, but this was unlikely, as Burchard and others would have remarked upon the telltale buboes that accompany this illness. As for the story of Cardinal Adriano believing he had been poisoned, this may well have been true, although the cardinal would have had nothing to support his belief beyond his own suspicions. Even Giustinian, with his ear so close to the ground, indicated his belief in the poisoning story—though this was in a private letter rather than in his official dispatch, and was backed by no evidence. All this does little more than indicate that he too was taken in by this most plausible of rumors, which so many believed because they wanted to believe in it.

Nearly all authoritative historians of the period dismiss the rumor of poison, largely on account of the "delayed action" of the illness. However, in spite of strong arguments in favor of malarial fever, there would seem to be more of an element of doubt than is generally conceded.

Despite Alexander VI's notoriety, his legacy was not entirely negative. He may have been an unprincipled character, but he was also a forceful one. The ambassadors in Rome who were privy to his debauched behavior did not respect him as a man, but they knew better than to disrespect his cunning and his power. During his eleven-year reign, spiritual regard for the papacy plunged to a nadir, yet his devious political machinations resulted in considerable temporal influence for the Holy See. At the outset of Alexander VI's reign, Charles VIII had marched through Italy with scant regard for the man who sat on St. Peter's throne. Yet by the time the army of Louis XII marched on Naples five years later, any powerful foreign invader knew that he needed the pope's backing if he was to achieve lasting success in his aims. Even the Spanish understood this. Yet while maintaining a difficult balance between the French and the Spanish, Alexander VI also managed to further his own covert, yet extremely ambitious, aims. He may not have lived to see the achievement of his ultimate aim—a powerful united Italy under Borgia rule—but he had set his son on the path towards this goal. Now it was all up to Cesare Borgia.

19

The Election of a New Pope

INITIALLY, ALEXANDER VI had seen his favorite son, Cesare's younger brother Juan, Duke of Gandia, as his main benefactor, with Cesare being little more than the clerical instrument in his plans. Yet from the moment of Juan's murder (quite possibly by Cesare), it became clear that any relationship between the pope and his new heir would not be one of easy subservience. When Cesare launched into his campaigns in the Romagna, Alexander VI's hold on his son was becoming tenuous and problematic, maintained largely by threats and the power of the papal purse strings. By the high summer of 1503, Borgia would seem to have got the upper hand in their relationship. Yet despite their occasional explosive quarrels, and even the threat of excommunication, it has to be stressed that Cesare remained dedicated to his father's notion of a lasting Borgia destiny and made his every move with his father's guiding idea in mind. As he would later confide to Machiavelli: "I was fully ready for the death of my father, and had made every preparation for it, but it never occurred to me that I myself would be fighting death at the same time."

As Cesare Borgia lay at death's door in the Vatican, the political situation could not have been more fraught. Upon news of the pope's death, the French army, now under the command of Francesco Gonzaga, the Marquis of Mantua, had been ordered to halt its march south to Naples. The vast, unruly French army ground to a standstill at the small city of Viterbo, forty miles north of Rome, arriving with such effect that the Cardinal of Viterbo would later report: "The whole city was in a ferment; the confusion was such that it seemed as if everything was going to pieces." Meanwhile the Spanish commander Gonsalvo de Cordova withdrew a large force from the siege of Gaeta and ordered it to march north under the command of Prospero Colonna. The Spanish halted their march at Marino, on the edge of papal territory just ten miles from the outskirts of Rome.

The Eternal City stood in peril: both of the two powerful foreign invaders now had a vested interest in securing the election of a pope who was sympathetic to their cause. Whoever held the papacy in all likelihood held the key to who ruled Italy.

On August 19, the day of the pope's funeral, Cesare suffered a serious relapse. The shops were all boarded up and the main streets of the city silent and empty, apart from the mass of quiet onlookers gathered outside St. Peter's waiting for the funeral procession. According to Giustinian, many were now clearly hoping that Cesare would soon be following his father to the grave. Rumors quickly began to spread that members of the Orsini and the Colonna clans were making their way towards the city with the intent of taking back the residences from which they had been dispossessed by the Borgias. Already, Cesare had ensured that members of the Borgia family had been moved into the Castel Sant' Angelo for safekeeping. Amongst these were his mother, Vannozza, as well as two of Borgia's previously unacknowledged illegitimate children and several more of Alexander VI's children, along with some of their mothers. Although the infant Rodrigo was not mentioned amongst this colorful clan, he too was almost certainly included in their number. If the Borgia dynasty was to be established, it would require as many loyal family heirs as it could muster.

After the pope's funeral, rival gangs began marching through the streets shouting slogans for the Orsini, the Colonnas, and the Borgias. A showdown seemed imminent. Yet neither the Orsini nor their supporters realized that before relapsing, Borgia had already taken measures to outwit them, sending out feelers to the Colonnas for a truce, offering them back all their confiscated lands and fortresses in return for their support.

For two days Borgia clung to life, and by the third it looked as if he might recover. He may have been too ill to move, but his plans were already coming into effect. On August 22 his loyal private secretary Agapito Geraldini, now acting as his envoy plenipotentiary, signed an agreement with the Colonnas in his master's name. The following day Prospero Colonna left the Spanish forces under his command at Marino and marched with his own Colonna contingent into Rome to support the 12,000 Borgia troops under Don Michele. When the Orsini arrived in Rome later that day with 400 cavalry and 1,500 infantry, they found themselves outmaneuvered and outnumbered. The following day they retreated from the city, venting their spleen by ransacking a number of undefended Borgia houses whose inhabitants had taken refuge in the Castel Sant' Angelo.

Meanwhile the situation beyond Rome was deteriorating fast. Seeing that Borgia was powerless to defend his ducal lands in the Romagna, The Marches, and Umbria, his enemies began to move in. The Venetians, who had always been mistrustful of Borgia's dukedom so close to their borders, now supplied Guidobaldo of Urbino with troops so that he could march south and attempt to retake his territory. Meanwhile Florence seized its chance to neutralize the Borgia threat to Tuscany by providing a contingent to their *condottiere* ally Jacopo d'Appiano to assist him in taking back his lordship of Piombino. At the same time, the Florentines encouraged the Baglionis to march on Perugia.

Yet back in Rome, Borgia still remained all-powerful, despite his weakened physical condition and occasional lapses into delirium. The College of Cardinals, which was now the official ruler of Rome during the interregnum before the election of a new pope, was so mistrustful of Borgia that its members refused point-blank to enter the Vatican. Instead, it met amidst the Gothic pillars of the church of Santa Maria Sopra Minerva, a mile away across the Tiber in the city of Rome itself. Even here, it was fearful of embarking upon the conclave to elect a new pope. The Church was paralyzed, and it soon became clear that such a state of affairs could not be allowed to continue.

If the papal election was held under the present circumstances, it was evident that Borgia would impose his chosen man and in effect have the new papacy in his pocket. Although it was not realized at the time,

Borgia saw this as the prelude to taking over the papacy himself, when the opportunity arose. Yet for the time being he was in no position to make such a daring, unprecedented, and final move—the ultimate in the strategy that he and his father had devised together. Neither the Spanish nor the French would have tolerated it. Indeed, Borgia now found himself facing opposition from the representatives of all Christendom: the world was waiting for a new pope, and the College of Cardinals had to be free to hold its conclave without external interference.

A deputation representing all the foreign embassies, under the leadership of Giustinian, entered the Vatican with the aim of persuading Borgia to leave. Though still severely debilitated, Borgia was nonetheless able to negotiate. He would leave, but only under two conditions. First, he was to be reappointed as *gonfaloniere* of the papal forces—a post that had automatically fallen into abeyance with the death of Alexander VI. Second, Venice was to be prevailed upon to cease its aggressive moves against his dukedom. On August 22 Giustinian and his delegation agreed to these conditions, as long as Borgia swore his allegiance to the papacy—at present in the form of the College of Cardinals, and later in the form of whoever was elected as the new pope.

On September 2 Borgia finally decamped from the Vatican, accompanied by a large armed escort under the command of Don Michele. Borgia himself was said to have been carried in a litter with closed crimson curtains, borne on the shoulders of eight liveried men, each armed with a halberd.* This was followed by Borgia's favorite black stallion covered with a black velvet coat adorned in gold with his ducal crown. Some of the spectators were struck by the resemblance to a funeral procession, a view that would have been reinforced had they been able to set eyes on Borgia himself. By this stage he was a shadow of his former self. His limbs were emaciated, his head a mere skull drained of flesh, all showing the effects of his persistent battle against the fever that even now still threatened to overwhelm him. The soles

---

* A short lance headed by an axe and a reverse-blade spike.

of his feet had become so swollen that he would have been unable to stand, even if he had possessed the strength to do so. Likewise, the face that just ten years previously had caused him to be called "the handsomest man in Italy" was now like that of a cadaver, its skin disfigured with the telltale blotches of syphilis. Yet although Borgia may have appeared as a ghost of the man he had once been, the inner man remained as ever, his ruthless will unimpaired. Except when he relapsed into an exhausted delirium, he was still very much in control of himself, still fired by his ambition for power—the man who was in control of himself still sought to control Italy.

The funereal appearance of Borgia's retreat from the Vatican was reinforced by the mournful family procession that followed the closed crimson curtains of Borgia's litter and his bowed black stallion. The retinue was led by his mother, Vannozza, followed by a gaggle of illegitimate Borgia children (this time definitely including the infant Rodrigo). Witnesses to this grim but colorful retreat reported that it also carried away heavily guarded strongboxes and chests containing all the Borgia treasure, while the Mantuan ambassador noted that the retinue included "women of every kind."

At least for the time being, Rome was no longer to be the central Borgia stronghold it had been throughout the reign of Alexander VI. Yet even in retreat Borgia retained his treacherous guile. Prospero Colonna was waiting for him across Rome at the gate known as the Porto del Popolo. From here Colonna would escort Borgia to Tivoli, ten miles to the east of the city, where the Spanish army was now encamped. By allying himself with the Colonnas, Borgia had allied himself to Spain and would be expected to used his Spanish cardinals to ensure the election of a new pope who looked favorably upon the Spanish cause. To reinforce this assumption, and reassure Colonna's spies, who would have observed him leaving the Vatican, Borgia had sent his artillery ahead across the Tiber. Yet no sooner had he been carried out of the Vatican than his procession turned off and slipped out of the Porto Viridaria beside the Vatican Gardens. At the same time, Borgia's artillery turned in its tracks and headed back across the Tiber.

Outside the Porto Viridaria, Borgia was met by his advance guard, who escorted his procession north to the Borgia fortress at Nepi, which was close to where the French army was now encamped. Colonna soon realized what had happened: he had been tricked, and Borgia was going to side with the French.

When Borgia reached Nepi, he received a succession of messages from all parts of his dukedom. Guidobaldo had retaken Urbino on August 28; four days later Venetian troops had occupied Cesenatico, and then moved on to Cesena. But Borgia's capital had rallied under Sansavino and held true to the Borgia cause. Despite this popular display in Borgia's favor, on September 3 Pesaro had fallen to its former ruler, Giovanni Sforza, Lucrezia's slandered former husband. Three days later, Rimini had also fallen. Meanwhile Florence was aiding the formidable Caterina Sforza's son Ottavio Riario in his attempt to retake Imola and Forli, which had so far held out for Borgia. Florentine assistance to Jacopo d'Appiano had allowed him to retake Piombino. And still the news came in: on September 9 Gianpaolo Baglioni finally took Perugia, and Vitelli forces had then retaken the family stronghold of Città di Castello.

Yet the situation quickly underwent a dramatic transformation. Once Louis XII was satisfied that Borgia had remained loyal to the French, he dispatched messengers to the Romagna, The Marches, and Umbria announcing that Borgia was "alive and well and the friend of the King of France." Anyone attempting to annex the territory of the Duke of the Romagna was thus an enemy of Louis XII. Venice withdrew its forces, and Florence immediately sent word declaring its allegiance to Borgia. Defiantly, but with foreboding, Guidobaldo of Urbino and Gian-paolo Baglioni of Perugia formed a league for the protection of their recaptured cities. It looked as if Borgia's unexpected decision to side with the French had saved his dukedom.

Yet by this stage Borgia had other concerns. Leaving the hot, malarial air of Rome for the cooler, healthier atmosphere of the hill town of Nepi had brought about a slight recovery in his health, which meant that he was able to concentrate his depleted energies on the papal election that was soon to take place in Rome. It was vital that this produce a pope who was malleable to the Borgia cause. To this end, Borgia had selected as his candidate the Spaniard Giovanni Vera, Cardinal of Salerno. Vera had been one of Borgia's tutors, and in 1501 Borgia had appointed him governor of Fano, where he had followed Borgia's instructions to the letter, to such an exent that Fano had remained loyal to the new Duke of the Romagna whilst nearby Urbino and Pesaro had returned to their former rulers. Even though Borgia had abandoned the Spanish cause, Vera knew that he could rely upon the support of the eleven Borgia-appointed Spanish cardinals, who comprised around one-third of the cardinalate. As early as August 21 Giustinian had written to Venice, "I have heard on the best authority that last Sunday eleven cardinals swore to Borgia that they would have Cardinal Vera elected, or else they would bring about a schism."

The papacy had been riven by schisms in the medieval era, and until little over half a century previously there had been an alternative pope in Avignon. Thus causing a schism would have been a major step, but not an unprecedented one. However, it would seem that either Giustinian was exaggerating or, more likely, Borgia was bluffing. Borgia was in no position to bring about such a break, but the very prospect of one might have frightened some of the uncommitted cardinals to his cause.

In fact, the election was wide open. Neither those cardinals in favor of the French nor those in favor of the Spanish could muster an overall majority. Between these two camps remained a rump of Italian cardinals, all of whom were known to be willing to cast their vote for the highest bidder. Giustinian reported that Borgia's eleven cardinals were "doing their best to win over Cardinals Caraffa, Riario, and Pallavicini to their cause. And I also know for a fact that Borgia has taken steps to prevent Cardinal Giuliano della Rovere from arriving in Italy, either by land or by sea."

Cardinal della Rovere, Alexander VI's sworn foe within the Church, had found himself in a dire situation following the election of his enemy as pope—the event that he had fought tooth and nail to prevent. As a result, he had felt in such danger that he had eventually fled from Rome, and finally from Italy altogether, in fear of his life. In exile he had plotted to bring about Alexander VI's downfall, but to no avail: the pope had outwitted him at every turn. Now Cardinal della Rovere was returning to confront the Spanish faction. This he knew was supported by Alexander VI's son, who just eight months previously had deposed his young nephew Francesco della Rovere as ruler of Sinigallia, and had then befouled the city with his treacherous murders. The della Roveres were also closely related to the dukes of Urbino, and the cardinal had been a devoted friend of the talented Guidobaldo of Urbino during the latter's youth. Cardinal della Rovere was bent on revenge, and had every reason to return to Rome for the papal election.

For the last six years he had been in exile in France and was naturally expected to support the French candidate, Louis XII's powerful and ambitious chief counselor, Cardinal d'Amboise. Borgia knew that once the cardinals were behind closed doors in their conclave, della Rovere might well engineer himself into the position of becoming a compromise candidate for the papacy. Whatever happened, this had to be prevented, and the most effective way of doing so was to prevent della Rovere from entering Italy in the first place. But Cardinal della Rovere had foreseen this, and managed to elude Borgia's men, arriving in Rome on September 3, the very day following Borgia's retreat from the Vatican.

After covert consultations with other cardinals, della Rovere quickly realized that the situation was just as he had hoped. It was possible that neither the French nor the Spanish would be able to muster the sufficient two-thirds majority. He saw that he was now the leading Italian compromise contender, and just two days after his arrival he told Giustinian:

> I have come to Rome on my own account, not to support other candidates. I shall not vote for Cardinal d'Amboise. If I am not voted pope myself, I hope that whoever does succeed will do their utmost to maintain peace in Italy and do the best he can in the interests of religion.

The last remark was intended as a coded warning. Della Rovere now did the rounds, explaining to all who would listen that if the French took over the papacy, they would in all probability move the

Leonardo da Vinci self-portrait drawn in later life around 1515,
possibly during his final stay in Rome

Portrait of Niccolò Machiavelli by Santi di Tito

Portrait of Cesare Borgia by Altobello Melone

Portrait of Rodrigo Borgia,
who became Pope Alexander VI

Detail from *Disputation of
St. Catherine* by Pinturicchio.
The model for St. Catherine
is thought to be Lucrezia Borgia,
sister of Cesare.

Portrait of Luca Pacioli by Jacopo de' Barbari. The young man in the background is possibly Guidobaldo, Duke of Urbino.

Portrait of Pope Julius II by Raphael

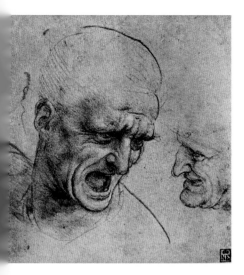

Above and right: Studies for
the *Battle of Anghiari* fresco

A copy of Leonardo's *Battle of Anghiari*, thought to be by Rubens

The Palazzo Vecchio, Florence

papal seat back to Avignon. This particular argument proved highly persuasive to many of the other Spanish and Italian cardinals.

On September 10 Cardinal d'Amboise himself arrived in Rome. This was the man who had been made a cardinal by Alexander VI and had received his cardinal's red hat from the hands of Cesare Borgia himself, on his visit to the court of Louis XII. This was also the man who had been told by Machiavelli that the French did not understand Italian politics. Upon his arrival in Rome, d'Amboise immediately let it be known that he expected the support of Borgia's Spanish cardinals.

Another arrival in Rome on September 10 was Cardinal Ascanio Sforza, whose vote for Borgia's father had notoriously been bought by a mule train laden with treasure. As a brother of Ludovico "Il Moro" Sforza, he had been imprisoned after Louis XII had taken Milan, but now he had been released in order to vote for Cardinal d'Amboise. Yet upon his arrival in Rome this popular cardinal had been given a rapturous welcome, which had immediately set him thinking about his own chances of ascending to St. Peter's throne as a compromise candidate.

Borgia continued watching these proceedings from his fortress at Nepi, being kept informed by regular messengers of how events were unfolding. His spies were everywhere, and he knew almost everything. The rest he surmised. He had realized by this stage that his first choice, Cardinal Vera, was unlikely to attract the necessary two-thirds majority of the votes. Besides, Louis XII had now made it plain that he expected Borgia to deliver the votes of his eleven Spanish cardinals to d'Amboise. Borgia knew that his Spanish cardinals would be reluctant to support any French candidate, but insisted that initially they should at least appear to support d'Amboise. Later, they would have to make quite sure that on no account was either Cardinal Giuliano della Rovere or Cardinal Ascanio Sforza to be allowed to succeed. Cardinal Sforza may once have been responsible for Alexander VI ascending to the papacy, but Borgia did not forget that Sforza had consequently betrayed his father by rallying the Colonnas and the Orsini to the cause of the French, when Charles VIII was making his way towards Rome, leaving the pope in a perilous position. The Sforzas, on their own account, were by this time no friends of the Borgias, especially after the grotesque travesty of Lucrezia's divorce from Giovanni Sforza, Lord of Pesaro. The past was now returning to haunt Borgia, with a vengeance.

On September 16 the conclave to elect Alexander VI's successor began, with the thirty-seven cardinals retiring for their secret negotiations beyond the reach of the outside world. The first ballot took place five days later, with Cardinal della Rovere receiving the most votes (fifteen) and Cardinal d'Amboise receiving thirteen. Amidst the subsequent horse-trading it soon became clear that neither of these two was likely to gather the necessary two-thirds majority. According to Giustinian, "The moment d'Amboise realized that he could not be elected, he decided to prevent the election of anyone who was not his choice." Fortunately for Borgia, neither d'Amboise nor Sforza favored della Rovere and they were determined that he should not be elected. D'Amboise and Sforza still nurtured their own secret hopes of becoming pope, but realized they would have to bide their time until the next conclave. The obvious answer was to elect a compromise candidate, whose age and general infirmity ensured that he would not live for long. D'Amboise and Sforza agreed that their votes, and those that came with them, should support the candidacy of the aged and ailing Cardinal Piccolomini of Siena. On September 22 the second ballot duly took place and Piccolomini was elected pope, taking the name Pius III. In the words of Giustinian:

> The previous life of the new Pope had been characterized by his many exemplary acts of compassion and charity. This encouraged the people to hope that his reign would be the very opposite to that of Alexander VI, and as a result they were filled with joy when they heard the result.

Other observers were filled with joy when it was noticed that at the ceremony in St. Peter's the new pope was so decrepit that he was incapable even of kneeling and had to be carried to the altar.

The new pope was obligated to d'Amboise and the French for his election, as well as to Borgia's Spanish cardinals, who had also voted for him. Such was Pius III's gratitude that when he moved into the papal apartments, he passed on those he had previously occupied to d'Amboise. But would his gratitude to the French and Spanish cardinals result in him confirming Borgia as *gonfaloniere* of the papal forces? So much rested on this, and Borgia was quick to send urgent representations to the pope pointing out the benefits of his confirmation as *gonfaloniere*. Borgia knew what Pius III wanted to hear, and assured him that as long as he was *gonfaloniere* there would be peace in the Romagna, and indeed throughout the papal territories.

But the opposition was quick to present its own case. During the days immediately after Pius III's election he received requests from Cardinal della Rovere for the restitution of his nephew to Sinigallia, as well as from Cardinal Riario requesting the return of his nephew to Imola and Forli. At the same time, Pius III also received visits from Borgia's Spanish cardinals, whose votes had proved so vital to his election: these pleaded Borgia's case. As did d'Amboise, pointing out that Borgia was now under the protection of the French.

Pius III was eventually convinced, and on September 25 he sent word that when Borgia returned to Rome, he would be confirmed in his post. He also sent word admonishing the Venetians for invading the papal lands of the Romagna, and a message to Gianpaolo Baglioni requesting that he and his Perugia league desist from their actions against the papal territory under the protection of Borgia. When Borgia heard news of this, he rejoiced. It appeared that the new pope was wholeheartedly backing him. However, Pius III's support was not quite as unequivocal as it seemed. The day after he confirmed Borgia in his post as *gonfaloniere* of the papal forces, the pope told Giustinian:

> Because of the pressure put on me by the Spanish cardinals and
> others who speak on behalf of Borgia, I have written orders
> recommending Borgia to the people of the Romagna. Yet I will
> give him no further encouragement, because I do not wish to
> be seen as a warlike pope, but instead as one who brings peace
> to Christianity. . . . I do not wish that anyone whom we favor
> should wage war in Italy. . . . I wish Borgia no harm, for it is

the duty of the Pope to have compassion on all. . . . Yet I foresee that through Divine punishment he will one day come to an evil end.

No matter the pope's private misgivings, Borgia was well satisfied. He had been confirmed as the ruler of the Romagna, and he now prepared to return to Rome to be confirmed by the pope himself as *gonfaloniere* of the papal forces. But before he could do so, he had first to face up to a serious problem. Gonsalvo de Cordova had been furious when he heard that Borgia had defected to the French, and had immediately sent word ordering all Spanish soldiers under Borgia's command to leave his service at once. Although these were some of Borgia's most loyal troops, it soon became clear that they were not willing to serve in a force that might well bring them into conflict with their own countrymen. At a stroke, Borgia lost many of his finest soldiers, including the bulk of his heavy cavalry and some of his most trusted and able Spanish commanders, such as Ugo de Moncada. Fortunately, the formidable Don Michele chose to remain at his side.

Borgia now faced a difficult dilemma: Should he return at once to the Romagna in order to consolidate his position within the dukedom? Or should he return to Rome, to have his position officially confirmed by the pope and thus re-establish the power base at the center of Italian politics that had once been maintained by his father? The vast majority of the Romagna was now back in Borgia hands, though Guidobaldo still held Urbino and had recently taken Sinigallia, whilst Perugia remained under Baglioni's rule. But Borgia chose to ignore this situation. Instead, on October 2 he set out from Nepi for Rome, arriving in the Holy City at dusk on the same day. An indication of the importance he attached to this move can be seen by the fact that he brought with him his mother and the Borgia children, and rode at the head of the thousand or so troops that remained to him. It was evident that Borgia intended to make Rome his own. The powerful cardinals della Rovere and Riario immediately hurried to the Vatican, demanding of Pius III that he condemn Borgia's move. The Orsini and the Colonnas, together with Gonsalvo de Cordova and the rest of Borgia's enemies, had all believed that he remained at death's door, and were alarmed at his appearance when he arrived. As Giustinian reported on October 6: "Borgia is far from being as ill as all believed. He speaks in his arrogant manner, and promises that he will soon have back all his possessions in the Romagna."

Borgia presented himself at the Vatican and did his best to charm Pius III. The new pope was known to be impecunious, and was delighted when Borgia offered him sufficient cash to ensure that his coronation ceremony, and the consequent celebrations, would be as lavish as was expected of the pope by the people of Rome.

On October 8, 1503, Pius III was duly crowned pope, and at the same time, he officially appointed Borgia *gonfaloniere* of the papal forces. A few days later Borgia moved into the Castel Sant' Angelo, bringing the Borgia children with him. He had returned with a vengeance. The Orsini, the Colonnas, Gonsalvo de Cordova, and all his other enemies could only look on in dismay. Borgia now appeared more powerful than ever, established with his troops in the Vatican, and with a weak pope in his pocket. With the backing of the grateful French, he would now be able to continue with his aim of making himself the major power in Italy. Once the situation in the Romagna was resolved, it looked as if Florence would at last fall into his clutches.

20

Squaring the Circle

A S EARLY AS July 1503 the Signoria of Florence had viewed the worsening political situation with some alarm. Florentine troops had been withdrawn from the siege of Pisa, and the secret scheme for the diversion of the River Arno had been shelved, leaving Leonardo without a source of income. At this point, the Signoria stepped in and offered him a public commission to paint a large fresco on the wall of the uncompleted Grand Council Chamber on the first floor of the Palazzo della Signoria. This commission was almost certainly suggested by Machavelli. The final agreement drawn up between the Signoria and Leonardo was even cosigned by Machiavelli, who may also have chosen the subject of the projected fresco. This was to be the Battle of Anghiari, which had taken place in 1440 near Borgo San Sepolcro, when a force of around 2,500 Florentines defeated a similar force from Milan under the command of the *condottiere* Niccolò Piccinino. Written into one of Leonardo's notebooks is a detailed description of this battle in another hand, which is recognizable as that of Agostino Vespucci, Machiavelli's friend and assistant. It has been suggested that this description was originally composed by Machiavelli, as it bears certain resemblances to his portrayal of this battle in his *History of Florence*, which he wrote almost twenty years later. Most scholars consider this unlikely. The two descriptions of the battle do indeed have similarities, but this is only to be expected, as they both appear to describe the same event. But the one penned in Leonardo's notebook ends:

There then began a great slaughter of men. None escaped other than those who had been the first to flee and those who managed to hide. The battle continued until sunset, when the Florentine commander decided to recall his soldiers so that they could bury the dead. Afterwards a memorial to the victory was erected.

On the other hand, Machiavelli's description in his *History* reads:

In this great defeat, and the entire battle which lasted from two until six in the afternoon, not more than one man died. And he perished not from wounds or from any honorable blow, but because he fell off his horse and was trampled to death.

In an attempt to account for this somewhat lackluster method of combat, in which several thousands of men "fought" for four hours, without any fatalities on either side, Machiavelli drily explained in his *History*, "At this time men were accustomed to fighting in great safety, mounted on horseback and covered in armor. No harm came to them because they were so protected, and when they could no longer fight they were able to surrender."

Despite the absence of valor, there was a serious point to the victory at Anghiari. As Machiavelli pointed out, the defeat of Milan had no serious effect on that powerful city, but "if the Florentines had lost the day, all of Tuscany would have fallen into the hands of the Duke of Milan." Such was the prime reason for Machiavelli's choice—to bolster the city's patriotic pride. This was especially necessary in its present time of need: instead of threat from Milan, it now stood under threat from Borgia.

Over a decade previously, whilst he was still living in Milan, Leonardo had written in his notebook instructions to himself on how to depict a battle:

If you show a man who has fallen to the ground, you must depict where he slipped on the dust, which has now been turned into mud by the blood. And you must show the tracks of the horses and the men who have passed over this blood-smeared earth. A horse will be dragging behind it the body of its dead rider....

Men fleeing in a rout will be shrieking through their open mouths. The ground must be littered with all kinds of weapons: broken shields, lances, stubs of shattered swords and other such things. . . . There could also be a riderless horse plunging into the enemy, its mane flying in the wind, inflicting severe wounds with its hooves. Or maybe a wounded man lying on the ground trying to protect himself with his shield, while his enemy leans over him trying to deal a killing blow with his sword. . . . Be sure not to leave a single level spot that is not trampled with blood and gore.

This was Leonardo's attempt to imagine a battle, before he had actually witnessed one. It concentrates on detail and particular incidents. But now, during his time with Borgia, he had witnessed such things at first hand—the slaughter in Fossombrone; possibly soldiers running in murderous riot through the Borgo at Sinigallia; and perhaps other incidents of men possessed by blood-lust. He had experienced the "most brutal madness" of war, and the awful power and fury of it had terrified him.

Leonardo's studies for *Battle of Anghiari*.

All this can be seen in the preliminary sketches that he made for *The Battle of Anghiari*. These go far beyond the artistic instructions he had given himself years beforehand on "how to paint a battle," and they certainly exceed the "historical description" he had been given of the battle itself. In Leonardo's sketches, the group scenes are characterized by a confused melee, where the fighting figures appear to be losing their individuality as they are caught up in a vortex of violent struggle. What we are seeing is not a frozen moment in the battle, but a glimpse into the midst of the turmoil as the battle ensues.

As well as these glimpses into the heart of battle, Leonardo also produced a number of sketches depicting individual faces of men in battle. By contrast, these are clear, capturing the moment with almost photographic accuracy—as the soldiers grimace and snarl, shout and swear. These very different views of battle were eventually blended in a fully realized scene that was intended to form the centerpiece of Leonardo's finished picture. Here four horsemen, their rearing wide-eyed steeds crammed head to head, fight awkwardly and desperately for the standard, its flag falling across their struggling bodies and the horses' manes. Such is the dramatic intensity that one can all but hear the cries and shouts of the men, the whinnying of the horses, the ringing clash of swords, the thuds of the hooves. The faces of the combatants grimace in expressions that vividly portray their simultaneous aggressive rage and mortal terror.

There appears to be an element of catharsis in all this: Leonardo was setting down not only the fear he had felt when witnessing such scenes, but also the emotional involvement he had unwittingly sensed, as his human empathy drew him into what he was seeing before his startled eyes. He had experienced the "most brutal madness" stirring in his own blood, and he knew that no matter how he might seek to renounce such violence, it was there within him too.

These drawings explain, as much as anything can, Leonardo's ambivalence—how the gentle, peace-loving artist who set free caged birds could have worked for the brutal, treacherous murderer Borgia, designing engines of destruction, ingenious bladed machines for slicing men and horses in two, as well as all manner of missiles, guns, and

weapons of death. *The Battle of Anghiari* was to be Leonardo's answer to
what he had experienced with Borgia.

Leonardo began working on *The Battle of Anghiari* around October
1503. On the twenty-third of that month the Signoria ordered that he
be given the key to a large disused building within the grounds of the
Santa Maria Novella monastery, to the west of the city center. The
building, known as the Sala del Papa (Pope's Hall), was in a state of
disrepair, with a leaking roof and ill-fitting windows, leaving the hall

Leonardo's studies for *Battle of Anghiari.*

itself exposed to drafts and rain. Despite this, Leonardo moved in,
setting up house with his assistants (amongst whom was Salai) in the
rooms leading off the large main hall. To the wall of the hall he
attached a patchwork of sheets of paper, intended for a full-scale
preliminary sketch of the fresco. And here he gradually immersed
himself in his ideas for what was intended to be his largest and most
ambitious fresco since *The Last Supper.* Yet as with that previous work,

he soon found his mind drifting on to other topics. He was now no longer at the beck and call of a capricious master, constantly on the move as he followed the campaign hither and thither through central Italy. At last he was once more free to pursue his thoughts wherever they led him.

The long fallow months he had spent with Borgia now gave way to a cornucopia of intellectual ideas, schemes, projects, and inventions, all of which began to spill across sheets of paper and the pages of his notebooks. Doubtless Leonardo was also committing to paper some of the ideas that had occurred to him whilst he was in the saddle during his travels with Borgia. Significantly, even the margins of the large sheet on which Vespucci had written out a heroic "historical" description of the Battle of Anghiari soon became covered in drawings of his project of the moment. These were of hinges that he intended for the wings of a flying machine. It is known that Leonardo renewed his interest in flight almost as soon as he returned to Florence in March. During the spring, he began making entries in his notebook that were intended to become a treatise entitled *On the Flight of Birds:*

> Birds that fly swiftly, keeping the same distance above the ground, are in the habit of beating their wings downwards and behind them. . . . The speed of birds is retarded by the way they open and spread out their tail. . . .

Leonardo thought that writing about flight "seems to be my destiny," stemming as it did from his earliest memory about a kite that had flown down onto his cradle. Possibly his first ambition had been to fly like a bird. More prosaically, he is known to have been inspired by the thirteenth-century English natural philosopher he calls "Rugiere Bacone" (Roger Bacon), whose *On the Marvellous Power of Art and Nature* contained a passage about "a flying machine with a man seated in the middle who can make an engine turn so as to cause its artifical wings to beat the air and fly like a bird."

Leonardo's ambition and imagination would certainly have been fired by Bacon's conclusion concerning the building of machines:

> Many such machines were made in antiquity, and have certainly been constructed in our time too, all except perhaps a flying machine, which I have never seen, nor have I heard of anyone who has built such a thing, although I do know of an expert who has worked out a way to build one.

Leonardo thought his method through from first principles:

> A bird is an instrument that works according to mathematical laws, and man is capable of constructing such an instrument that moves in a similar fashion, but he lacks the power to make such an instrument fly. . . . We can thus say that such an instrument constructed by man lacks nothing but the power of a bird. Therefore the power of a man must be adapted so that it imitates the power of a bird.

It is clear that at this stage Leonardo envisioned building an orni-thopter,* which would operate by means of mobile flapping wings. As early as 1478, during his first period in Florence, he had made a faint drawing of what appears to be a mechanical bird's wing attached to a cockpit. On the other side of the sheet is a zigzag line and the note, "This is the method by which birds descend," which presumably came from his observations.

He soon began conducting experiments: "In order to test a wing properly make one with a structure of net and cane, covered with paper. This should be 20 *braccia* [around 40 feet] long and equally broad." But there is no hint of any actual attempt at flight until Leonardo reaches Milan and takes up residence amidst the large, all but deserted rooms of the Corte Vecchia, where he sets to work in secret:

---

* From the ancient Greek *ornitho* for "bird" (as in ornithology) and *pteron* for "wing."

Barricade up the top room, and there construct a large and tall model. This could be taken up to the roof above, which is in every way the best place in Italy to launch it from. And if you stand on the roof beside the tower, the people working across on the dome of the Cathedral will not be able to see you.

His instructions to himself become more explicit, and he soon begins imagining and referring to his invention as if it already exists:

Remember that your flying machine must imitate a bat, whose membranes connect the framework of its wings. . . . If you imitate the wings of feathered birds . . . the feathers are separate and the air passes through them.

There is then an entry that reads: "Tomorrow morning, the 2nd January 1496, you will have both the leather strap made and the test." Was he preparing to carry out a test flight with his flying machine? There is no further mention of any test, which suggests that even if he had this in mind, it did not take place.

When Leonardo returned to Florence in 1503 after serving with Borgia, he once again took up his obsession—this time bringing his imagination to bear on what it might actually be like to fly. In his notebook he writes:

Describe swimming under water, which will be like the flight of a bird through the air. A good place for this is where the mills flow into the Arno, at the weir by the Ponte Rubaconte.

He even considers how things might go wrong. Under the heading "To Escape the Perils of Destruction," he writes:

The machine might be destroyed in two ways. Firstly, it could break up. Secondly, it might turn on its side, or nearly so, because it must always descend at a very shallow angle whilst it is almost exactly balanced at its center.

Earlier in Milan, he had already decided: "You must carry out your experiments with the machine above a lake, and you must wear tied around your belt a long inflated wineskin, so that if you land on the water you will not drown."

Later he seems to have abandoned this idea, for in Florence he announces confidently in his notebook, in a tone suggesting that he might be writing drafts for some public proclamation, that he is planning a launch up in the mountains to the north of Florence, beyond Fiesole: "The first flight of the great bird from the summit of Mount Ceceri will fill the universe with astonishment, all writings will be full of its fame, bringing eternal glory to the place where it was made." Another draft reads: "From the mountain which is named after the great bird,* the famous bird will start its flight which will fill the world with its great fame."

Did this flight ever take place? If it did, it certainly did not fill the world with wonder or bring lasting fame to its creator or his native city. No mention is made of such an experiment, either in the surviving notebooks of Leonardo or in contemporary chronicles. Yet there is one tantalizing reference, which appears half a century later, in a work by the celebrated mathematician Girolamo Cardano, whose father, Fazio, was a friend of Leonardo's. Girolamo wrote how the invention of manned flight was one of the arts that remained hidden from men, explaining how "it has turned out badly for those who tried it. Leonardo also attempted to fly, but his efforts were in vain."

During this period Leonardo also made further maps of the Arno basin: the diversion project was on hold, but there was a possibility that the scheme would be restarted during the summer of 1504. For this, the Signoria would require the necessary figures—how much earth would need to be dug, a feasible time plan, the required number of

---

* That is, Mount Cerceri: in medieval Tuscan dialect *cerceri* meant "swan."

men balanced against the cost of wages, and so forth. All this was a matter of simple mathematics, but Leonardo also embarked upon deeper researches into this subject. Luca Pacioli was in Florence during this time, and it may well have been the mathematical monk who encouraged Leonardo to embark upon certain unsolved problems. Over the last few years Leonardo had been studying *The Elements* of Euclid and some works of Archimedes that had introduced him to the problem of squaring the circle. Put simply, this ancient problem involved constructing a square that had the same area as a given circle, using only the methods of Euclidean geometry. This had defeated mathematicians through the ages: even Archimedes' solution had proved unacceptable. Leonardo soon became fascinated, trying out some ingenious suggestions inspired by Archimedes, incorporating his own practical engineering skills. Yet as Pacioli must have pointed out to him, these hardly conformed to the exacting rigors of Euclidean geometry—in fact, they were neither correct nor original.

Possibly stung by Pacioli's comments, Leonardo decided to take up the challenge in earnest. Various notebooks show that he frequently returned to this problem, with a number of increasingly ingenious geometrical drawings, including polygons inserted into circles and various arrangements of triangles and lunes intended to account for the missing areas where the sides of the polygon did not meet the curves of the circle's circumference. But none of them seemed to work. Then one November night he sat down with his notebook and a candle at his desk, determined not to rise until he had come up with a solution. It is possible to trace Leonardo's series of ingenious and beautiful designs, as he tried to improve upon Archimedes' faulty solution— until finally he cracked it! In the margin he records the exact time of his discovery:

On the night of St. Andrew's Day I eventually finished squaring the circle: by then my candles were finished, the night was finished, and so was the paper I was writing on. This conclusion came to me at the end of the final hour of the night.

Alas, he was deluded: he had not managed to overcome the difficulty that had rendered Archimedes' answer invalid. Squaring the circle was in fact impossible, though this would not be understood until nearly four hundred years later.*

Leonardo's quixotic attempt to square the circle may be seen as analogous to his need to reconcile his pacifism with his work as a military engineer, or his wish to fly free of the earth by becoming lighter than air. Yet such a range of pursuits as those embarked upon by Leonardo was perhaps bound to involve inconsistencies of one kind or another. What is most amazing is that so many disparate interests could be followed by a single mind at the same time. How could Leonardo manage to examine this multitude of different subjects with such persistence? Geometry, the flow of water, how to float on water, how to travel beneath water, how to divert a river, the facial expressions of men in battle, how to arrange their wild flailing anarchy into an aesthetically balanced composition, how to piece together a large machine that mimicked the flight of a bird, how to construct an engine that could drive such a machine—all this, and much more, is found in his notebooks, his sketches, his jottings for this period alone. How was it humanly possible for such single-mindedness to be simultaneously allied to such multifariousness?

The answer lies in the fact that Leonardo saw all these activities and interests as part of the selfsame enterprise. Behind such apparent disparateness lay a single unifying idea. At first, this seems to have been little more than an inarticulate instinct, pressing him in all directions, yet at the same time holding together everything in his mind. Only gradually would this powerful but inchoate idea surface into articulate consciousness, and even here it would appear in a number

---

* Not until 1892 would it be proved that it was impossible to square the circle. In that year it was proved that π (used in the formula to find the area of a circle) was transcendental—that is, not algebraic, not the root of any polynomial with rational coefficients. In a simplified generalization, this meant that it was impossible to give an exact equivalence between a number for the area of a square and a number for the area of a circle, which included π, whose value was by definition not exact.

of different guises. This was what Leonardo would call his "science of painting."

Looking, seeing, depicting, describing—these were the way to truth. And all this required the visual experience of painting, but most of all experience:

> All sciences are vain and full of errors that are not born of experience, mother of all certainty, and are not tested by experience, that is to say, that do not at their origin, middle, or end pass through any of the five senses.

But supreme amongst the senses was vision, which found its greatest expression in the eye of the artist. "Painting presents the works of nature to our understanding with more truth and accuracy than do speech or writing. . . . [Painting is] a science representing the works of nature. . . ." This leads him to the conclusion: "Therefore painting is philosophy."

The painter was thus the supreme scientist-philosopher, able to depict the world in its minutest details, and to record its most intimate and private workings. This clear-eyed *vision* of the world—of the world in all its variety and entirety—was the way to truth. Indeed, it was the truth. Here we can see Leonardo groping towards an articulation of the scientific ideal that would come into being more than a century later with Galileo. Leonardo's expression of belief in the clarity of vision, which could examine everything, was the guiding principle that held together his many pursuits. The more we see of the world and its workings, the more we see of the truth.

Curiously, Machiavelli's ideas were at this time beginning to coalesce in a remarkably similar fashion. He too saw the truth as a matter of clear-sightedness, of untrammeled and unflinching vision. However, Machiavelli's emphasis was not so much on the painter's vision as on the vision that focused upon human behavior. Leonardo and Machiavelli would seem to have discussed their relative views of the world during their time together in the Romagna, each reinforcing some central element in the other's view. They may even have continued these conversations after their return to Florence in early 1503. The similarity between their separate approaches to the world is remarkable. Leonardo sought to understand how things worked and how things are in the material world around him; Machiavelli sought to understand how things worked and how things are in the human world around him. They both sought a scientific vision. Leonardo would record the truth of what he saw, attempting to discover a science in seeing. Machiavelli was at this point also searching to discover a science in seeing, but the truth he sought to discover lay in the way human beings behaved. He had observed Borgia and his treacherous commanders; he had observed Louis XII and his chief adviser d'Amboise; he had seen how Soderini and the Signoria sought to save the city of Florence from its enemies. There had to be a science, some kind of method, in the way politics worked, if only he could see it. How should the successful leader set about achieving his ambitions? How had Borgia managed to overcome all the obstacles in his path? What advice should be given, what assessment of the situation should be made? How should it be done? . . . But before he could reach any conclusions on such matters, Machiavelli would find himself embarking upon a further harsh lesson in the art of politics. The naive vision of ruthless power that he had formed in his mind—the vision of Borgia, resplendent in his prime—would now undergo a wholly unexpected corrective.

On October 18, 1503, news reached Florence that, less than one month after his election, Pope Pius III had died. Florence's very existence as an independent republic now hung in the balance: it all depended upon who was elected as the new pope. Gonfaloniere Piero Soderini called a hasty meeting of the Signoria, which came to a rapid conclusion: Machiavelli should be sent to Rome to observe the papal elections, where he was to keep in close contact with Cardinal Francesco Soderini, who would be Florence's representative in the conclave. Whatever happened, Machiavelli was to consult with Cardinal Soderini and send regular dispatches back to Florence as often as he could, containing all the relevant information that he could gather.

21

A Changed Man

WHEN MACHIAVELLI ARRIVED in Rome on October 27, 1503, he found that Borgia's situation had changed dramatically. The Orsini had brought their forces back to Rome, and these now outnumbered Borgia's depleted militia, leaving him virtually under siege in the Castel Sant' Angelo. In their determination to avenge themselves on Borgia, the Orsini had even gone so far as to abandon their long-standing alliance with the French, and had followed the Colonnas in joining with Gonsalvo de Cordova and the Spanish. And now they had been joined by Baglioni and his men, who were equally hell-bent on revenge, informing Giustinian that they were in Rome "to lay hands on the Duke ... whom at all costs they desired to put to death."

The situation had looked desperate for Borgia. The French army, still camped around Viterbo in preparation for the resumption of its march on Naples, was in no mood to become involved in an invasion of the Holy City, just to rescue Borgia. His only real hope lay in joining up with the forces of the ever-loyal Don Michele, who had remained at the fortress of Soriana in the countryside north of Rome. They could then march together for the Romagna to rally Borgia's followers and consolidate his territories. Many considered that he should have done this in the first place; it looked as if coming to Rome had been a mistake.

At one point, Borgia had led his men out of the Castel Sant' Angelo, with the aim of reaching Don Michele, but the way had been blocked by the Orsini. After a bloody skirmish in which several men died, Borgia and his forces found themselves outnumbered and were forced to retreat to the safety of the Castel Sant' Angelo. The Orsini troops then went on the rampage, looting and pillaging all the Borgia properties they could find in Rome.

Ironically, Borgia had only been rescued from his desperate situation by the death of Pope Pius III. Now, all in Rome had turned their attention to the election of a new pope, and the Orsini forces were prevailed upon to leave the city, as was the custom prior to a conclave, so that the "discussions" prior to the papal election could be conducted without threat or coercion. Money was once again to be the determining factor, as the horse-trading between the rival factions got under way. This time the bargaining was more naked and more extravagant than ever in its opening stages. Where previously votes had covertly been acquired for thousands of ducats, they were now openly being bought for tens of thousands. As Giustinian reported: "There is no difference between the papacy and an eastern market: everything goes to the highest bidder." Once again, three familiar figures emerged as the most powerful candidates: Cardinal Giuliano della Rovere, Cardinal Ascanio Sforza, and Cardinal Georges d'Amboise.

Such was the situation that greeted Machiavelli upon his arrival in Rome, and he reported back to Florence:

> Borgia is much sought after by those who wish to be Pope, because of the Spanish cardinals, who are of his faction. Hence many cardinals have been to talk to him every day in the Castel Sant' Angelo, so it is thought that whoever becomes pope will be indebted to him, and he lives in the hope of being favored by the new Pope.

Machiavelli suspected that Borgia favored a compromise candidate, the obscure Cardinal Pallavicini, whom he would be able to dominate; and if it was not possible to muster enough votes for Pallavicini, Borgia would presumably throw his votes behind Cardinal d'Amboise, thus allying himself even more closely with the French. The eleven Spanish cardinals who could be relied upon to vote according to Borgia's wishes appeared to hold the balance amongst the thirty-seven cardinals expected to enter the conclave. But it soon emerged that Cardinal della Rovere was promising everything to everybody in a desperate bid to gain votes. Despite his long-term hatred for the Borgias, whose threat to his life had previously forced him into exile, the cardinal now even approached Cesare Borgia. According to Johannes Burchard, who remained papal master of ceremonies during the interregnum, on Sunday, October 29, Cardinal della Rovere held a meeting at the Vatican that was attended by Borgia and his eleven Spanish cardinals. In return for Borgia delivering the votes of the Spanish cardinals, Cardinal della Rovere undertook to reappoint Borgia as *gonfaloniere* of the papal forces and allow him to retain all his possessions in the Romagna, on condition that he support the new pope in all his dealings. All this would be sealed by a marriage between Borgia's young legitimate daughter Louise and the cardinal's nephew Francesco della Rovere, the thirteen-year-old former ruler of Sinigallia. Borgia readily agreed. He had thus got all he wanted, despite della Rovere being his sworn enemy.

On October 31 the thirty-seven* cardinals filed into conclave. According to Giustinian, who as Venetian ambassador had played an integral role in the pre-election bargaining, Cardinal della Rovere had by this juncture either bought or been promised the votes of most of the Italian cardinals and all the Venetian cardinals, as well as those of the Spanish cardinals, and those of Cardinal d'Amboise and the French cardinals. The conclave was to prove "the shortest known in all the long history of the Papacy," and the following morning, to the cheers of the people of Rome, Cardinal della Rovere was proclaimed pope. Giving a clear indication of what kind of pope he intended to be, the strong-willed Giuliano della Rovere broke with all precedent by choosing to rule under what was simply the Latinized version of his own name. So Giuliano became Pope Julius II.

---

* Machiavelli gave the figure as thirty-five, while others say there were thirty-six, but the authoritative Ludwig Pastor, in his forty-volume *History of the Popes,* insists that there were thirty-seven cardinals, citing Burchard.

Portrait of Julius II by Raphael.

Despite the cheers of the people, Julius II was not a popular man. During his previous period in Rome he had been widely hated by any who had stood in his way, for they had simply been trampled down as a consequence; he was also feared by those who knew him and understood the vehemence of his will. His many rich bishoprics had made him very wealthy, and he made sure that wherever possible he got his own way. (No candidate for the papacy had ever won by such a margin.) Although fifty-nine years of age and suffering from gout, he remained a vigorous man. The celebrated portrait by Raphael shows him with a flushed face, flowing white beard, and intense eyes, but his pensive expression in this painting is deceptive. Those who came into contact with the new pope, including Giustinian and the Florentine ambassador, soon learned to become fearful of his violent rages. They found diplomatic dealings with him extremely difficult and left a rather more revealing portrait, claiming that Julius II

> had the nature of a giant. Anything that he had been thinking overnight has to be carried out immediately next morning, and he insists on doing everything himself. When he encounters resistance, he breaks off the conversation. When anyone says something with which he disagrees, he interrupts the speaker by ringing a little bell which he keeps on a table next to him.

Yet on one point most were agreed: Julius II was very much the antithesis of his erstwhile enemy Alexander VI. He was just as unscrupulous as many senior churchmen of his time, but he believed in the good of the Church, rather than just the good of the della Rovere family or that of his supporters, amongst whom was now included Cesare Borgia. Indeed, on the very day of Julius II's election, he invited Borgia to take up residence once more in the Vatican.

Machiavelli was quick to spot the omens, writing just three days after Julius II's election, "Borgia allows himself to be carried away by the rash confidence he possesses—to the point where he believes that the promises of other men are more to be relied upon than any of his own promises." Machiavelli predicted, "He will be deceived, owing to the natural hatred which His Holiness has always felt for him. The Pope will not readily forget the ten years' exile he was forced to endure."

On November 2, just a day after the election of Julius II, Machiavelli received an express communication from Florence, bringing sensational news that had not yet reached Rome. The death of Pius III, followed by a report that Borgia had been forced to take refuge in the Castel Sant' Angelo, had encouraged Venice to launch another attack on the Romagna, and several of the previous lords had retaken their cities. Forlì and Rimini had fallen, and Giovanni Sforza had retaken Pesaro. Such had been the success of the Venetian campaign that of all Borgia's main cities only Imola, Faenza, and Cesena remained in the hands of his loyal followers.*

Machiavelli hurried to consult with Cardinal Soderini, and was told to take his letter to the pope. As Machiavelli reported in his dispatch, "I went to His Holiness and read him your letter." Julius II proved surprisingly unworried, saying that "all this had only happened because people had been ignorant of his election. Matters would take a very different course as soon as news that he had become pope reached the Romagna." Machiavelli took a less sanguine view: if Venice overran the Romagna, the whole of central Italy stood in danger. With this in mind, he next reported the news to Cardinal Sforza, who was in company with several senior cardinals. After informing them of what had happened, Machiavelli proceeded to:

> remind them that it was not just the liberty of Florence that was threatened, but also that of the Church. If Venice further increased its power by occupying all the papal lands of the Romagna, the pope would end up becoming nothing more than the chaplain of the Venetians. And it was their business to take this matter seriously, since one of their number was very likely to become a future pope.

He then reminded them "not to forget that it was Florence that had brought all this to their notice, and that in this matter Florence offered them what little assistance it was in the city's power to give. The cardinals showed that they understood the importance of this matter, and promised to do all that was possible."

Cometh the hour, cometh the man: the man of this moment was undoubtedly Machiavelli, who can be seen coming of age as a statesman in the course of these (and the following) meetings. His reading and handling of the situation reveal him as a master diplomat. He knew

---

* There remained some confusion here, as in some cases the city itself had fallen, while the *rocca*, the central walled fortress, still held out. This led to conflicting reports. For instance, although the city of Forlì had been taken, its *rocca* still held out for Borgia.

his place—that of a mere envoy—yet he was not abashed by the eminence of those to whom he reported. He understood the new pope's inexperience and knew precisely how to stir the cardinals into action, simultaneously impressing upon them the loyalty of Florence and cunningly suggesting that it was Florence to which they owed a debt in this matter—when in fact it was Florence that was utterly dependent upon whatever action was taken by the Church.

Finally, in the greatest test of all for his burgeoning skills, Machiavelli took the news to Borgia "in order to find out whether Florence could place any hope in him, or should instead fear him." Machiavelli found himself confronted by "an excessively agitated" Borgia,

> who complained bitterly about your Lordships [that is, the Signoria], saying you had always been his enemies, and that it was you rather than the Venetians whom he blamed for this state of affairs. He said that with just a hundred men you could have secured his cities, but you did nothing to support him. He swore that he would make sure you were the first to regret this. . . . He would no longer be deluded by you, but would let his territories go to the Venetians. Then Florence would be ruined, and it would be his turn to laugh. As for Florence relying upon French protection, this was just a dream: the French would either lose in Naples, or they would be too busy there trying to rescue their own situation to render any assistance to Florence.

Having delivered himself of this lesson in realpolitik, Borgia launched into a bitter tirade: "He spoke with words full of poison and anger. I could easily have argued with him, and replied to his charges, but I thought it best to try and calm him down, before managing as adroitly as I could to break off the interview, which felt as if it had gone on for a thousand years."

Machiavelli's final remark, though exaggerated, brings home the reality of this confrontation. Facing up to Borgia in a rage was no mean feat, especially when he was at the end of his tether, on the very brink of desperation. This was a violent, occasionally deranged personality who had thought nothing of murdering his most loyal commanders. A mere envoy, from a city that he felt had betrayed him, was small fry compared to the relatives, dukes, and cardinals he had seen put to death in the most excruciating fashion.

Machiavelli must have felt sure of himself, and sure of the strange rapport he had established with Borgia during their time together in the Romagna. Borgia had certainly impressed Machiavelli, and the perceptive admiration of this wily, independent-minded intellectual may well have touched Borgia, proving curiously reassuring in the midst of the treacherous, ever-shifting world in which he operated, especially now that he no longer had his father behind him.

Over the next few days events unfolded fast. Borgia expected to be named by Julius II as *gonfaloniere* of the papal forces at the first official meeting of the pope and his cardinals at the consistory, but on November 10 Machiavelli reported, "This meeting took place yesterday, but from all accounts that I have been told, neither Borgia nor his affairs were mentioned." Machiavelli therefore concluded, "Borgia's situation remains as uncertain as ever, and many well-informed sources are suggesting that he may yet come to a bad end, although in fact the new Pope has always been regarded as a man of his word."

Later in the same dispatch, seemingly written some hours after the above, Machiavelli reported that Borgia was now busy raising troops, "and according to some of his men he has also sent orders to northern Italy enlisting soldiers there too. It appears that he is raising these troops so that when he is once more made Gonfaloniere of the Papal Forces he will launch a campaign to recover his territories in the Romagna." In a second dispatch written even later on the same day, Machiavelli reported that Borgia's troops were preparing to leave for Ostia, where they planned to take ship for northern Italy to join up with his other contingent of newly recruited troops. Borgia himself

is getting ready to leave, and has obtained letters from Cardinal Soderini, Cardinal d'Amboise, and even the Pope himself, all addressed to Your Lordships. . . . He said that I should write to you too, informing you that he is sending one of his own men to get a safe-conduct allowing his troops to cross Florentine territory on their way to the Romagna. He has asked me to recommend that you do this, and asks you to reply as soon as possible.

This left the Signoria in an extremely difficult position. If they granted Borgia a safe-conduct, there was no telling what he might do once he marched into Florentine territory. Yet if they did not grant him a safe-conduct, he would construe this as an act of aggression and was liable to invade instead. What answer could they possibly give?

To make matters worse, it now emerged that Julius II had informed Borgia that he could use the papal galleys at the port of Ostia to transport his troops up the coast to La Spezia to join his newly recruited forces for the march on the Romagna. Even Giustinian could not fathom what was going on: "When I talk with the Pope he tells me how much he wishes for Borgia's downfall. Yet he publicly lends him the Papal galleys to take his soldiers wherever he wishes, and behaves towards Borgia as if once again the Pope was his father." However, a few days later Julius II would confide to Giustinian that "he expected Borgia and his troops to be attacked and defeated." The new pope was showing his political inexperience: he appeared to have no real grasp of the situation. Did he hope Borgia would be defeated by the Venetians? This was not only unlikely, but if it did happen, the papal lands of the Romagna would then be absorbed into Venetian territory and— just as Machiavelli had foreseen—the pope in Rome would be in danger of being reduced to a mere vassal of Venice. Or did Julius II hope that Borgia would be attacked and defeated by the forces of Baglioni and Vitelli, which were now stationed in Umbria? This was hardly likely, for two reasons: they were not powerful enough to defeat Borgia, and they were too far away. It looked as if Borgia could now do as he wished.

The next day Machiavelli wrote that Borgia had summoned him, "and I found him in a very different mood from my previous visit." This time there was no bluffing, no threats, no anger: Borgia was once more his resolute self. He confirmed to Machiavelli that "he is taking action to prevent the Venetians from becoming masters of the Romagna, and the Pope is ready to assist him."

In Florence, the Signoria was evidently paralyzed with indecision, for two days later Machiavelli was forced to write with some urgency: "Borgia is impatiently awaiting your word regarding his safe-conduct. It is impossible for me to know how to respond to him until I know what you have decided. . . . Without a reply, I am left dangling and have no idea what to do."

On November 14, Borgia received news from Florence. The Signoria had finally made up its mind: it refused a safe-conduct allowing Borgia to cross Florentine territory so that he could reach the Romagna. Machiavelli was informed that such was the feeling amongst the citizens of Florence that they would rise up rather than allow the Signoria to grant such a safe-conduct, no matter who recommended it. The terror and consternation that had been inspired by Borgia's campaign just two years previously, when he had threateningly marched his army to within ten miles of the city walls, were still fresh in people's minds.

This unexpected news proved much more of a blow to Borgia's fortunes than anyone at first realized. Borgia had evidently been bluffing when eight days previously he had assured Machiavelli that the French would not come to Florence's rescue because their army was too involved in its campaign against the Spanish in Naples. Borgia was now utterly reliant upon French backing and could not afford to antagonize Louis XII, who had strictly forbidden Borgia any further forays into Florentine territory. Only with the backing of the pope and the powerful French Cardinal d'Amboise, as well as the permission of the Signoria itself, would he have been able to get away with once again crossing into Florentine territory. Suddenly all Borgia's plans had collapsed: it looked as if he could no longer reach the Romagna.

Later that same day Machiavelli wrote in his dispatch to the Signoria, "Cardinal Soderini is beginning to doubt whether Borgia will leave Rome after all. When he visited Borgia he found him a changed man." Gone was the self-confident braggart of old, and instead he had found Borgia "paralyzed with indecision, become suspicious of everyone, and appearing generally unhinged in his behavior." Machiavelli knew Borgia too well to jump to any hasty conclusion, and prudently suggested that this transformation of Borgia's character "may be due to the natural volatility of his personality. On the other hand, he is used to having the luck of the devil, and this totally unexpected collapse of his fortunes may well have stunned and unnerved him." In order to find out more about what had happened to Borgia, Machiavelli began making inquiries. He heard that Cardinal Hernia,* the Spanish cardinal known to be closest to Borgia, "believes that Borgia has lost his wits, for he seemed no longer to know what he wanted to do, appearing confused and irresolute."

Despite this apparent nervous collapse, Machiavelli wrote on November 19: "By the grace of God, and to the great relief and satisfaction of everyone, Borgia has left Rome for Ostia." To show that he intended to pursue his campaign regardless, Borgia had also sent some of his Roman troops marching north towards Florentine territory:

> So Borgia told me, these forces consist of seven hundred mixed cavalry. Also, when the wind changes, allowing him to sail, he will embark with four or five hundred more for Spezia. . . . There is reason to fear that, owing to his annoyance at your actions towards him, he may decide to disembark at Pisa and give them assistance [in their war against Florence]. . . .

Borgia was dividing his troops, and the actual intention behind his apparently inconsistent and irrational moves was unclear. Many thought that this time he really had gone mad, and as Machiavelli reported, "at the moment everyone here in Rome is laughing at him. We will just have to wait and see which way the wind blows him."

Despite all Borgia's apparent irrationality, there still remained the strong possibility that the different contingents under his command would link up in northern Italy and then march across the north of Florentine territory to Cesena, which was still holding out for Borgia.

---

* In some texts, he is referred to as the Bishop of Elna.

From here he could launch his campaign to retake the Romagna. Becoming aware of this possibility, Julius II soon regretted allowing Borgia to depart from Rome, and, according to Machiavelli, "the Pope is unable to sleep on account of his worries over what to do about the Romagna." But when news reached Rome that Faenza had fallen to the Venetians, Julius II was finally emboldened to act, and on November 22 he dispatched Cardinal Soderini to Ostia with a demand that Borgia surrender Cesena and Imola, as well as any other castles remaining to him in the Romagna, into the hands of their rightful owner, the Church.

But Borgia had now swung into a state of defiance: he was preparing to embark upon the campaign that in his eyes was but the first step towards reinstating him once and for all as a major power in Italy. On November 23 Machiavelli reported:

> Early this morning a messenger arrived for the Pope from Cardinal Soderini in Ostia, announcing that Borgia refused to hand over his castles to Julius II. His Holiness was furious, and sent men from the Papal Guard with orders to arrest Borgia, and he is now held a prisoner. The Pope also wrote to Perugia and to Siena, ordering these cities to plunder and disarm at once any of Borgia's soldiers found marching across their territories towards Florence. I am not yet certain how much of all this is true, but will find out from Cardinal Soderini on his return.

It was soon confirmed that Borgia was being held a prisoner. But how could he possibly have allowed himself to be arrested? Evidently the strain of the last weeks of crisis and ever-fluctuating fortune, coming as they did before he had properly recovered from his debilitating and near-fatal illness, were beginning to take their toll. At Ostia, Borgia had been residing on one of the papal galleys, which was under the command of the pope's captain Mottino, who colluded in the arrest. Borgia's mood had plunged once more at the news of the fall of Faenza; he was at a low ebb and was caught by surprise. At the same time his soldiers, feeling themselves leaderless under their vacillating commander, chose not to respond to his arrest. Blow had followed upon blow, until at last Borgia appeared to be a broken man.

On November 26 Machiavelli reported that rumors of all kinds were flying about Rome, and he had received some particularly astonishing information from a reliable but unnamed informant:

> He said that he was with some others having an audience with the Pope in his chamber at eight o'clock last night, when two messengers suddenly arrived from Ostia. All those having the audience were asked to leave, but when my informant was in the next-door room he managed to overhear what the messengers from Ostia told the Pope. They bore news that Borgia had been thrown into the Tiber, just as the Pope had commanded. I can neither confirm nor deny this news. Yet even if it has not already happened, it will before long.

Machiavelli continued in deepest sarcasm. "So we can see that this Pope is already becoming a man of honor and repaying his debts [to those to whom he owed his power]. No sooner has he penned his word on a document than he uses the blotter to erase it."

Yet it quickly emerged that Borgia had not been killed. On orders from Julius II, the entire papal guard was dispatched to Ostia to bring Borgia back to Rome. Rumors continued to fly around the Eternal City, and when Borgia still did not arrive, some concluded that he had indeed been killed, while others were certain that he had escaped. On November 27 the man whom Julius II had dispatched to the Romagna, to report on what was happening there, arrived back in Rome. According to Machiavelli:

> He reported that there is little support for the Church in the Romagna. In Imola the people still favor Borgia, while Borgia's commander in the *rocca* at Forli is planning to strengthen his fortress and promises to hold out "for as long as Borgia lives." This news angered the Pope.

Two days later Borgia was brought under armed guard to Rome. He appeared a shadow of his former self, dejected and in despair,* his bedraggled troops trailing disconsolately behind him. Surprisingly, instead of condeming Borgia to the dungeons of the Castel Sant' Angelo, Julius II lodged him in living quarters in the Vatican. To the intense discomfort of Cardinal d'Amboise, the pope asked him to receive Borgia as a "guest" in his apartment, which was then placed under heavy guard. Borgia was now put under great pressure to divulge the passwords to the fortresses that remained loyal to him in the Romagna. Without these, it was known that their commanders would refuse to accept any orders to surrender, even if these purported to be in Borgia's name. But Borgia resisted this attempt to strip him of the last of his possessions.

Imola, Forli, and Cesena may have remained holding out in the Romagna, but on other fronts there was nothing but bad news for Borgia. On December 1, whilst Machiavelli was in the midst of an audience with Julius II, "news arrived that Don Michele had been taken prisoner, and his force disarmed, by Gianpaolo Baglioni on the border between Florentine territory and Perugia. His Holiness expressed his delight at this development, which was entirely in accord with his wishes." Next day Machiavelli wrote, "It is difficult to forecast Borgia's fate, but his prospects look evil."

By now, Julius II had summoned to Rome Guidobaldo of Urbino, whose Montefeltro family was closely linked by marriage to the pope's della Rovere family. Despite the thirty-two-year-old Duke of Urbino's lack of military experience, and the fact that he was becoming increasingly debilitated by gout, Julius II had decided to appoint him in place of Borgia as *gonfaloniere* of the papal forces.

On December 2 a meeting was arranged between Guidobaldo and Borgia in the apartments of Cardinal d'Amboise. This was the first time Borgia had encountered Guidobaldo after he had treacherously seized Urbino and deposed the young duke just a year and a half previously in June 1502. Now the tables were turned. Guidobaldo's report of

---

* Some reports claimed that he was in chains and weeping. See, for instance, the dispatch by Cattaneo, the Mantuan ambassador, dated December 22, 1503.

this meeting describes how Borgia fell to his knees before him, groveling and begging for his forgiveness. Borgia even claimed that he had only tricked Guidobaldo and taken Urbino on orders from his father Alexander VI. With a show of magnanimity, Guidobaldo raised Borgia and embraced him. In return for such compassion, he then insisted that Borgia give back to him all the treasures that he had looted from Urbino, especially the many priceless volumes and historic manuscripts that he had stolen from the palace library. (It appears likely that not all of these had been loaded onto the mule trains that crossed the mountains to Cesena; at least one or two of the copies of ancient Greek scientific and geometric manuscripts had almost certainly passed into the hands of Leonardo, who—unbeknownst to the Duke of Urbino—had by this stage added them to his collection in Florence, where he and his friend the mathematical monk Luca Pacioli were even now consulting them in the course of their researches. Perhaps on account of Leonardo's absorption in such problems as squaring the circle, the return of these manuscripts to their rightful owner was somehow overlooked.)

At the end of his meeting with Borgia, Guidolbaldo demanded the passwords to the cities that Borgia still held in the Romagna, and at long last Borgia surrendered them.

This description of the encounter between Guidobaldo and Borgia accords with Guidobaldo's extensive report of this meeting, which was dispatched back to Urbino a few days later. However, the account that Guidobaldo gave Giustinian immediately after the meeting made no mention of Borgia falling abjectly to his knees and begging forgiveness, which suggests that this particular humiliating event did not take place. Either way, the essential tenor of the meeting must have been metaphorically close to such a capitulation, for Borgia certainly promised to return all of Guidobaldo's treasures and gave up the withheld passwords with no hint of coercion. Many now foresaw the end of Borgia, and feared the reprisals that would inevitably follow upon his demise. Around this time his mother, Vannozza, bequeathed her Roman house and all her property to the church of Santa Maria del Popolo, on the condition that her home became a sanctuary and that she could live there under the protection of the Church until she died.

Yet all was not quite what it seemed. Borgia, in connivance with his remaining loyal supporters, had covertly arranged for a succession of wagons to carry out of Rome the considerable amount of concealed treasure that remained in his possession in the city; this was to be shipped north to Lucrezia in Ferrara. At the same time, a convoy of mules secretly left Cesena, laden down with all the treasure seized for Borgia by Don Michele from Alexander VI's chamber on the day of his death. This was said to include such priceless papal relics as the jewel-encrusted mantle of St. Peter, vast quantities of gold plate and precious stones, as well as "a cat in gold with two most notable diamonds as its eyes." All this too was intended for Lucrezia's safekeeping in Ferrara. Unfortunately for Borgia, spies quickly discovered what had happened. The wagons from Rome were intercepted as they passed through the countryside of Tuscany. At the same time, Bentivoglio sent a detachment of troops from Bologna to scour the northern Romagna, and they ambushed the mule train from Cesena, seizing all the treasure, which was swiftly dispatched to Bentivoglio in Bologna.

On December 4, two days after Borgia had revealed the passwords, his last remaining loyal commissioner, Pedro d'Oviedo, accompanied by a papal commisioner, set out with the passwords for the Romagna to take possession of Borgia's remaining strongholds. Borgia had placed his hopes on being allowed to leave Rome in the company of Cardinal d'Amboise, who was returning to the court of Louis XII in France. Yet when d'Amboise departed on December 9, Borgia was not permitted to accompany him. Julius II wished to be certain that Borgia's cities had surrendered, and word of this had not yet come through. In fact, d'Oviedo and the papal commissioner had been delayed by heavy snowfalls that had blocked the passes across the Apennines, and only managed to reach Cesena on December 14. By now its citizens had been persuaded by their prudent administrator Antonio di Sansavino that in the interests of their own safety they should displace him in favor of a ruler who was favorable to the pope and was willing to plead with His Holiness on their behalf. They had followed Sansavino's selfless advice somewhat reluctantly, and only because they feared for their lives: here, as in many other places throughout the Romagna, Borgia's rule had been popular. The invasion by the

Venetians, and the reinstatement of many of the former tyrants, had quickly seen a return of the anarchy and vendettas that had so beset the region in former times. Despite the surrender of the majority of the citizens of Cesena, others had taken refuge in the *rocca*, where Borgia's loyal Spanish commanders, the brothers Pedro and Diego Ramires, had continued to hold out, swearing allegiance to their master as long as he drew breath.

When Pedro d'Oviedo entered the *rocca* and presented the Ramires brothers with Borgia's passwords, they refused to surrender, claiming that Borgia could only have imparted them under duress. They swore that there would be no surrender as long as Borgia remained in captivity. They even went so far as to declare that, in bringing such a message, d'Oviedo had revealed himself as a traitor. He was seized and tortured, before being put to death; later his body, bloodied with knife wounds, was seen dangling from the battlements.

When news of this reached Rome on December 19, Julius II was all for casting Borgia into the dungeons of the Castel Sant' Angelo, but the Spanish cardinals beseeched him not to resort to such a desperate measure, which would surely have presaged his murder. Julius II, mindful of how much he owed the Spanish cardinals for his election, relented. Instead Borgia was transferred to a more secure apartment; ironically he was now lodged in the very room where Don Michele, on his orders, had garrotted Lucrezia's second husband, Alfonso, Duke of Bisceglie.

Julius II's motives were not entirely compassionate. By this stage he had reached the point where he wished to make sure that Borgia was utterly ruined. The seizure of Borgia's wagons in Tuscany and his mule train in the Romagna was evidently not the end of the matter. Borgia's previous intention to raise so many troops at short notice in northern Italy indicated that he still held considerable cash assets in that region, and almost certainly had further treasures secreted elsewhere. Consequently Julius II sent word urging Borgia's enemies to demand compensation for the damage he had done to them and their territories. As a result, Guidobaldo of Urbino put in a claim for 200,000 ducats.* Julius II's

---

* At the time of Julius II's accession, the official papal revenues for a year still amounted to around 300,000 ducats.

friend Cardinal Riario put in a claim for 20,000 ducats on behalf of the Riario family, who were now heirs to Imola, Forli, and Sinigallia. Meanwhile the Signoria in Florence began drawing up a list of compensations that it felt the republic was owed, and others soon followed suit.

In the meantime Julius II began preparing a legal case against Borgia, so that he could be tried for his murders. In pursuance of this, on December 14 the pope ordered the arrest of the former majordomo in the household of Cardinal Michiel, whom Alexander VI had ordered to be poisoned in April before seizing his palazzo and all his treasures in order to finance Borgia's campaign against Siena. At the same time, Julius II ordered the Signoria in Florence to keep the captive Don Michele under the strictest guard. The pope knew that the ever-loyal Don Michele had been privy to Borgia's darkest deeds, and he intended to use all information "extracted" from this source to build up a damning case against Borgia.

Yet why was Julius II going to all this trouble, when now that he had Borgia in captivity he could simply have had him murdered—as Alexander VI would doubtless have done? Before taking any precipitate action, Julius II wished to obtain from Borgia all his ill-gotten treasures, as well as his territorial possessions that belonged to the papacy. Mindful of his own political inexperience, the pope was also reluctant to create such a precedent so early in his reign. Murdering Borgia before he had been tried and condemned might well have alienated the Spanish cardinals, as well as displeasing Louis XII. Borgia had once had powerful friends, and as such had to be treated with care.

As Florence was no longer in immediate danger from Borgia, Machiavelli's reports from Rome were now mainly concerned with the situation in Naples, where the French were still engaged in fighting the Spanish for possession of the kingdom. Recently the fighting had swung both ways, with a number of sporadic indecisive confrontations, especially along the strategically important River Garigliano, which reached the sea some twelve miles down the coast from Gaeta. By this stage both armies were running short of cash, and were becoming hampered by erratic and inadequate supply lines; Machiavelli also reported that "there is much sickness." There had been an outbreak of plague in

Naples, and syphilis continued to ravage the soldiery; but the conditions and the lack of supplies were beginning to take their toll. Even in the south of Italy the winter was severe, with the countryside swept by freezing rains, the worst in living memory. The Spanish troops besieging the French at Gaeta had eventually been forced to withdraw, "being unable to endure any longer the privations they were suffering and greatly reduced by want." This was to be Machiavelli's final dispatch from Rome. On December 16 he was informed by the Signoria that his mission was over, and he set off back for Florence.

On December 28 Gonsalvo de Cordova defeated the French at a major battle fought on the banks of the Garigliano. Three days later the French garrison at Gaeta surrendered, and with that perished all Louis XII's hopes of taking Naples. Cesare Borgia's French allies were no longer the force in Italy they had once been. They now held only territories in the north of the country, far from Rome. As Machiavelli had previously observed in one of his dispatches: "It looks as if little by little Borgia is sinking into his grave."

Part 4

Consequences

22

Return to Florence

FROM THIS POINT on, the paths of Borgia, Machiavelli, and Leonardo began to diverge more widely. After leaving Rome in mid-December 1503, Machiavelli would never again set eyes on Borgia—though this charismatic figure would eventually come to play a decisive role in Machiavelli's future. Likewise Leonardo: having left Borgia's employ, he would have no further dealings with him. Yet the experience of those hectic months with Borgia would leave an indelible mark on Leonardo's character. As for the two Florentines, back in their home city Machiavelli and Leonardo would remain in contact, with Machiavelli continuing to play an important role in influencing the Signoria's dealings with Leonardo.

Machiavelli's first feelings on his return to Florence were relief at being back home amongst his old cronies, and joy at seeing his family again. The latter would have been something of a mixed blessing, however. Marietta was not pleased at her husband's frequent absences on his missions. Despite this, she was now beginning to gain a deeper understanding of certain aspects of her husband's character—probably from gossip passed on by women friends who had overheard snatches of conversations about "Il Macchia" amongst Machiavelli's cronies. Gossip spread fast in a close-knit community such as Florence, and Machiavelli's circle of friends amongst the civil servants at the Chancery would have been no exception. Marietta would have known, or at least strongly suspected, that her husband was in the habit of forming liaisons when he was posted to a particular spot for any length of time. On his six-month mission to the court of Louis XII in 1500 there are indications that he had an affair with a courtesan. This may have been two years before he was married, but his behavior remained much the same afterwards. We know from his witty letters to his friends that he retained the habit of visiting prostitutes in the cities through which he passed, behavior that was commonplace for a man traveling without his wife in Italy during this period.

It is unlikely that Machiavelli had any opportunity to form a lasting liaison during his months of travel with Borgia in the Romagna, though it is difficult to imagine him remaining celibate. Certain wives, widows, and other women would have been available to Borgia's officers during their stay at Imola, and Machiavelli's keen ear for intelligence of all sorts would certainly have enabled him to identify the women of the city who were covertly accessible. On the other hand, during his three-month stay in Rome in 1503 to observe the papal elections he probably formed a rather more lasting liaison with one of the many scores of courtesans who were available to diplomats.

Yet Machiavelli's philandering had a double-edged aspect. The evidence suggests he was aware that Marietta knew of his peccadilloes, and that this caused him in turn to suspect her of being unfaithful to him. Machiavelli was away during the summer of 1502 when Marietta was delivered of their first child, a daughter named Primerana. Then he was away—this time on his mission to Rome—when Marietta gave birth to a son, named Bernardino, in early November 1503. There is no doubt that this time Machiavelli suspected that he may also have been absent at the conception of this son. He had only arrived back in Florence from his mission to Borgia at the end of January, and Bernardino was born at the beginning of November, almost exactly nine months later (give or take a few days). In the early months, when Marietta's pregnancy had first become evident, that "give or take a few days" must have given him cause to ponder. He had certainly intimated his suspicions to his friends, as can be seen from the letter sent to him in Rome on November 11 by his friend Luca Ugolini:

My dear old pal—Congratulations! Now we know for certain that your Marietta did not deceive you, for your new son is the spitting image of you. Leonardo da Vinci himself could not have painted a truer likeness.

Marietta too must have been aware of his suspicions, for she wrote to Machiavelli in Rome begging him "to come back soon." She too knew that the moment he set eyes on Bernardino all his suspicions would be dispelled.

During the first days of January 1504 news reached Florence of Gonsalvo's victory over the French at Garigliano and the subsequent French surrender of Gaeta. This defeat of Florence's ally was disastrous news. The only consolation was that Piero de' Medici—the ousted ruler of the city, who had constantly been scheming for his return to power— had been drowned in the River Garigliano whilst attempting to flee with the French forces across its flooded waters.

Once again Florence was in jeopardy. What would now become of the city's French allies, whose support had so long guaranteed its independence? Would the Spanish seek to drive the French out of Italy altogether, leaving Florence at the mercy of any invader?

On January 14, 1504, Machiavelli was entrusted once more with a vital mission, this time to France. He was given the following instructions, which were taken down in his own hand, dictated by a member of the Signoria:

> You will proceed to Lyons, or wherever the French court happens to be, and present yourself to Valori [the Florentine ambassador], who will advise you of the latest situation. You will also inform him fully of your instructions. . . . One of the chief objects of your mission is to observe with your own eyes first-hand what preparations the French are making.

These preparations were with regard to troops to be dispatched to Italy, which could be used for the defense of France's ally Florence. It was stressed that Machiavelli must:

Report as soon as possible back to us with news of these matters, also giving your assessment of them. And if the preparations seem to you inadequate, by way of being insufficient in strength, uncertain in nature, or simply too slow, then you must make it abundantly clear to His Majesty that we are simply not in a position to provide enough forces for our own defense. In which case, if we cannot rely upon immediate and considerable assistance, we will be forced by circumstance to turn elsewhere and ally ourselves with someone who can protect us. For the preservation of the liberty of our state must be our prime concern, as we are sure he must understand.

The Signoria then went on to outline the situation that faced Florence:

We are threatened, on the one hand, by the Venetians, and on the other hand by the Spanish, who are acting in concert with one another. You must be sure to make His Majesty understand how things stand with us: we are at war with Pisa in the west and Venice threatens us to the east. At the same time, all our other neighbors, who are so badly disposed towards us, are now even more so after the defeat of the French army in the Kingdom of Naples. These neighbors have allied themselves with the Spanish, or are making preparations to do so. Meanwhile our troops are scattered in different places, with the rest defeated in Naples whilst in the service of His Majesty. Likewise we are threatened by recent events in the Romagna.

The repetition and tone of these instructions would seem to betray the agitation of whoever was dictating them to Machiavelli, as well as the speed at which they were being dictated. Machiavelli was to leave at once, and it is no exaggeration to say that as far as the members of the Signoria were concerned, the fate of Florence was being left largely up to his judgment. He was to respond to Louis XII as he saw fit.

(And if things went wrong, he was the one who would be blamed: a situation that could place him in mortal danger on his return.)

Machiavelli's departure was in fact delayed until January 20, when he set out posthaste. Once again "so eager for riding," he bragged to the Signoria that he would be at the French court in six days. In the event, he reached Lyon after seven days' riding, with a day's stopover at Milan to consult the French governor Charles d'Amboise (older brother of the cardinal). Machiavelli explained Florence's predicament, whereupon d'Amboise reassured him that Gonsalvo would not invade Florence, for if he did the French would respond—"without any doubt," he added emphatically.*

In Lyon, Machiavelli and ambassador Francesco Valori did their best to obtain an audience with Louis XII, but this proved impossible. The strain of maintaining the campaign against the Spanish in faraway Naples had proved too much for Louis XII, and when news of the defeat at Garigliano, together with the surrender of Gaeta, had reached Lyon he had suffered a nervous collapse, from which he had not yet recovered.

Instead, Machiavelli and Valori managed to gain an audience with Louis XII's chief adviser, Cardinal d'Amboise. They explained to him the delicacy of Florence's position, but d'Amboise "listened to Machiavelli with increasing displeasure, to the point where he soon became visibly angered." Understandably, from his point of view, d'Amboise was furious that Florence should adopt this attitude when France was in the midst of such difficulties.

The next day, Cardinal d'Amboise was calmer and informed Florence's

---

* In his dispatch to Florence dated January 22, Machiavelli quoted d'Amboise in the French of the period—*Non de rien dotté*—indicating that he could understand French and was not dependent upon interpreters, who could be unreliable. He had learned some French during his earlier mission to the French court in 1500, and his 1502 dispatches from Borgia's court in the Romagna gave the impression that he made use of this when gaining intelligence conversing with the officers in charge of the French contingent. However, precisely how fluent Machiavelli was remains unclear. Characteristically, he would not have been above implying to the Signoria greater linguistic skill than he actually possessed, much as he was not averse to exaggerating his amorous escapades in his letters to his friends.

two-man delegation that negotiations were now under way between France and Spain, with the aim of arranging a truce. This was duly signed on February 11. According to the agreement, there was to be a three-year truce between France and Spain, with each side nominating its allies in this pact. To the relief of Valori and Machiavelli, France named Florence amongst its allies. The city was safe, for the time being. Machiavelli was now free to return to Florence, but decided to delay his arduous trip back across the Alps. Instead, he spent his time calling upon the various powerful figures and ambassadors at the French court, gathering snippets of intelligence. A close inspection of the dispatches to Florence reveals that this information was little more than court political gossip. More important, there appears to have been some question as to whether the treaty had actually been ratified, but this was soon cleared up. On February 25, Machiavelli finally assured the Signoria that he already "had one foot in the stirrup, ready to ride back to Florence."

Despite this assurance, Machiavelli was not to leave until early the following month, and even then he took his time, covering the route in short stages and at a leisurely pace. It has been suggested that an amorous adventure may have accounted for his apparent reluctance to leave the French court. Be this as it may, it is clear that Machiavelli in fact reveled in his role at the court. Like so many intellectuals before and after him, he was overly impressed by men of power. Admittedly, none of the figures at the French court impressed him quite as much as Cesare Borgia had in his prime, but in Lyon he was intrigued to observe the mechanics of power within the most prestigious court in Europe. In the Romagna, with Borgia, Machiavelli had seen action—history in the making. At Lyon he was able to observe the background to such history, the subtle machinations that played out behind the scene of action. He was beginning to realize that any philosophy of power would have to take account of such matters. Even a leader in the Borgia mold would need to understand such things if he was to retain the power he had seized. It had been precisely Borgia's lack of expertise in this sphere that had been his downfall.

Despite Florence's vulnerable position throughout this period, it was arguably the time of the city's greatest glory. Less than two months after Machiavelli's return, he would have witnessed one of the city's most sensational artistic events. For three years the local-born young sculptor Michelangelo had been working in seclusion in a large warehouse near the cathedral, sculpting an eighteen-foot block of finest Carrara marble, which was gradually taking the shape of a superb, almost three times life-sized statue of *David*. This had been commissioned by Gonfaloniere Soderini, and its subject was of great significance to Florence—David was an emblem of the free republic that resisted the Goliath kingdoms and autocratic powers in Italy who threatened her, as well as those who were constantly scheming to overthrow the democratic government and replace it with the Medici rulers.

In May 1504 twenty-nine-year-old Michelangelo finally completed the statue. In order to remove it from the warehouse the wall had first to be knocked down. It then took no fewer than four days to haul the carefully boxed-up statue on rollers along the quarter-mile of uneven stone-slabbed streets to the site where it was to be placed—in the piazza in front of the Palazzo della Signoria, the seat of the city's government. When the statue was finally unveiled it caused a sensation, not only because of its bold nudity, but also because of its striking beauty and sheer originality. In the words of Michelangelo's fellow Florentine and near-contemporary Giorgio Vasari, "without any doubt this figure has put in the shade every other statue, ancient or modern, Greek or Roman." The Renaissance was now beginning to emerge in its full originality, surpassing and casting aside the classical exemplars that had initially so inspired its artists, poets, and thinkers.

Alongside Leonardo's scientific and anatomical researches in his notebooks, and Machiavelli's evolving thoughts on political philosophy, Michelangelo's *David* was like nothing that had gone before. Even as Florence had stood under threat from the predatory ambitions of Borgia, it had been emerging as the center of an entirely new development in human self-understanding, knowledge, and expression. Just as the city-states of ancient Greece had produced the beginnings of western civilization—in philosophy, the arts, and the sciences—when their liberty stood under greatest threat, so Florence and the vulnerable city-states of early-sixteenth-century Italy were now leading western civilization into a new era.

Astonishingly, Michelangelo's *David* was not the only supreme Renaissance icon being created in Florence during the early months of 1504. Leonardo too was at work on his own artistic masterpiece. During the summer of 1503, while Leonardo had been involved in plans for the diversion of the Arno as part of the continuing war against Pisa, Machiavelli had managed to secure for him the commission for the vast sixty-foot by twenty-four-foot fresco of the Battle of Anghiari, for which he had begun making preliminary sketches. In the midst of all this disparate activity Leonardo embarked upon what was to become his best-known work—now generally known as the *Mona Lisa*.

The *Mona Lisa*.

By the summer of 1504 this portrait was beginning to emerge as the painting we know today, with the central figure, her hands crossed, her head half turned to gaze directly out at the viewer. Mona Lisa is wearing a veil over her hair, lending her an incongruously Spanish air. Such a look was very much the height of fashion during these years, and had been inspired by the Spanish veil that Lucrezia Borgia had worn on her marriage to Alfonso d'Este in 1502, another oblique effect that the Borgias had upon Leonardo.

Behind Mona Lisa is the rising misty landscape of the upper Arno valley, through which Leonardo had traveled during his employment by Borgia. But it is not only the background that appears to recede into a hazy atmosphere. Not the least attraction of this painting is that the more one looks at it, the more elusive its image appears to become, an effect which is in part achieved by the *sfumato* technique that Leonardo frequently employed in his paintings.* In his *Treatise on Painting*, Leonardo writes: "In the streets as evening falls, or when the weather is gloomy, observe what delicacy and grace appear in the faces of men and women." Yet Leonardo's *sfumato* does not obscure; on the contrary, it lends the figure of Mona Lisa that soft luminosity which draws the eye and so beguiles the mind.

The most elusive element is of course the celebrated smile. This has been described in all manner of ways. It is as if Mona Lisa is smiling beneath her skin, an expression that has not quite come to the surface of her face. If we physically attempt to mimic this effect, we become aware of the subtleties involved, and it is here that Leonardo's anatomical investigations came into their own. Indeed, some critics have proposed that he was merely attempting to suggest the full anatomy of a face in all its bone structure and intricate musculature, and then clothing it in skin. Even Leonardo himself insisted that "painting has to do with natural philosophy" (that is, science). However, such purely materialistic description does no justice to the deeply mysterious effect of the all-but-hidden smile, which is open to so many interpretations that these in effect render it something of a mirror of the viewer. Some see it as a contemplative smile, suffused in deep spirituality—one even going so far as to call it "a womanly equivalent of Christ." Others see in it a dreamy sensuality, or an idealized picture of the young mother who Mona Lisa may well have been—reading into her face the qualities of compassion, understanding, the constancy of a mother's love.

---

* *Sfumato* is the technical term used to describe the technique of softening outlines and making the colors and tones of the paint shade into one another, producing a slightly misty effect. The Italian word *sfumato* has its own variety of vague meanings—ranging from "soft" or "shaded" to "vanished"—with its connotation of *fumo* or smoke.

Vasari's short biography of Leonardo is not always reliable, but even its exaggerations appear to have grown out of the gossip of Leonardo's contemporaries, several of whom Vasari knew personally. According to Vasari, Leonardo

> employed singers and musicians or jesters to keep her full of merriment and so chase away the melancholy that painters usually give to portraits. As a result, in this painting of Leonardo's there was a smile so pleasing that it seemed divine rather than human.

A likely story? Something like this—without the jesters, perhaps— could explain how Leonardo inspired a tranquil ease in his sitter, but gives no hint of how he actually achieved that most mysterious of expressions.

Which leads us to the question: who precisely was Mona Lisa? Earlier, Vasari plainly states: "For Francesco del Giocondo Leonardo undertook to execute the portrait of his wife, Mona Lisa." Hence the names usually associated with the painting: *Mona Lisa* and *La Gioconda*. At the time Leonardo began the painting, del Giocondo was a prosperous thirty-five-year-old silk and cloth merchant who also had interests in haberdashery. He had married Lisa eight years previously when she was fifteen, and by now she had borne him two sons. All this sounds plausible enough: both Francesco del Giocondo and his wife, Lisa, appear in the contemporary records. But if this Lisa was the subject of Leonardo's portrait, why did he never deliver it to del Giocondo, who would have paid good money in advance and would certainly have demanded delivery? The contemporary Florentine records also relate how del Giocondo treated a painter who owed him money, recovering the debt by having all the paintings in the artist's studio seized. Although Leonardo would never deliver this painting to whoever commissioned it, the *Mona Lisa* was not seized from his possession, which casts doubt on its being a portrait of La Gioconda.

There is evidence that suggests that the sitter might have been a mistress of the profligate Giuliano de' Medici, the youngest brother of

Piero de' Medici, the former ruler of Florence who drowned at Garigliano. In a travel journal kept by the secretary of Cardinal Luigi of Aragon, he describes a visit that they made many years later to the aged Leonardo in his studio. Here they were shown "a portrait of a certain Florentine woman, portrayed from life at the request of the late Magnificent Giuliano de' Medici." Presumably this was a description given to the cardinal by Leonardo himself. Apparent support for this identification comes in the form of the so-called nude *Mona Lisa*, which has vanished, although its one-time existence is confirmed by extant copies.* The respectable Francesco del Giocondo is unlikely to have commissioned such a portrait of his wife. If Mona Lisa was in fact Giuliano de' Medici's mistress, this would account for the painting remaining in Leonardo's possession: Giuliano did not collect the painting of his mistress because in the meantime he had got married. However, there is one serious drawback to this explanation. Leonardo could not have started painting the *Mona Lisa* in Florence for Giuliano de' Medici in 1503, as the Medici were in exile, and would remain so for another decade. This would seem to rule out Giuliano's mistress as the subject. Yet there remains the unresolved question of Cardinal Luigi's description, presumably stemming from Leonardo himself. Even more intriguing is the fact that the cardinal's visit to Leonardo's studio took place in 1517, and the curious evidence that this is the first known reference to the *Mona Lisa*. Astonishingly, Leonardo makes no discernible reference to this work in his notebooks, though there are a number of remarks that suggest what he might have intended in this painting. Take, for instance, "If poetry describes the working of the mind, painting considers the working of the mind in movement." By this "movement," Leonardo meant the movement of the body—especially in such subtle nuances as the movement of the eyes, the lips, the facial muscles in Mona Lisa's smile. This is no frozen expression: in Leonardo's painting it appears very much as a movement—a fluidity, an expression that has not yet quite surfaced.

* One, generally thought to have been painted by Leonardo's assistant Salai, is in the Hermitage at St. Petersburg. Although its pose resembles that of the *Mona Lisa*, it is entirely lacking the delicate subtlety of Leonardo's work.

There remains one final fascinating possibility. In the words of Leonardo's French biographer Serge Bramly:

Some claim the *Mona Lisa* resembles its painter. Could it have been a posthumous portrait of his mother? If this was the case, Leonardo never revealed the identity of the original, or else sent contemporaries off on false trails, since he had always been extremely discreet about Caterina.

Could this have been his attempt to capture some childhood vision of perfection—the young Caterina, his mother, motherhood? This might explain why Leonardo never finished his greatest work, keeping it in his possession throughout his ensuing travels, all the while returning to work on it for brief periods. Leonardo's block about completing his work had grown imperceptibly over the years, leaving gaps in the immaculate clarity of his ever-expanding vision. Instead of an ordered program of investigation, his notebooks reveal project after project taken up piecemeal, then abandoned before completion in favor of some other investigation, only to be taken up once more: flying machines, anatomical investigations, grotesque faces, geometrical figures, maps, torrents, calculations—a cornucopia of originality, forever diverting its flow from one channel to another, stopping, and turning aside to something else.

All this adds to the significance of the single occasion when he let drop that revealing suggestion concerning why so much of his work remained incomplete: "I will not publish nor divulge such things because of the evil nature of men." Previously Leonardo had been willing to divulge plans for the most gruesome war machines, without apparent thought for the consequences. But now his regard for his work had undergone a significant change. Instead of putting it to use for an employer, he wished to suppress it—or at least part of it. What had happened to him? What had made him wish to do this? Had he perhaps undergone some traumatic experience? As we have speculated, some deeply disturbing event may well have caused him to write these fateful words in his notebook. And from this time on, the block that had previously been a mental tic now deepened to become a psychological flaw. The utter clarity of each individual vision would remain, yet the whole would be lost in incoherence. The science of perception—that unifying philosophy of vision that drove him to see and investigate so much—would never be realized amidst the overall disorder of his work.

Leonardo would make several attempts to overcome this disorder. He would make lists, and plans to collect the separate elements of his notebooks under subjects, then begin sequencing them. But something, "the evil nature of men," would prevent him from bringing this task to completion so that he could pass it on to the world. It must have been something he had experienced whilst working for Borgia. During the massacre at Fossombrone? Amidst the mayhem at Sinigallia? After the atrocities at Sam Quirico? Or had this been a more cerebral event: some crushing realization, perhaps? We can imagine Leonardo drawing those three portrait sketches of Borgia as he lay stretched out in his chair before the fire in his chamber. Perhaps, whilst he attempted to reconcile the absolute clarity in which he saw Borgia's features with the mortal aura of mayhem, murder, incest, and betrayal that enveloped him, he had understood that such clarity of perception could never be innocent, in the end. So there would be no end—he would retreat from this, leaving the ultimate horror unseen, the final vision unfinished, the overall scheme uncompleted. Instead of overall order, overall chaos.

23

Coaxing Water

THE SIGNORIA CONTINUED to have their doubts about Leonardo's scheme to divert the Arno. However, due in large part to Machiavelli's lobbying of Gonfaloniere Soderini, it was decided to go ahead with the practical implementation of the scheme in the summer of 1504. It was to be a bold and massive undertaking, but Leonardo remained confident that it could be done. In his notebook, there is an initial draft of his instructions.

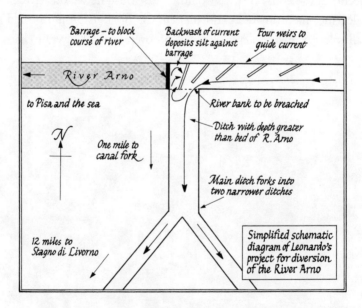

Simplified diagram of Leonardo's project for the diversion of the River Arno.

The river that is to be diverted from one course to another must be coaxed and not treated roughly or with violence. To do this a sort of weir must be inserted into the river, then another one further downstream jutting out beyond it, and similarly third, fourth, and fifth weirs, so that the river may discharge itself into the channel made for it, and by this means it may be diverted.

Basically, this was to be done in separate well-defined stages. First, to the south of the river a large, wide ditch would be dug, which was deeper than the bed of the Arno. Next, as Leonardo had instructed in his notebook, weirs would be inserted in the river to help guide the current towards its south bank. This bank would then be breached, causing the main current of water to flow into the ditch. And last, a barrage would then be erected, preventing the weakened flow of the Arno from continuing downstream, and diverting the rest of the water into the ditch. The back-eddies from the flow of the river would then deposit silt against the base of the barrage, thus strengthening it. This would render the new course of the river more permanent, and less susceptible to sabotage by the Pisans.

Leonardo's original calculations estimated that the initial single ditch would need to be one mile long and thirty-two feet deep, before it forked into two lesser ditches. To dig this out would require the removal of around one million tons of earth. This, and the subsidiary work, he estimated would take 54,000 man-days. If this was not feasible, he could construct an excavating machine that would reduce both the time and the manpower required.

In Leonardo's notebooks there is a drawing of just such a machine: a huge mobile digger, mounted on wooden rails and powered forward by a windlass. In front of the machine are two semicircular arrays of containers, one above the other, with each layer having up to a dozen containers. The precise function of these containers—if indeed they are such—is unclear. In the absence of any mechanical devices that have not been included in the drawing, it would appear that they were to be filled by teams of digging men. Each of the two levels is served by a swinging

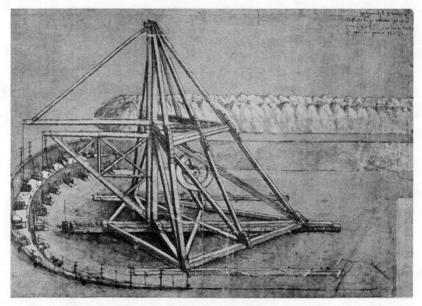

Leonardo's digging machine.

crane for the regular removal of containers filled with excavated earth. The machine would thus allow scores of men, or perhaps even a hundred or so, to continue digging in coordinated teams without having to haul the earth up the steep sides of the excavated ditch. The proportions given by Leonardo for the width of the ditch being excavated by the men in this machine conform exactly to his specifications for the Arno diversion ditch. His preparations and calculations were characteristically thorough and meticulous. But would they work in practice?

A Florentine master of works called Colombino was appointed chief hydraulic engineer, with the task of supervising the project on-site and executing Leonardo's plan. At the same time, Machiavelli's assistant and friend, the diarist Biagio Buonaccorsi, was deputized to liaise between Colombino and Machiavelli on the Ten of War, the council that was officially responsible for the project.

Work started on-site, which was protected by a garrison in the fortress of La Verruca, on August 20, 1504. A nearby abandoned tower was dismantled to provide material for the weirs, and according to Buonaccorsi's report:

A camp was established ... and *maestri d'acqua* were summoned. They said they required two thousand workers, and a quantity of wood to construct a weir to hold the river in, and divert it along the two ditches to the Stagno, and they promised they could complete the project within thirty or forty thousand man-days, and in this hope the project was begun ... with two thousand workmen hired at one *carlino** a day.

Even at this early stage discrepancies had begun to appear. Colombino's estimates for the total man-hours differ significantly from Leonardo's. Evidently Colombino intended, or had been advised, to make economies. The unending war against Pisa had left the Florentine exchequer at a low ebb, and he may well have received covert instructions regarding costs from the Signoria. However, despite Colombino hiring fewer men, the Signoria found it increasingly difficult to meet their wages, and soon a trickle of disenchanted laborers began to melt away and head back across country for Florence. On top of this, the project required a thousand soldiers to guard the laborers from attack by foraging Pisan columns.

According to Colombino's estimate, the entire project should easily have been finished within three weeks, yet by mid-September there was no sign of completion. Reports now began reaching Machiavelli that further deviations from Leonardo's plans were being made by Colombino. By September 20, Machiavelli was becoming seriously worried by the slowness with which the project was progressing, to say nothing of Colombino's eccentric engineering ideas. Machiavelli wrote impatiently to one of Colombino's deputy *maestri d'acqua:*

> Your letter of yesterday informed us about the ditch; if today, after so many promises, its mouth will be widened, this will please us; if not, without hoping any longer, we will nevertheless believe that you have done or are doing everything possible.

---

* A *carlino* was worth around one-twentieth of a florin. Leonardo paid his apprentice assistants approximately two *carlinos* a day.

Evidently Machiavelli now consulted Leonardo, for the letter he wrote the next day shows a much clearer grasp of the situation:

> Your delay makes us fear that the bed of the ditch is shallower than the bed of the Arno; this would have negative effects and in our opinion it would not direct the project to the end we wish.

Sure enough, when the breach was opened, the flow of water into the ditch was hardly as expected. Buonaccorsi reported: "The waters never went through the ditches except when the river was in flood, and as soon as it subsided the water flowed back."

Yet as Buonaccorsi's words imply, there had been an even more major divergence from Leonardo's plan. Buonaccorsi's earlier report had spoken of the river being diverted "along two ditches to the Stagno." Leonardo had instructed that the river should be diverted along one large deep ditch, which only after a mile would be split into two ditches. But Colombino insisted that the two ditches should lead directly out of the Arno. Either this was due to a serious misunderstanding or Colombino simply thought he knew better than Leonardo.

So Colombino had ordered two ditches to be dug. He had then disregarded Machiavelli's instructions (almost certainly originating from Leonardo) that any ditch should be deeper than the bed of the Arno. According to Buonaccorsi's report: "The greater of the two ditches was sixty feet wide and fourteen feet deep, and the second forty feet wide and as deep as the other." Yet Leonardo had specified that his single ditch should be thirty-two feet deep. One can only assume that, farcically, Colombino thought that having two ditches, each of half the depth, would solve the problem.

Then it got worse. In the first days of October Tuscany was swept by a violent storm, accompanied by torrential rain. As a result, the level of the Arno rose dramatically, its waters becoming such a torrent that the Florentine ships blockading the mouth of the river as part of the siege of Pisa were swept away and eighty men drowned.* The effect of the torrent was catastrophic: water spilled into the ditches with such force that the walls of both ditches collapsed, releasing a deluge of water across the plain to the south, destroying several farms in its path. And still the main flow of the river remained undiverted.

When one of the commanders in charge of the Florentine soldiers guarding the site saw what had happened, he finally lost all patience with the project, and sent word to Florence demanding that he and his force be recalled at once. This was followed by further desertions amongst the unpaid laborers. By mid-October the entire project was abandoned, with the remaining disgruntled laborers, together with their protective soldiers, trudging their way through the mud of the flooded Arno valley back to Florence. The Pisans immediately ventured out from behind the walls of their city and began filling in the ditches. As Buonaccorsi summarized in his report:

> In the end the project took far more time and money than anyone had forecast, and all to no avail. As it turned out, after eighty thousand man-days it had not even reached halfway.

The entire enterprise had cost 7,000 ducats, leaving the exchequer empty.

Not surprisingly, all this was to have serious political repercussions. Gonfaloniere Soderini was already becoming increasingly unpopular, and many had begun to regret that the city had appointed him for life. The opposition to Soderini was led by Alamanno Salviati, a member of one of the leading Florentine families. Many disenchanted citizens, of all classes, had begun to look back with nostalgia to the days of the glorious pageants thrown by Lorenzo the Magnificient. Such sentiments were encouraged by Salviati and his supporters, who were themselves receiving covert support from Rome, where the drowned Piero de' Medici's younger brother, Cardinal Giovanni de' Medici, had now risen to become a figure

---

* Some sources claim that the boats were guarding the mouths of the two ditches. Although this is possible, it seems unlikely, given the size of the ditches and the fact that they were being guarded by soldiers on land.

of considerable importance, being a close friend and loyal supporter of the new pope, Julius II.

The Signoria held Piero Soderini fully responsible for the costly fiasco of the Arno diversion project, blaming him for putting forward the idea in the first place—even though it had initially been suggested to him by Machiavelli, who had in fact been persuaded to adopt the idea by Leonardo.

Although Machiavelli and Soderini worked closely together, it appears that the *gonfaloniere* was not particularly well disposed towards Machiavelli, unlike his brother Cardinal Francesco Soderini, who was now the Florentine ambassador in Rome. Whilst Machiavelli had been on his mission to Rome, he and the cardinal had become particularly close, to the point where Machiavelli had invited Francesco Soderini to become godfather to his newly born son Bernardino. Although Gonfaloniere Soderini was not close to Machiavelli, he nonetheless recognized Machiavelli's exceptional diplomatic, political, and administrative skills. He often sought Machiavelli's advice—to such an extent that jealous colleagues in the administration had taken to referring to him as Soderini's *manino.**

These latest political developments placed Machiavelli in a precarious position. Salviati was head of the faction that had almost certainly been responsible for Machiavelli's surprise election to a senior post in the administration when he was just twenty-nine. Although in his youth the young poet Machiavelli had become close to the Medici circle, he was certainly no covert supporter of a Medici restoration, and did in fact have complete loyalty to Gonfaloniere Soderini and the continuation of Florence as a democratic republic. Even so, Soderini found it politic to inform Machiavelli that for the time being he was not to report for work at the Palazzo della Signoria. Had he been dismissed, or was this just a temporary enforced leave until things blew over?

On October 26, Cardinal Soderini wrote to Machiavelli from Rome:

---

* Literally "little hand," this was also the word for a "back-scratcher." In other words, Machiavelli was seen as Soderini's lackey.

My highly esteemed and very dear friend,

It caused me great pain to learn that your project for the waters of the Arno has ended in disaster. There is no doubt in my mind that this was the fault of Colombino and his engineers, who failed to obey their instructions. . . .

Gonfaloniere Soderini often used his brother Francesco to convey his true feelings to Machiavelli on difficult matters, and this was almost certainly the case here. Having reassured Machiavelli that he was hardly to blame for the fiasco, Cardinal Soderini advised him to look upon the aftermath philosophically: "Maybe it was God's will that it should end thus, and we should see it all as part of a greater and better scheme whose purpose remains unknown to us."

Despite such noble sentiments, Machiavelli was nonetheless out of favor, out of a job, and in political limbo. He now made what at first sight might appear to be a surprising choice: he returned to writing poetry. Machiavelli had in fact not abandoned the idea that one day he would fulfill his youthful dream of literary fame. Indeed, in many ways his work had provided him with numerous opportunities to practice his craft and hone his style. The clarity and precision of the dispatches written on his missions revealed his originality as well as his independence of mind, while his more informal letters home gave scope for his wit and imagination (not least in their exaggeration). His mocking self-awareness, his psychological analysis of the figures he encountered, and his vision of the historical events unfolding around him may not have been literature in themselves, but they certainly could have been turned into such, and he appears to have borne this in mind for quite some time. All this is inevitably speculative—but events such as the drama of his first chilling candlelit encounter with Borgia at the palace in Urbino would surely have stirred his poetic imagination.

Sometime around the end of October 1504, Machiavelli launched into writing the long historical poem that would be called *Decennale primo* (The First Decade). We know that on his missions he habitually traveled with "his saddlebag stuffed with books," and this wide reading would certainly be reflected in his literary style. The *Decennale primo* was written in the same terza rima form that Dante had chosen for his *Commedia Divina* (Divine Comedy), and there are indications that Machiavelli started this work with similarly lofty ambitions. His aim was nothing less than to capture in chronicle form the history of Florence and Italy during the previous decade (1494–1504). He describes the events from the fall of the Medici and Savonarola's republic through to the ascension of Pope Julius II and the stalemate of the war with Pisa, attempting to give them the poetic permanence of a classical epic such as Homer's *Odyssey* or Virgil's *Aeneid*. In the event, this proved to be an ill-advised aspiration for the out-of-practice thirty-five-year-old poet. The complexities and subterfuges of Italian politics during this period did not lend themselves to epic form: this was no era of heroes or mythic adventures. As a result, Machiavelli's chronicle was in many places hardly poetry at all—more a compressed, occasionally metaphorical record of events. Thus Borgia's first Romagna campaign:

> So the Duke [Borgia], beneath the flag of three lilies [that is,
>   with the aid of French troops]
> Mastered Imola and Forli
> And took away from them a woman [Caterina Sforza] and
>   her three sons.

To be fair, not all Machiavelli's 550 lines are quite so clumsy and prosaic. More important, this was (amongst other things) an early attempt to place Borgia in some kind of epic setting. It may have failed, but this impulse to realize Borgia as an illustrative figure would persist. What began here as an awkward poetic sketch would over time grow into a fully fledged and significant psychological portrait, against the background of an all-too-real history, occupying a central role in *The Prince*, the work for which Machiavelli would forever be remembered.

Possibly in an attempt to deflect criticism, Machiavelli boasts in his introduction to the *Decennale primo* that he had completed it in such haste that it represented "the labors of Italy for ten years and my own for fifteen days." Surprisingly, Machiavelli dedicated this poem to Soderini's opponent Alamanno Salviati—suggesting even more strongly that he had owed his position in the administration, at least to begin with, to the Salviati faction. However, this appears to have been evidence of a particularly difficult balancing act by Machiavelli—for the last verse of the *Decennale primo* contains an unmistakable reference to his belief in Soderini's leadership of the Florentine ship of state as it was at present constituted:

> We place our trust in the skillful steersman,
> In the oars, in the sails and the rigging . . .

Although Machiavelli invested high literary ambitions in his *Decennale primo*, there is no doubt that he also used it to try to regain his job. This was but the first instance in which Machiavelli sought to combine lofty aims with low subterfuge—a characteristic literary trait that would achieve its apex in *The Prince*.

Leonardo was during this time at work on the *Mona Lisa*, the masterpiece for which he too would forever be remembered. So far as is known, Leonardo managed to escape serious blame for his part in the Arno fiasco. Even so, the summer of 1504 was not to be a good time for him. As he recorded in his notebook: "On Wednesday at seven o'clock died Ser Piero da Vinci, on July 9, 1504, Wednesday, around the seventh hour." The death of Leonardo's father, just like the death of his mother, elicited no direct expression of emotion. Yet once again there is the telltale repetition. Despite his lengthy absences from Florence, Leonardo evidently maintained some kind of deep, if distant, relationship with his father. He even recorded his father's death again, in another notebook, as if for emphasis (he surely cannot have forgotten his earlier entry): "On July 9, 1504, Wednesday, at the seventh hour, died Ser Piero da Vinci, notary at the Palazzo del Podesta,* my father—at the seventh hour, aged eighty years, leaving ten sons and two daughters."

Around this time Leonardo withdrew from public view, and he appears to have distracted his feelings (whatever they were) by immersing himself in his work. Thus he became more and more absorbed in the

---

* Palace of Justice—that is, the law courts.

greatest challenge of his artistic career: the delicate and skillful task of representing Mona Lisa's expression. Yet all this meant that he increasingly began to neglect his public commission from the Signoria. Leonardo had already been paid a considerable advance for the vast fresco of the Battle of Anghiari that was meant to cover the bare wall of the new Grand Council Chamber in the Palazzo della Signoria. Not surprisingly, word of Leonardo's dilatoriness soon reached the Signoria, to the particular vexation of Gonfaloniere Soderini. Here was another project in which Machiavelli had persuaded him to invest good public money, which was now in such short supply.

24

Borgia's Gamble

IN ROME, POPE Julius II continued to hold Borgia under heavily guarded house arrest in the Vatican. The pope was becoming increasingly enraged at his inability to gain possession of the Romagna castles that remained loyal to Borgia, to such an extent that some of Borgia's closest sympathizers soon began to fear for their lives. Cesare's relative Cardinal Ludovico Borgia and Cardinal Francesco Remolino (both appointed by Alexander VI) fled for Naples, taking with them Cesare's younger brother Jofre, Giovanni Borgia (the mysterious "Infans Romanus"), and two of Cesare's illegitimate children.

Ironically, it had been the defeat of Borgia's allies the French at Garigliano—news of which had reached Rome early in the New Year of 1504—that probably saved Borgia's life. Spain's power was now in the ascendant, and Julius II knew that he owed his very election to Borgia's Spanish cardinals. He could not afford to risk offending the Spanish by any rash act of revenge against Borgia. Even so, the new pope was determined not to see Borgia released.

Meanwhile, his besieged castles in the Romagna obstinately continued to hold out against the somewhat ineffective papal forces of Julius II, now under the command of the new *gonfaloniere* of the papal forces, Guidobaldo of Urbino. Chief amongst Borgia's strongholds were the formidable *rocca* at Forli and the *rocca* at Cesena, which had recently been reinforced by Leonardo. Julius II had by now recognized that, apart from this ring of strategic fortresses held in Borgia's name, the remaining "papal states" that had been retaken by their former rulers were very much under Venetian influence, so much so that they were in danger of being annexed by Venice altogether. If Julius II was to have any hope of retaking the Romagna states for the papacy, he realized that he desperately needed the fortresses held in Borgia's name. With extreme reluctance, the willful Julius II was forced to enter into negotiations with Borgia.

Yet Borgia appeared in no hurry to reach an agreement. According to several reports, he was once again a changed man. Despite remaining under house arrest in the Vatican, the indecisive, apparently broken figure whom Machiavelli had left in Rome had now become transformed into his old self. According to Giustinian, "his spirit does not bend": he was willing to hold out against Julius II for as long as it took. Far from ruing his situation, Borgia passed his time idly watching his friends and attendants gambling with dice, and paying rapt attention to their games of chess. The Mantuan ambassador Cattaneo reported how, soon after his negotiations with Julius II had begun, Borgia invited a group of courtiers to dine with him, jovially reassuring them during the meal, "Don't be afraid of being poisoned." When one of his guests marveled at how he "was always full of confidence," he replied, "The more I am in adversity, the more I fortify my spirit." All this suggests that when Machiavelli was with him during November and December, Borgia was still suffering from the debilitating effects and mood swings wrought by his illness and its psychological aftermath.

As Borgia continued to drag out the negotiations between himself and Julius II, the thwarted pope started to become ill with suppressed rage. It is worth bearing in mind that Julius II was the man of whom the Venetian and other ambassadors wrote:

> He has not the patience to listen quietly to what you say to him. . . . It is almost impossible to describe how strong and violent and difficult to manage he is. . . . His impetuosity and his temper annoy those who live with him. . . . He inspires fear. . . . [He has] no moderation either in will or conception; whatever was in his mind must be carried through, even if he himself were to perish in the attempt.

One can only marvel at Borgia's apparent insouciance in the face of such a man, who had the power of life and death over him. The negotiations between the pope and his prisoner were conducted by the most influential Spanish figure in Rome, Cardinal Vera of Salerno, the man Borgia had once wished to see elected pope. Warily the cardinal conveyed the proposals and delaying counterproposals between the two negotiators. Faced with such tactics, Julius II succumbed to an unexpected weakness, which would be described by an ever-observant ambassador: "No one has any power over [Julius II], and he consults few, or none. . . . He changes his mind from hour to hour." Even one as skilled in diplomatic subterfuge as Giustinian remarked: "These affairs of [Borgia] are more complicated than a labyrinth."

However, it was not Julius II's indecisiveness but Borgia's recklessness that eventually led him to make the first mistake. Exasperated beyond measure by the inactivity imposed on him by his house arrest, Borgia finally appeared to sign his own death warrant—informing Julius II that in fact he had no control whatsoever over his commanders who continued to hold out in the Romagna. The murderous behavior of the Ramires brothers at Cesena towards Borgia's messenger only seemed to reinforce this point. In which case, Julius II surely had no need of Borgia and could safely order his execution. This was indeed a foolhardy game to play, but Julius II was not willing to call Borgia's apparently suicidal bluff. He was convinced that Borgia remained in communication with the Romagna, sending secret instructions by way of the Spanish cardinals.

Yet the pope could discover no evidence of such messages, and dared not move against the Spanish cardinals. Such was his isolation and lack of troops, and such was Spain's increased power in Naples, on his very doorstep no less, that his papacy was in danger of being rendered all but impotent. As a last resort, Julius II even considered the possibility of bribing Borgia with an offer of comfortable early retirement. Possibly in response to a secret offer on behalf of Borgia's loyal sister Lucrezia in Ferrara, Julius II approached her father-in-law Duke Ercole, the ruler of Ferrara, to determine whether he was willing to provide "honorable imprisonment" for Borgia. But the pope's offer was hastily rejected by Ercole, who wanted nothing to do with Borgia.

All of Italy was watching, and few would have dared to take sides. The outcome of the duel was still far from clear. Here was the man who had been elected pope negotiating with the man who had intended to make himself pope, declare himself a hereditary pope, and transform a secularized papacy into a powerful Italian state, with the ultimate aim of ruling all Italy. Yet Julius II too had great ambitions for the papacy. As Machiavelli would observe:

> Once in possession of all the Romagna ... he had in mind new ways of accumulating wealth which had not even occurred to Alexander VI or his predecessors. He wished to expand the power of the papacy further, was determined to take Bologna, crush the Venetians and to drive the French out of Italy.

Towards the end of his life Machiavelli judged the two men who had most impressed him during his long diplomatic career to have been Cesare Borgia and Pope Julius II. What was taking place in Rome during the early weeks of 1504 was nothing less than the old era bargaining with the new, for the highest of stakes. Borgia was not yet defeated, and Julius II was not yet in control. It was a struggle to the death: one false move, and the one who made it was not likely to survive.

Such was the air of mutual antagonism and deep suspicion surrounding the negotiations that the details are difficult to ascertain. Each of the ambassadors would hear the latest whispers from their inside contacts and would write posthaste to their home cities. Thus contradictory dispatches sped throughout Italy: Ferrara, Venice, Florence, Mantua, Naples, and the French in Milan all received their own unique secondhand version of events.

As far as it is possible to gather, on January 18, 1504, Cardinal Vera managed to broker an agreement between Julius II and Borgia. According to this, Borgia would order the surrender of his castles in the Romagna, on condition that he was allowed to go free and retain all his assets. This implied first that Julius II would cease his campaign to have Borgia prosecuted and sued for vast sums of compensation by various rulers, and second, that Borgia would retain the 300,000 ducats that were being held for him by bankers in Genoa. It is uncertain whether Julius II had any intention of keeping to the first condition, and unclear whether he knew of the sum involved in the second (an amount equivalent to the entire papal revenue that he could expect during his first year in office).

Indeed, the "agreement" proved so elusive that it was not actually signed until January 29. This may have been intended to make the agreement more binding, and did in fact clarify that Borgia's castles would have to be handed over within forty days. Even so, this did not prevent Giustinian from reporting on February 8 that "Borgia's situation is extremely desperate and no one gives much hope for his life." At every hour of the day Borgia wore his sword at his belt, only taking it off when he went to bed, whereupon he would lay it by his pillow. He himself had once ordered a murder in this very chamber: he knew what to expect.

Despite such forebodings, on February 15 Giustinian reported, "Borgia will leave for Ostia tomorrow night." This report seems to have been a little premature.* Other sources suggest that it may have been a day or two later before Julius II finally consented to Borgia's release. He was to be held at the port of Ostia in the custody of the senior Spanish dignitary Cardinal Carvajal, who was under strict orders not to allow Borgia his freedom until the surrender of the Romagna fortresses had taken place.

Borgia was observed reveling in his release from confinement, galloping his horse up and down the banks of the Tiber as he waited for the galley to take him to Ostia. However, Julius II had a surprise for Borgia when he reached Ostia; he was marched under armed escort from the quayside and confined within the formidable walls of the *rocca*. Although he was free to roam within the castle, this imprisonment was considerably more austere than his confinement in the Vatican apartment.

---

* For the most part, I have adhered to Giustinian's version of events. As indicated earlier, the reports by other ambassadors differ materially in both detail and interpretation.

There was no dicing, no chess or convivial dinner parties here. Borgia vented his spleen by setting off the cannons on the battlements, firing cannonballs out over the nearby deserted dunes.

Even if it was not on Borgia's express orders, he must surely have been aware of what would happen next. On February 29 couriers carried news from the Romagna to Julius II that Borgia's commanders once again refused to surrender their fortresses until they knew for certain that Borgia was a free man. On hearing this news Julius II exploded with rage, telling the couriers that "they could go and give the castles to the Turks, the Venetians, or whoever they wanted. He had them chased from the audience chamber and was in such a fury that he retired to bed."

Even Borgia was now becoming impatient. Not until he was free would he be able to embark upon any plans to repair his situation. On March 10 a new agreement was reached, by which Borgia promised to pay the Ramires brothers 3,000 ducats each to surrender the *rocca* at Cesena and the nearby strategic *rocca* at Bertinoro. He also agreed to pay 15,000 ducats to Mirafonte, commander of the *rocca* at Forli, to induce him to surrender.

Borgia's promises to surrender Cesena and Bertinoro appear to have been genuine, but the surrender of Forli would have meant the disappearance of his last stronghold in the Romagna. More pertinently, Borgia had transferred to Forli all the treasures that he had looted from Urbino. These had not yet been returned to Guidobaldo, as promised: such valuables could be used as collateral against which money could quickly be raised for the rapid recruitment of troops in the Romagna.

The Ramires brothers accepted their 3,000 ducats each, surrendering the *rocca* at Cesena and that at Bertinoro to the papal forces. The city of Cesena, Borgia's former capital, was now completely under the control of the Church. The reforms put in place by Sansavino were quickly dismantled and replaced by ecclesiastical rule. Instead of elected councillors, the administration was now placed in the hands of authoritarian priests who did not answer to the people, but to the decree of distant Rome. The citizens of Cesena had no choice but to submit grimly to the new regime, which soon found itself under threat. Now that Borgia's soldiers had abandoned the *rocca*, the Venetian troops advanced, setting up camp menacingly beneath the city walls.

Yet all was not entirely lost for Borgia. As ever, none could have foreseen his next move. At Forlì, Mirafonte was duly offered his 15,000 ducats, in the form of paper securities. As hardened mercenaries, Mirafonte and his men were accustomed to being paid in hard cash. They did not trust paper securities, and the 15,000 ducats in this form were contemptuously rejected—as Borgia knew they would be.

In mid-April news of the surrender of Cesena and Bertinoro reached Ostia before it reached Rome, just as Borgia had organized. Cardinal Carvajal appeared convinced that Borgia had fulfilled his side of the bargain and allowed him to go free without waiting for permission from Julius II.

As gradually becomes clear, Cardinal Carvajal's role in these proceedings was Byzantine, to say the least. Not without reason was it said of him, "He is sincere in nothing." At forty-nine years old he harbored hopes of one day becoming pope, and was determined to make sure that in all power struggles involving the Church he emerged on the winning side. This was just the sort of man with whom Borgia enjoyed dealing. Yet Carvajal also appears to have been party to a plot by Julius II to have Borgia "released" onto a papal galley that would deliver him to France. Borgia must have got wind of this, probably through Carvajal himself, but had no intention of going to France. Although Louis XII remained nominally Borgia's ally, he had begun to tire of Borgia's behavior, especially now that he no longer had the backing of the pope. The divergence between French aims and the ambitions of Louis XII's protégé was becoming glaringly apparent. Louis XII had decided not to order his troops to prevent Venice, or Julius II, from moving into the Romagna, and the French maintained their alliance with Florence. Borgia might have been welcomed in France, but his ability to indulge in independent action would have been severely curtailed by Louis XII. Indeed, Borgia's presence was awaited with some impatience in northern Italy, where he was expected to serve with the French contingent. He would certainly not have been allowed to operate on his own accord to regain his territories in the

Romagna. Julius II had understood this—hence the papal galley standing by in Ostia.

Borgia had realized that his hopes now lay with his ancestral Spain. An indication of this can be seen in the fact that he had sent the Borgia children with Cardinal Ludovico Borgia for safekeeping to Naples, whose entire territory was now firmly under Spanish rule. If Borgia retook the Romagna with Spanish blessing, the power of Julius II in Rome would be neutralized and Spain would extend its sphere of influence well into central Italy. The position of the French in northern Italy would be considerably weakened, and Florence would once again be at Borgia's mercy, this time with no last-minute recourse to any powerful ally.

Even so, Borgia realized that he would have to take precautions before arriving in Naples, which was now being governed for the Spanish by Gonsalvo de Cordova, a man who was no friend of Borgia's. On the other hand, Borgia was Spanish and felt sure that Gonsalvo's ultimate rulers, King Ferdinand and Queen Isabella of Spain, would see him as working for Spanish interests in Italy. He decided to approach Cardinal Carvajal on this matter. It did not take long for the ever-resourceful cardinal to make contact with Gonsalvo, through the intermediary of the two Spanish cardinals at present in Naples—namely, Cardinal Borgia and Cardinal Remolino. A promise of safe-conduct for Borgia was soon forthcoming from Gonsalvo.

Unfortunately, things had moved so fast that the galley that was to take Borgia from Ostia to Naples was still confined to Naples harbor by spring storms. Borgia was aware that his freedom, to say nothing of his life, could well be in danger if he remained in Ostia and took matters into his own hands. Early on the morning of April 19 he slipped undetected out of Ostia as soon as the city gates were opened. With an escort of just three trusted attendants, he rode swiftly thirty miles south along country roads to the remote little harbor of Nettuno. Here he took a small fishing boat and continued sixty miles along the coast, keeping close to the shore, before beaching the boat some thirty miles north of Naples. He then made his way on horseback to the city.

It took Borgia nine days to cover the 120 or so miles to Naples, indicating that he was concerned more with stealth than speed. His premature disappearance from Ostia would have caused Julius II to mount an all-out search, with his men scouring the countryside, but Borgia managed to elude them. The indications are that whilst traveling he reverted to his old habit of wearing a mask. This would not have been as unusual as it seems: long-distance riders traveling at speed—such as couriers—habitually shielded their eyes and covered the lower part of their face against the dust raised by passing horses' hooves. But there is evidence that Borgia had another reason for covering his face. According to Cardinal Carvajal, whilst Borgia had been in Ostia he "had been in some pain, and he seemed to me to be suffering from the French disease [syphilis]. . . . His face was blotched and disfigured with pustules." While there is no reason to doubt Carvajal's physical description, his diagnosis would seem to have been incorrect. The disease that had struck Borgia down the previous summer (and proved fatal for his father, Alexander VI) had almost certainly been tertiary malaria, an illness that is now known to cure the symptoms of syphilis. It is therefore likely that Borgia had begun to suffer from a recurring bout of his malaria, which might have been exacerbated by the unaccustomed physical inactivity of his prolonged period under house arrest in the Vatican apartment. Even so, there is no denying that Carvajal's description bears an uncanny resemblance to the symptoms of syphilis. If his diagnosis was correct, this would lend weight to the disparaged theory that Alexander VI and Borgia were in fact poisoned: the scandalous rumor that spread through Rome at the time may yet prove to have been true.*

Borgia rode into the city of Naples on the morning of April 28 and went at once to the palazzo of his relative Cardinal Ludovico Borgia, where a large apartment had already been set aside for his residence. Here he was reunited with his young brother Jofre, his two illegitimate sons, and sympathizers such as Cardinal Remolino. The importance with

---

* The definitive answer to this question will only come to light if material from the cadavers of Alexander VI and Borgia can be subjected to DNA testing, which can reveal the presence of poison as well as some illnesses. Although such tests seem unlikely to take place at present, it is worth noting that permission has recently been given for the Medici tombs in Florence to be opened for DNA testing.

which Borgia's entry into Naples was viewed can be gauged from the fact that on the very evening of his arrival he was visited and "greeted with marks of respect by Gonsalvo de Cordova as representative of the King of Spain."

Borgia was not surprised by Gonsalvo de Cordova's change of attitude towards him. Prior to their falling-out in the late summer of 1503, when Borgia had suddenly abandoned the Spanish commander and switched his allegiance back to Louis XII of France, Gonsalvo and Borgia had formed something of an alliance. This had involved secret negotiations, during which Gonsalvo had assured Borgia that when the time came for him to move on Florence, the Spanish commander would join him. In return, Borgia had apparently promised Gonsalvo that he would make him Lord of Pisa. In Naples, these plans would be revived.

Swapping the post of Viceroy of Naples for that of Lord of Pisa was not quite the comedown it might have appeared. Gonsalvo realized that his position as ruler of Naples was not only subordinate, but also temporary. It would come to an end when King Ferdinand and Queen Isabella of Spain were confirmed as monarchs of the Kingdom of Naples. In Pisa, he would be able to establish his own lordship, in an alliance with the rising star of Borgia.

Borgia became a regular dinner guest at Gonsalvo's headquarters in the Castel Nuovo. It was Borgia's intention to assemble an expeditionary force, sail up the coast, and land at Piombino or Pisa. Unfortunately, for the time being Borgia remained cut off from his funds in Genoa, but Gonsalvo promised his assistance. As a result, within weeks Borgia had assembled a force of 3,000 infantry, complete with artillery. These were to be conveyed up the coast in eight ships, and Borgia's quarter-masters were soon to be seen assembling twelve cannons on the quayside ready for loading aboard. The magnitude of Borgia's plans gradually became clear, and word soon reached Rome. According to Giustinian's dispatch to his masters in Venice, who had good reason to be kept informed of Borgia's plans for the Romagna, Borgia's aim was to land at a Tuscan port and march his forces across Tuscan territory to Modena. Here he would send word to his sister Lucrezia in nearby Ferrara, which was now dangerously sandwiched between the republic of Venice and the territory that Venice had occupied in the Romagna. Lucrezia was to explain to her father-in-law, Duke Ercole of Ferrara, that it was in his best interests to join Borgia in his campaign to reinstate himself as Duke of the Romagna. Only such an alliance would ensure the survival of Ercole's dukedom.

All this posed a major threat to the plans of Julius II, who made his own countermove, sending word to Florence that Borgia's imprisoned Spanish commander, the notorious Don Michele, should be brought forthwith to Rome. Don Michele arrived on May 22 and was at once escorted to the papal dungeons, where he was subjected to torture on the rack. Julius II was determined that Don Michele should reveal incriminating evidence of Borgia's involvement in the murder of his younger brother the Duke of Gandia, and in the assassination of Lucrezia's husband, Duke Alfonso of Bisceglie (which had in fact been carried out by Don Michele himself). However, despite enduring the extreme agonies of the rack, Don Michele refused to incriminate Borgia, claiming that both these murders were carried out on orders from Alexander VI. At least in the case of his favorite son, Gandia, this was palpably untrue, but Don Michele must have felt there was little harm in blaming the dead pope—this would be of no use to Julius II. What Julius wanted was to blacken Borgia's name, especially in the eyes of King Ferdinand and Queen Isabella of Spain, who would then order Gonsalvo to seize Borgia and prevent him from setting out with his expeditionary force from Naples. Borgia was quickly to realize the seriousness of this development, and sent word to Rome offering 10,000 ducats for Don Michele's release. Julius II dismissed this offer and ordered Don Michele's torture to be intensified. Yet still Borgia's most loyal commander refused to reveal any incriminating evidence about his master.

Despite this disappointment, the pope was soon given what promised to be heartening news. During the last week of May he received intelligence that Borgia's treasurer was attempting to smuggle the assets from his bank account in Genoa to Naples, and word had it that 300,000 ducats had reached Rome. Julius II immediately ordered papal agents to scour the city: the sanctuary where Borgia's aging mother, Vannozza, had taken refuge was ransacked, as were any premises even remotely suspected of housing Borgia sympathizers. Meanwhile spies in the households of the Spanish cardinals were questioned, and the cardinals' palazzi were kept under the strictest surveillance, day and night. Despite all these efforts, nothing was found.

Meanwhile developments in Naples were moving fast. On May 24 the Florentine ambassador Pandolfini sent an alarming dispatch to the Signoria: Gonsalvo had given permission for Borgia to embark, and his convoy was ready to set sail for either Pisa or Piombino.

On the evening of May 26, Borgia arrived at the Castel Nuovo to take his leave of Gonsalvo. According to Gonsalvo's sixteenth-century biographer, who appears to have drawn on a contemporary report:

> Borgia was to stay in the Castel Nuovo overnight, having made all the preparations for his departure on the morrow. Late that night he left his room to take his leave of Gonsalvo, for he planned to rise early in the morning. He instructed his manservant: "As it is late, you may withdraw to your quarters." But his manservant replied, "You may sleep, my lord, but I have been instructed to keep watch outside your door. I am not permitted to sleep." When Borgia heard this he understood at once what it meant, and let out a loud cry, "Santa Maria, I am betrayed! Lord Gonsalvo has dealt me the cruelest of blows. . . ." The commander of the garrison of the Castel Nuovo then appeared and ordered a guard to be posted at Borgia's door.

Instead of being Gonsalvo's guest, Borgia now found himself Gonsalvo's prisoner. The arch-betrayer, the murderous deceiver of Sinigallia, had himself been betrayed.

Yet how could this have happened? How could the safe-conduct given by Gonsalvo de Cordova, who as a Spanish nobleman held honor above all else, have proved so worthless? Borgia had committed a major blunder: in the midst of all his recent travails, his desperate game of bluff with Julius II, his adventurous escape from Ostia, and his determination to reach the Romagna whilst Mirafonte still held out at Forlì, he had overlooked the politics of the larger picture. In the past, he had relied to a large extent upon his father, Alexander VI, to deal with the overall Borgia strategy. As pope, Alexander VI had sat at the center of a diplomatic network that spread far and wide; and the qualities that had enabled him to acquire the papacy in the first place had made him highly adept at dealing with the complexities of Italian politics, playing on its ever-changing alliances and long-nursed rivalries to his own advantage. Although in his last years he had proved increasingly unable to restrain his son's impulsive behavior, he had still managed to smooth over the ensuing diplomatic crises. Now Cesare Borgia was no longer backed by such a master of intrigue, and without Alexander VI his neglect of developments in the overall political situation had led to his downfall.

During the previous months, the political situation in Italy had undergone a subtle but profound change. On his accession, Julius II had appeared weak, both militarily and politically. His outmaneuvering of Cardinal d'Amboise in the papal election had alienated the French, and his need for the votes of the Spanish cardinals had left him reliant upon Spain, the new rising power in Italy. Trapped between these two foreign powers, the papacy had appeared all but impotent. Yet unbeknown to Borgia, Julius II had succeeded in establishing himself in a position of considerable influence. Borgia had not realized that King Ferdinand and Queen Isabella of Spain were keen to form close and friendly relations with the pope, a situation that Alexander VI would instantly have apprehended. The joint Spanish monarchs were intent upon making Spain into the major power in Europe. In pursuance of this aim, they wanted the pope to give dispensation so that their daughter Catherine of Aragon could marry her deceased husband's brother, the future King Henry VIII of England. They also keenly wished the pope to legitimize their investiture as king and queen of Naples.

Just over a month after Cardinals Borgia and Remolino, along with the younger members of the Borgia family, had fled from Rome to Naples in December 1503, Ferdinand and Isabella had sent word to their viceroy Gonsalvo that they had no wish to see the Kingdom of Naples become a center for refugees opposed to Julius II. Then on May 11, just two weeks after Borgia's arrival in Naples under safe-conduct, Julius II had sent a secret dispatch to Gonsalvo. In this, the pope had requested the Viceroy of Naples to keep a strict watch over Borgia's behavior, and to prevent him from taking any action against the Church, whilst at the same time using his influence to persuade Borgia to order the surrender of Forli. To reinforce this message, Julius II also wrote that same day to the King and Queen of Spain, pointing out his displeasure at the actions of two of their subjects. He blamed Cardinal Carvajal for letting Borgia go free from Ostia, and he blamed Gonsalvo for permitting Borgia to reside in Naples and plot against the Church.

Gonsalvo, who did not even like Borgia, appeared to be in an impossible situation. On Borgia's account he found himself under attack from both the pope and his masters in Spain—yet bound by his honor to uphold the safe-conduct he had given to Borgia. Eventually, he found it expedient to betray Borgia, and an ingenious justification would be provided for this, according to which "the safe-conduct [was] alleged to have been given over the signature of the Catholic sovereigns . . . on their behalf by Gonsalvo." So it was not in fact Gonsalvo's safe-conduct at all: here was a justification worthy of Borgia himself, even if under the circumstances he was unlikely to have appreciated its particular finesse.

On May 29, three days after Borgia was taken prisoner, he was isolated from all contact with the outside world: his mistress was escorted from his chamber and he was removed to the most secure cell in the Castel Nuovo. This was the notorious *Il Forno* (The Oven), which lived up to its name more than ever during the long sweltering days of the Neapolitan summer.

Gonsalvo's instructions, from both Spain and Rome, were to persuade Borgia to order the surrender of the *rocca* at Forli. This would effectively have put an end to his political role in Italy: without the Romagna, he would have no base from which to launch his forces, no foundation on which to build his ambitions. Mirafonte showed no signs of surrendering Forli on his own accord; indeed, he remained contemptuous of the papal forces under Guidobaldo of Urbino, who despite besieging the *rocca* were unable to prevent Mirafonte from remaining in contact with his allies. Mirafonte seems to have sent regular messages to the

Spanish cardinals in Rome, as well as to Cardinals Borgia and Remolino in Naples, who themselves somehow appear to have remained in contact with Borgia, despite his solitary confinement in *Il Forno*. Even Julius II was unable to prevent this state of affairs: from the outset of his communications with Gonsalvo, he had written that the Viceroy of Naples should observe the strictest secrecy in all his dealings with the Vatican, "because these [Spanish] Cardinals have intimates within His Holiness's Chamber, and are advised of everything." Gonsalvo must have heeded this, for Borgia received no prior warning of his arrest. Yet ironically, now that he was confined, he proved able to communicate as far afield as Forli, which he showed no signs of being willing to surrender.

After two weeks with no progress, Gonsalvo decided to try a different strategy. Assured that he had the backing of King Ferdinand and Queen Isabella, he sent word to Mirafonte that he would order the confiscation of Mirafonte's Spanish estates if he did not surrender. But still Mirafonte held out. Gonsalvo continued to have no personal contact with Borgia, leaving him to sweat it out in *Il Forno*, only communicating with him when necessary through envoys.

At the beginning of July, Gonsalvo presented a new offer to Borgia. If he surrendered Forli, Gonsalvo promised to set him free. Astonishingly, Borgia agreed to this offer. Did he really trust Gonsalvo, after all Gonsalvo had done to him? Or had he come to the conclusion that further resistance was useless? On July 4 an armed detachment was dispatched to Venice to collect the 15,000 ducats promised to Mirafonte when he surrendered the *rocca*. On July 29 Borgia's signed order for the surrender arrived at Forli. Nonetheless, Mirafonte spent almost two weeks considering his options. Then on August 10 he finally communicated that he was willing to surrender. Next day the gates to the *rocca* swung open, and according to Bernardi, the contemporary chronicler of Forli, Mirafonte appeared, "mounted on his horse, in full armor, lance in hand, preceded by his attendant, with an air of proud defiance." At his side rode his deputies, and behind him marched 200 of his crack archers and militiamen beneath the banner of Cesare Borgia, "all proclaiming their allegiance with loud cries of 'Caesar! Caesar!'" As they passed through the streets of Forli and out into the countryside of the Romagna, the heavens opened and a violent rainstorm broke over them, which Bernardi ascribed to "the malignant celestial juxtaposition of the Sun and the Moon."

Despite these gloomy omens, the citizens of Forli and those standing by the wayside were sorry to see the Spanish leave. Already the Romagna was returning to its old ways. The petty tyrants ruled the cities, and lawlessness had returned to the countryside. Ancient vendettas were reactivated, while once more footpads (robbers) roamed the highways and byways. Borgia's brief rule had proved a mere respite, rather than the first step towards a new era. As Mirafonte and his proud band of men left the Romagna, they were sent greetings dispatched by Lucrezia Borgia from Ferrara, congratulating them on their valiant defense of the last territory remaining to the former ruler of the Romagna.

Back in Forli, Guidobaldo of Urbino hastened into the *rocca* to retrieve the treasures that Borgia had purloined from the palace at Urbino. The sight of the books from his father's library was said to have brought tears to his eyes. Whilst Guidobaldo was thus occupied, agents of Julius II set about seizing the rest of the treasure, hurriedly packing it onto mules for shipment to the Vatican.

When news of the surrender of Forli reached Naples on August 20, Gonsalvo did not keep his promise to release Borgia. It is difficult to see how even Borgia can have expected that he would do this. So why did Borgia give away his last bargaining chip and surrender Forli? There would seem to be only one conclusion: during his solitary confinement within the suffocating heat of *Il Forno*, he must have momentarily lost his nerve and succumbed to that same state of irrationality and irresolution into which Machiavelli had seen him sink around the time of the papal elections in Rome. Borgia was still just twenty-eight years old, and without the psychological reassurance of his father's backing he had little experience in how to act when fortune turned against him.

Again and again we have seen how Machiavelli remarked that Borgia appeared blessed by fortune. So many of his boldest and most decisive actions were accompanied by luck. In the light of his experience with Borgia, Machiavelli would come to regard *fortuna* as one of the necessary requirements for political success. On the other hand, its absence could be fatal, and in so many different ways. A man without the confidence inspired by *fortuna* was liable to make disastrous decisions. When his luck ran out, Borgia had become irrational and irresolute: his decisions—to trust when he should have distrusted—had brought about his downfall. Machiavelli would never forget the example of Borgia: both in his success and in his failure.

On August 20, 1504, Borgia was marched aboard a galley that was waiting to take him to Spain. To add insult to injury, when his galley put to sea it was escorted by an armed flotilla under the command of Prospero Colonna, the leading member of the aristocratic Roman family whose power the Borgias had tried so hard to destroy—the very man whom Cesare Borgia himself had deceived on more than one occasion. This time there was to be no possibility of deception. Borgia was to be delivered into the hands of King Ferdinand and Queen Isabella, who had already made plain to their ambassador in Rome their feelings towards him: "we regard [him] with deep displeasure, and not for political reasons alone. For, as you know, we hold the man in abhorrence for the gravity of his crimes." Their Spanish majesties intended to put Borgia on trial for his life, for the murder of his brother the Duke of Gandia and of his brother-in-law Alfonso, Duke of Bisceglie. They had assured Julius II that Borgia would never again be permitted to set foot on Italian soil.

25

Machiavelli's Militia

FLORENCE REMAINED BESET with problems. The Arno diversion plan had ended in disaster, and Pisa continued to hold out, blocking the city's overseas trade. Yet the new situation in Italy had placed Florence in even greater peril, leaving it standing between the opposing powers of France and Spain. Florence may have been allied to France, but for the moment Louis XII was in no position to rescue the city if it was attacked. Meanwhile, the new alliance between Julius II and Spain could only presage danger.

The small city-states on the borders of Tuscany now saw their chance to encroach on Florentine territory. In late 1504 the Signoria began receiving intelligence of a serious development. With the covert support of the Venetians in the Romagna, and almost certainly encouraged by Julius II, a mercenary army was being raised by the *condottiere* Bartolomeo d'Alviano with the express purpose of invading Florence.

By now Machiavelli was back in favor and had been reinstated. Early in 1505 he was dispatched by the Signoria to sound out which of the city-states on the borders of Florentine territory remained her allies and which were now of more questionable loyalty. Baglioni of Perugia and Petrucci of Siena both protested their friendship, but Machiavelli had come well informed and his probing questions revealed to him that they were both poised to take advantage of Florence's weakness. In the midst of this mission, news reached the Signoria that Gonsalvo de Cordova in Naples was planning to send troops to Pisa. Then d'Alviano made his move, marching north with his mercenary army up the coast of Tuscany, apparently making for Pisa. There was no time to lose, and Gonfaloniere Soderini ordered the Florentine mercenary army under Ercole Bentivoglio to march for the coast to cut off d'Alviano. On August 17 they encountered the forces of d'Alviano at San Vincenzo, sixty miles southwest of Florence. After several hours of fighting, d'Alviano's ill-disciplined mercenaries succumbed. A few managed to flee the battlefield, but most surrendered to Bentivoglio's forces, whereupon they were disarmed and taken captive, along with their baggage train and supplies.

Overly encouraged by the ease of this victory, Soderini decided upon a bold strategy, ordering Baglioni to march his troops north to Pisa. Here he was to launch a full-out attack and take the city. This had to be accomplished before the arrival of Gonsalvo's troops, and prior to the beginning of the autumn rainy season (which during the previous year had finally put an end to the Arno diversion project).

This was an optimistic strategy, to say the least, but Machiavelli was dispatched from Florence to join up with Baglioni, in order to make sure that Soderini's orders were fulfilled. By September 6 the Florentine army was in place before the walls of Pisa, setting up its eleven artillery pieces. The following day at dawn the artillery barrage against the walls began. Within days, two large breaches had been opened in the ancient city walls. Now it was time to take advantage of these breaches and storm the city.

However, owing to the incompetence of the besieging Florentine army, the Pisans had now been reinforced by 300 of Gonsalvo's foot soldiers, who had disembarked at Piombino, marched north, and entered Pisa under cover of darkness through a side gate. Heartened by this support, the Pisans easily repelled the first Florentine attempt to rush the breaches in the walls. Another attempt followed, but it soon became clear that the Florentine mercenaries had no stomach for any further dangerous assaults. Despite all orders, and threats, they refused to budge. In the end, Baglioni decided that he and his men had endured enough, and on September 14 he dismantled his guns and withdrew his army. The mercenaries then dispersed, returning home to their different territories for the winter.

As a result of this farce, Soderini faced widespread criticism in Florence and decided to turn to his secretary to the Ten of War, Machiavelli. For some time now Machiavelli had been suggesting that the only solution to Florence's military problems was for the city to raise its own militia, recruited from amongst the people. This idea had been inspired by what he had seen whilst on his mission to Borgia in the Romagna three years previously. Borgia's recruitment of "one man per household" and his success in training these men into disciplined soldiers had resulted in a substantial corps of loyal troops from all over his dukedom, which had also played its part in underpinning the political reforms introduced by his "President of the Romagna," Sansavino.

Machiavelli's idea of a locally recruited militia had been bitterly opposed by the ruling families, who feared that such an army was liable to take over the city at any time it chose. Its very presence was also likely to encourage those who sought sweeping democratic reforms, which would nullify the behind-the-scenes influence of the leading families and other powerful factions. Florence's quasi-democracy depended upon a precarious balance of power between rival groups, and any move that sought to destabilize this was invariably resisted by the powers that be. Memories of the autocratic rule of the Medicis, as well as the weakness and instability of Savonarola's recent theocratic republic, were still fresh in people's minds. Consequently, Machiavelli's military proposal had been resisted from the start. Even when Soderini had been in favor, the idea was opposed by too many powerful factions for it to be implemented. But now there seemed to be no alternative, if the city was to fight for its own survival. Eventually Soderini managed to persuade the Signoria and their backers amongst the powerful factions, and Machiavelli's scheme was given the go-ahead.

Even so, there were to be strict reservations. The troops for the militia were to be recruited from the countryside: the dangers of a trained and armed militia recruited from within the city were plain to all. In December 1505 Machiavelli was eventually dispatched north to the snow-covered mountains of the Mugello valley to begin his recruiting drive. As ever, he was happy traveling, though this time his "spirit so eager for riding" was reduced to a more humble means of transport.

As he wrote to the Signoria on January 2, 1506, "these north winds . . . teach me to go about on foot." Winters in the Mugello can be bitterly cold, and this was evidently no exception. With alacrity and efficiency Machiavelli moved down through the valley, recruiting in the towns along his way. Yet this was no simple task, as he made clear in his dispatch from Pontassieve on February 5:

> In the entire commune of Dicomano I have recruited two hundred men, which I expect to have to reduce to one hundred and fifty. There are two main difficulties here: one being the incorrigible habit of disobedience amongst these people and the other being the hostility which exists between the people of the village of Petrognano, who live on one side of the mountain, and those of Campana, who live on the other. I signed up as many able-bodied men as I could from Campana, but in Petrognano and Castagneto, who are united against Campana, none were willing to sign up. However, later on some fifty of them came to me, along with their leader, the son of one Andreaso. After much discussion amongst themselves, they said they were willing to sign up as long as this son of Andreaso was in charge of them.

Then there were the difficulties of arming the new recruits of one district without having them attack their defenseless rivals. "It is impossible to train the men of the two districts at the same time, as they are a considerable distance from one another." In answer to nagging criticisms from the impatient Signoria, Machiavelli replied irritably:

> I have not been able to complete this task with any greater dispatch. And if anyone thinks he can do it better, let him come and try. Then he will find out just what it is like to collect up and bring together such a bunch of peasants, especially of this sort.

Machiavelli returned to Florence in early February with the first batch of recruits; there he made them "exercise and drill in the Swiss manner."* They were then equipped with uniforms and took part in the parade on February 15, as part of the annual pre-Lenten Carnival. The Florentine diarist Luca Landucci described the occasion:

> There was a parade in the Piazza della Signoria of four hundred infantrymen who had been recruited by the Gonfaloniere from amongst the peasants in the countryside. These soldiers each had a uniform consisting of a white waistcoat, a pair of red and white stockings, a white cap, leather shoes, an iron breastplate and a lance, and some had arquebuses.† They were formed in battle groups, each with a constable in charge, to lead them and teach them how to use their weapons. Although they were soldiers, they would still live in their homes, only reporting for duty when there was a call to arms. There was an order for many thousands to be recruited in this fashion throughout our territory, so we should have no need of foreign mercenaries. And this was held to be the finest thing which had ever been organized by the city of Florence.

Machiavelli had put considerable thought into his militia, and he realized that it would remain ineffective unless Borgia's example was followed to the letter. But this would require grasping the nettle, and to this end he made a highly controversial suggestion to Soderini. The soldiers of the new militia would only combine into a successful fighting force if they were put through a training course as tough and effective as that employed by Borgia for his recruits in the Romagna. And for

---

* The Swiss militiamen were widely regarded as the finest in Europe during this period, and Machiavelli doubtless wished to emulate their method of training. In this very year Swiss mercenaries would be taken on by Julius II to guard the Vatican, a task that they perform to this day, dressed in the same colorful medieval uniform.

† The word Landucci uses is *scoppietti*, which is usually translated here as "musket." However, the musket was only developed from the more primitive arquebus several decades later. It has been suggested that these recruits were more likely to have been armed with bolt-firing crossbows, and that this was what Landucci in fact meant. Even so, *scoppietti* seems to refer to an explosive weapon of some kind, with its connotations of *scoppio* "explosion" and *scoppiettare*, "to crackle" or "backfire."

this they would require none other than Borgia's notorious commander Don Michele. Inevitably, Soderini took some persuading in this matter. Don Michele had only recently been held prisoner in the city dungeons, before being passed on to Julius II. After being tortured to no avail, Don Michele had recently been released.

Machiavelli's proposal caused a sensation. Many amongst the leading families suspected that Soderini was paving the way to imposing a tyranny in Florence, and that Don Michele would be employed by the *gonfaloniere* "to remove the citizens who were his enemies." Machiavelli remained convinced that the end the city sought—namely, a strong local militia—could only be achieved by the most effective means, even if this meant employing a commander of the lowest moral character. The new Florentine militia would not be compromised by the immorality of the means employed to command it and train it efficiently. On the other hand, such means might well prove ineffective without a ruthless commander to enforce them, in which case the end would not be achieved. This was an argument that Machiavelli had seen embodied in Borgia himself: effectiveness rather than moral consistency should be the aim. Here we see emerging the pluralism that would come to characterize Machiavelli's political thinking. Many would regard his arguments here as being essentially hypocritical and immoral, and centuries would elapse before it was recognized that such pluralism is central to western thought. Soderini was unable to convince the leading political factions in Florence regarding Machiavelli's choice, but he himself understood the force of Machiavelli's argument. As a result, he managed to push the proposal through the Signoria, and Don Michele was hired.

There is a persistent story that the uniforms for Machiavelli's militia were designed by Leonardo, and there may well be some truth in this, given their friendship and Leonardo's eminence as a military adviser. By this time Leonardo had finished the large cartoon for *The Battle of Anghiari,* which he had drawn on sheets of paper attached to the wall in the run-down Sala del Papa in the grounds of the Santa Maria Novella monastery. To his own satisfaction, he had solved the compositional problems involved in such a large and complex scene, and he now returned to the far more intriguing problem of Mona Lisa's smile—involving as it did not only psychology and anatomy, but also painterly skills of the highest order. We know that he also continued to study mathematics with his friend the monk Luca Pacioli, as well as pursuing further, ever-branching paths of knowledge in the privacy of his notebooks. However, there remained one persistent motif during this period—namely, the idea of manned flight.

At one point in his notebooks Leonardo reminds himself: "Swimming in water teaches men how birds fly in the air." By now he had evidently practiced swimming underwater at the weir by the Ponte Rubaconte. Then he goes further, imagining what it would be like to fly:

> If the north wind is blowing and you are gliding above the wind, and if in your straight ascent upward that wind is threatening to overturn you, then you are free to bend your left or right wing, and with the inside wing lowered you will continue a curving motion. . . .

This is so detailed as to suggest that possibly the experimental flight from Mount Cerceri did in fact take place (as suggested by the autobiography of the mathematician Girolamo Cardano, who would have been a child at this time). The tenor of these details also suggests that it was Leonardo himself who flew the machine. Other entries on nearby pages of the same notebook (*Turin Codex*) support this view, for here he writes of "the fury and impetus of the descent . . . Let no one encumber himself with iron bands, for these are very soon broken in twisting. . . ." A few pages later we read that he recommends wearing

> bags whereby a man falling from a height of six *braccia** may avoid doing himself harm with a fall into water or onto the ground. These bags should be strung together like rosary beads and worn on one's back.

* That is, approximately twelve feet.

The notebooks from this period also provide us with glimpses of Leonardo's daily domestic life, in the form of shopping lists and accounts. Here we learn that he and his household of assistants lived on a diet that included peppered bread, mushrooms, eels, meat, wine, apricots, ricotta, and the like. The meat would have been for his assistants; although Leonardo was himself a vegetarian, evidently he did not expect such abstinence from his hungry young helpers. His attitude towards animals—setting free caged birds, and so forth—may have been similar to that of the thirteenth-century St. Francis of Assisi, but it was highly unusual in the Italy of that period. Anyone who could eat meat did, and was glad to do so. Vegetarianism was for the destitute, and even they participated in the public feasts at festivals and carnivals when meat was served. The Carnival, which preceded Lent, was intended as a last feast of meat before the Lenten fast—hence its name *carne vale* ("farewell meat").

As a result, word of Leonardo's vegetarianism had spread far and wide, almost as wide as his public renown as an artist and sage. One instance of this can be seen when a decade later the Florentine traveler Andrea Corsali wrote back to his native city from as far away as India describing "a gentle people called Guzzarati [that is, Gujarati] who do not feed on anything that has blood, nor will they allow anyone to hurt a living thing, like our Leonardo da Vinci."

The shopping lists and accounts in Leonardo's notebooks are often written in another hand, evidently by one of his assistants. For instance:

The morning of Santo Zanobio the 25 of May, 1504, I had from Lionardo Vinci [*sic*] 15 gold ducats and proceeded to spend them thus. Saturday . . . clothes 13 *soldi*, barber 4 *soldi*, eggs 6 *soldi*, debt at the bank 7 *soldi*, velvet 12 *soldi*. . . .

The significant phrase here is "debt at the bank," implying that Leonardo was having to pay interest on a loan. He must have been broke. Had he spent all the money he had earned from Borgia, or had Borgia not paid him? He does not seem to have had any other source of income. Leonardo's seeming lack of concern about completing his public commission for the fresco of the Battle of Anghiari had so exasperated Soderini and the Signoria that payments to the artist had been stopped. Yet still he persisted in busying himself with his own preoccupations. Then in September 1504 the Signoria sprang a surprise on Leonardo. At Soderini's prompting, they commissioned Michelangelo to paint a mural of the Battle of Cascina on the wall facing Leonardo's blank, unfilled wall in the Grand Council Chamber of the Palazzo della Signoria. This was meant to be a companion piece to Leonardo's *Battle of Anghiari*, but all quickly recognized what was afoot. Here was a direct challenge to Leonardo: this would surely spur him to complete his fresco.

By now, the fifty-two-year-old Leonardo, painter of such renowned works as *The Last Supper*, was very much regarded as Florence's artistic old master. On the other hand, the twenty-nine-year-old Michelangelo, sculptor of the spectacular statue *David*, was viewed as the young up-and-coming genius of the city. Whose fresco on the walls of the Palazzo della Signoria would prove to be the best? This was to be "the battle of *Battles*," and the evidence of victory would be plain for all to see.

Temperamentally Leonardo and Michelangelo were poles apart. The contemplative, scientifically minded Leonardo, the self-educated illegitimate boy from the country with his peacock sensibility for fine clothes, had little in common with the son of a respected Florentine magistrate whose family had aristocratic pretensions. The classically educated Michelangelo had rebelled against his family to become a sculptor; his face was ugly, he dressed in coarse clothes covered in dust and chippings from his sculptures, and he had an intense, religious sensibility. Both Leonardo and Michelangelo were utterly dedicated to their own different interpretations of art and the world, and both were homosexual—Leonardo accepting his sexuality, while Michelangelo remained tortured by his. It is almost certain that they recognized each other's homosexuality, which must have added a certain frisson to their instinctive disaffection and rivalry. This is best illustrated by an incident that almost certainly took place around this time, and was passed on by the artist Giovanni di Gavina, who knew Leonardo:

One day Leonardo was walking through the Piazza San Trinità with Giovanni di Gavina and they passed the benches in front of the Palazzo Spini, where a group was arguing over the meaning of a passage in Dante. They called over Leonardo, asking him to explain it for them. At that moment, Michelangelo also happened to be passing by, and Leonardo told them: "There's Michelangelo, he'll explain it for you." Michelangelo took umbrage at this, thinking that Leonardo had intended to insult him, and replied angrily to Leonardo: "Explain it yourself. You think you're so clever—you design a great horse to cast in bronze, and then find you can't do it.* So you just abandon it, leaving it for someone else to do. Well you won't pass on your ignorance this time." Leonardo was ashamed and his face turned red with embarassment. As Michelangelo turned on his heels and stormed off, he called back to Leonardo: "And to think of it, those idiots in Milan actually believed you could do it."

Upon receiving his commission to paint *The Battle of Cascina* in the Palazzo della Signoria, Michelangelo moved his studio to a workshop in the Dyers' Hospital at San Onofrio, where there was sufficient space for him to begin work on the large cartoon for his fresco. Leonardo was probably none too pleased about the subject Michelangelo had been given. The Battle of Cascina was arguably the more popular subject: this had been the Florentine victory that marked the end of an earlier Pisan war almost 150 years previously. Its choice doubtless reflected an element of wish-fulfillment on the part of the Signoria, to say nothing of the citizens of Florence, who were growing heartily sick of paying for the seemingly unending war against Pisa. Even without the recent glory of his *David*, Michelangelo had the public on his side, or so Leonardo would have seen it.

Not only did Leonardo dislike Michelangelo, but he also disliked his style, which exaggerated the musculature of the figures to gain effect. Around this time Leonardo would write in his notebook, in what appears

* An allusion to the *gran cavallo* in Milan, which Leonardo never finished.

to be a slighting reference to Michelangelo's style: "You should not make all the muscles of the body too conspicuous . . . otherwise you will produce a sack of walnuts rather than a human figure."

Yet still, Leonardo could not bring himself to complete his commissioned mural of the Battle of Anghiari. His block about finishing projects may well in this case have been reinforced by its subject matter. He had now witnessed the ferocity of actual armed combat, which had given him a traumatic insight into human nature. It is indicative that in his notebook he had written of "the evil nature of *men*" (*delli omini*) in the plural—rather than, say, the more general "man" (*uomo*) or "humanity" (*umanità*), suggesting that an actual evil or malicious image of men may have inspired this comment.

Michelangelo, on the other hand, quickly set to work on his preparatory cartoon, which was pinned to the wall in the Dyers' Hospital, and he had completed this by February 1505. According to Vasari, "When they saw the cartoon, all the other artists were overcome with admiration and astonishment." But Michelangelo was not able to complete this project, for he was now summoned to work in Rome by Julius II, who three years later would commission him to paint the ceiling of the Sistine Chapel.

Leonardo was almost certainly amongst the artists who viewed Michelangelo's cartoon and were "overcome with admiration and astonishment," though his feelings may well have been tinged with other less adulatory emotions. At any rate, something spurred Leonardo to return to work on his own cartoon, which was finished by early summer of 1505. The sculptor and goldsmith Benvenuto Cellini, who was born in Florence in 1500 and later saw both cartoons, would write that Michelangelo's "showed all the actions and gestures [of the soldiers] so wonderfully that no ancient or modern artist has ever reached such a high standard." Indeed, he was so struck by this work that in his opinion, "Although the divine Michelangelo later on painted the great chapel of Pope Julius* he never reached half the same perfection; his genius never again showed the power of those first studies." Of Leonardo's cartoon

---

* That is, the Sistine Chapel.

Cellini wrote that it was "as divinely executed as words may express," and of the two cartoons, he said, "they served as a school for all the world." Such was the "battle" between Florence's two greatest artists. Unfortunately, we have to take Cellini's word for this, as neither of the cartoons has survived, except in the form of copies by later artists, which have little of the characteristic styles of either Michelangelo or Leonardo.

Having completed his cartoon, Leonardo was at last ready to start on the fresco itself. Before the high blank wall of the Grand Council Chamber in the Palazzo he rigged up an ingenious scaffolding apparatus of his own invention, which could be raised and lowered in the same way as an accordion expands and contracts. Leonardo himself described what happened next:

On June 6, 1505, a Friday, at the stroke of the 13th hour [that is, around 9.30 a.m.], I began to paint in the palazzo. The moment I set down my paintbrush, the weather took a serious turn for the worse and the church bells began tolling. The pieces of paper forming the cartoon began to fall apart. My water jug broke, spilling in front of me. Suddenly the weather grew even worse, and the rain bucketed down until the evening, turning day into night.

Leonardo was not a superstitious man, but this Friday at the thirteenth hour, his start on the fresco was evidently accompanied by spectacular ill omens. Or did he perhaps contrive to see it as such? Did he wish to blame a fateful event beyond his control for his artistic failure?

Other sources make no mention of any such incident as the reason Leonardo never completed the *Battle of Anghiari* fresco, but several of them suggest that the cause of his inability to finish the fresco was the oil he chose to use. The contemporary historian Paolo Giovio, who is not always reliable, suggests that the preliminary coating Leonardo applied to the wall was "irremediably resistant to paints prepared with walnut oil." A contemporary Florentine source suggests that Leonardo used poor-quality linseed oil, whilst another claims that he followed a recipe for mixing colors from a classical text by Pliny the Elder, which he had failed to understand properly. Apparently he had experimented with this in the Sala del Papa, making use of a fire that was intended to dry the paint, but the fire he used in the Grand Council Chamber was not close enough to dry the upper section of the wall, so that the colors ran. The latter explanation, involving Pliny the Elder, has an ominous ring: it is just the kind of daring experimental project that Leonardo would have delighted in attempting.

A copy of Leonardo's lost *Battle of Anghiari*, attributed to Peter Paul Rubens.

At any rate, Leonardo was certainly not prevented from painting the *Battle of Anghiari* fresco by the intervention of calamitous omens on the very day he began painting. We know from a number of anonymous copies made at the time that Leonardo did in fact probably complete the central section of the fresco, which depicts the soldiers battling for the standard. There is a copy of this scene attributed to the seventeenth-century Dutch artist Peter Paul Rubens, which shows the intertwined mounted soldiers slashing at one another furiously with their swords whilst grappling with the pole and flag of the standard itself. Such is the intensity and masterly composition of this copy that one can only lament the loss of the original.

Leonardo's self-justifying story, which he had told himself in his notebook, about the ill omens accompanying his fresco suggests that he was now becoming more aware of his unconscious block about finishing his work. After all, this was not the first time his apparent technical incompetence had ensured the eventual sabotage of his finest art. In Milan, in the monastery of Santa Maria delle Grazie, the paint of *The Last Supper* was already imperceptibly beginning to peel from the wall. Now, ten years later, after his upsetting experience with Borgia, this self-defeating impulse was apparently becoming more intense.

This must have been a time of dejection for Leonardo. His Arno diversion scheme had been swamped by floodwaters, and now his great fresco had been blighted by ill omen (or so he wished to persuade himself). As happened on occasions of distress, Leonardo began to cover the pages of his notebook with images of apocalyptic deluges. These would have served as a reminder of fearful childhood experience, as well as an obsessive repetitive exaggeration of events closer at hand— images in which he would realize his fears, give vent to his spleen, and achieve catharsis. He would write of these deluges with similar intensity:

> Let the dark and murky air be torn apart by the clash of contrary winds, let the sky be dense with continuous rain mingled with hail, carrying hither and thither an infinite number of branches torn from trees. . . . The swollen waters having burst the banks will plunge forward in monstrous waves and these will destroy the walls of cities. . . . Then the ruins of the highest buildings will collapse, throwing up into the air huge columns of debris, rising up like smoke or wreathed clouds against the falling rain.

Having vented his spleen and once again achieved equanimity, Leonardo returned to more lofty preoccupations, to what his biographer Charles Nicholl so aptly characterized as "flights of the mind," imagining himself soaring with the ease of a swimmer through the upper air— perhaps anticipating what it would be like in one of his flying machines, possibly even describing what it had been like:

The bird that mounts upward always has its wings above the wind, and does not beat them, and moves in a circular motion. And if you want to go westward without beating your wings, and the wind is in the north, make the incident movement straight and below the wind, and the reflex movement above the wind. . . . The bird descends on the side where the tip of the wing is nearer to its center of gravity.

As Nicholl also points out, this page in Leonardo's notebook has an eerie feature, filled with metaphorical resonance. Behind Leonardo's crabbed mirror-writing it is possible to make out a faint red-chalk drawing of a man's head. This is almost certainly a portrait of Leonardo drawn by one of his pupils—staring out from behind his words like a ghostly presence: the bearded face framed within his long flowing locks. The gentle bearded sage has over the centuries become the iconic Leonardo we know. However, this is in fact the earliest drawing we have of him—if indeed it is him—with a beard. Growing a beard is often an indication of a sea change in personality, the reflection of some profound psychological development. Here too would appear to be further evidence of the transformation that took place within Leonardo following his time with Borgia.

By early 1506 Leonardo had grown tired of his native city, of all the blame for wasting precious public money on his diversion scheme; of being constantly hounded by Soderini and the Signoria to resume work on the fresco that he had already mentally given up on; of being regarded as a charlatan and a failure by young upstarts such as Michelangelo. In February he presumably watched Machiavelli's militia parade through the piazza in the smart red and white uniforms he had designed, but already he must have been longing to escape.

Rescue came in the form of a message from the French governor of Milan, Charles d'Amboise, who insisted that Leonardo must now return to the city that he had left almost seven years previously. When Leonardo had hurriedly departed in 1499 he had left behind him a copy of his original *Virgin of the Rocks*, which he had painted with his friend and fellow Florentine exile, the artist Ambrogio de Predis. The

Confraternity of the Immaculate Conception, which had commissioned this copy, subsequently claimed that the painting was unfinished. A court case had ensued, which had finally reached the attention of Louis XII in France. The court eventually decided that the painting was indeed unfinished, and Charles d'Amboise informed the Signoria in Florence that Leonardo should return to Milan to complete his commission. The Signoria had no wish to offend their ally, and on May 30, 1506, Leonardo was reluctantly given permission to leave Florence, on a surety of the 150 florins that he now had in his bank account at Santa Maria Nuova. (Where had this come from? Had the back pay he was owed by Borgia finally been sorted out?) Leonardo also had to undertake to return to Florence within three months, so that he could finish the fresco of *The Battle of Anghiari,* for which the Signoria had already paid out so much.

Despite these measures, the indications are that Leonardo had in mind a rather more prolonged absence from his native city. Before departing early in June, he gathered together all his notebooks into bundles and placed them in storage at the Ospedale di Santa Maria Nuovo. After the failures, disappointments, and sheer terrors of the last few years he was once more off to Milan and a new life, much as he had first set out with Lorenzo the Magnificent's blessing some sixteen years previously.

During the summer of 1506 the political situation in Italy took another ominous turn. With Borgia out of the way, Julius II was determined to restore all the territories of the Romagna, and beyond, to papal rule. His first aim was to mount a military campaign to dislodge Bentivoglio from Perugia, and then to march north to take Bologna. Having pressured a reluctant France into supporting him with military aid, and having cowed Venice into remaining neutral, he then sent word to Florence that it too should send him troops in his campaign to "rid Italy of tyrants." Soderini was extremely reluctant to withdraw Florentine forces from the siege of Pisa, so he decided to send Machiavelli on a mission to Julius II. Machiavelli's unenviable task was to play for time, all the while assuring Julius II that he had Florence's full support.

In the early hours of August 26, 1506, Julius II conducted a public

Mass and blessed the crowd gathered at the Porte Santa Maggiore, before riding out of Rome at first light, at the head of his troops on the march north to regain the lost papal fiefdoms. To impress upon one and all the sanctity of his cause, and to ensure that there was no plotting in his absence, the pope was accompanied by his twenty-four cardinals, as well as the colorful Swiss soldiers of his new papal guard.

That same early morning Machiavelli set out from Florence. As ever, he must have ridden hard, for he had covered 150 miles by the following evening, when he met up with the papal forces at Nepi, the former Borgia stronghold. Julius II had appropriated the Borgia fortresses north of Rome and evidently intended making a tour of inspection on his way towards his initial destination of Perugia. Machiavelli succeeded in gaining an audience with the pope that very evening, and had another meeting the next day. As Machiavelli commented in his subsequent dispatch:

> His Holiness explained that his army would consist of three kinds of troops—the ones he had with him at present, the expected French contingent, and your troops from Florence. . . . I replied to him in a becoming manner, confining myself to entirely general terms.

Despite Machiavelli's practiced diplomacy, it was clear to him that Julius II understood his brief. Clearly, things were going to be difficult for the Florentine envoy. To make matters even more so, Machiavelli would also have noticed amongst Julius II's accompanying cardinals the prominent position occupied by Cardinal Giovanni de' Medici, the brother of Piero de' Medici, the deposed ruler of Florence. Cardinal Giovanni was the second son of Lorenzo the Magnificent, and as Piero de' Medici was now dead, he was the leader of the Medici cause, whose sworn aim remained to evict from Florence the republican government that Machiavelli represented. Machiavelli had published poetry in a book with Lorenzo the Magnificent, and it is likely that he had known the young Giovanni de' Medici personally. Machiavelli's acceptance of a post in the republican government would thus have been seen as a gross betrayal. It would soon become evident that the jovial and cultured Cardinal de' Medici was very much a favorite of the new pope, a development that did not augur well for Soderini's government in Florence.

Despite these setbacks, Machiavelli managed to attach himself closely to the pope's immediate entourage. The following evening, when Julius II reached the former Borgia fortress of Civita Castellana, Machiavelli was able to report that he walked directly behind the pope "as he viewed the fortifications and marveled at the excellence of their construction." Julius II would order the completion of this imposing fortress, which had been begun by Alexander VI. With Cesare Borgia out of the way, it looked as if Julius II now had it in mind to fulfill the Borgia dream— only in the name of the Church.

26

Borgia in Spain

CESARE BORGIA HAD arrived as a prisoner in Spain in late August 1504, being taken ashore in chains at Villanueva del Grano and transferred to the remote fortress of Chinchilla, 700 feet up in the mountainous hinterland of Valencia. Although Borgia was Spanish by lineage, for him this was a foreign country. He found himself alone, accompanied only by his loyal squire Juanito Grasica. He was also penniless, and abandoned by his powerful ally Louis XII, who had finally lost all patience with Borgia when he refused to present himself at Milan in readiness for the intended French march to retake Naples. As a result, Louis had stripped Borgia of his French title, the Duke of Valentinois, as well as the estates that went with it and the incomes they provided. Meanwhile all Borgia's other funds now lay beyond his reach, covertly held in various Italian banks, which he knew Julius II was making every effort to trace.

Regardless of the odds, Borgia now made a desperate bid to escape. According to one report, when he was taking the air on the turret under personal escort from the governor, de Guzman, Borgia suddenly hurled himself on the governor and attempted to throw him over the battlements. Owing to the debilitating effects of his illness and incarceration, his renowned strength and determination failed him, enabling de Guzman to overpower him. Another report had Borgia descending by knotted sheets from his cell, only for the sheets to break, causing him to fall and fracture his shoulder, so that he was quickly overcome by the guards.

Either way, in the summer of 1505 Borgia was transferred to the most secure prison in Spain, the fortress of La Mota at Medina del Campo, the city that was also one of the residences of the Spanish court. La Mota had a central keep, which could only be reached by a single gate, with the entire fortress surrounded by a deep defensive ditch. Not only was Borgia now 300 miles from the Mediterranean coast, but he was under the close attention of the entire Medina garrison. According to diplomatic reports arriving back in Italy, he had become a broken man who spent his time gazing from the narrow window of his cell high up in the keep, watching the falcons circling though the air below.

Meanwhile his sister Lucrezia was distraught, and turned to God, praying for his release. In a more practical move, she continued to use all her influence, writing to Julius II and even going so far as to plead with Borgia's sworn enemy Guidobaldo of Urbino to intercede with the pope. The Spanish cardinals in Rome also attempted to persuade Julius II to release him, but nothing came of all these efforts. Then support for Borgia emerged from an unexpected quarter—namely, his long-suffering French wife Charlotte (mother of his legitimate daughter Louise), who had not set eyes on her husband since he had left France five years previously, just three months after they had been married. Charlotte (formerly d'Albret) had persuaded her brother Jean d'Albret, King of Navarre—whose kingdom straddled the northern Pyrenees between France and Spain—to send word to the Spanish court petitioning for Borgia's release.

King Ferdinand and Queen Isabella had assured Julius II that Borgia would never be allowed to return to Italy. However, after Queen Isabella died at Medina in November 1505, it soon became clear that Ferdinand was more interested in using Borgia as a bargaining pawn to further his interests in Italy. When Ferdinand received intelligence from his spies in Naples that his viceroy Gonsalvo de Cordova was contemplating treachery by retaining Naples for himself, he considered the possibility of using Borgia to lead a force against Gonsalvo. Yet how would he be able to control Borgia, once he was free? Ferdinand decided to dispense with this plan, and sailed for Italy himself in September 1506.

Despite the hopelessness of Borgia's situation, the conditions of his incarceration were now in fact improved. This was due to the prison governor, de Cardenas, who admired Borgia and was aware that in the changing Spanish political situation it was still possible that Borgia might end up as commander of the royal troops, and thus his commanding officer. Consequently, de Cardenas saw to it that Borgia was provided with several manservants, and a personal chaplain, to assist his squire Juanito Grasica. Borgia's personal chaplain was hardly overworked, and was soon persuaded to occupy his time conveying messages to de Cardenas. In no time, Borgia had gained access to a rope.

During the night of October 25, less than three months after his incarceration in La Mota, Borgia let himself down the high walls of the keep towards where his chaplain and three armed men with horses were waiting at the bottom of the deep defensive ditch far below. But the alarm was raised, and before Borgia could reach the ground the rope was cut. Borgia fell to the ground, badly injuring himself, but the men waiting for him managed to bundle him onto a horse, and together they rode off. Galloping through the night, they made their way sixty miles north across the remote mountains to a castle on the estate of de Cardenas. Here Borgia hid for a month, attempting to recover from his injury, before setting off with his escort north to the coastal port of Castres. By now there was a hue and cry for Borgia throughout the land. On top of this, he can hardly have recovered from his injuries, for a witness at Castres (who at the time had no idea who he was) would later describe Borgia as "a man doubled up, with an ugly face, a big nose, dark." Only just ahead of their pursuers, Borgia and his men took ship at dawn, sailing east along the coast for the safety of Navarre, but a storm blew up, forcing them to beach their boat at a remote fishing village. Here they eventually managed to secure mules, which carried them over a mountain trail into the kingdom of Navarre. On December 3 Borgia appeared "like the Devil" at the court in the capital, Pamplona, where he was welcomed by his brother-in-law Jean d'Albret, the king. Ironically, this was Borgia's first visit to the very city where he had controversially been appointed bishop some fifteen years previously.

Despite being pursued throughout Spain, Borgia had managed to get news of his escape to Lucrezia at Bologna as early as November 23, in a note defiantly signed, "Cesar, Duke of the Romagna." Word of his escape caused a sensation as it spread to courts throughout Italy. When the people of the Romagna heard the news, there was public rejoicing: Borgia would soon return to set them free of their oppressors. Julius II was in Bologna, which he had occupied in early November. He feared there would be an uprising in the Romagna, and took immediate steps to prevent Borgia from making contact with any sympathizers in the region. In January 1507 he managed to intercept a courier returning from Ferrara to Pamplona conveying news of Lucrezia's delight that her brother had at last reached the safety of Navarre.

Borgia now set about planning how to regain the lost lands of his dukedom. The coffers of the kingdom of Navarre were empty, and Jean d'Albret was unable to help him directly. However, at Borgia's prompting he did write to his relative Louis XII suggesting that Borgia should be paid the considerable dowry that he had been promised in 1499 by the French king on his marriage to Charlotte d'Albret. Yet despite this appeal to his honor, Louis XII refused to support Borgia in any way. He had by this time formed an alliance with Julius II and King Ferdinand: he was not willing to upset the peace of Italy and endanger his possessions in northern Italy just for the sake of Borgia.

Untypically, it was Borgia who now proved his loyalty. Civil war had broken out in Navarre, and Borgia volunteered his services to his brother-in-law the king in his struggle against the treacherous Beaumonte, Count of Lerins. In January 1507 Jean d'Albret appointed Borgia commander of his forces, and early in the following month Borgia led his troops into the field. Recovered from his injuries and his illness, and once again at his vigorous, self-confident best, Borgia cut an impressive figure amongst the short, stocky men of Navarre. An eyewitness would remember him as "a big man, strong, handsome, and in the full flight of his manhood."

In early March, Borgia marched on the border fortress of Viana, 100 miles southwest of Pamplona, which was held by Luis, the eldest son of Beaumonte. The fortress was only lightly garrisoned, and Borgia knew that if he laid siege to it, Beaumonte was bound to mount a bid to rescue his son. Borgia and his troops reached the town of Viana below the fortress as night was falling on March 11. The spring rains had arrived in a torrential storm and high winds. Borgia surmised that Beaumonte would not attempt to relieve the fortress until dawn, and set a light guard. But under cover of the driving rain a column of Beaumonte's men, along with a mule train of supplies, managed to make their way through the town towards the fortress. Borgia was woken at dawn by a scene of confusion as the detected column of Beaumonte's men fled through the streets on horseback with Borgia's men riding in hot pursuit. Hastily pulling on his chain mail and breastplate, Borgia clambered onto his horse and rode after them. Such was his enthusiasm that he soon caught up with his column of men. As they rode on in pursuit, Borgia drew clear of his men, heedless of how far the others were receding behind him. Meanwhile Beaumonte was surveying the scene from a nearby hillside and ordered three of his knights to ride down and protect the rearguard of his fleeing men.

As Borgia galloped on alone into a ravine he was ambushed by the three knights. In the ensuing melee one of Beaumonte's knights managed to plunge his lance under Borgia's arm at a point where it was unprotected by his armor, savagely wounding him and at the same time unseating him from his horse. Borgia staggered to his feet, but was quickly overwhelmed by his three assailants, who fell on him with their daggers, stabbing him to death in a frenzy.

Not realizing who he was, the knights then stripped him of his shining crested armor, chain mail, boots, and fine garments—leaving him bloodied and naked with more than two dozen stab wounds. In a parting gesture, one of the knights placed a flat stone over the exposed genitals of his butchered body.

Borgia had died, on this obscure field of battle, on March 12, 1507, at just thirty-one years old. When news of his death reached Italy, its rulers—from Naples to Milan—breathed a sigh of collective relief. Only in Ferrara was his parting mourned. When Lucrezia received the news of the death of her beloved brother, she is reported to have cried out, "The more I turn to God, the more He turns away from me." She maintained her composure until she finally retired to her chamber, where she was heard calling out his name, again and again, in an agony of grief.

Some years beforehand, the contemporary historian Andrea Bernardi had reported how when Borgia had ridden at his enemies he had cried out, "Better to die in the saddle than in bed." But it took a sister's empathy to understand the truth behind these words. Lucrezia is said to have suspected that in his despair at the final failure of all his ambitions, Borgia's recklessness had been a form of suicide.

Borgia was dead, but his name would live on as an exemplar—in a manner he could never have foreseen. The man responsible for this would be his friend Machiavelli, who had seen him in action and understood how he had so nearly succeeded in his huge ambition. For Machiavelli, only such a man could save Italy from its self-destructive wars, which threatened to tear it apart in the midst of its great cultural renaissance. But it would be some years before Machiavelli would fully come to this realization, articulating clearly and decisively in his mind the qualities that were required if Italy was to be led into the classic greatness of another Roman era.

Machiavelli had remained with Julius II and his army as it moved up through Italy during the late summer and autumn of 1506. Regularly he sent back his dispatches to the Signoria in Florence, and on September 13 he was with the pope on his triumphant entry into Perugia. He then followed the papal forces into the Romagna as they moved north to attack Bologna. Julius II appeared to be sweeping all before him, and Machiavelli reported how on October 3 His Holiness bragged to the assembled envoys at his court that "he had an army that would make all Italy tremble, let alone Bologna." Machiavelli was not impressed. Two days later at Cesena the Florentine envoy was present when Julius II reviewed the papal forces under their *gonfaloniere*, Guidobaldo of Urbino. Machiavelli had by now acquired something of an eye for military matters, and reported proudly back to the Signoria, "I cannot refrain from informing your Lordships that if you could but see the troops of the Duke of Urbino, and the others under the Papal banner, you would not be ashamed of our own troops, nor would you underestimate them."

With regard to the matter of Florentine forces joining up with those of Julius II, Machiavelli continued to procrastinate as best he could, with the pope becoming increasingly impatient at Machiavelli's inability to commit himself. As previously, Machiavelli was only accredited with the rank of envoy, with no power to make decisions of his own accord, thus ensuring that he could not be browbeaten by the pope into any commitment that Gonfaloniere Soderini and the Signoria were unwilling to back. Towards the end of October, in the hope of appeasing the pope, the Signoria dispatched to the peripatetic papal court a representative with full ambassadorial powers, and Machiavelli was allowed to return home.

Along with his other administrative duties, Machiavelli continued to oversee the Florentine militia, in between being sent by Soderini on a number of diplomatic missions. The most important of these was in December 1507, when he was dispatched north into Germany to the court of Maximilian I, the Holy Roman Emperor. News had reached Florence that Maximilian I was planning to evict the French from northern Italy, and then march south to be crowned as Holy Roman Emperor in the traditional ceremony by the pope. Florence remained allied to the French, and any Florentine mission to the court of Maximilian I would require experienced and accomplished diplomatic skills. Machiavelli fulfilled his role well, but it would be a long, tricky task and he would not be back in Florence until June 1508.

In the course of his work as an envoy, Machiavelli had encountered a wide range of rulers—from petty tyrants to the most powerful men in Europe. Such meetings had allowed him to exercise his psychological and political insight. As a result, his understanding of the qualities required for statesmanship and leadership was growing ever more profound. But Machiavelli was also concerned with the general historical picture, and on his return to Florence he wrote a "Report on the State of Germany," which outlines with remarkable perception the strengths and political weaknesses of the German nation during this period:

> The reason why the private citizens are rich is, that they live as
> if they were poor. . . . Nobody cares for what he has not, but
> only for what is necessary to him, and these necessities are very

much less than ours.... Moreover, the cities know that the conquest of Italy would not be for their benefit, but for that of the princes, who can personally enjoy that country, which they could not do. And where the benefit is unequal, people are not willing to bear unequal expenses; and thus opinions remain undecided, without being able to determine the events that are yet in the future.

This work is diplomatic reporting of the highest order, yet it is also shot through with Machiavelli's propensity to philosophize and propound what he sees as the theory that underlies his experience.

This element in his writings came increasingly to the fore after his months in the Romagna with Borgia, and may well have resulted from his long conversations with the like-minded Leonardo, whose notebooks often reveal a similar propensity to seek scientific laws and make generalizing philosophical statements. Despite the advances of the Renaissance, the prevailing ethos of this period remained very much medieval, especially in matters of theory. Advances in scientific and political thinking were hampered by insistence upon appeal to the authority of the classical authors. To a large extent, what Aristotle said governed science and such political thinking as there was. Leonardo and Machiavelli were both believers in learning from experience, rather than accepting the pronouncements of some ancient authority: they adhered to what we would call scientific method. Leonardo sought the laws that underlay scientific experience, and in much the same way Machiavelli was searching for laws that underlay political experience. What were the most effective rules in politics? What was the best way to attain—and keep—power?

Yet for the moment Machiavelli had little time for such theoretical matters. Early in 1509 the Signoria decided to make a final determined effort to bring the long war against the besieged city of Pisa to a successful conclusion. Machiavelli's militia was to be given its baptism of fire, and on March 4 he arrived at the front to supervise his men beneath the walls of Pisa. This he did with such enthusiasm that orders soon had to be sent from Florence beseeching him to remain in his headquarters and not endanger his life by spending so much of his time amongst the frontline troops.

The Pisans quickly realized the impossibility of their situation, now that they were faced with an army that was enthused to fight for its cause. Word had spread of Machiavelli's recruiting trips around the countryside, and of the rigorous training undergone by the new Florentine militia: this was a patriotic army, rather than an army of cynical mercenaries. On March 14 the Pisans dispatched envoys to parley with the Florentines under a flag of truce, but Machiavelli quickly recognized the evasive tactics of the Pisan envoys for what they were and broke off the negotiations.

Hostilities now resumed, with the Florentine militia divided into three camps before the walls of Pisa. The running of such an army required considerable liaison and logistics if it was to maintain an effective siege and prevent the breakouts that had previously bedeviled the besieging army and rendered the blockade so ineffective. Inevitably, Machiavelli would have little time for writing his usual exhaustive regular dispatches back to Florence, so the Signoria sent two commissioners to assist him, as well as to report back to Florence on his activities. According to one of their early reports, Machiavelli "hovered everywhere throughout the armies." Discipline, supply lines, tactical liaison—Machiavelli oversaw them all.

By mid-May the Pisans had decided they had endured enough, and new negotiations were opened. On June 4, 1509, the surrender was signed; and four days later Machiavelli, his commissioners, and the Florentine militia entered Pisa. The war, which had dragged on intermittently for fifteen years, was at last over. As a colleague wrote to Machiavelli from Florence: "A thousand congratulations on the great acquisition of this noble city, for it may be truly said to have been your work." His friend Agostino Vespucci wrote to him:

> Here it is not possible to express how much delight, how much jubilation and joy, all the people here have taken in the news of the recovery of that city of Pisa: in some measure *every man* has gone mad with exultation; there are bonfires all over the

city, although it is not yet three in the afternoon, just think what they will do this evening after nightfall. . . . I do not know what to say. I swear to God, so great is the exultation we are having that I would write a Ciceronian oration for you if I had time.

June 1509 would prove the high point of Machiavelli's life.

27

Leonardo's Loss

B Y CONTRAST, MACHIAVELLI'S friend Leonardo had left Florence in 1506 under something of a cloud. Although Gonfaloniere Soderini had insisted that he must return to Florence within three months, Leonardo harbored little intention of complying with this stipulation. His arrival in Milan had been like returning home. Charles d'Amboise, the French governor of Milan, proved enchanted by Leonardo and soon housed him in his old quarters in the Corte Vecchia. Leonardo and his Florentine friend Ambrogio de Predis quickly finished the copy of *The Virgin of the Rocks* for the Confraternity of the Immaculate Conception, but in the course of this Leonardo seems to have fallen out with de Predis. He now found the whole business of painting for commissions, with the inevitable deadlines involved, irksome. He wished to devote his time to scientific studies, though he did dutifully agree to design a country villa for d'Amboise. Possibly in recognition of this, d'Amboise managed to secure for Leonardo an annual stipend of 400 ducats from Louis XII. In gratitude, Leonardo undertook a feasibility study with regard to linking Milan to Lake Como by way of a navigable canal that would also provide the city with fresh water.

Early in 1507 Leonardo learned of the death of his beloved uncle Francesco da Vinci, on whose farm he had spent his youth. When Leonardo's father, Piero, had died in 1504 he had left nothing for Leonardo in his will, which only benefited his legitimate sons. Francesco, on the other hand, left everything he had to Leonardo. His half-brothers were furious and blocked Leonardo's inheritance, contesting Francesco's will in the courts. As a result, Leonardo was forced to return to Florence in August 1507 to defend his inheritance. However, before setting out he made sure that d'Amboise sent an official communication to the Signoria, insisting that he be allowed to return to Milan when the case was finished.

The court hearings dragged on for months. The indications are that during this period Machiavelli made contact with his old friend, for several of Leonardo's court documents are copied out in the hand of Machiavelli's friend Agostino Vespucci. Machiavelli was presumably delegated by the Signoria to discuss with Leonardo the vexed question of the unfinished *Battle of Anghiari* fresco, but this came to nothing and in all likelihood their conversation passed on to more congenial intellectual topics. At this stage Leonardo and Machiavelli adhered to a remarkably similar outlook on life—one that was both rare and dangerous during this period. Indeed, such were the rarity and similarity of their views that it is almost inconceivable they did not—at this and earlier stages in their friendship—share their ideas and in the course of these communications influence each other. By now Leonardo's philosophy was well developed:

> All our knowledge has its origins in our perceptions. . . . In nature there is no effect without cause. . . . Experience never errs; it is only your judgments that err by promising themselves effects such as are not caused by your experiments. . . . Science is the observation of things possible, whether present or past; prescience is the knowledge of things which may come to pass.

The last sentence, in particular, could just as easily have been written by Machiavelli. By understanding the truth about how the world worked, we were capable of seeing what was likely to take place in the future. Machiavelli's philosophy may have developed to the point where it was all but identical to that of Leonardo, but their fields of observation were altogether different. Machiavelli studied the world of men, rather than the world of nature:

Since my intention is to say something which will be of practical use to the inquiring mind, I have thought it proper to represent things as they are in real truth, rather than as they are imagined. . . . In this way, my aim is to draw up an original set of rules . . . which will be of use. . . .

Significantly, both these philosophies were devoid of Christian morality, or indeed any morality at all in the ethical sense of respect for good and abhorrence of evil. Leonardo's voracious appetite for perceptual experience and understanding, leading to inventiveness, appeared unhindered by the moral paradoxes in which it involved itself. His pacifism and his vegetarianism in no way impeded his invention of machines whose purpose was military destruction and killing. Interestingly, his realization of "the evil nature of men" only caused him not to *publish* certain of his ideas. It did not prevent him from continuing his investigations into such things. This distinction is of particular importance. He had experienced humanity's evil nature during his time with Borgia, and his subsequent increasing inability to finish his work—to render it fit for public view, or "publication"— would seem to indicate that, at least on one level, unconscious moral scruples did in fact come into play. He had understood that his driven personal quest to perceive and understand the world was amoral, and his moral sense prevented him from making public the products of this drive—whether they were artistic or scientific. Such was the nexus that would now begin to affect his character in a more and more divisive fashion.

An immediate effect of this now became manifest during his return to Florence to defend his uncle's will. Amidst all the legal wrangling there was little time for concentrated original work. Consequently, Leonardo decided to collect his bundles of notebooks that he had stored in the Ospedale di Santa Maria Nuova. With the best of intentions, he would set about ordering their contents with a view to publication. This was evidently to be a major project, for he even records the day on which he began the process, his aims in doing so, and the difficulties involved:

Begun in Florence . . . on 22nd day of March 1508. This will
be a collection without any order, taken from the numerous
sheets which I have copied in the hope of later classifying them
in order, according to the subjects with which they deal. But I
believe that before I come to the end of this task, I shall have
to repeat the same things many times. So, dear reader, do not
blame me for this, because the subjects are many and memory
cannot retain them all, and say, "I shall not write this because
I have already written it."

Amidst the muddle of the manuscripts, and the attempt to order them,
it is not hard to see the underlying contradictory impulses. As on other
occasions, Leonardo's repetitions would appear to suggest deeper feelings.
There is no doubt that he wishes to organize the material, but there
is also the feeling that it might prove impossible to do so. He desperately
wants to publish his thoughts so that they are intelligible to others
("dear reader"), but finds himself beset with difficulties in the attempt
to do so ("do not blame me").

For the time being, in an effort to succeed at his project, he wonders
if perhaps he should limit himself to a number of short treatises culled
from entries in his notebooks. Instead of the full-blown "science of
perception" that is growing in his mind, he will confine himself to
observations on subjects such as the art of painting, the movement of
water, mechanics, anatomy, and so forth. He ponders on the order of
these treatises: "The book of the Science of Mechanics must precede
the Book of Useful Inventions—Have your Books on Anatomy bound
separately!" Yet he still hankers for some overall structure, which he
compares to building a house: "The order of your book must proceed
according to this plan: first come the simple beams, then those which
must be supported from below, then those which must in part be
suspended, then those which need to be wholly suspended. Then the
beams which support other weights." His impulse to publish becomes
overwhelmed by self-imposed complications, by his wish to convey his
vision in its entirety, setting everything in the context of everything else.
Things that might on their own be put to use for "the evil nature of

men" will be seen in the context of the whole, with the intention of enlightening and conveying the miraculous nature of the world as a whole.

On the other hand, by conveying his vision in its entirety he will of course reveal the paradoxes inherent within it. Revealed will be the pacifist who writes:

> If any man could have discovered the utmost power of the cannon, in all its various forms, and have given such a secret to the Romans, with what rapidity would they have conquered every country and vanquished every army, and what reward could have been great enough for such service!

Also revealed will be the designer of fearsome and destructive military machines who writes:

> The caterpillar is an emblem of virtue for all humanity: The caterpillar, which by means of assiduous care is able to weave around itself a new dwelling place with marvelous artifice and fine workmanship, afterwards emerges from this with painted and lovely wings, with which it rises towards heaven.

Yet he shows that he is aware of this irreconcilable duality in his nature when he describes:

> The hypocrisy of the crocodile: This animal catches a man and straightway kills him; after he is dead, it weeps for him with a lamentable voice and many tears. Then, having done lamenting, it cruelly devours him. It is thus with the hypocrite, who, for the smallest matter, has his face bathed with tears, but shows the heart of a tiger and rejoices in his heart at the woes of others, while wearing a pitiful face.

Leonardo's self-awareness is such that he realizes his situation. He is caught on the horns of a dilemma: his vision only comes into its own when it is seen as a whole, yet this vision in its entirety is a self-defeating contradiction. He longs to publish all the marvels he has seen, discovered, and understood, but the contradictions within him prevent him from publishing them. The more he organizes his work, the more he discovers complexities that prevent him from doing so.

Machiavelli, who shared Leonardo's philosophy, was to prove capable of overcoming this dilemma. Ironically, it was Borgia, the very man who had so heightened and exposed the contradictions within Leonardo, who would provide the solution for Machiavelli: "I know of no better precepts to give a new prince than ones derived from Borgia's actions." For politics to become a true science, it would have to accept the amorality of science, allowing the ruling prince to act regardless of any apparently self-defeating complexities.

Finally, after almost a year, Leonardo was free to leave Florence. The court delivered its verdict on Francesco's will in Leonardo's favor, and by July 1508 he had hurried back to Milan. There was good reason for him to return so hastily—he had fallen in love.

Leonardo was by now fifty-six years old, and his feelings for the rascally Salai appear to have mellowed into a rueful acceptance of his wayward behavior over the eighteen or so years since they had first met. There is no doubt that at one stage Leonardo's relationship with Salai had been sexual. This is confirmed by Leonardo's well-informed fellow artist, the Milanese Giovanni Lomazzo, who is usually reliable. In a dialogue that Lomazzo wrote, Leonardo is asked about Salai: "Did you ever play with him that 'backside game' which Florentines love so much?" And Leonardo replies: "Many times! You should know that he was a very fair young man, especially around the age of fifteen." But by now Salai was twenty-eight, and although his waywardness certainly still involved petty theft, for the most part his peccadilloes did not upset Leonardo as before. Their relationship was no longer sexual, perhaps no longer particularly affectionate on Salai's part.

As a result, there must have been a certain emotional emptiness at the heart of Leonardo's life. Then one day, probably when he was

Melzi's drawing of Leonardo.

traveling through the countryside working on plans for the Lake Como–Milan canal, he encountered a fifteen-year-old aristocrat called Francesco Melzi, whose father was a captain in the Milanese militia serving under the French king Louis XII. Melzi would become a pupil in Leonardo's studio, joining his household along with Salai and other young apprentices. He was described as a "count," though his family may well have been poor—even so, it was highly unusual for a young nobleman to become apprenticed to an artist, even one as renowned as Leonardo. Lomazzo and others allude to Melzi's own skill as an artist, and this may well account for the fact that he was able to become Leonardo's pupil. Melzi's talent is confirmed in the various works that are attributed to him, especially the fine red-chalk profile portrait of Leonardo in his new "sage" guise, replete with long hair and flowing beard. This drawing has a well-observed individuality, though it is without the psychological depth of the iconic full-face drawing generally attributed to Leonardo himself. Melzi's portrait dates from August 1510 and is signed "Francesco Melzi at seventeen years old." Being of a good family, Melzi was also well educated, and would soon take over Leonardo's secretarial chores.

Vasari describes Melzi as "a very beautiful boy, who was much loved by Leonardo," and this is confirmed by Lomazzo and others. Leonardo's French biographer Bramly identifies a portrait of him with a serious young face and thick hair falling down over his shoulders, though the identity of the sitter in this portrait is disputed by others.

Leonardo appears to have been smitten as soon as they met, sometime in early 1507. When he had to leave for Florence in August of that year to defend his uncle's will, he wrote frequently to Melzi in Milan, but to little avail. One of these letters he drafted in his notebook:

Good day, Sir Francesco,

Why, in God's name have you not replied to a single one out of all the letters I sent you. Just you wait till I get back, and by God I will make you write until you're sick and tired of writing altogether.

Much can be gleaned from this brief communication. Its formal opening is the customary mode of address to one of noble rank, suggesting that Leonardo is either not fully sure of himself or being ironic—probably an element of both. This duality persists in the immediate informality of the letter itself, which reads as an uneasy mix of the jocular and the angry. It is both sympathetic and demanding, for as Bramly so succinctly puts it: "Leonardo was not used to expressing his feelings so openly." The final remark in the letter implies that Melzi had already taken on secretarial duties, and was in the habit of taking down letters to Leonardo's dictation.

As ever, when Leonardo is emotionally disturbed, he repeats himself: immediately following this entry in his notebook is a second draft of the same letter. This is altogether calmer ("My dear, Sir Francesco"), and much more characteristic in that it is all but inscrutably oblique (except perhaps to Melzi himself). This letter purports to be about the lack of communication from the president of the Milan Water Board about the Como canal project, but beneath the surface the message is equally urgent. "I wrote to the President [of the Water Board] and to you, and then I wrote again, and still received no reply. . . . Please have the goodness to write and tell me what has happened. . . . Would you please, for the love of me, urge the President . . ." and so on. It would seem that this was the letter that was actually sent. Either way, it is clear (to us, as it would have been to Melzi) that he was begging Melzi to write to him.

What the errant Salai made of all this is only hinted at. Salai's relationship with Leonardo may have long since cooled, but he seems to have retained his master's persistent and deep affection. Even so, it would have been out of character for Salai not to have given some indication of his disapproval of this young aristocratic interloper. Salai remained as Leonardo's somewhat untalented pupil, and also acted as his servant, running errands and doing the shopping. Under a shopping list dating from this period (presumably after one of Salai's misdemeanors), Leonardo writes a note to him, apparently begging him to desist from his jealous reprisals and make peace with his master: "No more war," wrote Leonardo, "I give in." At any rate, Francesco Melzi now appears together with Salai and other apprentices in Leonardo's lists of his household and its expenses, usually under the affectionate nickname of "Cecho" or "Cechino" (little Francesco).

On his return from Florence to Milan in 1508, Leonardo busied himself with various projects, ranging from designs for buildings (which were never built) to paintings (most of which remained unfinished), as well as an ambitious scheme for improving the network of canals stretching thoughout Milanese territory (which would be completed only after his death, but would rely heavily upon his foundation work). Most of all he returned to his scientific investigations and his notebooks. These investigations were as wide-ranging as ever, and included further plans to organize his material. In particular, he returned to the idea of a series of books on human anatomy. Around this time he would claim in his notebook, "I have dissected more than ten bodies." These bodies would have been the cadavers of people who had died in hospital or had been executed as criminals, passed on to him with the permission of the authorities. Although Leonardo was permitted to conduct dissections for the purpose of anatomical exploration, such activities were viewed with abhorrence by many—associated with all manner of popular superstitions concerning necromancy and the like. Also, in an age before refrigeration, the cadavers would soon begin to putrefy. As a result, Leonardo would conduct his dissections alone and in the cool of the night, and even he would occasionally succumb to the irrational. In his notebooks he speaks of "the fear of living at night-time in the company of these dead people, sliced open, their innards revealed and horrible to behold."

Leonardo would produce more than 200 anatomical drawings of astonishing detail and accuracy, in the course of which he made many discoveries that were far ahead of their time, as well as correcting many of the errors that had persisted through the medieval era since classical times. Where human anatomy was concerned, physicians still relied upon the authority of the second-century Greco-Roman physician Galen, some of whose dissections had been carried out on animals. In particular, Leonardo was to detect the circulation of the blood some 150 years before it was fully discovered and explained by the British physician William Harvey. Leonardo specifically wrote of "the continuous flow [corso continuo] of the blood through the veins," and came close to understanding the difference between arterial and venal blood: "The blood that returns when the heart opens again is not the same as that which closes the valves of the heart."

He also made important discoveries concerning the workings of the genitourinary system and the development of the human fetus, the latter being prompted by his attempt to discover the "great mystery" of life. In this, his thinking remained essentially medieval: he sought to discover "how the soul dwells within the body." Unable to find any physical trace of this elusive entity, he resorted to analogy, comparing

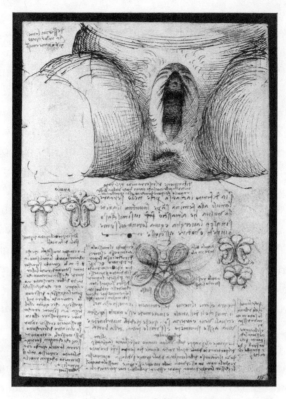

Leonardo's drawing of female genitalia.

the soul to "the air that causes the sound of music as it passes through an organ, and when the organ pipe bursts the wind passing through it ceases to have any good effect."

Leonardo would spend several years seeking the "great mystery" of life, in the realm of anatomy. In 1509, in the course of this quest, he would produce his well-known close-up drawing of a woman's vulva, whose distended proportions are unaccountably exaggerated. Leonardo seldom made such mistakes, and there would appear on this occasion to be no good reason for doing so—such as, perhaps, to exaggerate certain aspects in order to illustrate a specific scientific point. Leonardo's biographer Charles Nicholl has an explanation for his idiosyncrasy in this instance:

I am tempted to connect this strange exaggeration with Leonardo's earlier text about the "cavern,"* and to suggest that the fear he expressed about looking into that "threatening dark cave" was in part an unconscious confrontation with the disturbing mysteries of female sexuality. Within that Freudian sort of interpretation, the "marvelous thing" that might be glimpsed within the cave would be the mystery of generation and birth.

Leonardo's rich, resonant legacy invites such imaginative and ingenious readings, even if not all may find this particular instance convincing. Such speculation is, however, far preferable to the preposterous metaphysical flights and da Vinci codes that run so counter to the enlightened ethos of all that Leonardo strove to achieve.

In 1513 the Holy Roman Emperor Maximilian I (whom Machiavelli had visited five years previously) finally made good his threat and invaded northern Italy, chasing the French from Milan. As a close associate of the French, Leonardo found it prudent to leave, but he would not return to Florence. He records on the opening page of a new notebook: "On September 24, 1513, I left Milan for Rome with Francesco Melzi and Salai and . . ." He mentions two other pupils and a servant. He also took with him a number of unfinished paintings, as well as his bundles of disordered notebooks, all loaded onto a cart.

Once again he was forced to make a new beginning. To mark the occasion he drew in red chalk what is now regarded as his iconic self-portrait: the sixty-one-year-old sage, with domed forehead and long flowing hair merging into the flowing locks of his long beard. This is not the portrait of a happy man, or of one who is tranquil in old age. Look closely, and his face has a faint sneer, the corners of the lips downturned with life's disappointments. His eyes betray hurt and have a stoic aspect.

Italy was once more in the midst of a period of political turmoil.

---

* The dark mouth of the cave that he came across on a walk that hot summer's day in his youth; see page 13.

Much as Machiavelli had feared, in 1512 Julius II had dispatched the papal forces under Cardinal Giovanni de' Medici to take Florence. Gonfaloniere Soderini had fled and the Medici had once again taken over the city. As far as we know, Leonardo had no word of the fate of his friend Machiavelli. Then in early 1513 Julius II died and was succeeded by his close friend Cardinal de' Medici, who took on the name Leo X.

When Leonardo arrived in Rome he was soon made welcome by Leo X, who would have remembered him from amongst the circle of his father, Lorenzo the Magnificent. In those days the future Leo X had been a chubby but intelligent youth, of sufficient education to appreciate the many and varied talents of the artists, poets, and philosophers who had gathered at the Palazzo Medici in its heyday.

Leo X made sure that Leonardo and his pupils were housed in the Villa Belvedere in the grounds of the Vatican, and he was granted a regular income, which more than covered all his expenses. Yet elsewhere in Rome, Leonardo was not so highly regarded. He now looked old, and his art was out of fashion: he received no commissions. These were now all being snapped up by the younger generation of artists, who were coming into their prime. Leonardo's rival Michelangelo had just completed his frescos on the ceiling of the Sistine Chapel; and the young Raphael, whose portrait of Julius II was widely regarded as a masterpiece of psychological perception, was in constant demand.

Leonardo returned to his scientific studies, pursuing all manner of researches in notebooks that are now known to be lost. Giuliano de' Medici, the pope's younger brother, who had briefly taken over from Leo X as the Medici ruler of Florence but was now back in Rome, once more became Leonardo's patron.* Amongst other things, Leonardo designed for him a large parabolic mirror for capturing the sun's rays and turning them into heat. This source of solar energy was intended

---

* That is, if we assume that he was the unknown commissioner of the *Mona Lisa*. Even if this was not the case, it is almost certain that Giuliano de' Medici had at one time commissioned work from Leonardo. When Giuliano was a child, he also would have encountered Leonardo at the Palazzo Medici, when Leonardo was visiting his father, Lorenzo the Magnificent.

to boil the vats of water used for dyeing fabric in the Florentine textile industry, which was flourishing once again, now that the city had regained its overseas trade through Pisa. To assist him, Leonardo was assigned two young German artisans, known by the Italianized version of their names as Giorgio and Giovanni, who had experience with casting metal and making mirrors. Leonardo took an instant dislike to Giorgio and Giovanni, who proved as lazy and as cheeky as Salai, but with none of his redeeming qualities. The aging Leonardo was so upset with his new assistants that he became increasingly paranoid, suspecting them of spying on him and attempting to steal his ideas. He became solitary, stalking the corridors of the Vatican and musing alone in the gardens; at night he would lock himself in his studio, working through the hours of darkness. This was to be his undoing. Leonardo continued with his anatomical researches, dissecting cadavers; but such activity was banned in Rome, on orders from the Church. When his German assistants discovered what he was doing, they reported his activities to the pope. Leo X pardoned Leonardo, but warned him not to continue with his illicit dissections. The pope's sympathy was becoming a little stretched by Leonardo's willful behavior, especially with regard to paintings that Leo X had commissioned from him, which the artist showed little sign of completing. On one occasion, watching Leonardo dithering over the oils and varnishings that he was preparing, rather than getting on with the business of actually painting, the pope could not refrain from exclaiming exasperatedly: "Oh dear, this man will never do anything. Here he is thinking about finishing the work before he even starts it."

Leonardo's normally robust health began to fail during his time in Rome. In his notebooks he refers on several occasions to his "illness," his "malady," and so forth, which is also mentioned in the drafts of a letter to his patron Giuliano de' Medici in 1515: "my rejoicing at the news that you have recovered your health almost had the effect of curing me of my own illness." Despite this, Leonardo was well enough to accompany Leo X on his triumphal journey to Florence in November 1515, where the new Florentine pope was welcomed with scenes of genuine public rejoicing. The citizens had been touched that their new pope had named himself after the city's symbol, the lion. The accompanying extravagant celebrations were intended to remind them that, with the return of the Medici to power in the city, they could also expect a return of the glory days of Lorenzo de' Medici.

A week later the papal procession moved on to Bologna for an important diplomatic meeting with the new French king. Louis XII had died in January 1515 and had been succeeded by his twenty-one-year-old son-in-law Francis I, a tall, striking, and sympathetic character, renowned as much for his lust for women as for his lust for glory. On succeeding to the throne he had immediately set about gathering a vast army, with the aim of mounting a glorious invasion of Italy to recapture Milan. It had become apparent that the whole of Italy stood under threat from this invasion. There was nothing to stop Francis I continuing his march beyond Milan to take Florence and the papal territories of the Romagna.

Unsure of what to do, Leo X sent an envoy to consult in secret the most able political adviser he knew—namely Machiavelli, who was now living in disgrace outside Florence. Machiavelli advised the pope that his best (and perhaps only) hope lay in seeking an alliance with Francis I. Leo X ignored this advice, and instead asked Spain and the Holy Roman Emperor to join in a papal alliance to resist the French invasion. This proved catastrophic. In the summer of 1515 Francis I duly marched south across the Alps, defeating the forces of the papal alliance outside Milan. Leo X had been forced to dispatch a hurried message from Rome to Francis I, suggesting that they should meet for talks at Bologna.

In December 1515 the papal procession departed after its rapturous reception in Florence and proceeded towards its rather more uncertain reception by Francis I in Bologna. Leo X was determined to charm the cultured young French king, who was presented with one of Leonardo's most ingenious "entertainments": a mechanical lion that walked forward and opened its chest, revealing inside the French symbol of the fleur-de-lys—Leo the lion had France at heart. Despite such gestures, Francis I was not impressed by the overweight, middle-aged Leo X, who moved with a decidedly ungainly waddle and breathed heavily through his permanently open mouth. In the ensuing political discussions the French king drove a hard bargain, virtually dictating the terms of his agreement with the pope, though in a final gesture of goodwill he bestowed on Leonardo's patron Giuliano de' Medici the title of Duke of Nemours.

Leonardo must have been impressed by the striking Francis I. Wherever the young king appeared, all eyes were drawn towards him: he was over six feet tall—in an age when the diet ensured that few men grew above five foot six—and his noble features were if anything enhanced by his prominent nose. According to the Venetian ambassador, "the sovereign is so attractive that it is impossible to resist him." Here was another of the powerful young men in their early twenties to whom Leonardo would find himself strongly drawn—the last of a line that had begun more than fifty years previously with his young uncle Francesco in Vinci, and had gone on to include Lorenzo the Magnificent, Ludovico "Il Moro" Sforza of Milan and, most damaging of all, Cesare Borgia. Francis I, for his part, was fascinated by the aging genius-figure of Leonardo, with his flowing beard and distant, disillusioned, sagelike manner. It was as if Leonardo had somehow become overwhelmed by his impenetrable solitude. Indeed, Francis I was so touched and impressed by what he saw that he made Leonardo an offer of employment. Leonardo did not take it up, instead returning to Rome and remaining faithful to his patron Giuliano de' Medici. But when Giuliano suddenly died in March 1516, Leonardo realized there was nothing to detain him in Rome and decided to accept Francis I's offer.

In the autumn of 1516 the sixty-four-year-old Leonardo set out north from Rome, accompanied by Melzi and Salai. With him came the inevitable cart filled with unfinished paintings and bundles of papers. These were his worldly goods, including his notebooks, which he still had hopes of ordering into publishable form, as well as the *Mona Lisa*, which he continued to work on. He could not leave these behind, for he would never be returning to his native land. He could not have known this for certain, but he must have strongly suspected it and prepared his mind accordingly.

His first stop was Florence, the last time he would see his native city. His journey would have taken him close to the modest farmstead where Machiavelli was now living. There is no evidence that Leonardo called in to see his former friend, the man who had done so much for him whilst he had been in Florence. Leonardo had ended up casting in his lot with the Medici, the very ones whose return to Florence had been responsible for Machiavelli's disgrace.

In all, Leonardo's journey would take three months. On his arrival at Amboise, Francis I installed him in the small chateau of Cloux, close to the royal summer palace. Here Leonardo was granted a generous pension of 1,000 *écus soleil** a year. He was also accorded the title "first painter, architect and mechanic of the King," though he was not expected to perform any duties. The king wished for his company more than any works that Leonardo might produce. Some thirty years later the Florentine sculptor Cellini would be told by Francis I how "he was most enamored by Leonardo's wonderful virtues, and took so much pleasure in talking with him that few days passed in the year when he did not visit him." Cellini even goes so far as to give this as "one of the reasons why Leonardo did not manage to bring his studies to completion, despite the discipline with which he pursued this end."

Although Leonardo was now aided by the young Melzi, he was still unable to unable to assemble his notebooks into any kind of satisfactory order. Yet he continued to work, persisting in his researches, writing in his notebooks, occasionally returning to retouch his paintings: the *Mona Lisa, John the Baptist,* and *The Virgin with St. Anne.* As he wrote in his notebook: "Iron grows rust when it remains unused, stagnant water loses its purity and freezes over with cold. In the same way does inactivity sap the vigor of the mind."

Occasionally he would receive visitors. In October 1517 Antonio de Beatis, the secretary to the Cardinal of Aragon, recorded how they went "to see Messer Leonardo Vinci . . . the most celebrated painter of our day," who was "aged more than seventy years." Leonardo would in fact have been sixty-five, but his guise and demeanor were evidently those

---

* The golden *écu soleil* was, during this period, more or less equivalent to the golden florin of Florence or the golden ducat of Venice. In other words, Leonardo was now being paid around three times the amount he had needed to run his studio in Milan. On top of this, according to the register, Francis I made a generous allowance of 400 ordinary *écus* to "the Italian gentleman who is with Master Lyenard" (Melzi) and 100 *écus* "in a single payment to Salay, the servant of Master Lyenard de Vince."

of a very old man. Despite this, he must have made some progress in ordering his notebooks, for de Beatis records how Leonardo

> has composed a work on anatomy, especially as applied to the study of painting, applying as much to the external bodily members as to the interior muscles, nerves, veins, joints, intestines, and everything that can be explained, both in the bodies of men and in those of women. Never has the like of it been seen before. He showed it to us. . . .

De Beatis's next comments suggest that Leonardo still had it in mind to order and publish his notebooks: "He has also written (or so he said) innumerable volumes, all in the vernacular [that is, Italian], on hydraulics, on various machines and on other subjects, which, if published, will be useful and most delightful books."

But this was not to be. Leonardo had just eighteen months to live. In the words of Vasari, the nearest surviving source we have for this period in his life: "Finally, in his old age Leonardo lay sick for several months, and feeling that he was near to death. . . ." At the end, "he was joined by the king, who often used to pay him affectionate visits." Even now he remained the scientist: "having respectfully raised himself in his bed he told the king about his illness and what had caused it." Yet Leonardo remained greatly troubled by his failings and "protested that he had offended God and mankind by not working at his art as he should have done." This does not refer to his painting alone, but to all his "art," including his scientific studies, his notebooks, and his experimental machines. His failure to work at this "as he should have done" would thus refer to the lack of order in his work, which had prevented him from finishing his paintings as well as from passing on his findings to the world at large. This was the failure that had "offended God and mankind."

Vasari describes the end:

> Then he was seized by a paroxysm, the forerunner of death, and, to show him favor and soothe his pain, the king held his head. Conscious of the great favor being done to him, the inspired Leonardo breathed his last in the arms of the king.

Leonardo died at Cloux on May 2, 1519, at the age of sixty-seven. Vasari's description was written some thirty years after the event and has certain known inaccuracies: he, too, overestimates Leonardo's age by several years. Then there is the deathbed conversion that he describes, when Leonardo "earnestly resolved to learn about the doctrines of the Catholic faith and of the good and holy Christian religion. Then, lamenting bitterly, he confessed and repented."

A different story appears in the lines that were later removed from Vasari's first version, which described how Leonardo "formed in his mind a doctrine so heretical that he depended no more on any religion, perhaps placing scientific knowledge higher than Christian faith." Why did Vasari go back on this? Did someone point out to him that he had in fact been mistaken? Or did he perhaps find it expedient, for his own sake as well as for the memory of Leonardo, to omit such heretical words? Vasari was writing when the Counter-Reformation was being pursued by the Church with great vigor, and the freedom of thought possible in the High Renaissance was being purged in favor of a strict orthodoxy by the newly instituted Roman Inquisition. Either way, both Vasari's versions would seem to agree on one point: during his life, Leonardo did not believe in "the doctrines of the . . . Christian faith," until he may or may not have had to "learn" them on his deathbed.

However, the seemingly unlikely story of Leonardo dying in the king's arms may indeed have been true, and if not, it would certainly have been appropriate. Francis I loved Leonardo like a father: an honor that the king of a great nation had rarely before bestowed upon a mere genius.

The *Mona Lisa* famously ended up in Francis I's bathroom, but Leonardo left most of his possessions and all his papers to Melzi. Salai, who had made use of his proximity to the French king to sell tidbits of information to the Milanese ambassador, was left a small legacy. A year previously he had returned to Milan, where a few years later his roguish behavior would end in his being killed by a bolt fired from a crossbow, apparently in a duel.

A year or so after Leonardo's death, Melzi set off back for Italy, accompanied by a cart piled up with Leonardo's spilling notebooks.

During his lifetime Leonardo had published nothing but the drawings of geometric solids that had appeared in Pacioli's *De divina proportione,* which had eventually been published in Venice in 1509. Otherwise the list of Leonardo's surviving works is nothing less than tragic. None of his sculptures remain; his architectural drawings resulted in not one complete building; fewer than fifteen of his unsurpassed paintings have come down to us, some unfinished, others including work by other hands. And so it goes on. . . .

Once back in Italy, Melzi retired to his small family estate at Vaprio, some twenty miles northeast of Milan, where he began sorting through Leonardo's papers and notebooks, which are estimated to have contained more than 13,000 sheets. Working with two scribes, he managed to assemble a work now known as the *Treatise on Painting,* but for some reason even this remained unpublished at Melzi's death in 1570, whereupon Leonardo's notebooks were consigned to the family attic. Over the years they would be sold off, in no particular order, to visiting souvenir hunters, who sometimes sold them on, or passed them to other people who lost them. In time, several of Leonardo's notebooks found their way into the hands of various rich collectors, passing into collections in Italy, France, Spain, and even England. Of the original 13,000 sheets, only 6,000 or so have come down to us so far. In other words, we know less than half of what Leonardo thought, on paper, in his notebooks.

For the most part, Leonardo's cramped pages of pictures, diagrams, and notes would be regarded simply as miraculous curiosities, the wastepaper of genius. His mirror script is said to have been decoded 150 years after his death by Cassiano de Pozzo, secretary to a cardinal in Rome. Leonardo's discoveries and inventions would remain largely unappreciated, unseen by scholars or scientists, engineers or inventors, physicians or astronomers, or anyone who might have appreciated their worth and built upon them.

Gradually, over the years, his discoveries would be made and improved upon by others who were wholly unaware of the priority of their secretive predecessor. In 1543 the Flemish physician Andreas Vesalius would finish his *De humani corporis fabrica* (On the Structure of the Human

Body), which is generally recognized as the founding work of modern anatomy. This contained the first comprehensive published description of human anatomy, but nonetheless failed to incorporate and take account of several anatomical discoveries made half a century previously by Leonardo. Coincidentally, in the same year Copernicus would publish his heliocentric solar system, well after Leonardo had observed, in the previous century, "The sun does not move." In 1609, oblivious to Leonardo's work on optics and lenses, Galileo would at last develop his own version of the telescope. In 1628, building on Vesalius' anatomy rather than that discovered a century beforehand by Leonardo, William Harvey would discover the circulation of the blood, which Leonardo had understood to bring life to the body, such that "the flow of blood through the veins eventually makes these veins thicken . . . so that they prevent the flow of the blood," resulting in the cessation of life. All this, and so much more, he had discovered. The eye, the engines, the inventions . . . It has been surmised that if Galileo alone could have set eyes upon Leonardo's notebooks, entire fields in the history of science could have been opened up several decades—even centuries—before this in fact happened.

Leonardo's actual contribution to the history of science would be nothing. By a supreme irony, his notebooks would in fact remain ingenious oddities, just as their first collectors had so ignorantly regarded them. Filled with the ghosts of what might have been, in the end they became the blueprint of nothing. How much Leonardo's psychological inhibition about finishing his work, and publicizing it, was deepened by his experiences with Borgia is difficult to assess. But it was then that he seems to have experienced for the first time, in full manner, "the evil nature of men," which caused him to write amidst the diagrams and drawings, speculations and perceptions in his notebooks, the uncannily prophetic words: "I will not publish or divulge such things."

28

"Am I a Machiavel?"

IN MANY WAYS Machiavelli's legacy would be precisely the opposite of Leonardo's. As, indeed, would be the later course of Machiavelli's life. In June 1509, after witnessing the surrender of Pisa to his new Florentine militia, the forty-year-old Machiavelli had been the hero of the hour. But within months Florence would find itself in an even worse plight than war with Pisa.

As we have seen, Italy now stood on the brink of yet another convulsion. Pope Julius II had retaken the papal states of the Romagna, but it seemed that this was not enough to satisfy his ambitions. The French in Milan, to whom Florence remained allied, belatedly realized that they were under threat from the papal forces, which had been strengthened by a powerful contingent of Swiss mercenaries.

Meanwhile it was becoming clear that the pope's increasingly aggressive territorial ambitions were matched by his increasingly aggressive and volatile personal behavior. When Florence dispatched an ambassador to the papal court to offer his services as a mediator between the pope and the French, Julius II forbade him to speak and then flew into a rage, threatening to excommunicate him and raze Florentine territory to the ground. The Florentine ambassador was lucky; an envoy sent by the Duke of Savoy on a similar mission was peremptorily ordered to be flung into the dungeons and tortured. Prior to this, at Ostia, the pope had threatened to throw the ambassador from Ferrara into the sea with his own hands.

Julius II clearly had no intention of entering into negotiations with the French, and Louis XII's worst suspicions were confirmed when, in a fit of temper before the assembled ambassadors of the papal court, Julius II launched into a tirade about "delivering Italy from servitude and out of the hands of the French." Florence now stood between these two powerful armies: if the republic became involved, it faced war, destruction, and the final loss of its independence.

In June 1510 Machiavelli was dispatched once more to France with a brief to try and persuade Louis XII to let Florence remain neutral. This was a position that would have been of benefit to France, for if Florence sent its militia to join the French in Milan, as Louis XII insisted, the papal forces would immediately move to occupy Florentine territory, rendering the French position in Milan increasingly precarious. But the French would not listen to Machiavelli's arguments. Once more he had cause to complain that the French "knew nothing of statecraft."

Machiavelli returned to Florence despondent, and persuaded the Signoria that if the republic was to defend itself, the militia needed to be strengthened with cavalry. Machiavelli was at once ordered "to raise a detachment of light horse." In a move against the pope, Louis XII now encouraged the French cardinals to declare France independent of papal authority and summon a general Council of the Church at Pisa, with the aim of provoking a schism. In the summer of 1511 the first cardinals began to assemble at Pisa for the Council. Julius II was furious and blamed Florence for allowing the Council to be held on its territory.

In September Machiavelli was once more hurriedly dispatched to France, in an attempt to persuade Louis XII to move the Council from Pisa. By now hostilities had broken out between the French and papal forces in the Romagna, a conflict that threatened to engulf the entire region, with disastrous consequences for Florence. Louis XII proved ambivalent about moving the Council, and when Machiavelli returned to Florence in November he was dispatched to Pisa, where he miraculously managed, by means of subterfuge and cajoling, to persuade the cardinals to leave and reassemble their Council in Milan. This was more than fortunate, for the Council would summon Julius II to appear before it, and when the pope refused he would be declared suspended from office. Julius II had earlier responded to the Council by excommunicating all the cardinals who attended and confining a French cardinal who lived in Rome to the dungeons of the Castel Sant' Angelo. The pope now responded to his suspension from office by declaring that as the Council's members were excommunicated, their suspension of him was invalid. Such theological niceties aside, Julius II remained a powerful threat to the Florentine republic: he had already made it clear that he blamed Gonfaloniere Soderini for the "treacherous" position adopted by Florence, and would do all in his power to have him overthrown.

The papal army, which was by this stage led by the pope's trusted friend Cardinal Giovanni de' Medici, marched to Ravenna, where at Easter 1512 it confronted the massed forces of the French. By now the French were not alone in being supported by batteries of artillery, and the ensuing battle resulted in one of the worst slaughters in European history to that date, with possibly 25,000 being killed on the field, to say nothing of the countless wounded, many of whom would soon die. Technically, the Battle of Ravenna was a French victory, but the main consequence was that the French soon withdrew their army to the other side of the Alps. Much as Machiavelli had feared, Julius II now gave permission to Cardinal de' Medici to march on Florence and attempt to restore Medici rule.

Soderini ordered Machiavelli to prepare the city's defenses, and the 9,000-strong Florentine militia marched out to meet the papal forces, which were by this stage depleted to the point where they were outnumbered by the Florentine forces. However, the troops under Cardinal de' Medici consisted mainly of fearsome Spanish militiamen, much the same as those who had served so ruthlessly under Borgia. When the men of the Florentine militia found themselves confronted with such battle-hardened troops at Prato, some ten miles northwest of Florence, they simply ran away. With their blood up for a battle, the Spanish troops then stormed the defenseless town, whereupon there ensued two days of rape and slaughter, at the end of which nearly 5,000 lay dead.

News of the sack of Prato quickly reached Florence, where the terrified population prepared to surrender. Medici sympathizers in the city marched on the Palazzo della Signoria demanding Soderini's resignation, to which he consented. His last act was to dispatch Machiavelli to carry his official notification of the city's surrender to Cardinal de' Medici, asking only for safe passage into exile in exchange. This was agreed upon,* and on September 1, 1512, the Medici returned to power in Florence after an absence of eighteen years, with Leonardo's future patron Giuliano de' Medici later being installed as the city's ruler.

Machiavelli was seen as one of Soderini's closest supporters and would soon be stripped of his office, deprived of his Florentine citizenship, and fined 1,000 florins, which effectively bankrupted him. He was then banned from the city and exiled to his family smallholding seven miles south of the city walls, to a life of poverty and disgrace. At the age of just forty-three, Machiavelli saw his accomplished international career in ruins.

As if this were not bad enough, in February 1513 an anti-Medici plot was discovered in Florence, and on a list of twenty or so likely sympathizers the plotters had put down Machiavelli's name. When news of this discovery reached Machiavelli, he at once hastened to Florence to explain his innocence and his ignorance of any such plot. But the authorities arrested him and he was thrown into jail. Here he was subjected to torture in order to extract any information he might have had. The traditional means of torture in Florence during this period was the strappado. This involved both hands being tightly bound behind one's back and attached to a rope that passed up over a pulley. The rope was then hauled, suspending the victim high in the air with his wrists yanked up behind his back. But this was only the agonizing preliminary. The rope was then released, letting the victim fall, until the rope abruptly halted his descent, just before his feet could reach the ground, yanking his wrists further up behind him with such an excruciating jolt that it felt as if his shoulder was breaking or his arms were being wrenched out of their sockets—either of which sometimes happened.

Machiavelli was subjected to six "drops" of the strappado, but

---

* Despite this agreement, after Soderini left the city, Julius II dispatched papal agents to arrest him and bring him to Rome. During the ensuing chase Soderini managed to take ship and escape across the Adriatic to Ragusa (modern Dubrovnik), over which the pope had no jurisdiction.

confessed to nothing. (Four drops had been enough to make Savonarola confess that he was a heretic.) As Machiavelli later wrote to a friend about these tortures: "I have borne them so straightforwardly that I am proud of myself for it and consider myself more of a man than I believed I was." Had he confessed to anything—just to avoid further pain—he knew he would have been executed. Even so, he must have suspected that he would soon be following the two main conspirators into the execution yard. One morning before dawn he had been woken by the sound of the condemned conspirators being led to the scaffold, accompanied by the traditional small choir singing a hymn (this was intended to drown out the howls and curses of the condemned).

In extremis, Machiavelli wrote a poem addressed to the new ruler of Florence, Giuliano de' Medici, begging for forgiveness. In it he described his situation:

Giuliano, I have a pair of shackles clawing into my ankles
And the pain of six drops clawing into my back . . .
These walls are covered with lice
So big and fat they seem like butterflies . . .
Amidst the stomach-turning suffocating stench
Arise sounds like Jove and erupting Etna
Flinging thunderbolts to earth:
A metal door slams closed, a prisoner rattles his chains,
Another about to endure the drop
Cries out: "Too high off the ground!" . . .
But worst of all, to be woken near dawn
By the hymn accompanying the condemned . . .
I pray to you, let your mercy turn towards me
So that you may surpass the fame of your magnificent father
And that of your grandfather.

Machiavelli's pleas were ignored, and he was left rotting in his stinking, vermin-ridden cell, forgotten. Outside, the world went on. In Rome, Julius II died. Then on March 12 the news reached Florence that Cardinal de' Medici had been elected as the new pope, taking on the name Leo X, after the Lion of Florence. As part of the celebrations an amnesty was granted to prisoners, and Machiavelli found himself released. Like a specter, he slunk past the joyous crowds, trudging off down the long road out of the city through the countryside, back to exile in his farmstead.

Here he gradually recovered and began making a few attempts to put his life back together again. He wrote groveling letters to the Medici and their cronies in the new administration, offering his services. All he had ever done had been to serve the city of Florence; all he had ever done had been in its best interest, regardless of factions. His missives advertised his skills, begged for work, and swore his loyalty to the Medici. This last was not complete hypocrisy: any follower of the Medici would have known that it was, at least in part, true. Or had been. In his youth Machiavelli had been a visitor to the Palazzo Medici, and had published poems alongside those of Lorenzo the Magnificent. One of these poems had even been dedicated to the young Giuliano de' Medici: they must have known each other. And Machiavelli's sudden rise from nowhere to head the Second Chancery at the outset of his career, after the fall of Savonarola, had almost certainly had the backing of the moderate Medici faction.

Yet Machiavelli's letters were of no avail, so he decided to go one step further. He would devote his days of enforced inactivity to writing a book—one that distilled all that he had learned during his illustrious career in the service of Florence. He would show how indispensable his skills had been to his native city, so that it would offer to employ him once more. After all, had not the destiny of Florence depended more than once upon his diplomatic skills? Had he not traveled on missions to the greatest courts in the land, and beyond? He had conducted dealings with the most powerful men in Europe—Popes Alexander VI and Julius II, Louis XII, the Holy Roman Emperor Maximilian I, and not least Cesare Borgia, whom he had observed at close quarters on a daily basis, and who had on occasion taken the Florentine diplomat into his deepest confidence.

Machiavelli's experiences had led him to understand the difficult art of statecraft: now he would set down its principles in a book that showed all he had learned about politics, illustrating this with examples from his own experience, and comparing these with the great events of ancient history. This book he would dedicate to Giuliano de' Medici, who as ruler of Florence would surely recognize what Machiavelli had done for his native city, the city they both loved. Then once again he would be permitted to return to the great stage of international politics, from which he had only been removed by accident, by an unfortunate turn of events, by *fortuna*.

By contrast with his days of glory, Machiavelli described in a letter his present daily routine of humiliation and obscurity:

> I get up before daybreak, prepare the birdlime, and go out with a bundle of birdcages on my back . . . to catch thrushes. . . . I catch at least two, at most six birds. And that's how I spent the entire month of November. Eventually this pastime, although contemptible and alien to me, petered out at the end of the season—to my regret, even. Let me tell you what I do now with my day. I get up in the morning at sunrise and go into one of my woods that I am having cut down. Here I spend a couple of hours looking over the work done on the previous day and chat away with the woodsmen who are always involved in some dispute, either amongst themselves or with their neighbors. . . . Then I return [home] to eat with my family the meager fare that this poor farm yields. Afterwards I go to the inn, where I meet up with the innkeeper, together with a butcher, a miller, and a few kiln workers. I muck about with them for the rest of the day playing backgammon. Our games lead to endless disputes and much swearing—usually over nothing more than a penny—though you can hear us shouting as far as the next village. This is the way I blow the mold from my brain, cooped up as I am amongst my country lice—the only way I have of letting off steam and venting my anger at my fate.

What had happened to him was through no fault of his own. In his opinion: "Fate alone has been the cause of my injuries." But now was his chance to try and turn fate in his favor. Despite his lengthy complaints about life in the country, Machiavelli was not in complete despair. He was in fact living a double life. This too he described, with a writer's touch for vivid, evocative detail:

> When it's evening, I return home from the inn and retire to my study. Before entering I take off my everyday work clothes, which are covered with mud and filth, and go through the ritual of donning my robes of state. Thus fitted out in appropriate dress, I enter the venerable courts of the ancients, where they kindly receive me. Here I nourish myself on the food that alone is mine and for which I was born. Here I am bold enough to converse with the mighty, and to question them about the motives for their actions; whilst they, out of their gracious humanity, consent to answer me. For four hours I forget all my worries and boredom, I am afraid neither of poverty nor death. I am utterly absorbed in this world of my mind. And because Dante says that no one understands anything unless he remembers what he has understood, I have noted down what I have learned from these conversations. The result is a short book, called *The Prince*,* in which I delve as deeply as I can into the subject of how to rule—discussing the definitions of princedoms, the categories of princedoms, how they are acquired and how retained, and why they are lost.

For several years the ideas had been forming in his mind. Now it was as if his bitterness at his fate had stripped away the final veil of illusion, letting him see once and for all the true principles that lay behind political life. What had crystallized in his mind was a science— much the same as those ideas he had discussed with Leonardo. What Leonardo had sought was a science of the world, of the body, of machines, of art. . . . What Machiavelli sought was a science of the political world, of power, of human behavior.

* In fact, Machiavelli used the Latin term *De principatibus*, meaning "About principalities." This work would become known as *The Prince (Il Principe)*, the name it has retained through the centuries, and as such I have used this name throughout.

Previous descriptions of political life and society had sought an ideal prescription, such as Plato's *Republic* or the constitutions for city-states set down by Aristotle. But these had focused on the world as it ought to be. In many ways, they had all been descriptions of a utopia.* Machiavelli, on the other hand, chose to describe the world as he saw it in the here and now. Any ruling prince had to take account of how humanity in fact behaved, not how it ought to behave. He had to be prepared for the basest behavior: treachery, hypocrisy, vengeance, and so forth. And if he wished to remain in power, the prince would have to employ these qualities too—only more efficiently, so as to defeat his enemies. Such measures had to be applied ruthlessly, and scientifically.

Essentially, Machiavelli's advice to the prince was to "secure yourself against your enemies, conquer by force or by fraud, make yourself loved and feared by the people . . . destroy those who can or are likely to injure you." It is not difficult to see the specter of Borgia behind these words. Hypocrisy was essential: a prince may appear just and moral, but he must be prepared to act otherwise. He should take no half-measures. "People should be treated either with generosity or crushed; and when inflicting injury, make sure it is so great that the victim will be incapable of taking revenge."

The political existence of the prince was ruled by two aspects: Virtue and Fortune. However, these had no place for Christian virtues or even for the passive endurance of ill fortune that Christianity preached. Virtue (*virtù*) was not to be mistaken for the moral view of this word, but should be understood in its original ancient meaning, which had connotations of the Latin words *vir* (man) and *vis* (strength). Virtue, as Machiavelli used it, indicated virility, strength, power, manliness. Fortune (*fortuna*), on the other hand, was essentially a feminine principle, and its capriciousness should be treated as such: "It is better to be impetuous than cautious, for Fortune is a woman." Fortune was Fate,

---

* In fact, this word would first be used three years later, in 1516, when Thomas More published his *Utopia*. In keeping with the Platonic and Aristotelean tradition, More's work would seek to describe an ideal imaginary society.

in the ancient sense of this word, but was not to be viewed with any hint of ancient Stoicism: political expedience had no room for political correctness. "Because Fortune is a woman, to make her submissive it is necessary to beat her and force her. . . . Being a woman she favors younger men, because they are less cautious, and more filled with ardor, and because they overcome her with greater audacity."

Machiavelli's prescriptions were reinforced with specific classical examples and illustrated with relevant recent events. His aim was to build his political science upon empirical evidence. Thus reference was made to Alexander the Great as well as to Alexander VI, to Julius Caesar as well as to Julius II.* But Machiavelli's ultimate accolade was for Cesare Borgia, to whom he devoted most of Chapter 7, which was headed "New Princedoms gained with other men's forces and through Fortune." Here Machiavelli was able to show his prince in action, and the crucial error that led to his downfall. He demonstrated how Borgia benefited from having his father as pope, as well as from being backed by Louis XII. He was blessed by Fortune, which gave him the immense confidence necessary to embark upon his highly ambitious course. But Borgia soon realized the limitations imposed by French backing, when he was prevented from taking Florence. "As a result, he determined not to depend upon the arms and Fortune of others." Machiavelli then went on to commend Borgia's unexpected murder of his harsh commander Ramiro de Lorqua: this was done in order to make an example to the people and to separate Borgia from Lorqua's behavior. Next, Machiavelli described the audacity with which Borgia enticed his treacherous commanders to Sinigallia and ruthlessly destroyed them, in what would come to be regarded with admiration throughout Italy as "a most beautiful deception." Borgia was both the inspiration and the foundation upon which Machiavelli built his ruthless political philosophy.

Only then did Machiavelli show why Borgia failed. As Machiavelli had written earlier, Borgia had made allowance for the death of his

---

* Indicatively, and in true Renaissance fashion, both these popes consciously named themselves after their ancient namesakes. Julius II had of course also named himself after himself (Giuliano della Rovere), a declaration of intent worthy of a Machiavellian prince.

father, but not for the fact that he too would be at death's door at the same time. This led to his fatal mistake:

> The single thing for which we can blame him is the election of Julius II as pope. Here he made a bad choice. For as I have said, if he could not set up a pope to his liking, he should have prevented the papacy from going to one who was not. He should never have let the papacy go to one of the many cardinals he had injured, or would have cause to fear him. Men do you harm either because they fear you or because they hate you.

In Machiavelli's opinion, "Borgia should have thrown his support behind one of the Spanish cardinals for pope, thus securing the successful candidate's loyalty and alliance because of his indebtedness." Instead he chose to back Cardinal della Rovere, who would become Julius II: "so he blundered and brought about his ultimate ruin."

The final chapter of *The Prince* appeared to suggest Machiavelli's ulterior aim in writing this work. It was headed "An Exhortation to liberate Italy from the Barbarians." These "barbarians" were the foreign powers that had invaded Italy—France, Spain, and now the Holy Roman Emperor Maximilian I—whose armies were destroying the country Machiavelli loved. If this was indeed Machiavelli's motive, then the amorality he preached can be seen not as an end in itself, but as a means for a strong leader to take charge of Italy, drive out the foreign armies, and protect the freedom and security of its citizens. In this way, Italy would be returned to its former greatness, as in the era of the Roman Empire. Yet with such methods as Machiavelli advocated, the freedom and security of Italy's subjects would seem to be the prince's least concern: *The Prince* was an instruction manual for a dictator, rather than a liberator.

Machiavelli intended to dedicate *The Prince* to Giuliano de' Medici. The Medici were now one of the leading powers of Italy, with the Medici Leo X as pope and ruler of the papal states and Giuliano as ruler of Florence. For Machiavelli, Giuliano de' Medici with the backing of Leo X was to be the prince who would rule Italy and drive out her foreign oppressors. Unfortunately, although Machiavelli wrote *The Prince* in a matter of months during the winter of 1513–14, by the time he had completed it Giuliano de' Medici was no longer ruler of Florence, but had returned to Rome—where he would resume his role as Leonardo's patron before dying in 1516. So instead Machiavelli simply transferred the dedication to Giuliano's cousin Lorenzo de' Medici,* who had taken over as ruler of Florence. This was followed by the necessary adjustments to the text: the identity of the great prince who would lead Italy to liberation and greatness now appeared to be of little concern—the main point was that he recognized the author of this exemplary political work, appreciated his political expertise, and reinstated him to his former important post in the administration.

All this begs an important question. If Machiavelli did not really care who the prince was, did he really believe in the self-serving and ruthless advice that he was advancing? Did he really believe that this was the way to rule? In fact, during the ensuing years Machiavelli would write a much more serious, deeply considered, and lengthy book entitled *The Discourses*, in which he advocated a more humane and democratic republican government. Indeed, in this work he even goes so far as to distance himself from "those who generally dedicate their work to some prince," and instead advocates "new principles and systems" such as would be put in place by "the sagacious legislator of a republic . . . whose object is to promote the public good, and not his private interests."

So did Machiavelli believe a word of what he had written in *The Prince*? It would seem as if *The Prince* and *The Discourses* were in practice intended for different historical periods. The first was the prescription— the way to unite Italy and achieve its freedom—whilst the second was how the country was to be governed once this freedom had been achieved. Yet this assumption does not hold good. The prince had been given instructions on how to become an effective ruler, and these selfsame instructions also included details on how to avoid being deposed as a ruler. So we return to the question of whether Machiavelli in any way believed in the unprincipled and effective ideas he proposed in *The*

* Not to be mistaken for Lorenzo the Magnificent, who had been his grandfather.

Prince. Yet even to ask this is perhaps to miss the point. The irony is that, in writing *The Prince*, Machiavelli was employing unprincipled and effective ideas very similar to those that he proposed in the work itself. He was willing to do anything to get his job back. He was convinced that he was the best man for the job, and thus considered that any means he might use to get it back were justified—just as the prince was justified in using any means to achieve power, retain it, and use it to make Italy great again. But *The Prince* did not achieve its aim, and Machiavelli continued to languish out of favor, watching from afar as Italy veered on its disastrous course, beset on all sides by foreign powers.

No one was listening to him anymore. Just as predicted, in 1513 the Holy Roman Emperor Maximilian I had invaded Italy, evicting the French from Milan (and causing Leonardo to move south to Rome). Two years later Louis XII died and Francis I succeeded to the throne of France, intent upon retaking Milan and thus placing all Italy in peril. Faced with this crisis, the inexperienced Leo X had sent an envoy to consult in secret with Machiavelli. He may have been in disgrace now that the Medici had taken over Florence, but at least they recognized his worth. Machiavelli astutely advised Leo X to form an alliance with Francis I: this would safely have established the pope as the major power in Italy, even if he was reliant upon French backing. In Machiavelli's view, this move alone could save Italy. Instead Leo X chose to ignore Machiavelli's advice and form an alliance with Spain and the Holy Roman Emperor Maximilian I, thus further increasing the influence of foreign powers in Italy.

Machiavelli remained alone, in disgrace. But there is just a chance that he now received a final visit from a distinguished friend. With the death of Leonardo's patron Giuliano de' Medici in 1516, and the artist's subsequent decision to take up the offer of employment from Francis I, Leonardo set out north from Rome towards Florence. As he approached Florence, there is a possibility that he made the small detour necessary to call in and see his old friend Machiavelli at his farmstead in the country. On Leonardo's previous passage through Florence, fleeing from Milan to Rome in 1513, he would have heard of Machiavelli's downfall, as well as his exile to his smallholding in the nearby countryside.

At that time, Leonardo had been on his way to Rome to live under the protection of the Medici, the very people who had been responsible for Machiavelli's downfall: there could have been no question of any friendly meeting. Yet now, just three years later, things had changed. Leonardo might well have heard that Machiavelli had tried to ingratiate himself with Giuliano de' Medici, who had become Leonardo's patron. Now that Machiavelli too had thrown in his lot with the Medici, they could have renewed their friendship.

If this meeting between Leonardo and Machiavelli did take place, what might they have had to say to each other? Leonardo was old, disappointed, his legacy scattered in disarray through his jumble of notebooks, yet still pursuing his utterly original investigations, far ahead of any other in his time. Machiavelli was also disappointed, in disgrace, apparently a broken man, yet at the height of his intellectual powers, having just completed the work for which he would forever be remembered. Both of them were deeply affected, in their separate ways, by the horrific experience of their time with Borgia. Their memories of him would surely have entered any conversation they might have had. This was the last time that Machiavelli and Leonardo could possibly have met.

Three years later Leonardo would be dead. Lorenzo de' Medici would also die in 1519 and be succeeded as ruler of Florence by Cardinal Giulio de' Medici, the cousin of Leo X, who would reward Machiavelli for his secret advisory role to the pope by offering him a post in Florence. Yet this was hardly the senior administrative post for which Machiavelli had been hoping: he was appointed official historian and commissioned to write a history of the city. More encouraging was the fact that he was consequently sent on a number of minor missions. At the same time, he continued to act as occasional undercover adviser to Leo X. But for the most part the pope continued to ignore his advice, muddling through the complications of the Italian political stage, antagonizing almost everyone in the process. It was his extravagant behavior that provoked Luther in faraway Germany, thus leading to the Reformation, which would split Christendom in two. In 1521 Leo X died; many suspected poisoning by one of the numerous enemies he had made.

Two years later his cousin Cardinal Giulio de' Medici would be elected pope, taking on the name Clement VII. At last, in 1525, Machiavelli was reinstated by the Medici rulers of Florence and given a post as military adviser. He also continued to pass on occasional advice to the new pope; but Clement VII proved an even more inept pope than his cousin. By 1527 his political chicanery and dithering had so antagonized the Holy Roman Emperor Charles V that he dispatched an army south across the Alps to attack Rome. In May 1527 the Eternal City was sacked amidst scenes of rape and pillage not witnessed since the collapse of the Roman Empire. As a consequence of these upheavals, Medici rule in Florence collapsed and a new republican government was installed.

As soon as Machiavelli heard this news he hurried to Florence, filled with joyous anticipation. This was the day he had been dreaming of for five long years: now at last he would once more be given an appointment commensurate with his skills. Yet by a twist of *fortuna*, the new republican rulers would have nothing to do with him. Ironically, he was now tainted by his association with the Medici! On June 10 Machiavelli's former post as secretary to the Ten of War was given to another. This final disappointment proved a bitter blow. Machiavelli was fifty-eight years old, and the many years of hard traveling in all weathers, along with his years of disappointment, had taken their toll on his health. Ill and dejected, he retired to his farmstead in the country and took to his bed. Within days it became clear that he was dying. Despite this, when he was visited by his few close cronies, he insisted upon living up to his subversive role as "Il Macchia," telling them how in a recent dream he

> beheld in his sleep a crowd of famished and miserable people. On asking who they were he was told: the blessed souls in Paradise. Hardly had they vanished from his view than he saw instead a throng of grave-visaged men discussing political matters, and distinguished among them many illustrious philosophers of Greece and Rome. These were the souls condemned to eternal punishment. Being asked in which company he preferred to remain, he instantly replied: I would rather be in

Hell and converse with great minds upon State questions, than live in Paradise with the rabble I saw just now. . . . For in the latter he would meet no one but wretched monks and apostles, whereas in Hell he would be in the company of cardinals, popes, princes, and kings.

In less than a fortnight after his final disappointment, Machiavelli died, on June 21, 1527, at the farmstead outside Florence where he had written *The Prince*.

This work had not yet been published, though manuscript copies had already begun to circulate. Indeed, one of the reasons Machiavelli had fallen from favor with the republicans in Florence was that several leading figures had read *The Prince* and been horrified by the amorality of its content. In 1532, five years after Machiavelli's death, the first printed edition of the work appeared. It caused a sensation, with *The Prince*, as well as Machiavelli himself, becoming an object of public vilification. In 1557 the Roman Church issued its first Index of Banned Books: this included not only *The Prince*, but for good measure all of Machiavelli's works.

Already *The Prince* had begun to have a direct influence upon the practice of politics. An early example of this was seen in England, where in the very year that the work was first published, Henry VIII appointed Thomas Cromwell as his chief minister. Possibly during his previous travels in Italy, Cromwell had obtained a copy of *The Prince*, and upon his appointment he is said to have shown this to Henry VIII. The result was a transformation of Henry's rule into a ruthless pursuit of power. England broke with the Roman Church, declaring itself ecclesiastically independent. This was followed by the Dissolution of the Monasteries, which destroyed the Church's power base and brought Henry VIII vast revenues. No longer did he seek the pope's permission to divorce his second wife, but instead had her executed (a fate that would also befall his fifth wife). As a result of the new policy adopted by the king and his chief minister, the Archbishop of Canterbury would call Cromwell "an emissary of Satan." Yet it was this ruthlessness that laid the foundations for England's independence and greatness during the reign of

Henry's daughter Elizabeth I. Machiavelli had intended a similar greatness for Italy.

Machiavelli's influence would permeate political philosophy. A fine example of this appears in the work of Scottish philosopher David Hume, a quote that also appears in an essay by one of the founding fathers of America, Alexander Hamilton. As is evident, this applies especially to Machiavelli:

> Political writers have established it as a maxim, that, in contriving any system of government, and fixing the several checks and controls of the constitution, every man ought to be supposed a knave; and to have no other end in all his actions, but his private interest.

Machiavelli, like Leonardo, had recognized "the evil nature of men." Any political system that did not take account of this invalidated itself. Unfortunately, this recognition of humanity's evil nature could work both ways. Benito Mussolini always kept a copy of *The Prince* at his bedside, claiming, "Machiavelli was the greatest Italian philosopher . . . the teacher of all teachers of politics . . . but he did not have enough contempt for humanity."

Machiavelli had viewed politics as a science, and had set out his instructions accordingly. Follow the instructions and they will bring about the required result: cause and effect, the bedrock of the scientific world view. However, this view of politics entails the idea that there is a correct answer to each political problem. This notion that there is only one right solution in politics would give rise not only to Mussolini's fascism, but also to communism and any totalitarian political system. Indeed, it remains with us today in the western belief that free-market liberal democracy is the "answer" to the world's problems.

Ironically, *The Prince* can also be seen as an early instance of pluralism—the ability of a society, or even an individual human being, to retain within itself differing points of view. Machiavelli was one of the first to grapple with the inherent hypocrisy that springs from the pluralism that lies at the heart of the western world view. Christianity (like almost all religions) is essentially spiritual: our aspirations should be focused on the next world, and our behavior in this world should be governed by such qualities as compassion, meekness, humility, and love of one's neighbor. However, in the everyday secular world—the social and political world that we actually inhabit—we are expected to value precisely the opposite qualities. In order to succeed here we need ambition, greed, self-assertion, and so forth. This dichotomy is the unavoidable hypocrisy at the heart of western life: one that it has not always been easy for us to live with through the centuries. Some see it as our essential flaw, others as the inner contradiction that drives us.

Machiavelli was perhaps the first to accommodate this dichotomy, advising his prince to appear moral, yet to use the necessary immoral means in order to retain his power. This was the lesson he had learned from Borgia, and it was why *The Prince* was greeted with such outrage. The very strength of this outrage would seem to confirm the book's honesty: it touched an unacknowledged truth within us.

Only posthumously would Machiavelli achieve the aim that would have satisfied the two most powerful elements in his life: his ambition and his subversiveness. There is a further irony here, which envelops not only Machiavelli, but also Leonardo and Borgia. All three denied the spiritual outlook of the preceding medieval era, yet they would each, in their separate ways, become emblematic of an eternal aspect of the human spirit—the artist, the philosopher, and the warrior.

Notes

The following references are organized first by page, followed by the start of the quotation, and then by source.

Prologue: A Unique Constellation

1 "Your lordships should . . ." Machiavelli dispatch to Florence, June 22, 1502, signed by Soderini, but written in Machiavelli's hand. For Machiavelli's works I have usually relied upon the texts as printed in *Opere di Machiavelli*, ed. Sergio Bertelli, 11 vols (Milan, 1968–72). Volumes 6–8 contain his dispatches in chronological order. English translations of Machiavelli's works, which do not always match my own, can be found in Machiavelli, *The Chief Works and Others*, trans. Allen Gilbert, 3 vols (North Carolina, 1965).

1 "to install himself . . ." Machiavelli dispatch dated "before daybreak," June 26, 1502.

2 "by the light of a single . . ." Garrett Mattingly, "Machiavelli" in *The Penguin Book of the Renaissance*, ed. J. H. Plumb (London, 1964), p. 64. This description is collated mainly from Machiavelli's writing, as well as Mattingly's own researches into the life of Borgia.

2 "I am not pleased . . ." See first note, p. 1.

2 "made Florentines tremble . . ." Machiavelli, *Decennale primo*, lines 514–6.

4 "colossal outlines . . ." Jacob Burckhardt, *The Civilization of the Renaissance in Italy*, trans. Middlemore (London, 1937), p. 75.

5 "Am I politic . . ." William Shakespeare, *The Merry Wives of Windsor*, Act III.i.104.

1: Leonardo Learning

11 "Writing in such detail . . ." Leonardo, *Codex Atlanticus* [from now on abbreviated *Cod Atl*], 66v-b.

12 "Many children . . ." Leonardo, *Cod Atl*, 145a.

12 "I have witnessed . . ." *Manuscript F, Institut de France, Paris,* 37b [from now on abbreviated: e.g. *MS F,* 37b]; also *The Literary Works of Leonardo da Vinci,* ed. Jean Paul Richter, 2 vols (New York, 1970), # 1338. I have included the latter, as it is a more readily available source; this contains Leonardo's Italian, alongside an English translation to which I have not always adhered. [From now on abbreviated: e.g. Richter, *Literary Works of Leonardo,* # 1338.]

13 "While you are alone . . ." and "You should say . . ." Both Institut de France, Paris. *Treatise on Painting* 2038 27b-a; see also Richter, *Literary Works of Leonardo,* # 494. All up to # 705A are in vol 1.

13 "Driven by my . . ." Richter, *Literary Works of Leonardo,* # 1339.

14 "Men will seem to see . . ." Richter, *Literary Works of Leonardo,* # 1293; *Cod Atl,* 145a.

17 "Design for a device . . ." Leonardo, *Cod Atl,* 34r.

17 "Paulus crosses . . ." Cited in G. Uzielli, *La Vita e i tempi di Paolo dal Pozzo Toscanelli* (Rome, 1894), p. 233.

18 "my map of . . ." Richter, *Literary Works of Leonardo,* # 1444; *Cod Atl,* 120a.

19 "They fled in terror . . ." Machiavelli, *Istorie fiorentine,* bk VIII, sec. 6–7.

21 "little devil" etc. See Charles Nicholl, *Leonardo da Vinci* (London, 2004), pp. 270–1.

21 "the perfect type . . ." Cited in D. S. Chambers, *A Concise Encyclopedia of Renaissance Italy* (London, 1981), p. 300.

22 "the justice of . . ." Leonardo, *MS H,* 406.

23 "fires stones . . ." Notebook sheets in *Royal Library Collection, Windsor,* folio 12652 [from now on abbreviated: e.g. *W,* 12652].

23 "the cruelty of men . . ." Richter, *Literary Works of Leonardo,* # 1296; *Cod Atl,* 370b.

23 "a method of letting . . ." Leonardo, *MS B,* 64.

23 Evidence that Leonardo began thinking about a canal during this period is cited in Roger D. Masters, *Fortune Is a River* (New York, 1998), p. 44.

24 "He would arrive . . ." Matteo Bandello, *Opere,* 2 vols, ed. F. Flora (Milan, 1934), vol. 1, p. 646.

25 "this restless masterpiece" Cited in Nicholl, *Leonardo,* p. 293.

25 "all that could . . ." Giorgio Vasari, *Le opere,* ed. Gaetano Milanesi, 9 vols (Florence, 1878–85), vol. 5, p. 424.

25 "Let no one . . ." Richter, *Literary Works of Leonardo,* # 3.

29 "Look up . . ." See Baldassare Taccone, *Coronazione e sposalitio de la serenissima regina Maria Bianca* (Milan, 1493), p. 99.

29 "his passing was . . ." and "it became impossible . . ." Machiavelli, *Istorie fiorentine*, bk VIII, sec. 36.

31 "boasted that the Pope . . ." This remark was recorded by the contemporary Venetian historian Domenico Malipiero, *Annali Veneti* (Florence, 1843 edn), p. 482.

31 "Sell what you . . ." Cited in Nicholl, *Leonardo*, p. 319.

32 "Memorandum to Maestro . . ." Richter, *Literary Works of Leonardo*, # 1563; Leonardo, *Cod Atl*, 230b.

34 "The Duke has lost . . ." Richter, *Literary Works of Leonardo*, # 1414; Manuscript L, Institut de France 0.

34 "I recall with sadness . . ." Saba da Castiglione, *Ricordi* (Venice, 1554), p. 51.

34 "smashed it to pieces" Giorgio Vasari, *Lives of the Artists* (Harmondsworth, 1987), vol. 1, p. 264.

35 "He kept them . . ." and "This work not only . . ." Vasari, *Lives*, vol. 1, pp. 265–6.

35 "Leonardo's life is . . ." and "obligations to his majesty . . ." Letters 3 and 14, April 1501, from Novellara to Isabella d'Este, translated from the original MSS and cited in Nicholl, *Leonardo*, pp. 336–7.

2: Machiavelli: A Surprise Appointment

38 "I was born . . ." Cited in Roberto Ridolfi, *The Life of Niccolò Machiavelli*, trans. Cecil Grayson (London, 1963), p. 4.

39 "the streets were filled . . ." Machiavelli, *Istorie fiorentine*, ch. VIII, sec. 7–9.

40 "I have just been . . ." Machiavelli, letter to Ludovico Alamanni, December 17, 1517. Machiavelli's personal letters appear in vol. 6 of *Opere* (ed. Bertelli), see first note to p. 1. The best English version of his letters is *Machiavelli and His Friends*, ed. and trans. James B. Atkinson and David Sices (Northern Illinois, 1996).

40 "had been loved . . ." et seq. Machiavelli, *Istorie fiorentine*, ch. VIII, sec. 36.

41 "the islands beyond . . ." et seq. Cited in Frederick J. Pohl, *Amerigo Vespucci* (New York, 1944), p. 40.

41 "We arrived at . . ." Letter from Vespucci to Lorenzo di Pierfrancesco de' Medici, cited in Pohl, *Vespucci*, pp. 130–1.

42 "the dangers which . . ." Machiavelli, *Discorsi sopra la prima deca di Tito Livio*, bk 1, prologue.

42 "It is the rays . . ." *Codex Leicester* 2a; Richter, *Literary Works of Leonardo*, # 902.

42 "The sun does . . ." *W*, 12669a, Richter, *Literary Works of Leonardo*, # 886.

42 "Italy faced hard . . ." Machiavelli, *Decennale primo*, lines 1–3.

42 "tell of so many . . ." Machiavelli, *Decennale primo*, lines 4–6.

42 "prime mover . . ." Machiavelli, *Decennale primo*, line 51.

43 "the yoke that . . ." Machiavelli, *Decennale primo*, lines 25–8.

43 "persuaded by him . . ." Machiavelli, *Discorsi*, bk 1, ch. 11, sec. 5.

43 "showed his learning . . ." Machiavelli, *Discorsi*, bk 1, ch. 45, sec. 2.

44 "bonfire of the vanities" Described in Luca Landucci, *Diario fiorentino dal 1450 al 1516* (Florence, 1883), p. 168. The actual phrase is *"bruciamente della vanità,"* which is more literally "the burnings of the vanities."

44 "O prostitute Church . . ." Cited in F. Ludwig von Pastor, *The History of the Popes*, ed. F. I. Antrobus, 40 vols (trans. London, 1950), vol. VI, p. 17.

44 "savaging him . . ." Machiavelli letter, Florence, March 9, 1497, to Ricciardo Becchi in Rome.

44 "Savonarola was unarmed . . ." Machiavelli, *Il Principe*, ch. 6, sec. 5.

46 "sell him spiritual . . ." From the contemporary Florentine historian Francesco Guicciardini, *Storia d'Italia*, 4 vols (Florence, 1919), vol. 1, p. 246.

46 "spoke well . . ." Niccolò Machiavelli, dispatch to Florence, May? 1499, see *Le Opere di Niccolò Machiavelli*, 6 vols, ed. L. Passerini and others (Florence, 1873), vol. 2, p. 127.

47 "a breeding ground for all . . ." Machiavelli, *Discorsi*, bk 3, ch. 29, sec. 1.

48 "she always liked . . ." Machiavelli, dispatch to Florence, July 17, 1499.

48 "I manifested my feelings . . ." Machiavelli, dispatch to Florence, July 24, 1499.

49 Subsequent letters . . . See Roberto Ridolfi, *The Life of Niccolò Machiavelli*, trans. Cecil Grayson (London, 1963), pp. 29–30; and Pasquale Villari, *The Life and Times of Machiavelli*, trans. L. Villari, 2 vols (London, 1892), vol. 1, pp. 259–60.

50 "Let them be . . ." Cited in Ridolfi, *Machiavelli*, p. 35.

51 "his saddlebag . . ." See Sebastian de Grazia, *Machiavelli in Hell* (New York, 1989), p. 6.

51 "dying of laughter . . ." Cited in de Grazia, *Machiavelli*, p. 129.

51 "Bloody hell, Luigi . . ." et seq. Letter from Machiavelli to Luigi Guicciardini, December 8, 1509.

53 "haughtiness masks . . ." Machiavelli, letter to Francesco Vettori, August 26, 1513.

53 "The French are blinded . . ." Dispatch to Florence, August 27, 1500. Although these dispatches were signed by both the Florentine commissioners, Francesco della Casa and Niccolò Machiavelli, they appear to have been largely written by Machiavelli. Those after September 14 are signed by Machiavelli alone.

54 "The King complains ..." Dispatch to Florence, August 29, 1500.

54 "Concerning the matters ..." Cited in Sarah Bradford, *Cesare Borgia: His Life and Times* (London, 1976), p. 138.

55 "having long ears ..." Machiavelli, dispatch to Florence, November 21, 1500.

55 "for by this policy ..." Machiavelli, *Il Principe*, ch. 3, sec. 12.

55 "The Cardinal of Rouen ..." Machiavelli, *Il Principe*, ch. 3, sec. 13.

56 "From this it is ..." Machiavelli, *Il Principe*, ch. 3, sec. 14.

56 "was turning the Romagna ..." Machiavelli, *Decennale primo*, lines 292–4.

57 "they don't have women ..." Machiavelli, *Mandragola*, act V, sc. 6.

58 "The Florentines had been ..." Landucci, *Diario fiorentino*, p. 245.

60 "I am not pleased ..." Dispatch to Florence, June 26, 1502, signed by Soderini, but written in Machiavelli's hand. The following details of the two meetings with Borgia, and the conversation with the Orsinis, all come from the dispatch to Florence dated June 26, 1502.

62 "like an error or ..." Ridolfi, *Machiavelli*, p. 50.

3: The Pope and His Bastard

65 "pledge of the great ..." et seq. Cited in Bradford, *Borgia*, p. 23.

65 "the handsomest man ..." Cited by Michael Mallett, entry on Cesare Borgia in *Encyclopedia Britannica* (2002 edn), Micropedia, vol. 2, p. 386, col. 1.

66 "ardent mind" et seq. Paolo Giovio, *Istorie del suo Tempo*, trans L. Domenichi, 2 vols (Venice, 1555), cited in Bradford, *Borgia*, p. 24; also mentioned in W. H. Woodward, *Cesare Borgia* (London, 1913), p. 32.

66 The four laden mules et seq. From Stefano Infessura, *Diario della città di Roma*, ed. O. Tommasini (Rome, 1890), p. 282.

67 "The day before ..." The Ferrarese ambassador, cited in Bradford, *Borgia*, p. 30.

68 "Alexander sells ..." *Le Opere volgari di M. Jacopo Sanazzaro*, 2 vols. (Venice, 1741), cited in Bradford, *Borgia*, p. 29.

68 "a loud exclamation" Cited in Barbara Tuchman, *The March of Folly* (London, 1984), p. 78.

70 "His limbs were so proportioned ..." Francesco Guicciardini, *History of Florence and History of Italy*, trans. Cecil Grayson (London, 1966), p. 179.

71 For details re cannons, see Giovio, *Istorie*, vol. 1, pp. 53–5.

72 "an unspeakably terrible thought . . ." Guicciardini, *History*, p. 180.

72 "constantly pressed the King . . ." Guicciardini, *History*, p. 181.

73 "Not only did he lack . . ." Guicciardini, *History*, p. 149.

73 "On January 30 . . ." See *Le Journal de Jean Burchard*, trans. Joseph Turmel (Paris, 1932), p. 218. Burchard's *Diarium* was written in Latin, and a three-volume version was published by Thuasne in 1885. This, and the Italian translation by Cellani (1907–13), have various (differing) lacunae. The most reliable and readily available collation of these is Turmel's French translation, each of whose entries has numbered references to Cellani and Thuasne, for those who wish to check the earlier sources.

73 "All these Italians . . ." Various versions of this remark appear in a range of sources, including Guicciardini. It is said to have been overheard by Cardinal Giuliano della Rovere.

74 "The French were . . ." Cited in Bradford, *Borgia*, p. 50.

75 "had become afraid . . ." Machiavelli, *Decennale primo*, lines 52–4.

75 "marched onward . . ." Machiavelli, *Decennale primo*, lines 87–91.

77 "When the Pope . . ." See Burchard, *Journal* (Turmel), p. 292.

78 "the Pope had taken . . ." Cited in Bradford, *Borgia*, p. 70.

78 "saying how . . ." Machiavelli letter, March 9, 1497.

4: Cesare Rising

82 "He is well enough . . ." Cited in Bradford, *Borgia*, p. 81.

83 "wanted to remove . . ." Vasari, *Lives*, vol. 1, p. 263.

84 "a breeding ground for . . ." Machiavelli, *Discorsi*, bk 3, ch. 29, sec. 1.

86 "This castle, which . . ." Machiavelli, *The Art of War*, bk VII, sec. 5.

86 "Duke Valentino . . ." Sanuto, *Diarii*, cited in Bradford, *Borgia*, p. 112.

87 "If I could write . . ." Cited in Bradford, *Borgia*, p. 157.

88 "He was gravely . . ." See Burchard, *Journal* (Turmel), p. 305.

88 "Who hired these . . ." Cited in several sources, e.g. Woodward, *Borgia*, p. 180.

89 "stupefied by the suddenness . . ." This and Brandolinus' ensuing description are conflated from several sources; see for example Woodward, *Borgia*, pp. 180–1, and Maria Bellonci, *Lucrezia Borgia* (London, 2000), pp. 139–40.

89 "Her tears soon . . ." Bellonci, *Lucrezia Borgia*, p. 140.

90 "a brave and powerful . . ." This and the following from Collenuccio's dispatch to Ferrara appear in several sources; see for example Bradford, *Borgia*, pp. 136–7.

92 "At this time the city . . ." Biagio Buonaccorsi, *Diario dall'anno 1498 all'anno 1512* (reprinted Rome, 1999), p. 106.

94 "Whenever she is . . ." Cited in Bradford, *Borgia*, p. 160.

94 "Cesare murdered . . ." Several biographies cite this remark, but without giving any further details. I have included it because, even if it is apocryphal, it certainly reflects the popular opinion and feelings of the time— as confirmed, for instance, by the comments of the Venetian envoy Paolo Capello, cited in Bradford, *Borgia*, pp. 130–1.

95 "On Sunday evening . . ." See Burchard, *Journal* (Turmel), p. 310.

95 "lead the mares into . . ." Burchard, *Journal* (Turmel), p. 312.

96 "Alexander asked Cesare . . ." An envoy from Ferrara named El Prete, cited in Ferdinand Gregovorius, *Lucretia Borgia: According to Original Documents and Correspondence of Her Day*, trans. John Garner (New York, 1903), p. 218.

5: Treachery and Bluff

103 "having escaped with . . ." Cited from Guidobaldo's description of his journey in a letter written next day (June 28, 1502). For the full text of this letter in a translated version, see James Dennistoun, *Memoirs of the Dukes of Urbino*, 3 vols (London, 1909), vol. 1, pp. 401–4.

105 "was quaking heart and . . ." Machiavelli, *Decennale primo*, lines 343–5.

105 "This lord is truly . . ." Machiavelli, letter to the Signoria, June 26, 1502.

6: Obeying Orders

109 "boots," "a support for . . ." etc. See Richter, *Literary Works of Leonardo*, # 1420.

110 "Method for draining . . ." et seq. From notebooks: see Richter, *Literary Works of Leonardo*, # 1066, 1035, 609.

112 "Many treasures and . . ." Leonardo, *Notebook*, L, 91r.

112 "Stairs of the . . ." Richter, *Literary Works of Leonardo*, # 1040.

113 "Where is Valentino . . ." Richter, *Literary Works of Leonardo*, # 1420.

7: "Either Caesar or nothing"

116 "from your brother . . ." Cited in Bradford, *Borgia*, p. 186.

116 "Ought one to work . . ." Cited under entry "Epidemics, historical" by Peter L. Allen in the *Encyclopedia of AIDS* (New York, 1998).

116 "spent the whole night . . ." Bellonci, *Lucrezia Borgia*, p. 204.

117 "His Most Christian Majesty . . ." Niccolò da Corregio writing from Milan, August 8, 1502, cited in Bradford, *Borgia*, p. 187.

117 "that bastard son ..." Venetian ambassador to the French court, cited in Bradford, *Borgia*, p. 188.

119 "Sacred Majesty, I render ..." Andrea Bernardi, *Cronache Forlivese ... 1476 al 1517*, ed. G. Mazzatinti, 2 vols (Bologna, 1895), vol. 2, p. 14.

119 "Today at the twentieth hour ..." Letter written by one of the attendant physicians to Duke Ercole on September 8, 1502, cited in Bradford, *Borgia*, p. 190.

8: "A new science"

121 "that spirit of yours ..." Letter written by Vespucci, October 13, 1502, see *Machiavelli and His Friends*, ed. and trans. Atkinson and Sices, p. 50.

122 "whom you think ..." Letter written on September 8, 1502, by Machiavelli, on behalf of the Signoria, to Piero Soderini in Arezzo, cited in Ridolfi, *Machiavelli*, p. 268, n. 20.

122 "the world was always ..." Cited in Ridolfi, *Machiavelli*, p. 52.

122 "Urged on by genius ..." Villari, *Machiavelli*, vol. 1, p. 296.

123 "The Romans knew ..." This and subsequent quotes from *How to Deal with the Rebellious Citizens of the Val di Chiana* are taken from the translation by Linda Villari in Pasquale Villari, *Machiavelli*, vol. 1, pp. 296–7.

125 "Their curious way ..." Ridolfi, *Machiavelli*, p. 53.

126 "with his flaunted ..." Ridolfi, *Machiavelli*, p. 54. This description by Ridolfi owes a certain amount to the contemporary Florentine chronicler Bartolomeo Cerretani, who was in fact prejudiced against Machiavelli, but certainly knew his character.

9: Leonardo at Work

128 "the dovecote ..." Richter, *Literary Works of Leonardo*, # 1034.

128 "At the foot ..." Richter, *Literary Works of Leonardo*, # 1067.

128 "the chief realm ..." Richter, *Literary Works of Leonardo*, # 1046.

128 "in the library ..." Cited in Nicholl, *Leonardo*, p. 346.

129 "Make harmonies ..." Cited in Nicholl, *Leonardo*, p. 346.

129 "To all our lieutenants ..." et seq. The original of this document is in the Archivo Melzi d'Eril at the Villa Melzi on the shore of Lake Como at Bellagio. It is cited in most biographies of Leonardo: see, for instance, Serge Bramly, *Leonardo: The Artist and the Man*, trans. Sian Reynolds (London, 1992), p. 324–5.

130 "It has also been suggested ..." Several commentators make this point; I have relied upon Robert Payne, *Leonardo* (London, 1979), p. 181.

130 "At Porto Cesenatico . . ." and "The way in . . ." Richter, *Literary Works of Leonardo*, # 1044.

131 "The diggers . . ." Richter, *Literary Works of Leonardo*, # 1047.

131 "his notebook that covers this period . . ." This is notebook L, whose original is in the library at the Institut de France, Paris. For relevant early sketches, see in particular 24, 25r. The later, more fully realized drawings are in the *Codex Atlanticus* at the Ambrosian Library in Milan, especially 3, 4r. For the suggestion that a large earth-moving machine may have been constructed at Cesenatico in the summer of 1502, see the catalog for the exhibition *Leonardo, Machiavelli, Cesare Borgia* (Rimini, 2003), article by Enrico Fernandino Londei, pp. 53–71.

133 "a cruel and impetuous man . . ." Machiavelli, *Il Principe*, ch. 7, sec. 7.

133 "the most unheard of . . ." Villari, *Machiavelli*, vol. 1, p. 319.

133 "mild character . . ." See Dennistoun, *Memoirs of the Dukes of Urbino*, vol. 2, p. 11.

134 "a most learned . . ." Machiavelli, cited in Woodward, *Borgia*, p. 256.

134 "had placed in . . ." Cited in Bradford, *Borgia*, p. 216.

135 "those men who . . ." et seq. From letter to Ludovico Sforza cited in Richter, *Literary Works of Leonardo*, # 1340.

138 "One day Cesare . . ." Cited in Nicholl, *Leonardo*, p. 348, who gives the original reference as Pacioli, *De viribus quantitatis*, 2.85 (Biblioteca Universitaria, Bologna MS 250, 193v–194r).

138 "in a crate . . ." et seq. Leonardo's notebooks, *Codex Madrid*, II 4 b.

138 "Be sure that . . ." Leonardo's notebooks, *Cod Atl*, 43v b.

139 "most brutal . . ." Leonardo da Vinci, *Treatise on Painting*, trans. A. P. McMahon, 2 vols (Princeton, 1956), vol. 1, p. 110, sec. 266.

139 "One who by himself . . ." and answer. See Richter, *Literary Works of Leonardo*, # 1295.

141 *"Finestre da Cesena"* Richter, *Literary Works of Leonardo*, # 1043.

142 "And you, man . . ." Richter, *Literary Works of Leonardo* # 1140.

10: Borgia at Bay

145 There are few references to the clandestine meeting in Camerino—see, for instance, Michael Mallett, *The Borgias: The Rise and Fall of a Renaissance Dynasty* (London, 1969), p. 197. However, consequent events make it clear that a secret agenda was certainly agreed upon between Alexander VI and Cesare at this time.

146 "a man of a thousand ..." et seq. Machiavelli, *Decennale primo*, lines 406–8. Machiavelli's quotes regarding Liverotto come from *Il Principe*, ch. 8, secs 4, 5; Baglioni *Discourses* 1, ch. 27, sec. 2, etc. Other details are repeated in many sources, such as Villari and Ridolfi.

148 "in order not to be ..." Letter written by Gianpaolo Baglioni, October 11, 1502; see Machiavelli, *Opere*, 6 vols, ed. Passerini (Florence, 1873–7), vol. 4, p. 94 et seq.

149 "The castellan ..." Machiavelli, *Chief Works*, trans. Gilbert, 1965, vol. 1, p. 164.

150 "raging like a bear" Giustinian dispatch, cited in Bradford, *Borgia*, p. 193.

151 "the Florentines ..." Machiavelli, *Chief Works*, trans. Gilbert, 1965, vol. 1, p. 164. This was written sometime later, and may well have been intended for inclusion in future chapters of Machiavelli's *History of Florence*, hence his reference to himself in the third person.

11: Machiavelli's Mission

152 "collection of no-hopers" et seq. Cited in dispatch from Machiavelli to the Ten of War, October 7, 1502; see Machiavelli, *Opere*, ed. Passerini, vol. IV, p. 67. As before, in line with protocol, Machiavelli's dispatches were addressed to the Ten of War, but were intended for the *gonfaloniere* and the Signoria.

153 "The Signoria sent ..." E. R. Chamberlin, *The Fall of the House of Borgia* (London, 1974), p. 282.

153 "for at this court ..." Machiavelli to the Ten of War, first dispatch, October 20, 1502.

154 "onions" etc. See Roger D. Masters, *Machiavelli, Leonardo and the Science of Power* (London, 2002), p. 278, n.30.

154 "the chief man ..." Cited in Woodward, *Borgia*, p. 270.

154 "when they claim ..." et seq. From Machiavelli to the Ten of War, first dispatch, October 20, 1502.

156 "He has spent ..." Cited in Bradford, *Borgia*, p. 194.

12: The Ghost

160 For hodometer, see Kenneth D. Keele, *Leonardo da Vinci's Elements of the Science of Man* (London, 1983), p. 134, which reproduces the drawings from Leonardo, *Cod Atl*, 1 ra.

160 "makes the ear ..." Keele, *Leonardo da Vinci's Elements*, p. 134.

160 "Imola, as regards ..." Richter, *Literary Works of Leonardo*, # 1051.

161 "The Duke [Borgia] has so much ..." Machiavelli dispatch to the Signoria, October 9, 1502.

161 "made use of new ..." See Charles Yriarte, *César Borgia: sa vie, sa captivité, sa mort* (Paris, 1889), vol. 2, p. 140.

162 "a huge machine ..." From a description in the dispatches of Antonio Giustinian, the Venetian ambassador to the court of Alexander VI; see Bradford, *Borgia*, p. 211.

163 "to another who is ..." Machiavelli dispatch, November 1, 1502.

163 "lengthy conversation" et seq. Machiavelli dispatch, November 3, 1502.

163 "I am sure ..." et seq. Letter to Machiavelli from Agostino Vespucci, October 14, 1502; see also *Machiavelli and His Friends: Their Personal Correspondence*, ed. and trans. Atkinson and Sices (Northern Illinois 1996), p. 50.

164 "I think I can ..." Letter to Machiavelli from Biagio Buonaccorsi, October 15–18, 1502.

165 "The new *gonfaloniere* ..." Letter to Machiavelli from Biagio Buonaccorsi, November 5, 1502; for this and ensuing letter see also *Machiavelli and His Friends*, p. 51 et seq.

165 "The Signoria felt ..." Letter to Machiavelli from Biagio Buonaccorsi, November 15, 1502.

166 "Madonna Marietta sent ..." Letters to Machiavelli October 18, 1502, from Biagio Buonaccorsi.

166 "Your letters to Biagio ..." Letter to Machiavelli written around October 25, 1502, from Bartolomeo Ruffini.

166 "Madonna Marietta is cursing ..." Letter to Machiavelli December 21, 1502, from Biagio Buonaccorsi.

167 "My very dear Niccolò ..." Conflation of letters dated November 14 and 18, 1502, from Piero Soderini to Machiavelli.

167 "Shove it up your arse ..." Letter to Machiavelli dated December 21, 1502, from Biagio Buonaccorsi, see also *Machiavelli and His Friends*, p. 79.

13: Borgia Negotiates

169 "Now they are playing ..." Cited in Villari, *Machiavelli*, vol. 1, p. 311.

170 "It is impossible ..." Machiavelli dispatch, October 27, 1502.

170 "None of them would be ..." Machiavelli dispatch, November 10, 1502.

171 "He stabbed us ..." Machiavelli dispatch, November 28, 1502.

173 "Rarely, if ever ..." Bernardi, *Cronache Forlivese*, vol. 2, p. 9.

173 "All the cities ..." Machiavellli dispatch, November 16, 1502.

174 "I have made no attempt . . ." Machiavelli dispatch, November 22, 1502.

174 "so as to relieve . . ." Machiavelli dispatch, December 6, 1502.

176 "Percussion is less . . ." Leonardo, *Cod Atl*, 48 rb.

178 "Sluices should be constructed . . ." Richter, *Literary Works of Leonardo*, # 1001.

179 "examine and consider . . ." Machiavelli letter, October 1522: *Advice to Raffaello Girolami when he went as ambassador . . .*

179 "I think I should . . ." Machiavelli dispatch, November 8, 1502.

180 "all the ardor . . ." Villari, *Machiavelli*, vol. 1, p. 313.

180 "My intention is first . . ." Richter, *Literary Works of Leonardo*, # 1148 A.

180 "Besides realizing . . ." Machiavelli dispatch, December 6, 1502.

181 "I offered . . ." Machiavelli dispatch, December 10, 1502.

181 "devoured everything . . ." Machiavelli dispatch, December 14, 1502.

14: A Definitive Move

182 "Borgia's first move . . ." Giustinian dispatch, November 24, 1502; see Antonio Giustinian, *Dispacci . . . Ambasciatore Veneto in Roma dal 1502 al 1505*, ed. P. Villari, 3 vols (Florence, 1876), vol. 1, p. 223.

183 "Up till now . . ." et seq. Giustinian dispatch, December 2, 1502.

183 "the Pope is most unwilling . . ." Giustinian dispatch, December 17, 1502.

183 "What the devil . . ." et seq. Giustinian dispatch, December 23, 1502.

184 "customary diversions" et seq. Burchard, cited in Villari, *Machiavelli*, vol. 1, p. 328.

184 "After dinner . . ." See Burchard, *Journal* (Turmel), p. 349.

184 "had told the Cardinal . . ." *Ibid.*

185 "When I was at court . . ." et seq. Machiavelli dispatch, December 20, 1502.

186 "The Duke no longer . . ." Machiavelli dispatch, December 23, 1502.

186 "The suspicions that . . ." Giustinian dispatch to Venice, cited in Bradford, *Borgia*, p. 202.

187 "It is said that . . ." Machiavelli dispatch, December 23, 1502.

187 "with whom he was greatly taken . . ." cited in Bradford, *Borgia*, p. 202.

187 "This morning Lorqua . . ." Machiavelli dispatch, December 26, 1502. Although Machiavelli's dispatch appears to suggest that Lorqua's body was discovered on the morning of the 26th, most other sources indicate that this happened on the 25th. This apparent discrepancy is almost certainly because Machiavelli dated his dispatch on the day that he finished writing it.

188 "Because Borgia knew that . . ." et seq. Machiavelli, *Il Principe*, ch. 6, sec. 7.

188 "affecting the honor . . ." See Woodward, *Borgia*, p. 225, n. 2.

189 "If I know you . . ." Postscript to letter to Machiavelli from Buonaccorsi, December 22, 1502; see also Villari, *Machiavelli*, vol. 1, p. 320, n. 5.

189 "a highly secretive man . . ." Machiavelli dispatch, December 26, 1502.

190 "Liverotto da Fermo was . . ." From Machiavelli, *A Description of the Method used by Duke Valentino [Borgia] . . . Oliverotto da Fermo and Others;* see also Machiavelli, *Works*, trans. Gilbert, vol. 1, p. 166. *A Description of . . . Valentino* was written two decades after the events, and the picture it paints differs to a certain extent from the facts set down in Machiavelli's *Dispatches*, which were written at the time. For instance, in *A Description of . . . Valentino* Borgia leaves Cesena "about the middle of December," whereas the *Dispatches* record him leaving on December 26. These discrepancies may be minor; but Machiavelli's conception of Borgia is also different in the later version of events. In the *Dispatches* Borgia is shown reacting to the events taking place around him; but in *A Description of . . . Valentino* a somewhat idealized Borgia is shown to be in command of these events. Part of this discrepancy is due to the fact that at the time Machiavelli was not privy to Borgia's schemes. It is necessary to bear in mind that the seeds of the "ideal" Borgia who would emerge in Machiavelli's later works were sown during the period of these events. As far as possible I have tried to keep to the contemporary Borgia described by Machiavelli in the *Dispatches*, referring to *A Description of . . . Valentino* mainly to fill in knowledge of which Machiavelli was unaware at the time, but also to give hints of the deep impression that Borgia was making on Machiavelli.

190 "The Duke received . . ." *A Description of . . . Valentino*, and *Works*, trans. Gilbert, vol. 1, p. 166.

192 "That same day . . ." *A Description of . . . Valentino*, and *Works*, trans. Gilbert, vol. 1, p. 167.

192 "We are all awaiting . . ." Giustinian dispatch to Venice, January 1, 1503, cited and collated especially from Bradford, *Borgia*, p. 204; Villari, *Machiavelli*, vol. 1, p. 329; also Ridolfi and Woodward.

15: "An action worthy of a Roman"

194 "Riding south towards . . ." From Machiavelli, *A Description of the Method Used by Duke Valentino [Borgia] . . . Oliverotto da Fermo and Others;* see also Machiavelli, *Works*, trans. Gilbert, vol. 1, p. 167.

194 "Borgia winked . . ." *A Description of . . . Valentino*, and *Works*, trans. Gilbert, vol. 1, p. 168.

194 Et seq. There are various accounts of the events that took place at Sinigallia on December 31, 1502. Machiavelli heard of them directly from Borgia, but his two accounts (in *Dispatches* and *Description of the Method . . .*) differ in their details. Other accounts also disagree, but again only in the details. I have collated what I consider to be the most coherent and plausible account from both of Machiavelli's versions, and several others— including the unreliable version produced by Borgia himself and ones by Burchard and Buonaccorsi, as well as other contemporary sources, such as Sanuto, Sigismondo dei Conti, Padre Gratio, and others.

196 "Having remained a while . . ." From "A Florentine Account," cited in Bradford, *Borgia*, p. 205.

197 "This is what . . ." Machiavelli dispatch; see also Bradford, *Borgia*, pp. 205–6.

197 "The town is still . . ." et seq. Machiavelli dispatch, December 31, 1502.

198 "in most excellent cheer . . ." et seq. Machiavelli dispatch, January 1, 1503.

198 "They both behaved . . ." Machiavelli dispatch, January 1, 1503.

199 "perfidious rebellion and . . ." Borgia's letter to Perugia is cited in full in Dennistoun, *Dukes of Urbino*, vol. 2, pp. 6–8.

200 "began by saying that . . ." See Antonio Giustinian, *Dispacci Ambasciatore Veneto in Roma dal 1502 al 1505*, ed. P. Villari (Florence, 1876), vol. 1, pp. 304–5.

200 "the castellan . . ." See Dennistoun, *Urbino*, vol. 2, pp. 6–8.

201 "The Pope has become . . ." Giustinian dispatch, January 6, 1503.

201 "some in their red . . ." Giustinian dispatch, January 8, 1503.

202 "symptoms of derangement" et seq. Giustinian dispatch, February 15, 1503.

202 "his drink had . . ." Giustinian dispatch, February 21, 1503.

202 "in the Spanish manner" Cited in Woodward, *Borgia*, p. 284.

203 "The Duke's actions . . ." Machiavelli dispatch, January 8, 1503.

203 "an act worthy . . ." Louis XII, cited in Woodward, *Borgia*, p. 285.

203 "a most beautiful . . ." Paolo Giovio, cited in Bradford, *Borgia*, p. 207.

16: "What has happened so far . . ."

207 "in the worst possible . . ." Machiavelli dispatch, January 1, 1503.

208 "You know how anxious . . ." et seq. Machiavelli dispatch, January 10, 1503.

209 "We have done everything . . ." Alexander VI, cited in Bradford, *Borgia*, p. 209.

210 "Word has reached us . . ." Burchard, *Journal* (Turmel), p. 350.

211   "We hereby swear to God . . ." Borgia's ultimatum, cited in Yriarte, *Borgia*, vol. 2, p. 134.

213   "public madman" Cited in Bradford, *Borgia*, p. 210.

214   "When the Pope dies . . ." Machiavelli dispatch, November 8, 1502.

216   "Every day he . . ." Giustinian, cited in Bradford, *Borgia*, p. 211.

216   "mortars capable . . ." See Yriarte, *Borgia*, vol. 2, p. 140.

216   "At the siege . . ." Yriarte, *Borgia*, vol. 2, p. 140.

217   "so if you add . . ." Giustinian dispatch, March 29, 1503.

217   "Look at it . . ." Giustinian dispatch, April 13 1503.

218   "thus demonstrating . . ." Giustinian dispatch, May 31, 1503.

17: Leonardo at Work

220   "The Duke has so much . . ." Machiavelli dispatch to the Signoria, October 9, 1502.

221   "You can have . . ." Richter, *Literary Works of Leonardo*, # 1192.

221   "Where there is . . ." Richter, *Literary Works of Leonardo*, # 193.

221   "On the 16th . . ." Leonardo, *Forster Codices* (Victoria and Albert Museum, London), Notebook III, 88 a.

221   "Funeral expenses . . ." et seq. *Ibid.*

223   "From Buonconvento . . ." Richter, *Literary Works of Leonardo*, # 1052.

226   "The case of . . ." Richter, *Literary Works of Leonardo*, # 1347 A.

227   "All our knowledge . . ." Richter, *Literary Works of Leonardo*, # 1147–8.

227   "The bridge at Pera . . ." Richter, *Literary Works of Leonardo*, # 1109.

227   "Ask Bartolomeo the Turk . . ." *Ibid.*

228   "wanted to employ . . ." Ascanio Condivi, *The Life of Michelangelo*, trans. Alice Wohl (Pennsylvania, 1976), p. 37.

228   "A copy of a letter . . ." This letter first appeared in German translation in an academic article: see F. Babinger, *Nachrichten der Akademie der Wissenschaften in Göttingen* 52 (1952), pp. 1–20. It has since been cited in some sources in slightly differing English translations. See, for instance, Nicholl, *Leonardo*, p. 354.

229   "I know how . . ." et seq. Richter, *Literary Works of Leonardo*, # 1340.

230   "The Black Sea . . ." et seq. Richter, *Literary Works of Leonardo*, # 1108.

230   "The Sultan's secretaries . . ." Bramly, *Leonardo*, p. 459, n. 42.

232   "The one we find . . ." Luigi Capasso, cited at www.msnbc.msn.com/id/15993133. See also other entries related to "Leonardo's finger." For further information on the work of Luigi Capasso with regard to "Leonardo's fingerprint," see www.msnbc.msn.com/id/15993133.

233 "surmised that the . . ." For this and further information concerning Vebjørn Sand's modern Norwegian footbridge over the E-18, see www.vebjorn-sand.com/the bridge.htm.

234 "Saturday the 5th . . ." Richter, *Literary Works of Leonardo,* # 1530.

18: Machiavelli Uses His Influence

237 "Beyond the borders . . ." et seq., including words of the Byzantine emperor: Machiavelli, *Parole da dirle sopra la provvisione del danaio* . . . See Machiavelli, *Opere,* ed. Passerini, vol. 6, p. 279ff.; and Machiavelli, *Works,* trans. Gilbert, vol. 3, pp. 1441–2.

238 "being used by . . ." Cited in Masters, *Fortune Is a River,* p. 90.

241 "Leonardo da Vinci . . ." Cited in Carlo Pedretti, "La Verucca," *Renaissance Quarterly* 25 (4), 1972, pp. 417–215. See also Masters, *Fortune,* p. 95. The drawings of La Verruca (sometimes La Verrucola or other variations) are in *Codex Madrid* II 4r, 7v, 8r, and v.

242 "Leonardo, together with . . ." Pedretti, "La Verucca"; see also Masters, *Fortune,* p. 96.

242 "how by means . . ." et seq. Richter, *Literary Works of Leonardo,* # 1114.

243 "the most wicked act . . ." Richter, *Literary Works of Leonardo,* # 1140.

244 "the two were . . ." Giustinian dispatch, March 3, 1503.

246 "The Duke had . . ." Francesco Matarazzo, the Perugian chronicler; see (in another translation) *Chronicles of the City of Perugia,* trans. E. S. Morgan (London, 1905), p. 244.

248 "once expected the . . ." Ercole Strozzi, *Strozzii poetae* (Venice, 1513?), p. 31 et seq., cited in Burckhardt, *Renaissance,* pp. 304, n. 220.

249 "I will see . . ." Tommaso Gar, *Relazione della Corte di Roma,* vol. 1, p. 12, cited in Burckhardt, *Renaissance,* p. 61, n. 219.

249 "He, if anybody . . ." Burckhardt, *Renaissance,* pp. 61–2.

249 "the Pope and . . ." Giustinian dispatch, August 6, 1503; cited in Bradford, *Borgia,* p. 229.

250 "This month is . . ." et seq. See Pastor, *History of the Popes,* vol. VI, pp. 131–2, who had it from Sigismondo di Conti, though he suggests "there is some confusion in the dates."

252 "The Vatican was . . ." Giustinian dispatch, August 17, 1503.

252 "Borgia, who was sick . . ." Burchard, *Journal* (Turmel), p. 355.

253 "The skin of his face . . ." et seq. Burchard, *Journal* (Turmel), p. 359.

19: The Election of a New Pope

257 "I was fully ..." See Machiavelli, *Il Principe*, ch. VII, sec. 10.

257 "The whole city ..." Cited in Pastor, *History of the Popes*, vol. VI, p. 185.

261 "women of every ..." The Mantuan ambassador, cited in Bradford, *Borgia*, p. 235.

262 "alive and well ..." Cited in Bradford, *Borgia*, p. 236.

263 "I have heard on ..." et seq. Giustinian dispatch, August 21, 1503.

264 "I have come to Rome ..." Giustinian dispatch, 5 September, 1503.

266 "The moment d'Amboise ..." Giustinian dispatch, September 22, 1503.

266 "The previous life ..." Giustinian dispatch, September 22, 1503.

267 "Because of the pressure ..." Giustinian dispatch, September 26, 1503.

269 "Borgia is far from ..." Giustinian dispatch, October 6, 1503.

20: Squaring the Circle

270 "It has been suggested": By the renowned scholar Edmondo Solmi, amongst others.

271 "Then there began ..." Leonardo, *Cod Atl*, 75 r b.

271 "In this great defeat ..." et seq. Machiavelli, *Istorie fiorentine*, bk 5. ch. 33.

271 "If you show ..." Richter, *Literary Works of Leonardo*, # 601, # 2.

275 "Birds that fly ..." *Ibid.*

275 "a flying machine ..." et seq. Roger Bacon, *De mirabile poteste artis et natura* (Paris, 1542); a translation from the Latin by L. Tenney of this long letter by Bacon appeared in 1940, published by Kessinger. See references in Brian Clegg, *The First Scientist: A Life of Roger Bacon* (London, 2003), pp. 39–42, 221.

275 "A bird is ..." Richter, *Literary Works of Leonardo*, # 1126 D.

276 "This is the method ..." Nicholl, *Leonardo*, p. 150.

276 "Barricade up ..." Leonardo, *Cod Atl*, 361 b.

276 "Remember that your ..." Richter, *Literary Works of Leonardo*, # 1123.

276 "Tomorrow morning ..." Richter, *Literary Works of Leonardo*, # 1370 B.

277 "Describe swimming under ..." Leonardo, *Codex Leicester*, 13 r, 16 v.

277 "The machine might be ..." Richter, *Literary Works of Leonardo*, # 1124.

278 "You must carry out ..." Leonardo, MS B 74 v.

278 "The first flight ..." et seq. Richter, *Literary Works of Leonardo*, # 1428, 1428 A.

278 "it has turned out ..." Girolamo Cardano, *De subtilitate*, cited in several sources: see, for instance, Edward McCurdy, *The Mind of Leonardo da Vinci* (New York, 1928), p. 258; and Bramly, *Leonardo*, trans. Reynolds, p. 288.

279 "On the night . . ." Leonardo, *Codex Madrid*, 112 a.

281 "science of painting" See particularly Richter, *Literary Works of Leonardo*, # 2 et seq.

281 "All sciences are vain . . ." Richter, *Literary Works of Leonardo*, # 6.

281 "Painting presents . . ." Richter, *Literary Works of Leonardo*, # 7.

281 "Therefore painting . . ." Richter, *Literary Works of Leonardo*, # 9.

21: A Changed Man

283 "to lay hands . . ." Giustinian dispatch, cited in Bradford, *Borgia*, p. 244.

284 "There is no . . ." Giustinian dispatch, October 19, 1503.

284 "Borgia is much . . ." Machiavelli dispatch from Rome, October 30, 1503, to the Ten of War in Florence. (As before, these dispatches were of course intended for the *gonfaloniere* and the Signoria.)

285 "the shortest known . . ." Pastor, *History of the Popes*, vol. VI, p. 210.

287 "had the nature . . ." Collated from reports by the Venetian, Florentine, and other ambassadors; see Barbara Tuchman, *The March of Folly* (London, 1984), p. 93, and Felix Gilbert, *Machiavelli and Guicciardini* (Princeton, 1965), pp. 124–7.

287 "Borgia allows himself . . ." et seq. Machiavelli dispatch, November 4, 1503.

288 "I went to His Holiness . . ." and descriptions of his subsequent meetings: Machiavelli dispatch, November 6, 1503.

289 "in order to find out . . ." and the following quotes regarding the meeting with Borgia are also from Machiavelli's dispatch of November 6, 1503.

290 "This meeting took place . . ." et seq. Machiavelli dispatch, November 10, 1503.

291 "When I talk . . ." Giustinian dispatch, November 11, 1503.

291 "he expected Borgia . . ." Giustinian dispatch, November 18, 1503.

291 "and I found him . . ." et seq. Machiavelli dispatch, November 11, 1503.

292 "Borgia is impatiently . . ." et seq. Machiavelli dispatch, November 13, 1503.

292 "Cardinal Soderini . . ." et seq. Machiavelli dispatch, November 14, 1503.

293 "By the grace of God . . ." et seq. Machiavelli dispatch, November 19, 1503.

293 "at the moment . . ." Machiavelli dispatch, November 20, 1503.

294 "the Pope is unable to sleep . . ." Machiavelli dispatch, November 21, 1503.

294 "Early this morning . . ." Machiavelli dispatch, November 23, 1503.

295 "He said that . . ." et seq. Machiavelli dispatch, November 26, 1503.

295 "He reported that . . ." Machiavelli dispatch, November 27, 1503.

296 "news arrived that . . ." Machiavelli dispatch, December 1, 1503.

296 "It is difficult . . ." Machiavelli dispatch, December 2, 1503.

298 "a cat in gold . . ." See Zambotti, *Diario Ferrarese dall'anno 1476 sino al 1504*, entry for January 2, 1504, cited in Bradford, *Borgia*, p. 211.

300 "there is much . . ." Machiavelli dispatch, December 14, 1503.

301 "being unable to endure . . ." Copied from a report from Gaeta and included in Machiavelli's dispatch for December 16, 1503.

301 "It looks as if . . ." Machiavelli dispatch, December 3, 1503.

22: Return to Florence

307 "My dear old pal . . ." Letter to Machiavelli from Luca Ugolini in Florence, November 11, 1503; see also *Machiavelli and His Friends*, ed. Atkinson, p. 87.

307 "to come back . . ." Cited in Maurizio Viroli, *Niccolò's Smile: A Biography of Machiavelli*, trans. Anthony Shugaar (London, 2000), p. 194, though the extrapolation is mine.

307 "You will proceed . . ." et seq. Commission to Machiavelli dated January 14, 1504, at the outset of his second mission to the court of France. See Machiavelli, *Opere*, ed. Passerini, vol. 5, p. 3.

309 "listened to Machiavelli . . ." Valori dispatch to Florence, January 29, 1504. As ambassador, Valori signed most of the dispatches from the French court in Lyon to Florence. Their verbose style suggests that they were also written by Valori, though it seems likely that Machiavelli would have made his contribution. For this reason they are included in Machiavelli, *Opere*, ed. Passerini, vol. 5, p. 3 et seq.

310 "had one foot . . ." Machiavelli dispatch to Florence, February 25, 1504.

311 "without any doubt . . ." Vasari, *Lives*, vol. 1, p. 339.

313 "In the streets . . ." Richter, *Literary Works of Leonardo*, # 363.

313 "painting has to do . . ." Richter, *Literary Works of Leonardo*, # 23.

313 "a womanly equivalent . . ." Bramly, *Leonardo*, trans. Reynolds, p. 366.

314 "employed singers . . ." Vasari, *Lives*, vol. 1, p. 267.

314 "For Franceso del Giocondo . . ." Vasari, *Lives*, vol. 1, p. 266.

315 "a portrait of . . ." Antonio de Beatis, *The Travel Journal*, trans. J. R. Hale (London, 1979), p. 132.

315 "If poetry describes . . ." Richter, *Literary Works of Leonardo*, # 23.

316 "Some claim . . ." Bramly, *Leonardo*, trans. Reynolds, p. 364.

316 "I will not publish . . ." Richter, *Literary Works of Leonardo*, # 1114.

23: Coaxing Water

318 My diagram of Leonardo's project is a highly simplified and schematized version, based on several maps that appear in Leonardo's notebooks. See in particular *Codex Madrid II*, 52 v. 53 r.

319 "The river that is . . ." Richter, *Literary Works of Leonardo*, # 1008.

321 "A camp was . . ." Buonaccorsi's report to the Ten of War, cited in Nicholl, *Leonardo*, p. 359.

321 "Your letter of yesterday . . ." Machiavelli letter, October 20, 1504; see Roger D. Masters, *Fortune Is a River: Leonardo da Vinci and Machiavelli's Magnificent Dream to Change the Course of Florentine History* (New York, 1998), p. 128.

322 "Your delay makes . . ." Machiavelli letter, October 21, 1504; see Masters, *Fortune* . . . , p. 130.

322 "The waters never . . ." Buonaccorsi's report to the Ten of War; see Nicholl, *Leonardo*, p. 359.

322 "The greater of the . . ." Buonaccorsi's report, cited in Masters, *Fortune* . . . , p. 129.

323 "In the end . . ." Buonaccorsi's report to the Ten of War; see Nicholl *Leonardo*, p. 359.

325 "My highly esteemed . . ." et seq. Cardinal Francesco Soderini, letter to Machiavelli, October 26, 1504; see Masters, *Fortune* . . . , p. 135, or *Machiavelli and His Friends*, ed. and trans. Atkinson and Sices, pp. 106–7.

325 "his saddlebag . . ." See Sebastian de Grazia, *Machiavelli in Hell* (New York, 1989), p. 6.

326 "So the Duke . . ." Machiavelli, *Decennale primo*, L. 241–3.

326 "the labors of . . ." Machiavelli, *Decennale primo*, prologue.

327 "We place our trust . . ." Machiavelli, *Decennale primo*, L. 547–9.

327 "On Wednesday . . ." See Richter, *Literary Works of Leonardo*, # 1373. Neither Richter nor Nicholl includes Leonardo's repetition here, which is included in Bramly, *Leonardo*, p. 342, and can plainly be seen in the facsimile from *Cod Atl* F. 71 v b in *Il Codice Atlantico di Leonardo da Vinci: nell edizione Hoepli 1894–1904 curata dall' Accademia dei Lincei* (Milan, 2004), p. 218. However, all agree on the repetition in the following quote.

327 "On July 9, . . ." Richter, *Literary Works of Leonardo*, # 1372.

24: Borgia's Gamble

330 "his spirit . . ." et seq. Giustinian and Cattaneo, cited in Bradford, *Borgia*, pp. 261–2.

330 "He has not the patience . . ." Collation of reports from various ambassadors, cited in Pastor, *History of the Popes*, vol. VI, pp. 213–14.

331 "No one has any power . . ." Cited in Pastor, *History of the Popes*, vol. VI, pp. 213–14.

331 "These affairs . . ." Cited in Bradford, *Borgia*, p. 264.

331 "honorable imprisonment" See Woodward, *Borgia*, p. 358.

332 "Once in possession . . ." Machiavelli, *Il Principe*, ch. XI, sec. 5.

333 "Borgia's situation . . ." Giustinian dispatch, February 8, 1504.

333 "Borgia will leave . . ." Giustinian dispatch, February 15, 1504.

334 "they could go and . . ." Giustinian dispatch, February 29, 1504.

335 "He is sincere . . ." Cited in Pastor, *History of the Popes*, vol. VI, p. 387.

337 "had been in some pain . . ." Reported conversation with Carvajal in Giustinian dispatch, April 26, 1504.

338 "greeted with marks . . ." See Woodward, *Borgia*, p. 362; and Pastor, *History of the Popes*, vol. VI, p. 243.

340 "Borgia was to stay . . ." See Rodriguez Villa, *Cronicas de Gran Capitan* [i.e., Gonsalvo de Cordova] (Madrid, 1908), p. 434. The quote is taken from the main body of this work, which consists of an anonymous 600-page biography originally published in 1584.

342 "the safe-conduct . . ." See Woodward, *Borgia*, p. 268, n. 2.

343 "because these [Spanish] Cardinals . . ." Cited in Bradford, *Borgia*, p. 269.

343 "mounted on his horse . . ." et seq. Bernardi, *Cronache 1476–1517*, vol. 2, pp. 406–7.

345 "we regard [him] . . ." Letter of May 20, 1504, from the Spanish court to the ambassador in Rome, cited in several sources; see, for instance, Woodward, *Borgia*, p. 367.

25: Machiavelli's Militia

348 "one man per . . ." See Villari, *Machiavelli*, vol. 1, p. 398 and n. giving source.

349 "these north winds . . ." Machiavelli dispatch from the Mugello to the Signoria in Florence, January 2, 1506.

349 "In the entire . . ." et seq. Machiavelli dispatch from Pontassieve, February 5, 1506.

349 "exercise and . . ." Guicciardini, *Storie fiorentine*, ed. Palamarocchi (Bari, 1931), p. 277.

350 "There was a parade . . ." Landucci, *Diario*, p. 273.

351 "to remove the citizens . . ." Guicciardini, *History*, cited in Ridolfi, *Machiavelli*, p. 277, n. 33.

352 "Swimming in water . . ." Richter, *Literary Works of Leonardo*, # 1114 B.

352 "If the north wind . . ." See Nicholl, *Leonardo*, p. 399, citing *Turin Codex* 10v.

352 "the fury and impetus . . ." Richter, *Literary Works of Leonardo*, # 1124 A.

352 "bags whereby . . ." Richter, *Literary Works of Leonardo*, # 1125.

353 "a gentle people called . . ." Cited in Nicholl, *Leonardo*, p. 478.

353 "The morning of Santo . . ." Richter, *Literary Works of Leonardo*, # 1548.

354 "the battle of . . ." Cited in Bramly, *Leonardo*, p. 350, apparently from Cellini (see below).

355 "One day Leonardo . . ." From the manuscript by an anonymous sixteenth-century Florentine, often referred to as Anonimo Magliabechiano, because it is in the Florentine Biblioteca Nazionale Centrale under MS Magliabechiano XVII, 17 (c. 1542–8).

356 "You should not make . . ." Cited in Nicholl, *Leonardo*, p. 382.

356 "When they saw . . ." Vasari, *Lives*, vol. 1, p. 341.

356 "showed all the actions . . ." Benvenuto Cellini, *Autobiography*, trans. George Bull (Harmondsworth, 1998), p. 18.

357 "as divinely executed . . ." Cited in Villari, *Machiavelli*, vol. 1, p. 424.

357 "They served as . . ." Cellini, *Autobiography*, p. 18.

357 "On June 6, 1505 . . ." Leonardo, *Codex Madrid* II, 1r [Bramly, Nicholl, and others give the page as 2a; but it is unmistakably 1r, according to *Madrid Codices*, ed. Ladislao Reti (New York, 1974)].

357 "irremediably resistant . . ." Cited in Bramly, *Leonardo*, p. 348.

359 "Let the dark . . ." Leonardo, *Turin Codex*, 10v.

360 "The bird that mounts . . ." See Nicholl, *Leonardo*, p. 399, citing *Turin Codex* 10v; also Richter, *Literary Works of Leonardo*, # 1122 A.

361 "rid Italy . . ." Cited in Michael White, *Machiavelli* (London, 2004), p. 122.

362 "His Holiness explained . . ." Machiavelli dispatch to the Signoria from Civita Castellana, August 28, 1506.

363 "as he viewed . . ." Machiavelli, dispatch, August 28, 1506.

26: Borgia in Spain

366 "a man doubled . . ." Cited in Bradford, *Borgia*, p. 281.

366 "like the Devil . . ." This apt citation is included in a large number of relevant works and biographies of Borgia, yet no source is given.

367 "Cesar, Duke of . . ." See, for instance, Bradford, *Borgia*, p. 267.

367 "a big man . . ." Cited in Bradford, *Borgia*, p. 285.

368 "The more I turn . . ." Most of the biographies of Lucrezia repeat a

version of these words. See, for instance, Bellonci, *Lucrezia Borgia*, p. 258, where she also speculates on the possibility of Borgia's suicide.

369 "Better to ..." Bernardi, cited in Bradford, *Borgia*, p. 291.

369 "he had an army ..." Machiavelli dispatch to the Signoria, October 3, 1506.

369 "I cannot refrain ..." Machiavelli dispatch to the Signoria, October 5, 1506.

370 "The reason why ..." Niccolò Machiavelli, *The Historical, Political, and Diplomatic Writings*, trans. C. E. Detmold (Boston, 1882), vol. IV, pp. 384, 397, 401.

372 "hovered everywhere ..." Cited in Ridolfi, *Machiavelli*, p. 107.

372 "A thousand congratulations ..." Ridolfi, *Machiavelli*, p. 108.

372 "Here it is not possible ..." Agostino Vespucci to Niccolò Machiavelli from Florence, June 8, 1509; see *Machiavelli and His Friends*, ed. and trans. Atkinson and Sices, p. 180.

27: Leonardo's Loss

375 "All our knowledge ..." Richter, *Literary Works of Leonardo*, # 1147, 1148 B, 1153, 1148.

376 "Since my intention ..." Machiavelli, *Il Principe*, ch. XV, sec. 1.

377 "Begun in Florence ..." Richter, *Literary Works of Leonardo*, # 4.

377 "The book of the Science ..." Richter, *Literary Works of Leonardo*, # 7.

377 "The order of your book ..." Richter, *Literary Works of Leonardo*, # 8.

378 "If any man ..." et seq. Richter, *Literary Works of Leonardo*, # 1476.

378 "The hypocrisy of the crocodile ..." Richter, *Literary Works of Leonardo*, # 1241.

379 "I know of no better ..." Machiavelli, *Il Principe*, ch. VII, sec. 3.

379 "Did you ever play ..." et seq. Cited in Nicholl, *Leonardo*, p. 274.

381 "Francesco Melzi ..." This much-reproduced drawing is in the Ambrosiana Library in Milan, and the inscription reads in the original *"Francescho de Melzo di anni 17."*

381 "a very beautiful boy ..." Vasari, *Opere*, vol. IV, p. 35.

381 "Good day ..." Richter, *Literary Works of Leonardo*, # 1350. "Sir Francesco" is my translation of *"Messer Francesco,"* which would usually be translated as "Mister Francesco." I have chosen the other meaning of *messer*, as I think it better catches the mock formality and rank indicated by this phrase as Leonardo uses it in this instance.

381 "Leonardo was not ..." Bramly, *Leonardo*, p. 464, n. 22.

382 "I wrote to the President ..." Richter, *Literary Works of Leonardo*, # 1350.

382 "No more ..." Cited in Bramly, *Leonardo*, p. 369.

383 "I have dissected ..." Richter, *Literary Works of Leonardo*, # 796.

383 "the fear of living ..." Leonardo da Vinci, *Quaderni D'Anatomia* I–IV, ed. O. Vangesten etc., six vols (Norway, 1911–16), I 6r.

383 "the continuous flow ..." Richter, *Literary Works of Leonardo*, # 848.

383 "The blood that ..." Richter, *Literary Works of Leonardo*, # 850.

383 "great mystery" Cited in Bramly, *Leonardo*, p. 376.

383 "how the soul ..." Richter, *Literary Works of Leonardo*, # 1143.

384 "the air that ..." Richter, *Literary Works of Leonardo*, # 1141.

385 "I am tempted ..." See Nicholl, *Leonardo*, pp. 420–1.

385 "On September 24 ..." Richter, *Literary Works of Leonardo*, # 1465.

387 "Oh dear, this man ..." Cited in Vasari, *Lives*, p. 269.

387 "my rejoicing ..." Richter, *Literary Works of Leonardo*, # 1351.

389 "the sovereign is ..." Cited in Bramly, *Leonardo*, p. 397.

390 "first painter..." Cited by Ludwig Heydenreich in his article on Leonardo da Vinci in *Encyclopedia Britannica*, Macropedia (2002), vol. 22, p. 942.

390 "the Italian gentleman ..." et seq. Cited in Bramly, *Leonardo*, p. 399.

390 "he was most enamored..." et seq. Benvenuto Cellini, *Opere*, ed. B. Maier (Milan, 1968), pp. 858–60.

390 "Iron grows rust ..." Leonardo, *Cod Atl*, 289v c.

390 "to see Messer Leonardo ..." et seq. De Beatis, *Journal*, trans. Hale, p. 132.

391 "has composed a work ..." et seq. Antonio de Beatis, *Voyage de Cardinal d'Aragon*, trans. Havard de la Montagne (Paris, 1913), pp. 192–3.

391 "He has also written ..." De Beatis, *Journal*, trans. Hale, pp. 132–3.

391 "Finally, in his old age ..." et seq. Vasari, *Lives*, vol. 1, p. 270.

392 "earnestly resolved ..." Vasari, *Lives*, vol. 1, p. 270.

392 "formed in his mind ..." Cited in Bramly, *Leonardo*, p. 12.

394 "the flow of ..." Richter, *Literary Works of Leonardo*, # 848.

28: "Am I a Machiavel?"

396 "delivering Italy from ..." Cited in Ridolfi, *Machiavelli*, p. 118.

396 "knew nothing of ..." Cited by Ridolfi in his article on Machiavelli in *Encyclopedia Britannica*, Micropedia (2002), vol. 7, p. 628.

396 "to raise a detachment ..." Cited in Ridolfi, *Machiavelli*, p. 120.

399 "I have borne ..." Letter from Machiavelli to Francesco Vettori, March 18, 1513; see *Machiavelli and His Friends*, ed. and trans. Atkinson and Sices, p. 222.

399 "Giuliano, I have a ..." Machiavelli, *Opere*, Mondadori edn (Milan, 1949), vol. II, p. 747.

401 "I get up before . . ." Letter from Machiavelli to Francesco Vettori, December 10, 1513; see *Machiavelli and His Friends*, ed. and trans. Atkinson and Sices, p. 263 et seq.

401 "Fate alone has . . ." Letter from Machiavelli to Francesco Vettori, March 13, 1513; see *Machiavelli and His Friends*, ed. and trans. Atkinson and Sices, p. 221.

402 "When it's evening . . ." Letter from Machiavelli to Francesco Vettori, December 10, 1513; see *Machiavelli and His Friends*, ed. and trans. Atkinson and Sices, p. 263 et seq.

403 "secure yourself against . . ." Machiavelli, *Il Principe*, ch VII, sec. 10.

403 "People should be . . ." Machiavelli, *Il Principe*, ch. III, sec. 6.

403 "It is better . . ." et seq. Machiavelli, *Il Principe*, ch XXV, sec. 6.

404 "New Princedoms . . ." Machiavelli, *Il Principe*, ch. VII: heading.

404 "As a result . . ." Machiavelli, *Il Principe*, ch. VII, sec. 5.

405 "The single thing . . ." et seq. Machiavelli, *Il Principe*, ch. VII, sec. 12.

405 "An Exhortation . . ." Machiavelli, *Il Principe*, ch. XXVI: heading.

406 "those who generally . . ." et seq. Cited by Mary G. Dietz in her article on Machiavelli in *Routledge Encyclopedia of Philosophy*, ed. Edward Craig (London, 1998), vol. 6, p. 19.

409 "beheld in his sleep . . ." See Villari, *Machiavelli*, vol. 2, pp. 535–7. Villari himself in fact casts doubts on this story, although it is confirmed by at least two of Machiavelli's contemporaries, namely the historian Giovio and the Florentine letter writer Busini.

410 "an emissary of . . ." See Martin Haile, *The Life of Cardinal Pole* (London, 1910), p. 57, which uses a different transcription. The one I have included is the more common usage.

411 "Political writers . . ." See David Hume, *Theory of Politics* (London, 1951), p. 157. For this quote, and its use by Alexander Hamilton, I am particularly indebted to Michael White, *Machiavelli* (London, 2004), p. 278.

411 "Machiavelli was . . ." Alluded to in Laura Fermi, *Mussolini* (Chicago, 1961), p. 219, from Mussolini's essay *"Preludio al 'Machiavelli'"* in the journal *Gerarchia*, 1924, pp. 205–9.

Select Bibliography

For Machiavelli's works I have usually relied upon the texts as printed in *Opere di Machiavelli*, ed. Sergio Bertelli, 11 vols (Milan, 1968–72). Volumes 6–8 contain his dispatches in chronological order. English translations of Machiavelli's works, which do not always match my own, can be found in Niccolò Machiavelli, *The Chief Works and Others*, trans. Allen Gilbert, 3 vols (North Carolina, 1965), and more comprehensively in Niccolò Machiavelli, *The Historical, Political, and Diplomatic Writings*, trans. C. E. Detmold, 6 vols (Boston, 1882).

The most readily available and comprehensive source for Leonardo's notebooks is *The Literary Works of Leonardo da Vinci*, ed. Jean Paul Richter, 2 vols (New York, 1970). This has text in Leonardo's Italian, and abbreviations, as well as Richter's translation, to which I have not always adhered. There are several, variously illustrated versions of the codices, some of which are facsimiles. Particularly relevant to this period of Leonardo's life are Manuscript L (whose original is at the Institut de France in Paris), *Codex Atlanticus* (Ambrosian Library, Milan), *Codex Turin* (Royal Library, Turin), *Codex Leicester* (formerly *Codex Hammer*, now in the Gates Collection, Seattle), and the more recently discovered sheets known as *Codex Madrid* (which is not in Richter, and is at the National Library, Madrid).

The most illuminating contemporary sources for Cesare Borgia and his father, Alexander VI, are to be found in the dispatches of Machiavelli (see above); the dispatches of the Venetian ambassador to the papal court, Antonio Giustinian (see below); and the diary kept by the papal master of ceremonies Johannes Burchard (see below for various editions).

Anonimo Magliabechiano, Florentine Biblioteca Nazionale Centrale, MS Magliabechiano XVII, 17 (c. 1542–8).

Roger Bacon, *De mirabile poteste artis et naturae* (Paris, 1542).

Matteo Bandello, *Opere*, 2 vols, ed. F. Flora (Milan, 1934).

Antonio de Beatis, *Voyage de Cardinal d'Aragon*, trans. Havard de la Montagne (Paris, 1913).

Antonio de Beatis, *The Travel Journal*, trans. J. R. Hale (London, 1979).

Maria Bellonci, *Lucrezia Borgia*, trans. Bernard Wall (London, 2000 edn).

Andrea Bernardi, *Cronache Forlivese . . . 1476 al 1517*, ed. G. Mazzatinti, 2 vols (Bologna, 1895).

Sarah Bradford, *Cesare Borgia: His Life and Times* (London, 1976).

Serge Bramly, *Leonardo: The Artist and the Man*, trans. Sian Reynolds (London, 1992).

Biagio Buonaccorsi, *Diario dall'anno 1498 all'anno 1512* (reprinted Rome, 1999).

Le Journal de Jean Burchard, trans. Joseph Turmel (Paris, 1932).

Johannis Burchardi, *Diarium*, 3 vols (Thuasne, 1885).

Jacob Burckhardt, *The Civilization of the Renaissance in Italy*, trans. S.G.C. Middlemore (London, 1937).

Saba da Castiglione, *Ricordi* (Venice, 1554).

Benvenuto Cellini, *Autobiography*, trans. George Bull (Harmonsdworth, 1998).

E. R. Chamberlin, *The Fall of the House of Borgia* (London, 1974).

D. S. Chambers, *A Concise Encyclopedia of Renaissance Italy* (London, 1981).

Chronicles of the City of Perugia, trans. E. S. Morgan (London, 1905).

Brian Clegg, *The First Scientist: A Life of Roger Bacon* (London, 2003).

Ascanio Condivi, *The Life of Michelangelo*, trans. Alice Wohl (Pennsylvania, 1976).

James Dennistoun, *Memoirs of the Dukes of Urbino*, 3 vols (London, 1909).

Encyclopedia of AIDS (New York, 1998).

Laura Fermi, *Mussolini* (Chicago, 1961).

Felix Gilbert, *Machiavelli and Guicciardini* (Princeton, 1965).

Paolo Giovio, *Istorie del suo Tempo*, trans. L. Domenichi, 2 vols (Venice, 1555).

Antonio Giustinian, *Dispacci Ambasciatore Veneto in Roma dal 1502 al 1505*, ed. P. Villari, 3 vols (Florence, 1876).

Sebastian de Grazia, *Machiavelli in Hell* (New York, 1989).

Ferdinand Gregovorius, *Lucretia Borgia: According to Original Documents and Correspondence of Her Day*, trans. John Garner (New York, 1903).

Francesco Guicciardini, *Storia d'Italia*, 4 vols (Florence, 1919).

Francesco Guicciardini, *Storie fiorentine*, ed. Palamarocchi (Bari, 1931).

Francesco Guicciardini, *History of Florence and History of Italy*, trans. Cecil Grayson (London, 1966).

Martin Haile, *The Life of Cardinal Pole* (London, 1910).

David Hume, *Theory of Politics* (London, 1951).

Stefano Infessura, *Diario della città di Roma*, ed. O. Tommasini (Rome, 1890).

Kenneth D. Keele, *Leonardo da Vinci's Elements of the Science of Man* (London, 1983).

Luca Landucci, *Diario fiorentino dal 1450 al 1516* (Florence, 1883).

Leonardo da Vinci, *Treatise on Painting*, trans. A. P. McMahon, 2 vols (Princeton, 1956).

Leonardo da Vinci, *Madrid Codices*, ed. Ladislao Reti (New York, 1974).

Leonardo, Machiavelli, Cesare Borgia, exhibition catalog; see article by Enrico Fernandino Londei (Rimini, 2003).

Il Codice Atlantico di Leonardo da Vinci: Nell edizione Hoepli 1894–1904 curata dall'Accademia dei Lincei (Milan, 2004).

Machiavelli and His Friends: Their Personal Correspondence, trans. James B. Atkinson and David Sices (Northern Illinois, 1996).

Machiavelli, *Opere*, 6 vols, ed. L. Passerini and G. Melanesi (Florence, 1873–7).

Domenico Malipiero, *Annali Veneti* (Florence, 1843 edn).

Michael Mallett, *The Borgias: The Rise and Fall of a Renaissance Dynasty* (London, 1969).

Roger D. Masters, *Fortune Is a River: Leonardo da Vinci and Machiavelli's Magnificent Dream to Change the Course of Florentine History* (New York, 1998).

Roger D. Masters, *Machiavelli, Leonardo and the Science of Power* (London, 2002).

Edward McCurdy, *The Mind of Leonardo da Vinci* (New York, 1928).

Charles Nicholl, *Leonardo da Vinci* (London, 2004).

F. Ludwig von Pastor, *The History of the Popes*, ed. F. I. Antrobus, 40 vols (trans. London, 1950).

Robert Payne, *Leonardo* (London, 1979).

The Penguin Book of the Renaissance, ed. J. H. Plumb (London, 1964).

Frederick J. Pohl, *Amerigo Vespucci* (New York, 1944).

Renaissance Quarterly (New York).

Roberto Ridolfi, *The Life of Niccolò Machiavelli*, trans. Cecil Grayson (London, 1963).

Le Opere volgari di M. Jacopo Sanazzaro, 2 vols (Venice, 1741).

William Shakespeare, *The Merry Wives of Windsor*.

Baldassare Taccone, *Coronazione e sposalitio de la serenissima regina Maria Bianca* (Milan, 1493).

Barbara Tuchman, *The March of Folly* (London, 1984).

G. Uzielli, *La Vita e i tempi di Paolo dal Pozzo Toscanelli* (Rome, 1894).

Giorgio Vasari, *Le opere*, ed. Gaetano Milanesi, 9 vols (Florence, 1878–85).

Giorgio Vasari, *Lives of the Artists* (Harmondsworth, 1987).

Rodriguez Villa, *Cronicas de Gran Capitan* [i.e., Gonsalvo de Cordova] (Madrid, 1908).

Pasquale Villari, *The Life and Times of Machiavelli*, trans. L. Villari, 2 vols (London, 1892).

Maurizio Viroli, *Niccolò's Smile: A Biography of Machiavelli*, trans. Anthony Shugaar (London, 2000).

Michael White, *Machiavelli* (London, 2004).

W. H. Woodward, *Cesare Borgia* (London, 1913).

www.msnbc.msn.com/id/15993133.

www.vebjorn-sand.com/thebridge.htm.

Charles Yriarte, *César Borgia: Sa vie, sa captivité, sa mort* (Paris, 1889).

Zambotti, *Diario Ferrarese dall'anno 1476 sino al 1504*.

Index

Adriani, Marcello, 163–4

Adriano da Corneto, Cardinal, 251, 254, 255

Albret, Charlotte d' (wife of Cesare Borgia), 82, 87, 365, 367

Albret, Jean, d' (King of Navarre), 365, 366, 367

Alexander VI, Pope (*earlier* Cardinal Rodrigo Borgia; father of Cesare Borgia): unfolding of grand strategy, 7, 144, 149–50, 247–9; forms Holy League, 30, 46, 75, 69; engineers downfall of Savonarola, 44; forms alliances with Louis XII (King of France), 46, 48, 80–1, 90, 92–3, 118; family's Spanish background, 64; and Vannozza de' Cattanei, 64; awards Cesare Borgia religious titles, 64, 68; and Giulia Farnese, 65, 68; increases influence in Spain, 65; rivalry with Cardinal Giuliano della Rovere (*later* Pope Julius II), 66, 68, 191; "buys" election to papacy (1492), 66–7; arranges marriages of Lucrezia and Cesare Borgia, 68, 80; institutes papal reforms, 69–70; and Charles VIII, 70–9; sexual behavior, 76, 89–90, 94–5, 192; makes Cesare Borgia *gonfaloniere* of papal forces, 80; makes Cesare Borgia Duke of Romagna, 91; arranges third marriage of Lucrezia Borgia, 94, 95–6; and Giovanni "Infans Romanus," 94, 116; seizes lands of

Colonna family, 106; tensions with Cesare Borgia, 143–4, 192, 209–10, 212–13, 215, 244, 246, 257; secret meeting with Cesare Borgia at Camerino, 144–5, 197, 210, 214; and La Magione conspiracy against Cesare Borgia (1502), 146–9, 214; confides in Giustinian (Venetian ambassador), 182–3; outmaneuvers Cardinal Orsini, 184–5, 192, 199–202; rapacious financial strategy, 217–18; negotiates with Sultan Bejazit II, 224; approves Leonardo's return to Florence, 234; devious negotiations with Spain, France, and Venice, 243–6, 248; plans for own death and burial, 250–6

Alfonso II (King of Naples), 70, 74

Alfonso of Bisceglie, Duke (second husband of Lucrezia Borgia), 80, 83, 88–90, 339, 345

Alidosi bridge (Castel del Rio), 226–7

Alviano, Bartolomeo d', 346–7

Amboise, Charles d' (French governor of Milan), 309, 360–1, 374

Amboise, Georges d' (Cardinal of Rouen): meetings with Machiavelli, 54, 55, 309–10; as cardinal 81, 265; fails in bid to become pope, 264–6, 284; supports election of Pius III, 266–7; supports election of Pope Julius II, 285, 341; and Cesare Borgia's house arrest, 296; leaves Rome for France, 298

LONGWOOD PUBLIC LIBRARY
800 Middle Country Road
Middle Island, NY 11953
(631) 924-6400
mylpl.net

LIBRARY HOURS

Monday-Friday	9:30 a.m. - 9:00 p.m.
Saturday	9:30 a.m. - 5:00 p.m.
Sunday (Sept-June)	1:00 p.m. - 5:00 p.m.